Contemporary Argentina

Contemporary Argentina

A Geographical Perspective

David J. Keeling

WestviewPress

A Division of HarperCollins*Publishers*

Copyright © 1997 by Westview Press, A Division of HarperCollins Publishers, Inc.

Published in 1997 in the United States of America by Westview Press, 5500 Central Avenue, Boulder,
Colorado 80301-2877, and in the United Kingdom by Westview Press, 12 Hid's Copse Road, Cum-
nor Hill, Oxford OX2 9JJ

Library of Congress Cataloging-in-Publication Data
Keeling, David J.
    Contemporary Argentina : a geographical perspective / by David J. Keeling
        p.   cm.
    Includes bibliographical references and index.
    ISBN 0-8133-8680-2
    1. Argentina—Economic conditions—1983– 2. Argentina—Economic
policy. 3. Economic forecasting—Argentina. 4. Argentina—Social
conditions—1983– 5. Argentina—Social policy. 6. Social
prediction—Argentina. 7. Regional planning—Argentina. I. Title.
HC175.K44   1997
330.982—dc21   97-4465
                                                                                                            CIP

The paper used in this publication meets the requirements of the American National Standard for Per-
manence of Paper for Printed Library Materials Z39.48-1984.

10   9   8   7   6   5   4   3   2   1

To DJ, with love.

*May our geographical explorations be many
and our experiences unforgettable.*

Contents

PART FOUR
ARGENTINA IN THE TWENTY-FIRST CENTURY

Tables and Figures

Figures

Preface

Between 1870 and 1930, Argentina consolidated its national territory, inserted itself into the world economy, and set out along a development path that paralleled the industrialized North Atlantic countries. Many thought that Argentina had a brilliant future. Unfortunately, between 1930 and 1990, Argentina suffered a reversal of fortune. Sixty years of political instability, economic mismanagement, and public service inefficiency propelled the country to the very brink of disaster. During the 1970s and 1980s especially, inflation ran rampant, foreign debt threatened to bankrupt the country, poverty increased exponentially, and urban growth went out of control. A brutal government campaign against perceived internal threats to Argentina's stability terrorized the populace during the late 1970s, resulting in massive human rights violations. This so-called "Dirty War" culminated in the military government's embarrassing defeat in 1982 at the hands of the British in a war over control of the Malvinas/Falkland Islands. Argentinos became painfully aware that their country had progressed from having a brilliant future to having a brilliant past. Moreover, a psychology of underdevelopment permeated Argentina's institutional structures, weakening the planning and organizational capabilities of the country (Gamba-Stonehouse 1992). Argentina struggled to find a place in the emerging political and economic global system.

Since 1990, however, Argentina has experienced perhaps the most significant period of change since federation in 1880. Under the leadership of President Carlos Menem and the *Justicialista* (Peronist) political party, contemporary Argentina is emerging from the chaos of long-term instability to reassert itself in the regional and global systems. With an eye toward the evolving world economy, Menem's government has pursued free market economic policies, regional economic alliances, state disengagement in many aspects of industry and services via privatization and deregulation strategies, and *rapprochement* with neighboring states. Menem and Domingo Cavallo, the Harvard-educated former economic minister, have argued that an infusion of new capital and a more open economy will propel Argentina toward a period of socioeconomic growth unmatched since the glory years of the late nineteenth century.

Economic and social restructuring are prompting changes in the way people look at the geography of Argentina. First, analysts, policy makers, businesspeople, and academics are focusing greater attention on the implications for Argentina of involvement in the contemporary global economy. Increasing recognition is being given to the role of international forces in reshaping the geography of Argentina. Moreover, globalization and regional integration processes are encouraging comparisons between Argentina's economic and social restructuring and change in Europe, North America, and Asia. Second, deindustrialization and an upsurge in the service sector have shifted the analytical spotlight to the locational characteristics of Argentina's economic restructuring programs. Previously, analysts focused primarily on macro-level processes, not on regional or local events. A more intensive analysis of national, regional, and local patterns of economic and social activity, against the backdrop of globalization, could shed light on the spatial dynamics of growth and change in Argentina. Finally, Menem's "economic surgery without anesthesia" is causing a critical reevaluation of the spatial impacts of social change in Argentina. Particularly important is the ongoing bifurcation of the country between a wealthy coastal region (Buenos Aires) and an increasingly impoverished interior. Although uneven regional development has been a dominant theme in Argentina's national evolution for at least the past 200 years, the problem has become particularly acute since restructuring began in 1990.

Despite the profound changes that are occurring in Argentina, the country remains on the fringe of geographic research. We know very little about the geographic processes that have shaped contemporary Argentina and even less about the spatial impact of the country's restructuring programs. The lack of an up-to-date geographic analysis of growth and change in Argentina, coupled with new theoretical developments in the way we view growth and change, have encouraged this volume and have influenced the selection of topics. The book's major objective is to present an account of the way in which local, national, and international trends in society and economy have reshaped the geography of Argentina in recent years. In addition, the book seeks to examine the potential impacts of these trends on development, growth, and change in Argentina's myriad and diverse localities for the remainder of the 1990s and beyond. Although the primary emphasis of the analysis is on economic change, the themes of social polarization, infrastructural decline, megacephalous urban growth, and rural poverty share center stage. Other related themes include concerns over environmental degradation, inadequate housing provision, weak land-use planning, changing geopolitical relationships, and inefficient transport networks.

Within the context of the primary analysis outlined above, this book also attempts to explode a number of myths or beliefs that have shaped perceptions about, and studies of, Argentina since 1945. The first myth portrays Argentina as a resource-rich country that should have developed (and still could develop) in the manner of the North Atlantic countries. In reality, much of Argentina is resource poor, and the global economy no longer demands the quantities of agricultural products historically yielded by the pampas. A second myth argues that since the nineteenth century Buenos Aires and the Pampeana provinces have sucked the marrow from the bones of the interior, exploiting its people and impoverishing its economies. However, the evidence shows that, at least during the twentieth century, the interior has received tremendous subsidies from the economic core, subsidies which ultimately hindered Argentina's national development. Moreover, massive migration from the interior to Buenos Aires and the Pampeana cities since 1945 has imported poverty to the economic core.

The myth of Europeanness is the third belief that has shaped profoundly the way Argentina is perceived both from within and without. The idea of Buenos Aires as the "Paris of Latin America" and of an Argentina ensconced among the ranks of the more developed countries of the global economy has permeated socioeconomic thought since the 1880s. Since 1945, however, Argentina has experienced the latinamericanization of significant portions of its territory, economy, and society. Development problems experienced by interior provinces are identical to the problems found today in many developing countries. A fourth myth portrays the interior of Argentina as plagued by a few isolated pockets of poverty. Yet the evidence suggests that only a few isolated pockets of development exist beyond the Pampeana core. Much of the interior is impoverished, isolated, underdeveloped, and wracked by socioeconomic and political inequalities. The final myth explored in this study is that Argentina's contemporary globalization strategies will encourage further democratization, spread the economic impetus of the core to the interior, increase national unity, and promote socioeconomic and political stability. This myth is challenged by the evidence presented in the following chapters.

The book is organized in four parts. The first introduces the main theme of socioeconomic change and its geographic impact. An overview of Argentina's geohistorical regional and international relationships provides a framework for understanding the country's present characteristics, problems, and linkages. The forces of globalization and the government's attempt to reconstruct Argentina's socioeconomic spaces then are examined against the backdrop of Argentina's geohistorical experiences. Part Two examines the geographical impact of change in Argentina, with a specific focus on events since 1990. This section takes a thematic approach by exploring three key components of development and change in the emerging global system: society and place; the capital-labor-production nexus; and transport and communication. The analysis highlights how these components have had different implications for disparate places, in part because of embedded characteristics and historical inertia. The spatial outcomes of these elements provide a framework in Part Three for distinguishing four major regions in Argentina. These regions and their constituent localities are responding in different ways to the forces of change in Argentina. The final part of the book draws on the analysis of the preceding chapters and attempts to assess the future prospects for both Argentina and its major regions against the backdrop of evolving patterns of demographic, social, political, and economic change. It concludes by highlighting the key policy issues at the regional and local levels and by revisiting the theme of Argentina's potential role in suprastate regional, hemispheric, and global networks.

Field research for the book took place during the northern summers of 1988, 1991, 1993, and 1994. These visits allowed me to experience first-hand changes in Argentina's economy and society and to understand more clearly the regional differences at work in the country. I point out to the reader that my own cultural, business, and academic backgrounds bias my interpretation of contemporary Argentina. Although I have enjoyed a relationship with this wonderful and intriguing country that spans three decades, I do not view Argentina through the same lens as would, for example, a native Argentino. My personal interests and biases have led me to focus on certain aspects of the country's development, perhaps to the exclusion of other significant changes. This does not mean that the processes I have excluded are unimportant. They are not. However, I have chosen to focus the analytical lens on certain themes to provide a more interconnected picture of Argentina and to tease out certain national, regional, and global processes that are helping to reshape the country.

I hope that the geographic interpretation of Argentina presented in this book stimulates interest, argument, and discussion about the country and provokes additional questions and research. Argentina is a fascinating, complex country that merits further analysis as its citizens attempt to cope with the dynamic forces of growth and change.

It is impossible to be completely up-to-date with the rapid changes that are occurring in Argentina. Official statistics and other data frequently are several years old upon release to the public. Moreover, researchers must use caution when evaluating official statistics and other data from Latin America. Many Latin American countries, including Argentina, have improved their methods of data collection and dissemination in recent years, yet statistics often can be unreliable and outdated. The development of a critical mass of information necessary to provide a long-term picture can be hindered by a lack of basic data and by an unquestioned reliance on official estimates. Many hypotheses about development processes in Argentina, for example, have been built on data that are not always confirmable or that diverge from estimations gleaned from other sources. In a parody of Gresham's law, as Jorge Schvarzer (1992:170) wryly notes, "poor information displaces good data in the circulation of ideas." Therefore, quantifications and data in this study serve primarily to illustrate trends and relationships. They are not meant to be definitive evidence of a particular process. Readers can remain reasonably up-to-date on Argentine economic and political events by perusing the *Review of the River Plate*, *Latin American Weekly Report*, monthly reports of Argentina's Ministry of the Economy, Works, and Public Services, the *Statistical Abstract of Latin America*, the annual *Statistical Yearbook of the Republic of Argentina*, and the various information sources available in cyberspace.

David J. Keeling
Bowling Green, KY

Acknowledgments

Many people have played an instrumental role in bringing this book to fruition. Juan Alberto Roccatagliata, general executive coordinator of the Argentine government's territorial restructuring program, provided logistical support, friendship, and innumerable introductions during my visits to Argentina. In Buenos Aires, Lucía Bortagaray, Mónica Guastoni, Norma Marino, Verónica Arruñada, Mabel Tamborenea Inza, Albina Lara, and Alberto Hugo Peláez at the offices of La Presidencia de la Nación provided valuable advice, data, and referrals. Marta Sanmarchi, Arturo Héctor Ramón, Luis Ainstein, Horacio A. Torres, Patricio H. Randle, César A. Vapñarsky, Carlos E. Reboratti, Elena M. Chiozza, Manuel Ludueña, Fernando López del Amo, María Adela Igarzabal de Nistal, and Alfredo Aguirre generously provided data, copies of their publications, and personal insights into the machinations of Argentina's government and society.

Geographers and students at the national universities in Mendoza, La Rioja, Salta, Tucumán, and Córdoba were generous with their time and personal knowledge of local events and processes. I especially thank Ricardo Capitanelli and Mariano Zamorano at the Instituto de Geografía de la Universidad Nacional de Cuyo in Mendoza. Carlos A. Ballistrieri at the Central National University of Buenos Aires Province in Tandil provided data about changes in Argentina's airline network. The librarians and staff at various provincial and local government offices (especially CONICET), and at the Commission for the Metropolitan Area of Buenos Aires (CONAMBA), the Center for the Study of the State and Society (CEDES), Center for Population Studies (CENEP), Center for Urban and Regional Studies (CEUR), Institute of Argentine Railroads (FIADF), Association for the Promotion of the Study of Territory and Environment (OIKOS), and the National Institute of Statistics and Census (INDEC), all in Buenos Aires, were generous with their time and expertise.

In the United States, Frank Richter and Ronald Sheck provided updated information on the privatization of Argentina's railroads and suburban transit systems. My colleagues in the Department of Geography and Geology at Western Kentucky University provided logistical support, advice, and encouragement. Tom Polanski, a geography graduate student, produced the maps, and Vince Arrell, also a geography graduate student, conducted library research. The interlibrary loan staff at Western, especially John O'Hara, diligently tracked down some of the more esoteric material. Special thanks go to Richard Pace in Western's Department of Folk Studies, Modern Languages, and Anthropology, who diligently reviewed and critiqued the manuscript's introductory chapters. *Muchísimas gracias amigo.* The staff at Westview Press provided valuable support, advice, and editing skills as the manuscript threatened to take on a life of its own. I particularly thank Barbara, Patricia, Elizabeth, Karl, and Jennie for their patience and support of the project as the weeks passed into months and then years! Finally, and most important of all, Dacia (DJ) Urquhart deserves special recognition for guiding me through the past two years providing love, encouragement, and copious quantities of tea and biscuits during my many excursions into cyberspace. All errors, interpretations, and nuances in translations from Spanish or other sources remain the responsibility of the author. Photographs are by the author unless noted otherwise.

DJK

Contemporary Argentina

PART ONE

Argentina in the Global System

1

Key Geographical Trends

For many Latin American countries, the gloomy prognosis that the 1980s would be a "lost decade" for socioeconomic development proved to be true. Rampant inflation, continued political upheaval, increasing social inequalities, and deteriorating infrastructure throughout the region retarded the development process and widened the gap between rich and poor. As the 1990s dawned, Latin American countries found themselves in a desperate struggle to redefine their role in a rapidly evolving and sophisticated global system. New regional economic alliances, the end of an ideologically bifurcated world order, and the spread of free-market capitalism and democracy forced countries such as Argentina to reappraise their policies, economies, and territorial spaces. In Argentina, Carlos Menem, newly elected as president in 1989, chose to pursue privatization, deregulation, and globalization strategies to reshape Argentina's position in the global economy. Dubbed "Menemstroika" or "Menemization" by many observers, these strategies were designed to open up Argentina's economy to regional and global competition, to pursue a policy of *rapprochement* with neighboring countries, to disengage the state from many aspects of the national economy, and to restructure society.

The implementation of restructuring policies in Argentina has begun to change the country in profound and fundamental ways. New social, political, and economic spaces are emerging out of the debris of the pre-1990s state to redefine Argentina's role in the world. At the same time, global, hemispheric, and regional forces are changing the map of Argentina at the sub-regional, provincial, and local scales. Tensions, strengths, and weaknesses in Argentina's bidirectional links along the local-global continuum of economic, social, and political relationships are having a direct impact on patterns of growth and change in the country. For example, tensions exist between Argentina's global integration strategies and domestic social policies, strengths are evident in the country's development of regional economic ties, and weaknesses continue in Argentina's transport links to both internal and external regions. To understand more clearly the role that Argentina is likely to play in emerging regional, hemispheric, and global networks, it is necessary to examine in detail the impact of these policies and linkages over space and through time. Geographers, in particular, are extremely interested in how changes in these linkages are reshaping patterns of interaction between people and the environment at the local and regional levels. Especially important is the problem of uneven socio-economic development among a country's constituent regions. In this chapter, I discuss the importance of uneven regional development in shaping the past, present, and future of Argentina. Then I develop a theoretical framework for analyzing the restructuring of the country's pillars of regional development. Chapter one concludes by setting out the four distinct spatial environments in Argentina that serve as contexts for understanding geographical expressions of change.

Uneven Regional Development

Pronounced inequalities between regions appear to be endemic to capitalist development. Differences in the living standards of places and regions are created as people, capital, and materials flow through and between regions. These differences can be exacerbated, reduced, or sustained depending on the particular historical, cultural, political, and economic contexts of specific regions. Many researchers view such differences, or uneven regional development, as a normal process in highly industrialized and urbanized societies (Storper and Walker 1989). Within the European Community, for example, clear disparities exist in the levels of transport provision between central Wales and southeast England, or between northern and southern Italy (Champion and Townsend 1990). It also is widely accepted that regional divergence in the quality of life in developing regions such as Latin America is the norm (Bennett 1980). Regional differences in Latin America are a legacy of the colonial experience and have been exacerbated by the development of export-oriented economies, the megacephalous growth of primary cities, and by declining levels of transportation. In many Latin American countries, the failure to address the problem of uneven regional development historically has proved to be the Achilles heel of national and regional socioeconomic policies.

Nigel Smith's (1984:ix) observation over a decade ago that "one can hardly look at the world today without perceiving that, at the hands of capital, the last decades have witnessed an emergent restructuring of geographical space more dramatic than any before" is even more pertinent in the mid-1990s. New regional economic arrangements, time-space relationships, geopolitical networks, and urban interactions are forcing Argentina to reevaluate both its national identity and its global role. For example, historic links to the North Atlantic economies are being realigned to cope with the forces of integration, deindustrialization, and the international division of labor. Internally, Argentina is struggling to redefine its regional development priorities in order to encourage activity deconcentration to interior cities and to reduce the overwhelming influence of Buenos Aires, the capital, over the country. Strategies designed to relocate federal government functions from Buenos Aires to an interior city also have been proposed in an attempt to reorganize Argentina's territorial dynamics. The present government of Argentina views regional change, especially the amelioration of regional disparities, as crucial to the successful socioeconomic restructuring of the country (República Argentina 1993).

Economic Cycles and Regional Change

Complex and shifting patterns of regional socioeconomic activity in Argentina may be related to the temporal rhythms suggested by international "Kondratieff cycles." A Russian historian, Kondratieff (1935) theorized the existence of short economic cycles of 3.5 to 11 years in length superimposed on deeper "long waves" of 47 to 60 years. These waves and cycles are caused by a complicated combination of political, social, economic, and technological activities and developments (see Taylor (1989) for a more detailed discussion). Considerable evidence exists to suggest that the world economy has passed through four major cycles since the late eighteenth century. Although considered ambiguous and open to a significant range of interpretations by many researchers, these cycles and their correlation with technological changes provide a useful framework for examining the evolution of Argentina's participation in the world economy. Peter Taylor (1989) has compiled a space-time information matrix that, by merging elements of the Kondratieff cycles with Immanuel Wallerstein's world-systems theory, divides the world economy into core, semi-peripheral, and peripheral components. This matrix helps us to interpret the distinct role that certain countries have played historically in the world economy. For example, Argentina's position on the global periphery explains why its regions and economy have been reoriented several times to serve wider needs within the world economy (Chapter 2). Prior to the late eighteenth century, the interior provinces and cities of Argentina dominated the country and were oriented to the Northwest and the Pacific. One hundred years later, the Atlantic coast region of Argentina centered on Buenos Aires controlled the country. The littoral region's rise to prominence was fueled by an export-oriented, agriculturally based economy geared to service the industrialized North Atlantic nations. In the twentieth century, regional change in Argentina has been driven, in part, by changes in core-periphery relationships. Britain's declining levels of investment in Argentina's transport networks between 1918 and 1945 played a crucial role in the inability of interior regions to develop stronger ties with neighboring countries. After 1945, the growth of industry in the country's major urban centers was related closely to the new global hegemony of the United States. The United States became Latin America's major source of capital, technical, and military assistance, as well as the region's most important market. U.S.-funded industrialization in Buenos Aires, for example, encouraged rural-urban migration flows and exacerbated the social and economic bifurcation of Argentina. More recently, the collapse of the bipolar world order and the development of new regional trading blocs have precipitated a realignment of Argentina's relationships with neighboring countries. New social and economic spaces are being created at both the suprastate and substate regional scales. Northwest Argentina, for instance, is once again looking toward the Pacific coast region, and northeast Argentina is experiencing new levels of interaction with neighboring Brazil and Paraguay.

The Emergence of a Bifurcated State

The most critical change to emerge from Argentina's geohistorical experiences is the creation of a bifurcated state. From a position of dominance in the late eighteenth century, the interior regions of Argentina, particularly the Northwest and Northeast, have fallen into an abyss of poverty, underdevelopment, and inadequate infrastructure. This occurred through a combination of political, economic, and social policies that devalued the so-called 'barbaric' interior to the benefit of the civilized and modern coastal region (Keeling 1992). Europeanized Buenos Aires and its pampas hinterland developed rapidly after 1850 to become an economic power-house and a Latin American showcase for civilization and modernization.

Since the 1900s, the northern provinces have suffered from depopulation, poor monocropping practices, inadequate investment, and collapsing infra-structure, despite significant financial support from the federal government. The 1950s and 1960s were particularly brutal to the economies and societies of the interior. Between 1953 and 1969, the Gross Domestic Product (GDP) per capita of the Northwest provinces plunged from 57 percent of the national average to under 36 percent (Table 1.1). In the Northeast, the GDP rate fell from 55.1 to 47.6 percent of the national average during the same period. Problems of grinding poverty, unem-ployment, inadequate housing, and a declining quality of life seemed to overwhelm both federal and provincial governments. The trends of social, economic, and population decline in the interior provinces continued unabated until the implementation of regional development policies in the 1960s and 1970s. Although the interior recovered slightly during the late 1970s and early 1980s as a result of these policies, high levels of poverty and underdevelopment in the interior are a central feature of Argentina's contemporary geography (Chapter 3).

Depopulation of the northern provinces' rural areas continues as economic restructuring benefits primarily Buenos Aires and its pampas hinterland. Table 1.2 shows that the Northwest provinces accounted for nearly 29 percent of Argentina's total population in 1869. This share fell to its lowest level, 10.2 percent, in 1970 before recovering slightly to 11.3 percent in 1991. Tucumán, the smallest of the Northwest's six provinces, lost 164,000 people during the 1960s alone (República Argentina 1971). Similarly, the Cuyo provinces declined from a 10.2 percent share of the national popula-tion in 1869 to a low of 6.4 percent in 1947, before recovering to 6.8 percent in 1991. In contrast, the Pampeana region including metropolitan Buenos Aires grew from 53.4 percent of the national population in 1869 to 68.7 percent in 1991, although a slowdown in this region's growth rate has been evident since 1970. Only Patagonia has shown consistent, if slow, growth since the nineteenth century, in part because of the region's status as a frontier zone.

The depth of Argentina's regional bifurcation, its precise definition, and the likely directions of change are key issues for this study. Also important are questions concerning the opening up of the Patagonian frontier, the

TABLE 1.1 Regional Disparity in Argentina's Gross Domestic Product Per Capita, 1953-1969

Planning Region	1953	1961	1969
National	100	100	100
Northwest	57.1	39.8	35.8
Northeast	55.1	52.1	47.6
Cuyo	91.5	79.8	89.3
Central	69.8	78.7	80.5
Pampeana	103.9	106.2	116.4
Comahue	105.4	96.9	98.6
Patagonia	163.4	188.7	148.0
Metropolitan	129.6	133.6	121.5

Source: After Ferraro (1973); Lara and Durán (1993a).

overwhelming influence that Buenos Aires and its immediate hinterland exert over Argentina, and the regional ramifications of *rapprochement* with neighboring states.

A Theoretical Framework

The contemporary global economy has been described as a historically unprecedented phenomenon (Friedmann 1993). According to Ash Amin and Nigel Thrift (1992), during the 1970s and 1980s an important shift occurred in the capitalist system, with a transition from an international to a truly global economy. Four characteristics define the contemporary global economy. First, industries now function on a global scale through the medium of global corporate networks. Second, oligopolistic, progressively centralized power has increased, helping to create important nodes in the global system. Third, new forms of joint ventures, subcontracting, and other types of networked organization and strategic alliances are contributing to the ongoing process of corporate decentralization. Finally, there is a new, more volatile balance of power between corporations, local governments, and national states. These new power

TABLE 1.2 Population Distribution in Argentina by Region, 1869-1991

Region	1869	1895	1914	1947	1960	1970	1980	1991
				Percent				
National	100	100	100	100	100	100	100	100
Metropolitan[a]	13.2	19.8	25.8	29.7	38.4	41.3	40.5	39.4
Pampeana[b]	40.2	47.3	47.8	42.1	33.3	31.2	30.2	29.3
Cuyo[c]	10.4	7.0	6.5	6.4	6.7	6.6	6.7	6.8
Northeast[d]	7.4	7.3	5.9	8.3	8.1	7.7	8.1	7.7
Northwest[e]	28.8	17.9	12.6	11.3	11.0	10.2	10.8	11.3
Patagonia[f]	-	0.7	1.4	2.2	2.5	3.0	3.7	4.5

[a] The Metropolitan region includes the Federal District of Buenos Aires, the 19 *partidos* (Counties) of the Suburban Inner Ring and, from 1960 onwards, the 32 *partidos* of the Outer Suburbs including Greater La Plata.
[b] The Pampeana region includes the provinces of Buenos Aires (including the 32 *partidos* of the outer suburbs of the city of Buenos Aires up until 1960), Córdoba, Entre Ríos, La Pampa, and Santa Fé.
[c] The Cuyo region includes the provinces of Mendoza, San Juan, and San Luis.
[d] The Northeast region includes the provinces of Chaco, Corrientes, Formosa, and Misiones.
[e] The Northwest region includes the provinces of Catamarca, Jujuy, La Rioja, Salta, Santiago del Estero, and Tucumán.
[f] The Patagonia region includes the provinces of Chubut, Neuquén, Río Negro, Santa Cruz, and Tierra del Fuego.
Source: República Argentina (1994).

relationships have resulted in the increased prominence of cross-national issue coalitions, where "fragments of the state, fragments of particular industries, and even fragments of particular firms" are united in a global network (Amin and Thrift 1992:574-575). Although debate continues over the precise nature of the new global economic order, most observers seem to agree that a reconstituted economic landscape is emerging, along with a realignment of class forces.

Moreover, in recent years the State's relative dominance in global affairs has given way to new space-time patterns where both the multinational and global and the regional-local scales have become more prominent.

Corporate, financial, and political activity at the global scale still play crucial roles in structuring daily life. However, geographers and others are finding that regional and local responses and restructuring processes have become equally important. Certainly, local and regional processes always have played a crucial role in structuring daily life, yet until recently they generally were given short shrift in the development of meta-theories and models about global change. In the 1990s, the forces of decentralization, devolution, and localization are counterbalancing the processes of globalization. As a result, the local-global continuum of social and economic relationships is realigning itself over space and through time, with major implications for regions and states. Yet treating global and local activities as contradictory forces is much too simplistic an approach. In practice, these activities are generating complex and dynamic tensions within and between social divisions and structures inside national states, tensions that are creating distinct spatial patterns of development, growth, and change.

Theorizing the relationships between various aspects of social division and structure remains extremely difficult, and no consensus on the best way to resolve the issues this raises has been reached over the last few decades. However, at the very core of understanding socioeconomic divisions within societies is the fact that they occur within the territories of national states. The theoretical point of departure for this study, therefore, is the key role of the Argentine state in social reproduction. As the earlier discussion pointed out, Argentina is divided in myriad ways. These divisions have immense practical importance for the way the country is articulated with the world economy, particularly to those people who live on the disadvantaged side of such divisions. The strategies and policies of Argentina's government thus become central to the way in which social divisions are created, reinforced, and recreated over space and through time.

The Argentine state's role in social reproduction includes not only coping with the multidimensional character of Argentine society, but also with relationships between Argentina and other states, supranational organizations (MERCOSUR, for example), and extra-state organizations (such as transnational or multinational corporations). Moreover, as Peter Taylor (1989) pointed out, the fact that national states function as components in an international state system has important constraining effects. He goes on to argue that, within the context of Kondratieff's long waves, the world economy both enables and constrains the actions of national states. In Argentina, for example, Carlos Menem's government is attempting to create a version of the dominant growth model (free-market capitalism) within the current phase in the evolution of the world economy. Yet although wider constraints on state actions are significant, Ray Hudson and Allan Williams (1995:18) caution that researchers should not "slip into a reductionist position which reduces national strategies to the effects of the global swings of long waves." Both national uniqueness and global interdependence are critical to understanding why there are specific impacts on Argentina's society as a result of state policy actions and why these impacts take the form that they do in different places.

A Framework for Analysis

Within the capitalist global economy, certain regions and subregions have emerged to function as significant focal points for transport, communication, and international economic activity. These regions, and more specifically their dominant cities, also serve as concentration points for global financial activity and can be distinguished by certain characteristics such as a concentration of multinational headquarter functions, a flexible and mobile labor force, major cultural infrastructure, and substantial flows of goods and information (Friedmann and Wolff 1982). In countries around the world such as Argentina, the regional context is being restructured to enhance these global characteristics and to capture the benefits of participation in the emerging system of world cities and regional trading blocs. If international and national processes are impacting differentially on different kinds of regions in Argentina, then these processes need to be identified, measured, and analyzed in a manner that will shed meaningful light on the spatial implications of restructuring.

The interplay between national uniqueness, regional processes, and global interdependence in Argentina can be synthesized in a basic model of regional growth and change (Figure 1.1). The model functions as a framework for analyzing regional restructuring within the context of global economic processes. A thematic-spatial approach treats the core components of regional growth and change as an interactive, integrative whole. This approach suggests that a highly generalized set of central relationships is at work in and among regions of many scales. Place, capital, and labor function as central pillars in local, regional and global economic systems. Interaction between these three components is inextricably intertwined with, and shaped by, social, political, cultural, and environmental forces. Changes in the ethnic and demographic character of place, for example, directly affect the interaction between place and the other pillars of

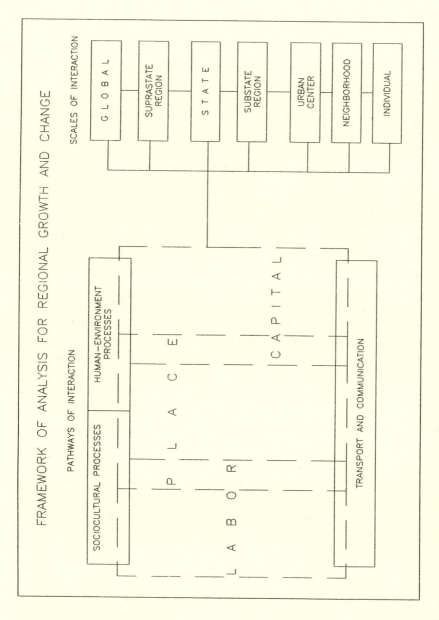

FIGURE 1.1 A Framework of Analysis for Regional Growth and Change.

development--labor and capital. Circuits of capital change as places become more impoverished, and the dynamics of labor change as local and regional populations age or relocate. The constantly expanding and contracting interface between the model's components, represented by the dashed lines, determines the strength of the relationship and its possible impact on a region. Weak interfaces between labor, capital, and place can serve to inhibit the development of relationships within the world economy and with the hierarchy of regions and urban centers. For example, if global or national capital has a weak interface with place, theoretically little regional restructuring is likely to occur. In Argentina, for example, the Northeast and the Northwest both are substantial regions, with about 2.8 and 3.7 million inhabitants respectively, yet they exhibit little physical evidence of a strong interface with the circuit of global or national capital. These regions are impoverished, underdeveloped, and isolated from the main pathways of regional-global interaction.

Finally, transport and communication operate as the foundation upon which the central pillars of the regional development process rest. Transport facilitates the movement of people, goods, and information in and among regions and is a necessary, though not sufficient, component of regional and global economic genesis, growth, and change. Weak linkages between transport, communication, and any of the three central pillars can have a deleterious spatial impact on the regional environment and can influence the process of growth and change in negative ways. With this general framework for analysis as a backdrop, we now can examine some of the major thematic and spatial characteristics of change in Argentina.

Restructuring Argentina's Pillars of Development

Society and Place

As the dynamics of Argentina's society are restructured, relationships between place, labor, and capital are altered irrevocably. Demographic data provide insight into how interactions between people, places, and regions in Argentina are changing over space and through time (Chapter 3). Although rural depopulation remains a serious challenge to policy makers, since the 1970s, the country has experienced a slowdown in the rate of internal migration as regional development policies attempt to focus activity on interior regional growth poles. Nonetheless, many of the northern provinces (for example, Corrientes, Entre Ríos, Santa Fé, and Santiago del

Estero) have experienced a relative decline in their share of Argentina's total population since 1960 (see Table 1.2). In contrast, several of the Patagonian provinces have seen their share of the national population increase since 1960, in part as a result of government policies to open up this frontier zone. The ethnic complexity of Argentina is changing as increasing numbers of migrants from contiguous countries and from overseas arrive in the major cities seeking economic opportunity. Guy Bourdé (1974) has termed this process the nationalizati'n or Latinamericanization of Argentina's society. The influx of mestizos and indigenous peoples from the interior, as well as Koreans, Japanese, and Vietnamese from Asia, is reshaping the social and cultural dynamics of Argentina and has precipitated what some have called the end of the European myth. Problems of uneven social and economic development continue to retard improvements in the quality of life for millions of Argentinos, particularly in the Northwest provinces. Over two million people in Argentina, nearly seven percent of the nation's population, subsist on less than US$100 per month. Many millions more hover critically around the poverty line. Critics of the government's privatization and globalization policies argue that Argentina's society is becoming increasingly polarized. Could increased social polarization lead to another period of explicit political conflict and urban violence?

Capital, Labor, and Production

Societal structure powerfully shapes the relationships between capital, labor, and production, which in turn shape and reshape places and regions in Argentina (Chapter 4). Investment capital is a crucial pillar of development, especially capital generated by the domestic economy. Historically in Argentina, capital has circulated predominantly in the primary city of Buenos Aires and in the agricultural industries of the Pampeana. Argentina's social and economic élite have preferred to invest capital surpluses in land, offshore banks, or in the conspicuous consumption of luxury imported goods, not in the development of technology and infrastructure. Failure to direct domestic investment capital into infrastructural projects over the past 100 years arguably has created a dependency on foreign capital that continues to this day. Argentina remains one of the most indebted countries in Latin America, with foreign institutional debts of over US$80 billion and a private debt burden of US$7 billion. The country is pursuing privatization policies in part because it starved public services of investment capital.

The restoration of these services requires billions of dollars in new capital, funds that the government does not have. Thus, the government has turned to the international financial market to raise the capital necessary to rebuild Argentina. Although billions of dollars in domestic capital have returned to Argentina from overseas since 1990, very little of this capital to date has been invested in productive infrastructural projects. The interior provinces in particular are suffering from a lack of capital for infrastructural development. Questions about the geographical impact of changes in Argentina's circuits of capital are important for understanding the potential long-term effects of social and economic restructuring.

Ongoing deindustrialization in the Buenos Aires region, coupled with attempts to encourage industrial development in the interior, continue to reshape relationships between cities and provinces. State-controlled industries and services with bloated bureaucracies and inefficient operations are being sold off to the private sector. Privatization of the railroads, airlines, electricity companies, telephones, ports, and a host of other services has reshaped the labor market in Argentina and has encouraged expansion into service, retail, and financial activities. However, urban and rural unemployment have risen dramatically as surplus labor continues to flood the job market, causing downward pressure on labor wage rates. Moreover, the liberalization of Argentina's regional and global trading links is causing a reappraisal of traditional labor practices and productivity rates. The government of Carlos Menem has stated unequivocally that a government-protected economy and labor force no longer are deemed viable in the regional and global market place of the 1990s. What type of long-term effects will economic restructuring and the consequent restructuring of trade and production patterns have on the various spaces of Argentina?

Transport and Communication

As the foundation for the three major pillars of regional development, transport and communication are critical to growth and change in Argentina. Transport and communication services and infrastructure facilitate and condition interaction between people, institutions, labor, capital, and the regional environments. However, since the nineteenth century, transport routes in the country have been dendritic in nature, geared to carry export products from the interior to the ports. In the more remote areas of the Northeast, Northwest, and Patagonia, transport provision historically has been poor and unsuitable for regional development (Roccatagliata

1992a). Moreover, successive transport policies have failed to address the lack of connectivity with neighboring countries and have reinforced Buenos Aires' dominant position within Argentina (Keeling 1993). Privatization of the transport and communication sector has caused a realignment of internal spatial arrangements, with important consequences for the locational utility of regions and places (Chapter 5).

The level of connectivity experienced by Argentina along the local-global continuum plays a crucial role in shaping relationships between the country, its neighbors, and regional urban centers. Transport and communication also help to shape the response of individuals and institutions to the forces of change. The long-term success of globalization forces in Argentina and the country's incorporation more fully into the world economy depend, in large part, on the government's response to increased demands for transport and communication services and infrastructure. What role, then, are transport and communication playing in the restructuring of Argentina's social and economic spaces?

Argentina's Spatial Dichotomies

As a result of the ongoing restructuring of Argentina's pillars of development, the country's map of spatial inequalities in the 1990s promises to be far more complex than at any time in the preceding decades. Before addressing Argentina's internal spatial dichotomies, a brief overview of the national setting helps to provide a context for regional change. The Republic of Argentina is located at the extreme southern end of the American continent. It occupies an area of 3.7 million square kilometers, which includes 964,000 square kilometers of continental Antarctic territory and South Atlantic Islands claimed by Argentina. The country's continental land mass stretches southward over 3,700 kilometers from the 22nd to the 55th parallel. Argentina borders Bolivia to the north, Paraguay to the northeast, Brazil, Uruguay, and the Atlantic Ocean to the east, and Chile to the west. A lengthy coastline extends from the Río de la Plata estuary to Tierra del Fuego (Figure 1.2). Argentina's vast territorial extension suggests a wide variety of climates from the subtropical north to the frigid Patagonian lands. The bulk of the country, however, lies in a predominantly temperate zone. Humid lands comprise one third of the country, of which 30 percent is subtropical forests and woods in the northeast and 70 percent is the pampas plains that cover some 600,000 square kilometers.

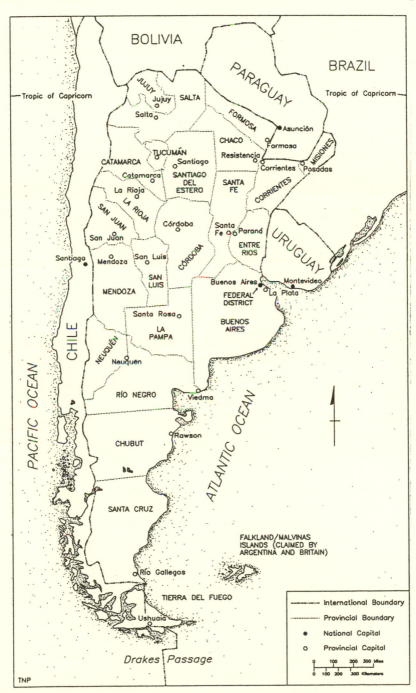

BOLIVIA

BRAZIL

PARAGUAY

—Tropic of Capricorn—

JUJUY

Jujuy
○

SALTA

Salta
○

FORMOSA

Tropic of Capricorn—

●Asunción

CHACO

Formosa
○

TUCUMÁN

Resistencia
○

CATAMARCA

Santiago
○

Corrientes
○

Posadas
○

MISIONES

Catamarca
○

SANTIAGO
DEL
ESTERO

SANTA
FE

CORRIENTES

La Rioja
○

LA RIOJA

SAN JUAN

Córdoba
○

San Juan
○

Santa
Fe ○

Paraná
○

URUGUAY

Santiago
●

Mendoza
○

San Luis
○

CÓRDOBA

ENTRE
RIOS

CHILE

SAN
LUIS

Buenos Aires
○

Montevideo
●

MENDOZA

FEDERAL
DISTRICT

La Plata
○

PACIFIC OCEAN

Santa Rosa
○

BUENOS
AIRES

LA
PAMPA

NEUQUÉN

Neuquén
○

RÍO NEGRO

Viedma
○

ATLANTIC OCEAN

Rawson
○

CHUBUT

SANTA CRUZ

FALKLAND/MALVINAS
ISLANDS (CLAIMED BY
ARGENTINA AND BRITAIN)

Río Gallegos
○

TIERRA DEL FUEGO

————— International Boundary

·········· Provincial Boundary

Ushuaia
○

● National Capital

○ Provincial Capital

Drakes Passage

0   100   200   300 Miles
0 100 200   300 Kilometers

TNP

FIGURE 1.2   Argentina.

The Pampeana is the dominant agricultural and industrial region of Argentina, accounting for 70 percent of the national population, 80 percent of the nation's agricultural production by value, and 85 percent of all industrial activities. The remaining two thirds of Argentina consists of arid or semiarid zones marked by prolonged dry periods. Organized as a federal representative republic, the country is politically divided into 23 provinces and a Federal Capital. Such great diversity in physical and human environments ensures that the impacts of growth and change in Argentina are temporally complex and spatially variegated. Indeed, dichotomies in Argentina's spatial development have plagued governments for over two centuries.

Defining a Regional Context for Analysis

A crucial and fundamental problem for understanding the spatial dynamics of change in Argentina and for creating policies designed to restructure and transform socioeconomic relationships has been the treatment of the country's diverse regions as static, homogenous units. Failure to consider the socioeconomic diversity and dynamism of Argentina's regions resulted in policies that focused the development impetus on Buenos Aires and its Pampeana hinterland. As a result, Argentina became a bifurcated society, characterized by extreme differences in the social and economic development of interior and Pampeana provinces.

Regions as Development Units. Prior to the 1960s, the concept of a region as a development unit did not exist in Argentina (Keeling 1994). Federal and provincial governments struggled for nearly a century after the independence movements of the early nineteenth century to define the exact external and internal boundaries of Argentina. Conflict still exists over extant boundaries, but the establishment of generally recognized territorial limits enabled federal, provincial, and local governments to develop formal administrative systems. To the extent that regions were considered at all, they always were seen as existing in relation to other Argentine regions and not to external regions. During Argentina's golden age of development (1880-1930), the organization and implementation of economic, social, and political policies strictly followed provincial political boundaries, even though planners, politicians, and the general public often thought in terms of commonly understood perceptual or vernacular regions--for example, the historic, colonial Northwest, or the desolate, frontier South. A strict territorial-hierarchical organization became embedded in the way planners and policy makers thought about Argentina and its constituent regions. Before World War II, government policies that addressed social and economic development issues emanated from Buenos Aires and were national in scope. Buenos Aires was Argentina. Moreover, development policies treated Argentina as a homogenous spatial unit, with little concern for functional differences or similarities among provinces.

Import-substitution industrialization policies adopted by Argentina during the global economic depression of the 1930s encouraged the government to group provinces in a consistent and practical way so as to facilitate statistical comparisons of development over long periods of time. Provinces were grouped based on the homogeneity of their economic activities (the agriculturally based Pampeana provinces of Buenos Aires, Córdoba, Entre Ríos, La Pampa, and Santa Fé), or on their natural geographic boundaries (the Northeast provinces of Corrientes, Chaco, Formosa, and Misiones) (Brodersohn 1967). From 1946 until the early 1960s, national planning agencies concentrated on sectoral development by focusing on the centralization and coordination of different economic sectors at the state level. Yet during this period, no changes occurred in either the theoretical or practical definition of regions. Provinces continued to be grouped together for statistical and administrative purposes.

In the 1960s, the desire of the Argentine government to ensure state security by firming up national claims to border territories spurred the establishment of formal development regions. For example, a strategic need to occupy and transform peripheral regions that were subject to possible claims or actions by Chile motivated the creation of urban growth poles in Patagonia (Morris 1972). Argentina's first major development plan formulated in 1965 established eight regions for the explicit purpose of planning, controlling, and stimulating the development of areas beyond the core metropolitan zone. These eight regions were defined according to their economic development potential and to their natural geographic boundaries. In practice, provincial boundaries demarcated the regions. Later plans reorganized development region boundaries to account for both the structural characteristics of the regions and the functional relationships among the regions' various structural elements. Nonetheless, political boundaries continued to play a central role in defining Argentina's regions.

Four dominant regions emerged from both perceptual and functional descriptions of Argentina during the 1970s and 1980s (Figure 1.3). From the viewpoint of Buenos Aires, the North came to be equated with poverty,

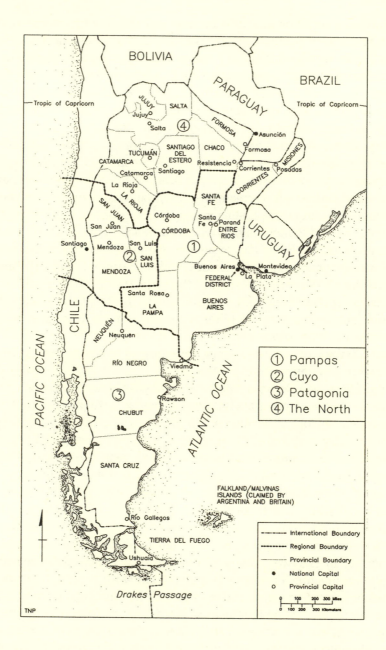

FIGURE 1.3 Argentina's Four Dominant Development Regions.
Source: República Argentina (1971).

backwardness, and non-Europeanness. Patagonia was perceived as the natural resource-rich underdeveloped frontier, an area with a mythology similar to the western frontier of the United States in the nineteenth century. To the west, the Cuyo had developed a somewhat ambiguous status as a gate-way to the Pacific and a growing agricultural zone populated by European immigrants, yet bracketed to the north and south by poverty. Finally, the pampas provinces were perceived as the heart of Argentina's economy, rich in agricultural wealth, dominated by Europeans, and inextricably inter-twined with the global economy.

Dividing Argentina's national territory into formal and functional regions for analytical purposes has preoccupied many of Argentina's geographers and planners since the 1950s. A variety of specific criteria, including geology, climate, morphology, economics, and regional development, have driven the definition and delimitation of regions. Although debate among Argentine scholars still occurs over the theoretical ways in which regions can be delimited, in practice the regions that have resulted from the use of these criteria remain defined by national boundaries and, in many cases, by provincial boundaries. Yet most functional regions did not come into being concurrently with the state or first-order civil division to which they usually are subordinated. Furthermore, regional inequalities generally do not originate or end at state boundaries.

Despite contemporary theoretical and practical challenges to conventional definitions of regions, development policies in Argentina continue to pose questions about particular regions without exploring the nature and significance of the region itself. Regions frequently are treated simply as acontextual spatial units. For example, Santillán de Andrés and Ricci's (1992) analysis of northwest Argentina never explains the significance of the Northwest as a cultural and spatial unit or even how the region evolved. Strategies designed to address regional inequalities will remain unsuccessful unless such concerns are addressed. Indeed, the failure of Argentina's regional development policies can be attributed in part to the lack of consideration given to the historical spatial, temporal, and cultural boundaries of the country's interior regions.

The challenge for planners, policy makers, and researchers is to rethink both the role and definition of regions in Argentina's development process. Regions should not be considered simply as geopolitical spaces with fixed and immutable boundaries (states or substate units, for example). Rather, regional contexts for analysis should be driven by the spatial and temporal incidence of growth and change within a distinct spatial milieu.

Relationships between sets of locations in resource, production, and human settlement systems change constantly. A good example of this concept is the creation, reproduction, and disappearance of the Salta-Potosí regions. The eighteenth-century relationships between the hierarchy of settlements focused on Salta in present-day northwest Argentina and the hierarchy of settlements focused on Potosí in Upper Peru (now Bolivia) created a single functional region that incorporated the territory between these places. As changes occurred both in the world economy and in political circumstances, the region restructured and finally disintegrated. Two new regions emerged out of the ashes of the old, partly as a result of the evolution of two separate states during the early nineteenth century with clearly defined boundaries and national ideologies. In the 1990s, these two hierarchies of settlements have few formal or functional links. However, sufficient interaction remains between Salta and Potosí for the functional boundaries of these two regions to overlap (Keeling 1994).

The geographical expressions of change in contemporary Argentina point toward the emergence of four distinct human-physical environments or regions, each with different challenges for planners and policy makers. Thus, the implications of socioeconomic restructuring are studied not in terms of the 23 provinces or the five standard planning regions that are commonly used in analyses of Argentina, but in terms of the collective issues that inextricably bind certain provinces and localities together. This does not mean that there are not important distinctions between, for example, Tucumán and Jujuy in the Northwest or between Tierra del Fuego and Chubut in Patagonia. Individual provinces and localities within regions all may exhibit different social and economic relationships. However, this division--although relatively crude and lacking in precision at the edges--corresponds much more closely to the realities of change in contemporary Argentina than the usual regional treatment.

The Megacity

Argentina's capital city and primary urban center continues to exert tremendous influence over the nation. Since the 1950s, the dominance of Buenos Aires over the country has created a serious planning problem and has encouraged megacephalous growth in the suburban areas of the city. Nearly 14 million people, or about 40 percent of the entire country's population, lived in the Greater Buenos Aires metropolitan area in 1996, an increase of about one million since the 1991 census. This represents a staggering concentration of humanity in one city when you consider that Argentina has 2.8 million square kilometers of continental territory. Excessive traffic congestion, deterioration of the physical environment, urban pollution, and increasing levels of poverty are eroding quality of life in Buenos Aires (Keeling 1996). In many ways, the city encapsulates the country's socioeconomic problems.

One of the more serious issues for the future of Argentina is the embedded belief that what is good for Buenos Aires is good for the nation. National planning often is driven by the context of Buenos Aires' problems and frequently treats Argentina as a homogenous planning space. Regional environments, cultures, and economic differences rarely are recognized explicitly in national policies. As James Scobie (1971) put it, Buenos Aires historically has been both city and nation (Chapter 6). Moreover, the pattern of megacephalous growth in Buenos Aires is being replicated in Argentina's provincial capitals. Each province has become dominated over the past 50 years by its own megacity, albeit at a different scale. For example, Greater Mendoza accounted for approximately 70 percent of the total population of Mendoza province in 1991, Salta accounted for 43 percent of Salta province's total population, and Greater Córdoba dominated the province of Córdoba with 45 percent of the total population. Thus, the problems created by the megacephalization of the provincial capitals relative to their respective province are similar to those created by Buenos Aires' dominance over Argentina.

Prosperous Agricultural Provinces

The Pampeana provinces comprise the economic core of Argentina. Agricultural production from the Pampas has provided the economic backbone of the country for over 200 years. However, in recent years, regional development strategies have attempted to deconcentrate industrial and commercial activities to the Pampeana. Today, Argentina's major ports, largest urban centers, most extensive transport networks, and major industrial plants are contained within a broad pampas arc that extends approximately 750 kilometers from the capital city. This dispersal of housing and employment growth from Buenos Aires to the urban centers of the Pampeana raises major questions about land-use planning and the role of agriculture in the economy (Chapter 7). Tensions between industrial, agricultural, and urban activities are evident as planners struggle to cope with the problems of growth in the prosperous Pampeana region. Moreover, these agricultural provinces must face the reality that the global economy no longer requires the quantities of agriculture produce that historically have formed the backbone of the country's wealth.

The Challenge of Transition Areas

The Cuyo provinces nestled in the foothills of the Andes face a particularly difficult period of transition as Argentina attempts to globalize its economy and society. Historically dominated by viticulture and light manufacturing, this subregion could play a major role in articulating Argentina with an emerging Pacific Rim. The cities and towns of the Cuyo lie closer to Chile and the Pacific Ocean than to Buenos Aires and the Atlantic. Moreover, the Cuyo provinces form an oasis of growth and development between the underdeveloped northwestern provinces and the emerging provinces of southwestern Patagonia. Could a major north-south Andean growth axis alter the economic space of Argentina and provide balance to a country dominated by Buenos Aires?

Patagonia also is an area of Argentina in transition. The government has tried growth pole strategies in recent years to encourage industrial and population growth. During the 1980s, for example, population increases greater than 30 percent were recorded throughout the region, with Tierra del Fuego exploding by over 150 percent. Yet major questions remain about the role Patagonia might play in the socioeconomic restructuring of the country's territory. Endowed with some natural resources, but hampered by inadequate communication infrastructure and poorly conceived regional development strategies, this frontier area is considered by planners and government officials alike as crucial to the long-term economic success of Argentina. What possibilities exist to develop the image and infrastructure of these transition areas, as a prelude to introducing modern economic activity to the major growth axes (Chapter 8)?

The Problem of Submerging Rural Areas

Some of the most compelling evidence of the consequences of socioeconomic restructuring in Argentina is found in the rural areas of the Northeast and Northwest. Grinding poverty, rampant unemployment, inadequate housing, poor education opportunities, and a substandard quality of life suggest that the short-term impact on outer rural areas of economic globalization has been mostly negative. Yet these places are positioned to take advantage of potential increased interaction with neighboring states and to benefit from an evolving Southern Cone regional trading bloc. Moreover, their distinct rural environments continue to attract tourists and to induce some elements of commercial agricultural and industrial growth (Chapter 9).

Many of the divisions and similarities between different regions of Argentina need a much deeper understanding, which can be provided by a detailed review of the country's international and historical position in the global system. As Nigel Thrift (1986:62) argued, few researchers have seemed willing to "come out of their national shells and take the wider view which would enable them to understand what is going on within their own countries." In the following chapter, I examine Argentina's past and present relationships at the regional and international levels in order to place in context the experiences of national and local socioeconomic growth and change.

2

The Development of Regional and International Relationships

Argentina's social, economic, and political spaces have been shaped historically by four distinct phases of international and national influence: colonization, mercantilism, industrial capitalism, and globalization. This chapter analyzes briefly the genesis, growth, and change of Argentina's regional and international relationships during these phases, extending from the arrival of the Spanish Conquistadors in the sixteenth century to the beginning of the 1990s. The framework used here for an analysis of the geohistorical evolution of Argentina in the world economy is provided by Peter Taylor's (1989) space-time information matrix, based on Kondratieff's description of economic long waves (Table 2.1). The matrix has been modified to explain local conditions within Argentina.

During the logistic curve that preceded the first Kondratieff wave (1536-1776), the Spanish colonized Argentina and established an urban network geared to support resource extraction. A two-pronged system of spatial development in Argentina based on the growth of agriculture and protoindustrial services characterized the region's evolution in the world periphery during the first Kondratieff wave (1776-1852). From the beginning of the second wave (1852) until midway through the 'B' cycle of the third wave, Argentina enjoyed 80 years of agriculturally based mercantilism. During the first half of the nineteenth century, the country emerged from a series of internal struggles, consolidated its national territory, and fully incorporated itself into the world economy. Railroads, wheat, and cattle became the driving forces in the solidification of Argentina's international relationships. The era of national industrialization, from 1930 until 1990, built on the foundations of a capitalist export economy rooted

TABLE 2.1   A Space-Time Information Matrix

Economic Cycle	Core
Logistic Curve	
A c.1450 - c.1600	Initial geographic expansion based on Iberia but economic advances focused on northwest Europe.
B c.1600 - c.1750	Consolidation of northwest Europe's dominance, with Dutch and then French-English rivalry.
Kondratieff Waves	
I A 1780/90 - 1810/17	Industrial Revolution in Britain, "national" revolution in France, and the defeat of France.
B 1810/17 - 1844/51	Consolidation of British economic leadership. Genesis of socialism in France and Britain.
II A 1844/51 - 1870/75	An era of free trade with Britain as the "workshop of the world."
B 1870/75 - 1890/96	Britain declines relative to Germany and the United States. Emergence of the Socialist Second International.
III A 1890/96 - 1914/20	Consolidation of German and U.S. economic leadership. Arms race.
B 1914/20 - 1940/45	Defeat of Germany, British Empire saved. US economic leadership affirmed.
IV A 1940/45 - 1967/73	United States as the global military and economic hegemon. New era of free trade.
B 1967/73 - 1990/92?	Decline of the U.S. relative to Japan and Europe. Nuclear arms race.
V A 1990/92? - ?	German reunification and the end of the Cold War. Development of multipolar regional trade blocs. Emergence of a truly global economy.

(continues)

TABLE 2.1 (continued)

Semiperiphery	Periphery: Latin America and Argentina
Relative decline of cities of central and Mediterranean Europe	Iberian Empires in the "New World." Spanish colonization in Argentina.
Declining areas now include Iberia, joined by rising groups in Sweden, Prussia, and the northeast U.S.	Retrenchment in Latin America, rise of Caribbean sugar. Expansion of Spanish control, with development of urban network in northwest Argentina.
Relative decline of whole semi-periphery. United States established.	Decolonization in Latin America. Atlantic ports open up in Argentina.
Start of selective rise in North America and central Europe.	Expansion of British influence. Conflict retards Argentina's development.
Semiperiphery reorganized; U.S. civil war, German and Italian unification.	Era of "informal imperialism" with growth of Latin America. Expansion of Argentina's agricultural economy.
Decline of Russia and Mediterranean Europe.	The classical age of imperialism. British investment in Argentina.
Entry of Japan and the Dominion States.	U.S. hegemony in Latin America. Early industrial growth in Argentina.
Socialist victory in Russia-U.S.S.R. established.	Import-substitution in Latin America. Political and economic crises in Argentina, rise of Peronist state.
Rise of Eastern Europe and "Cold War." Entry of OPEC.	Economic growth in Latin America. Rapid growth of Argentina's cities; disengagement from world economy.
Entry of "Asian Tigers" and new regional powers.	Latin American debt crisis. Economic and political collapse in Argentina.
Dissolution of the U.S.S.R. Globalization of economies.	New democracies in Latin America. Economic restructuring in Argentina.

Source: Adapted from Taylor (1989) and Becker and Egler (1992).

in agriculture and encouraged national-developmentalism during the Post-World War II Peronist period. During the fourth Kondratieff wave, Argentina suffered a reversal of fortune and became disengaged from the international system. As the world economy arguably moves into the 'A' cycle of a fifth Kondratieff wave, the Argentine state is restructuring the economy in order to rearticulate the country more forcefully with emerging regional trade blocs and with the truly global economy. The impacts of post-1990 globalization strategies on Argentina's society and economy are analyzed in part two of the study.

On the Margins of Empire (1536-1852)

Spanish exploration and settlement of the territory which became Argentina were part of a wider process of European maritime expansion during the fifteenth and sixteenth centuries known generally as the "Age of Discovery." Spurred in part by Iberian demand for booty wealth, fresh sources of slave labor, raw materials for a growing manufacturing sector, and finished goods for an increasingly voracious consumer society, the search for new routes to the Orient led Columbus and others to the Americas. Geography and European politics also played a crucial role in the occupation of southern South America by the Spanish. Rivalry between Spain and other European powers during the sixteenth century encouraged the Spanish Crown to seek out strategic positions on the southern landmass of the New World. The first attempt at settling Argentina occurred in 1536 on the right bank of the Río de la Plata, when Pedro de Mendoza established a garrison which eventually became known as Buenos Aires. The Spanish saw the Río de la Plata region as a possible Atlantic gateway between Spain and the perceived mineral riches of the Andean highlands. A fortified settlement along the Plata estuary could function as a barrier to possible Portuguese incursions into the region and as a possible administrative center for Spanish activities in the new territory (Rock 1985).

The second prong of Argentina's territorial occupation came from the Pacific coast. Preliminary explorations of the Northwest region began in 1535 after the Spanish had defeated the great Inca empire. Lima's establishment as the center of the Viceroyalty of Peru controlling all territory south of Panamá, and the 1545 discovery of silver at Potosí in present-day Bolivia, gave impetus to the creation of permanent settlements in Argentina's northwest. As with the initial incursions of the Inca into Argentina prior to the colonial period, several factors encouraged Spanish exploration of the Northwest (Scobie 1971, 1988; Rock 1985). First, the Northwest's indigenous societies could supply not only agricultural products for local and regional consumption (maize, potatoes, beans, squash, and quinoa), but also labor for the "rights of encomienda" (forced labor) granted to loyal Spaniards and for the Potosí mines. Second, the Spanish were eager to find and develop an alternative supply route to Upper Peru because existing maritime connections via Lima and Panamá were tenuous at best. Third, access to the Atlantic would enable a more rapid deployment of military reinforcements from Spain for the wars against Chile's Araucanian peoples. Moreover, the development of an Atlantic corridor also would protect the region against Portuguese incursions. Finally, competition between rival settlers in the Northwest and Asunción for control of both legal and illegal trade with Potosí and Brazil encouraged the solidification of transport and communication routes between Upper Peru, Mendoza, and the Atlantic coast.

The Spanish Crown's prohibition against trade with other towns in the Americas encouraged the new Argentine settlements to develop strong economic ties outside the region. As a dependency of the Viceroyalty of Peru, the region's trade was strictly controlled from Lima, a policy reinforced by the economic and political power of merchants in Spain (Scobie 1971). Official maritime trade links to the city of Sevilla in Spain were facilitated by the 5,000-kilometer major trunk route that connected Buenos Aires, the northwestern towns, Potosí, and the Incan capital of Cuzco to Lima (Figure 2.1). However, with few precious metals to exploit in Argentina and little European demand for temperate produce, the region's international commercial activity remained limited to a marginal role in Peru's mining economy (Crossley 1983). Corn, wheat, fruit, melons, grapes, honey, wax, cotton, and dyes were exported to Chile and Peru from the Northwest, while clothing, livestock (horses, cows, goats, and sheep), plants, and seeds were imported. Sheep and cattle products from the pampas grasslands around Buenos Aires also contributed to regional and domestic trade.

Absent strong international demand for Argentine products during the first two centuries of Spanish colonial rule, the country developed an economy of protoindustrial and agricultural self-sufficiency. Argentina grew as a peripheral region of the evolving European world economy, while the core countries of Western Europe consolidated their global trade dominance and began a period of intense rivalry. Relative economic isolation encouraged contraband trading with Brazil and with European interlopers and stimulated indigenous manufacturing, particularly in the urban centers of

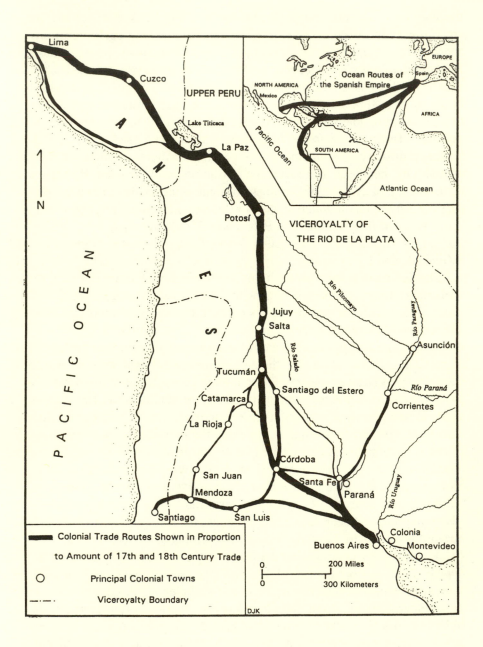

FIGURE 2.1   Colonial Transport Corridor in the Southern Cone.
Source: After Scobie (1971).

the Northwest. Tucumán supplied carts to the entire Río de la Plata region and cotton and woollen goods to Chile and Potosí. Mendoza developed as a center for the production of wine and dried fruits. Mules were bred in Mesopotamia and on the pampas, fattened in Córdoba and Tucumán, and sold by the thousands at the great annual fair in Salta. Livestock farming, however, would become the backbone of Argentina's later commercial economic success. The luxuriant natural pastures of the pampas and mesopotamia permitted the rapid multiplication of wild cattle and horses. Hides became the leading commercial product, with nearly 1.5 million exported annually by the 1780s. (Crossley 1983). Salt meat production for export also developed rapidly in the 1780s following the introduction of salt supplies from Patagonia.

Development of the Atlantic Coast

Spain's creation of the Viceroyalty of the Río de la Plata in 1776 centered on Buenos Aires coincided with the beginning cycle of Kondratieff's first wave (Table 2.1). With the introduction of "free trade" regulations in 1777-78, Argentina's Littoral opened up to the North Atlantic economy, dramatically changing the region's local, regional, and international trade relationships. The Atlantic coast region began to dominate political, social, and economic activities in Argentina. Trade relations between the interior provinces and neighboring regions weakened as Buenos Aires exerted more political and economic power over the Southern Cone. Forty years later, emancipation from Spain and political independence disrupted the economy of the entire region and led to a dramatic restructuring of traditional trade links. The creation of national political boundaries between Bolivia, Chile, Paraguay, and Argentina constricted the Northwest's primary commercial outlet and subjugated its urban centers to the Littoral and Buenos Aires. In addition, persistent internal strife between 1816 and 1880, the erection of interprovincial tariff barriers, and liberal trade between Britain and the Atlantic coast cities further increased the economic isolation of interior towns.

Argentina's peripheral role in the world economy during the 'B' cycle of the first Kondratieff wave weakened as a consequence of internal conflict. Moreover, the core-periphery pattern evolving at the global level began to develop within Argentina. Political and economic forces favored the emerging coastal zone focused on Buenos Aires, especially the concentration of agricultural wealth, political power, merchant dominance, and transport provision in and around the port city. Thus, the first half of the nineteenth century marked the beginning phase of a permanent shift in national emphasis from the Northwest to the Littoral. Although the demographic balance between the two areas remained steady, the urban nucleus of Buenos Aires began to set the pace of development that the Pampeana region would follow. Economically, the balance between coast and interior changed dramatically. As Aldo Ferrer (1967:67) noted, "the policy of free imports blocked any possibility of spreading (to the interior) the dynamic impulse generated by the Litoral's export expansion." Poor access to export markets and an extremely weak transport infrastructure prevented the interior provinces from generating surplus capital with which to purchase new technologies. Distance remained the major barrier for development of the interior, although local industries were protected from competition. However, industry in the Northwest stagnated, forcing the growing urban population increasingly into subsistence occupations (Ferrer 1967). By the middle of the nineteenth century, three distinct socioeconomic zones could be distinguished in Argentina: the dynamic, prosperous coastal area; the impoverished interior; and the frontier lands of Patagonia.

Integration into the World Economy (1852-1930)

The geography of Argentina began a period of profound transformation at the beginning of the "A" cycle of Kondratieff's second long wave (see Table 2.1). Argentina emerged from dictatorship in 1852 to enjoy a long period of semi-democratic constitutional government and rapid economic growth. Four processes played a dominant role in restructuring the national territory and articulating the country with the world economy: immigration, improved capital circulation, an agricultural revolution, and railroad construction. These processes were driven by the political and economic ideas of the elite and their growing power in newly independent Argentina, ideas nourished to maturity by European models and myths of progress and modernization. Agricultural wealth from the pampas provided the political and economic base that formed the foundation for Argentina's development ideologies. However, by adopting rather than adapting European ideas about "civilization" that stemmed from Enlightenment and Positivist philosophies, Argentina's policy makers embarked on a development path that reflected little or none of the local socioeconomic environment. Two powerful themes or myths emerged from this period that have shaped development policies and ideologies to this day: a belief that Buenos Aires represented the civilized, modernized European world and that the interior was backward and barbaric; and a belief that what was good for Buenos Aires was good for Argentina. In other words, the entire nation should aspire to be like the sophisticated, cosmopolitan, Europeanized capital.

Immigration

Immigration's role in reshaping Argentina is unique in the western hemisphere. The creole, mestizo, and indigenous character of Argentina transitioned into a "lumpy stew" of European settlers as over 3 million migrants arrived from overseas to seek their fame and fortune. From 1881 to 1890, and again from 1901 to 1910, Argentina experienced the highest intensity of immigration ever recorded in the New World (Crossley 1983). In 1869, only 12 percent of the country's population was foreign-born; by 1914, this number had reached 30 percent. However, a distinct spatial pattern in migration could be observed in Argentina. The country effectively became ethnically bifurcated between a European-dominated coastal region, and a mestizo- and creole-dominated interior. Few migrants from contiguous countries settled in Buenos Aires, the federal capital. Most moved to those Argentine provinces that bordered their native land. For example, 70 percent of Formosa's population in 1914 was Paraguayan and nearly 40 percent of the population of Misiones province was Brazilian or Paraguayan. In Jujuy province, Bolivians comprised 20 percent of the population, and Chileans comprised nearly 50 percent of Tierra del Fuego's population.

In contrast, over 90 percent of the European migrants to Argentina settled either in Buenos Aires or in the agriculturally developing provinces of the Pampeana. The 1914 census revealed that 57 percent of Argentina's 2.1 million European-born residents lived in the five Pampas provinces, while 33 percent resided in the city of Buenos Aires. In comparison, the western and northern provinces that had been demographically dominant during the eighteenth and nineteenth centuries attracted only 7.5 percent of Argentina's recent European immigrants. Moreover, the majority of European immigrants preferred to settle in the cities. In 1914, although only 53 percent of the country's population was considered urban, 78 percent of all Spanish-born and 70 percent of all Italian-born immigrants lived in urban areas.

Economic opportunities in Argentina shaped the distribution of immigrants. Although immigrants suffered from poor access to landownership after 1890, many became owners or tenants of livestock and crop farms on the pampas. In the urban centers of the Pampeana, however, nearly 70 percent of all commercial and industrial companies were foreign-owned by 1914, and immigrants comprised approximately half of all their personnel (Crossley 1983). The influx of migrants from both Europe and adjacent countries shaped Argentina's cities, towns, and villages in profound ways during the late nineteenth and early twentieth centuries. Yet the country emerged from this period divided, uncertain, and a little schizophrenic. As James Scobie (1971) observed, Argentina struggled with the image of sophisticated, prosperous Buenos Aires juxtaposed against an impoverished interior one hundred years removed from the cosmopolitan city.

Improved Circuits of Capital

Throughout the 'A' cycle of Kondratieff's third economic wave, speculative British capital and domestic capital generated by the agricultural bounty of the pampas spurred land improvements, port construction, urban redevelopment, and transportation advancements in Argentina. Britain's industrial success during the nineteenth century generated a tremendous capital surplus. British companies, institutional investors, and individuals looked beyond the island's shores for investment opportunities in agriculture and resource extraction, sectors necessary to feed Britain's growing urban populations and supply its huge industrial capacity. As the world leader in the development of railroad technologies, Britain also looked to export its transport capabilities overseas as the transport sector could provide important backward and forward linkages to British industry. Argentina appealed to British investors in part because of its dominant European ideology and heritage, its relative political-economic stability, its rich, flat pampas grasslands suitable for railroad construction and export-oriented agriculture, and its promise of high profits. By 1910, Britain's investments in Argentina were valued at nearly 300 million pounds sterling.

Improved circuits of capital in Argentina facilitated the harnessing of immigrant labor to maximize the country's agricultural potential. By 1914, over 8 percent of the world economy's foreign investment had been directed toward "lubricating the machine of Argentine agricultural production" (Crossley 1983:400). Railroads, port installations, public utilities, and irrigation projects absorbed 75 percent of this capital, while a further 20 percent was directed into trade, finance, loan agencies, banking, and merchant services. Yet despite this tremendous flow of capital into Argentina, only five percent of all foreign investment in Argentina by 1914 had gone directly into agriculture. Extensive, relatively inefficient agricultural production rather than intensive, efficient production dominated Argentina's economy. Nonetheless, the profits and rents that accrued to the pampas landowners were among the highest in the world, yielding what Flichman (1982:74-78) called an enormous "international differential rent." Excess rent stemmed from the availability of cheap labor, from the high yields that could be obtained from the fertile land with little capital investment, from the relatively close proximity of the ports, and from the absence of property or export taxes (Johns 1992). Unfortunately, little of the capital that flowed into Argentina prior to 1930 found its way to the interior provinces. Capital that did circulate through the interior primarily focused on the major urban centers, where it reached out almost exclusively to the sugar mills of the Northwest and to the vineyards of the Cuyo.

Argentina's Agricultural Revolution

New capital helped Argentina's agricultural economy convert rapidly to the production of vast quantities of cereals and high-quality meat products. The new republic quickly established itself as a leading player within the nineteenth-century world exchange economy. The introduction of better breeds of sheep allowed wool exports to rise from 7,700 tonnes in 1850 to nearly 150,000 tonnes by the turn of the century, although Patagonia eventually became the dominant sheep region as grains and cattle took over the Pampeana provinces. Meat-freezing plants and refrigerated ships stimulated the livestock industry and encouraged new grazing lands to be developed on the pampas frontier, in the north, and in Patagonia. Over one million kilometers of wire fencing reshaped the landscape as the pampas underwent conversion from an almost purely pastoral region to one of the leading cereal producers in the world economy (Crossley 1983). Cultivated acreage on the pampas increased fifteen-fold to almost 10 million acres between 1872 and 1895. Cereals totaled over 50 percent of total exports by value by the turn of the century, with wheat, maize, and flax dominating production. Immigrant labor in the form of tenant farmers, mortgages granted to farmers for land-fencing projects, government loans, and the expansion of the railroad network together made possible Argentina's agricultural revolution and its articulation with the world economy.

Although the production of pampas cereals and meat for the world markets functioned as the primary stimulus for Argentina's growth between 1852 and 1930, other components of the country's agricultural economy also played an important development role. Railroads and protective tariffs encouraged sugar production in the northwest provinces of Salta and Tucumán, where over 100,000 hectares of sugar cane were under cultivation by 1914. However, high production costs and a marginal climate limited the distribution of sugar to the domestic market. In the Cuyo provinces of Mendoza and San Juan, Italian immigrants and tariff protections combined to stimulate the wine industry, although, like sugar, the majority of production entered the domestic market. Cotton production in the Chaco region expanded rapidly after the First World War, with Argentina becoming the world's seventh-largest cotton producer by the 1930s. Agricultural production also stimulated industrial development, although industry remained small scale and geared primarily to food processing. Manufacturers in the major urban centers mostly produced simple consumer goods to satisfy domestic demand. Very little production of heavy machinery, capital equipment, transport technology, or luxury manufactured goods occurred in Argentina before the 1930s.

Railroad Construction

Between 1870 and 1930, the Pampeana became the social, political, and economic powerhouse of Argentina. Buenos Aires and surrounding provinces were closer perceptually and practically to London and Paris than to many interior areas. During the railroad construction era, much of the interior became peripheral to the growing power of the Pampeana as railroads focused on the port cities and began to tie the coastal region more closely to the world economy. A great deal of controversy surrounds the railroad's role in developing Argentina from a relatively isolated remnant of Spain's overseas empire to an important component of the world economy. The impact of product specialization and trade concentration on the country's social structure also has been debated quite vociferously (Scalabrini Ortiz 1957; Ferrer 1967; Ortiz 1964).

Economic, political, and social cleavages between the interior and the Littoral have been linked directly to Argentina's participation in the world economy. The argument generally presented is that the cereal and beef producing areas of the pampas captured the fruits of development, while the importation of European manufactures led to the ruin of handicrafts and small industries in the interior. As a result, Argentina evolved into two unequal and divided worlds (Scobie 1971; Shumway 1991). British-controlled railroads that transported export products to port and distributed European imports throughout the country often are presented as the agents of this bifurcation (Ortiz 1946; Cuccorese 1969; Scalabrini Ortiz 1983). The myriad narrow, economically focused analyses of the railroad's development powers, however, frequently have ignored many of the important geographic, political, and social processes that contributed to underdevelopment in the interior (Keeling 1992). Nonetheless, railroads, more than any other technological advance in the nineteenth century, epitomized Argentina's crusade to incorporate European ideologies into the development of the country. Politicians especially were convinced that the elimination of provincial isolation and insularity would promote national unification, which in turn would help articulate Argentina more forcefully with the world economy.

British capital built many of the railroad lines that snaked out across the flat pampas from the port cities to capture the economic potential of the interior and unify the nation. However, few intraregional railroads were constructed in the interior, and connections between interior provinces remained difficult and slow. For example, in 1914 approximately 73 percent of all the railroad lines in Argentina were located in the Pampeana region (Table 2.2). The British-owned companies that controlled most of the Pampeana railroad lines were concerned with profitability and annual rates of return, not with regional development and territorial integration. On paper, interior Argentina presented little profit potential for foreign investors, who remained content to let the Argentine government take the lead in railroad construction in more remote areas. However, neither federal nor provincial governments had the funds or the willingness to extend railroad lines beyond the provincial capitals.

Railroads facilitated the insertion of Argentina into the world economy but they did little to encourage the creation of a territorially dispersed hierarchy of market centers. The means of production in the interior remained small, deprived of technology, and poor. In contrast, the landowners' world of cities, industry, import, and export--a world that relied on a backward and exploited interior population--thrived and grew rapidly. Heralded originally as the social and economic salvation of the backward interior, railroads could not negate the culturally embedded influences of a regressive social system, unjust land tenure, exploitive labor conditions, political corruption, usurious credit practices, and technological underdevelopment.

Argentina's railroads could have stimulated interior development only as part of a strategy designed to produce an interconnected network of market towns. In order to insert interior provinces into the national, regional, and international economies, a coherent spatial, temporal, and social hierarchy

TABLE 2.2 The Distribution of Railroads in Argentina by Region and Political Division, 1914

Region/ Political Division	Kilometers		Percentage of National Network	
Pampeana				
Buenos Aires	12,086		37.2	
Córdoba	4,123		12.7	
Entre Ríos	1,183		3.6	
La Pampa	1,325		4.1	
Santa Fé	4,972	23,689	15.3	72.9
Northwest				
Catamarca	632		1.9	
Jujuy	530		1.6	
La Rioja	655		2.0	
Salta	375		1.2	
Santiago del Estero	1,458		4.5	
Tucumán	784	4,434	2.4	13.6
Cuyo				
Mendoza	1,176		3.6	
San Juan	340		1.0	
San Luis	965	1,241	3.0	7.6
Northeast				
Chaco	219		0.7	
Corrientes	924		2.8	
Misiones	57	1,200	0.2	3.7
Patagonia				
Chubut	86		0.3	
Neuquén	192		0.6	
Río Negro	411	689	1.3	2.2
National Total:		32,493		100.0

Source: Bunge (1918); República Argentina (1946).

of settlements was required that could function as production, trade, and service centers offering employment and access to other basic needs and opportunities. However, from the perspective of the federal government in Buenos Aires, the priorities of transport development during the railroad era had been to reach the provincial capitals, capture their industries, and bind the interior irrevocably to the fortunes of the capital (Keeling 1992). Although the government did invest in some infrastructural projects to encourage development of the interior's urban hinterland, particularly road and rail building in the Northwest, it proved to be too little, too late. Rural colonization schemes in Patagonia and the Northwest, for example, did help to diversify rural production, but the interior remained handicapped by inadequate distribution networks and poor communications.

The development of a transport network focused on Buenos Aires and the pampas ultimately restricted widespread social, political, and economic growth in the interior. By failing to take advantage of transport and trade opportunities with Bolivia, Brazil, Chile, Paraguay, and Uruguay, Argentina's government stymied any possible integrated or independent economic networks from emerging in the interior and alienated many interior residents. Most of the interior provinces, especially those of the Northwest, were condemned to future decades of a substandard quality of life with minimal access to the opportunities that could set the interior on a development course parallel to the Pampeana. The insertion of Argentina's economy into the international system had been achieved by subjugating the interior to Buenos Aires and the Pampeana provinces.

Argentina in the 1920s

Debate between structuralists, nationalists, and liberals over the ideological and practical implications of Argentina's participation in the world economy between the 1850s and the 1920s continues to rage. Structuralist critiques of Argentina's growth prior to the 1930s suggest that the country was ill-prepared to participate in the international financial and commercial system that developed after World War I (Bunge 1940; Ferrer 1967; Fodor and O'Connell 1973). They argue that the growing importance of the United States in hemispheric and global politics and trade after World War I meant an end to Argentina's traditional European financial and commercial links. Structuralists also point to serious exogenous and endogenous flaws in the pattern of export-driven development that had shaped Argentina up to the 1920s.

Nationalists and radicals argued that external penetration of Argentina's economy, coupled with inequities inherent in the core-periphery structure of the world economy, had compounded the problems of sectoral, social, and regional disparities associated with an agriculturally based export growth model (Scalabrini Ortiz 1957; Ortiz 1964). Poor agricultural productivity caused by undercapitalization, inequitable patterns of land ownership, and inadequate technology retarded the State's ability to cope with the profound social changes wrought by mass immigration, improved mobility, and rapid urban growth between the 1880s and the 1920s. Nationalists supported disengagement from an exploitive world economy in order to develop a strong national socioeconomic structure, while liberals continued to eulogize the benefits of export-led growth (Lewis 1993). Although recent research on landholding patterns on the pampas challenge many assumptions about the relative efficiency of Argentina's agricultural sector, there is little debate that the country remained highly dependent on exports of agricultural production and on imports of industrial and consumer goods. The real problem lay with the failure of the Argentine state to generate, implement, and sustain development policies that recognized the spatial, socioeconomic, and political complexity of the country. Nonetheless, Argentina's rapid growth during the second and third Kondratieff waves enabled it to become by 1930 one of the ten richest countries in the world, per capita.

Disengagement from the World Economy (1930-1990)

Between the 1930s and the 1980s, Argentina suffered from a combination of political upheavals, dictatorships, inept management of the national economy, megacephalous urban growth, and the increased social and economic bifurcation of the country. Coupled with the economy's conversion to a state-directed system driven by import substitution industrialization policies, by 1989 these problems had dragged Argentina down from 10th to 70th richest country in the world (Milberg 1993). Argentina's brilliant future had become instead a brilliant past. Explanations of the Argentine development paradox abound, with most citing missed opportunities, mismanagement, and a weak national political culture as the major themes of Argentina's economic history during the fourth Kondratieff wave (see, for example, Díaz-Alejandro 1970; Wynia 1992; Erro 1993). Colin Lewis (1993:110) focused on three principal interrelated causes of the country's decline: inconsistent political economic policy, a high level of sectoral conflict, and an exceptionally high degree of disarticulation between the national and world economies. These and other factors combined to disengage Argentina slowly but surely from the world economy after 1930. However, in terms of the long-term development of the country's socio-economic space, four processes stand out as critical: (1) increased state control over the means of production via import-substitution and nationalization policies; (2) the concentration of industrial activity in and around Buenos Aires; (3) the deterioration of the national transport network; and (4) a failure to develop strong regional and global trade relationships.

Import-Substitution Industrialization

Argentina's steady industrial growth prior to the 1930s was unplanned and unencouraged, simply a by-product of rapid population growth, an agricultural boom, and railroad expansion (Lewis 1990). Yet despite industrial optimism and growth, economic trends during the 1930s suggested that Argentina was headed in the wrong direction for future development. Compared to other industrialized countries, manufacturing in Argentina remained technologically backward, small-scale, poorly capitalized, inefficient, and dependent on government support for survival. A "push" and "pull" dynamic clearly was evident during the initial phase of Argentina's import-substitution industrialization (ISI). A shortage of imports and reduced capital investment in Argentina's industry caused first by global economic depression and then World War II provided a "push" for ISI policies. Even the agricultural elite supported ISI as a means of stabilizing exports and developing a more profitable and efficient sector. Unfortunately, ISI policies placed little emphasis on the export of manufactured consumer and capital goods. National political events in Argentina supplied the "pull" dynamic for ISI. Industrial development helped to create an urban middle class, which in turn became increasingly incorporated into society and began to share political power with the landowning oligarchy. In addition, the government intervened with loans, tariffs, and regulations designed to protect fledgling industries and to encourage self-sufficiency in the production of industrial goods for domestic markets. Over the long term, ISI encouraged factories to become more labor intensive rather than capital intensive (Lewis 1990; Lewis 1993).

Most Latin American countries pursued policies of internally directed growth after the 1930s. However, few adopted ISI policies as rigorous as those implemented by Argentina, particularly between 1945 and 1970. The introduction of tariffs, currency exchange controls, barriers against capital flows, and a host of other non-tariff trade barriers proved severe and poorly timed and served to isolate the national economy from global markets (Lewis 1993). Argentina's ISI policies were, in part, a reaction to events in the world economy. After World War I, many industrial countries erected tariff barriers to protect their domestic agricultural systems, which reduced Argentina's export earnings. Britain especially looked increasingly to agricultural and raw material production in the Commonwealth countries. Thus, with imported consumer goods expensive and difficult to obtain, native manufacturing was encouraged to expand. Argentina suffered, however, from several structural handicaps that limited the success of ISI policies. A run-down transportation system, inadequate heavy machinery and equipment, a lack of developed energy resources, the uneven development of light industries, the absence of a steel industry, and an impoverished interior market all combined to retard industrial growth (Scobie 1971). Nonetheless, by the end of World War II, Argentina boasted over one million industrial workers producing goods in nearly 85,000 factories (Table 2.3). Unfortunately, a further blow to industrial growth occurred during the Second World War, when Argentina's equivocal neutralist or pro-Axis attitudes severed the major supplies of capital goods from the United States.

As the world economy entered the fourth Kondratieff wave during the 1940s, import-substitution policies in Argentina were melded with social and institutional changes to reshape the country in profound ways. National developmentalism and Juan Domingo Perón's development of the social state are perhaps the most enduring legacies from this period. Perón nationalized much of Argentina's transport system, public utilities, and major industries, and led the drive toward domestic industrialization and economic independence (Rock 1993). The Peronist regime theorized that disarticulation from a world economy that drew primary exports from Argentina and returned goods manufactured in the North Atlantic countries would allow Argentina to develop its own national economic and social identity and to realign itself more advantageously in the core-periphery structure of the world economy. In addition, a more equitable process of national regional development would result from such a strategy. Although much of Argentina's industrial expansion under ISI policies was undercapitalized, inefficient, labor-intensive, and spatially concentrated, throughout the 1960s and 1970s manufacturing continued to increase its

TABLE 2.3 Patterns of Industrial Growth in Argentina, 1895-1946

Year	Number of Establishments	Annual Increase (%)	Number of Workers	Annual Increase (%)
1895	24,114	-	174,782	-
1937	45,263	10.6[a]	539,525	11.6[a]
1939	49,100	4.2	581,599	3.9
1941	52,445	3.4	684,497	8.8
1943	59,765	7.0	820,470	9.9
1946	84,905	14.0	1,058,673	9.7

[a] Relative to 1935 industrial census.
Source: After Lewis (1990).

share of Argentina's gross domestic product (GDP) at the expense of the primary sector (Table 2.4). Yet although agriculture lost its preeminent position in the overall structure of Argentina's economy, it remained a key earner of foreign exchange. Rural capitalists, however, tended to invest their profits not in the agricultural or manufacturing sectors, but in the financial markets. As a result, a serious under-capitalization of the agricultural sector would limit rural flexibility and productivity during the 1970s and 1980s.

Import-substitution industrialization faced built-in limitations in Argentina. The country's small domestic market (only 23 million people in 1970) quickly became saturated, leaving little incentive for domestic industry to expand. Although the urban middle class sector in Argentina was the largest of any Latin American country, increases in consumer buying power alone could not solve the country's industrial problems. Liberals argued that the only solution was to rearticulate Argentina with the world economy by throwing open the doors to free trade. From 1976 until 1981, under Economy Minister José Martínez de Hoz, ISI strategies gradually were replaced by policies that attempted to open the economy to international market forces. Under what Juan Corradi (1985:130) called "liberal militarism," the government introduced programs designed to

TABLE 2.4   Argentina's GDP by Sector, 1925 to 1990

Sector	1925-9	1950-4	1960-4	1970-4	1975-7	1990
			(Percentage)			
Agriculture	27.1	18.8	16.4	12.3	12.5	8.1
Mining	0.2	0.6	1.4	1.6	1.5	2.9
Industry	23.8	27.8	31.3	37.3	36.8	26.5
Utilities	0.5	1.0	1.5	2.5	2.9	1.9
Construction	3.9	4.5	3.7	4.3	3.7	4.4
Commerce	23.3	18.8	18.7	18.0	17.8	15.2
Transport	6.3	8.3	7.8	7.3	7.2	5.2
Finance	3.6	4.2	3.9	3.5	3.8	14.6
Services	11.3	16.0	15.3	13.2	13.8	21.2
Total:	100.0	100.0	100.0	100.0	100.0	100.0

Source: After Crossley (1983); República Argentina (1994).

rationalize Argentina's economy.

However, major capital investment did not materialize and the economy became rationalized to the point of deindustrialization. By 1982, industrial production had fallen below the level achieved in 1974, and manufacturing employment fell continuously from a peak index of 119.4 in 1975 (1970 = 100) to 73.0 in 1982 (IBRD 1987). The military's "Process of National Reorganization" program fell apart in 1981, and Martínez de Hoz's policies were reversed in part because of the class divisions that had become embedded in Argentine society since the Perón years. Labor-management relations had deteriorated badly throughout the 1970s, with strikes and absenteeism rates in the double-digits for many industries. This forced industrialists to reduce their dependence on workers by utilizing more labor-saving machinery (Lewis 1990). In a major policy reversal, the government reintroduced state controls over the economy and borrowed heavily overseas to keep unstable banks and industries from collapsing completely (Lewis 1990). Dynamic socioeconomic stagnation resulted throughout the 1980s.

Industrial Concentration in the Pampeana Region

Most industrial activity during the ISI period gravitated to the city of Buenos Aires and its surrounding *partidos* (counties). In 1935, the Greater Buenos Aires Metropolitan Area contained nearly 60 percent of the country's total industrial capacity, over 70 percent of its industrial workers, and nearly 70 percent of its industrial horsepower. During the period of national developmentalism, major industrial growth occurred primarily along the Río Paraná and Río de la Plata from San Nicolás in the north to Ensenada south of the capital. Development strategists headquartered in the Federal District of Buenos Aires gave little recognition to social, economic, political, and cultural diversity in the interior provinces. They pursued a homogeneous approach to national planning driven by the idea that the rest of Argentina should be like Buenos Aires. As James Scobie (1971: 235) so cogently observed, Perón's administration "deliberately depreciated rural occupations and promised bread and circuses for the urban masses." The national capital thus became the employment heart of Argentina, and even more people flooded in from the countryside and from neighboring states.

By 1960, over 80 percent of all manufacturing jobs were concentrated in the Pampeana provinces of Buenos Aires, Córdoba, La Pampa, and Santa Fé, and in the Greater Buenos Aires Metropolitan Area. Fifty-two percent of all commercial employment and 50 percent of all service jobs also were located in Greater Buenos Aires. The dominance of Buenos Aires and the Pampeana in the national economy encouraged massive rural-urban migration between 1945 and 1975. With few major industries in the interior and declining agricultural employment, hundreds of thousands of people migrated to the major cities. By 1970, 80 percent of Argentina's 23 million citizens lived in urban areas, with over 15 million people residing in eight major Pampeana cities. Rural depopulation spread from the Northwest provinces to the Northeast, Cuyo, and Patagonia. The concentration of people and industry in the Littoral region further exacerbated Buenos Aires' dominance over the nation and Argentina's socioeconomic bifurcation. The Northwest provinces in particular slipped deeper into poverty, isolation, and underdevelopment, a process caused in part by a deterioration in the national transportation network.

Transport Network Deterioration

Nationalization of the railroads, port facilities, and telephone networks in the 1940s formed a key part of Juan Domingo Perón's first Five-Year Plan

(1947-51) to increase Argentina's industrial capacity. The national transport and communication system had been designed to handle the commerce of the pampas and was completely inadequate for Perón's industrial aspirations. Barely 8,500 kilometers of paved roads existed in Argentina in 1945 and the railroads had suffered terribly from a lack of capital investment. Yet despite nationalization and government rhetoric about the importance of the transport sector, new investment in infrastructure did not occur. The railroad network continued to deteriorate, especially in the interior, and few major highways were constructed outside the ambit of the major Pampeana cities. Unlike Mussolini in Italy, Perón could not even boast that he had made the trains run on time. They often did not run at all! By 1960, annual losses of about US$280 million by the railroads comprised nearly 80 percent of the entire federal deficit (*Review of the River Plate* 1961)

A 1962 speech by President Arturo Frondizi (Instituto de Estudios de la Marina Mercante 1962:70) clearly recognized the extent of the railroad's problems:

> Argentina's railroad system no longer serves the needs of our economy. It was laid out for another Argentina, for the Argentina whose foreign trade was limited to the export of meat, hides, wool, and grain and to the import of machinery, fuel, and manufactured products. That Argentina exists no longer. Now there are manufacturing centers throughout all the interior, oil wells in the north and in the south, iron ore and coal and other mines distributed throughout the entire country. The railroad must connect these centers adequately and rapidly without the necessity of transshipment in Buenos Aires. It must be able to transport iron and coal from the south to the north, and livestock and fruit from one province to another.

Despite acknowledgment of the problems, however, little action took place to improve the transport network. For example, regional growth pole strategies implemented in the 1960s and 1970s to address interior underdevelopment largely failed because of inadequate transport and communication infrastructure (Keeling 1994). Government and private studies in the 1980s and 1990s concerned with Argentina's reinsertion into the global economy have argued consistently that inadequate transport and communication facilities remain the Achilles heel of the country's redevelopment strategies (Roccatagliata 1986, 1994; República Argentina 1993a). Most at risk are the interior provinces of the Northwest and Patagonia. Failure to address the country's deteriorating transport systems weakened not only internal socioeconomic relationships, but also trade links with neighboring countries.

Regional and Global Trade Relationships

The final process that helped to shape Argentina's regional and international ties between 1930 and 1990 was the continued ambivalence in political and economic relationships with neighboring countries. Enmity between Argentina, Chile, Brazil, Paraguay, Bolivia, and Uruguay has its roots in the colonial and early post-colonial periods. Conflicts over trade, territorial boundaries, and resources encouraged fierce competition in the region, which spilled over into the twentieth century. Boundary issues, for example, continue to plague the Southern Cone. Chile and Argentina came close to armed conflict several times during the 1970s and 1980s over disputed territory in Tierra del Fuego. Argentina's territorial ambitions over the Malvinas (Falkland) Islands, Antarctica, and Patagonia, coupled with recent flirtations with nuclear development for military purposes, all have helped to maintain a sense of wariness and distrust among the Southern Cone countries since World War II. In addition, extremely weak transport and communication services and infrastructure among Southern Cone countries since the 1850s have exacerbated the sense of national isolation and have encouraged interior dependence on the dominant city, which in turn looks to North America and Europe for ideologies, capital, and technology.

The type of economy developed historically in the Southern Cone encouraged North Atlantic ties to the detriment of intraregional relationships. A lack of economic complementarity between Argentina and its neighbors over the past 150 years, caused primarily by a reliance on agricultural production, has done little to encourage strong social, economic, or political ties in the region. The creation of independent national identities out of the Portuguese and Spanish colonial territories also played a powerful role in fostering enmity between political neighbors and rivals. However, with the end of the Cold War, and with the emergence of powerful regional trading blocs within the world economy (for example, the NAFTA, the EU, and the ASEAN group), Argentina and its neighbors began to pursue a policy of *rapprochement*. They have been motivated to cooperate in part by the economic and spatial reality of the 1990s: "divided we fall, united we prosper."

Globalization and the New Argentina

Argentina's relative regional and hemispheric isolation, and its continued reliance upon inefficient state-controlled industries and public services as the backbone of the national economy during the 1980s, seemed at odds with the dynamics of the evolving world economy. Change seemed inevitable for Argentina, although many observers feared that change could come violently. Before embracing the ideologies of economic globalization, the country hovered on the brink of socioeconomic disaster for most of the 1980s. Following the country's "Dirty War" during the 1970s and its ill-fated expedition to seize control of the Malvinas (Falkland) Islands in 1982, Argentina began the slow and painful process of democratic restoration. Raúl Alfonsín's election in 1983 marked a turning point in Argentina's history and held out the promise of better days for *porteño* (resident of the Federal District of Buenos Aires) and *campesino* alike. Although over the next few years the Alfonsín government clearly identified the major problem areas for national development, it seemed powerless to effect any serious economic change. Throughout the 1980s, the economy sputtered and misfired, foreign debt soared to unprecedented levels, and rural poverty continued to worsen. By 1989, the annual rate of inflation had reached nearly 5,000 percent, the consumer price index continued to grow exponentially, and the value and purchasing power of the national currency seemed to decline daily (Table 2.5). Food riots broke out in several major cities in protest over the country's economic collapse. Reports flooded in of desperate mothers instructing their hungry children to run into grocery stores and supermarkets, stuff as much food as they could swallow into their mouths, and flee the premises (*La Nación* 1989).

In the midst of this socioeconomic chaos, national elections pitted the candidate from Alfonsín's Radical party against a flamboyant and charismatic politician from the poor northwest province of La Rioja, Carlos Saúl Menem, who ran for election under the banner of the Peronist or *Justicialista* (Social Justice) party. Menem drew heavily on the rhetoric and political tactics of the party's controversial namesake, Juan Domingo Perón, drawing support from labor unions, working class urbanites, and the entrenched bureaucracy. Pre-election propaganda stated that welfarism, state intervention, and tariff protection--the very core of Peronist ideology-- would remain the conventional wisdom in Menem's public policies. Menem won the 1989 election in what seemed a "re-release of archaic populism and a remedy worse than the disease" (Corradi 1995:76). Indeed, during the first six months of the new presidency, nothing seemed to have

TABLE 2.5   Annual Rate of Inflation, Consumer Price Index Change, and Currency Exchange Rates in Argentina, 1980-1996

Year	Annual Rate of Inflation (Percent)	Consumer Price Index[a] (Base 1988 = 100)	Exchange Rate For the US Dollar (Selling Rate)[b]
1980	87.6	0.003943	Australes 0.000184
1981	131.3	0.008067	0.000574
1982	209.7	0.02136	0.002594
1983	433.7	0.0948	0.010540
1984	688.0	0.6889	0.068422
1985	385.4	5.32	0.6011
1986	81.9	10.112	0.9442
1987	174.8	23.39	2.31
1988	387.7	103.62	10.85
1989	4,923.6	9,112.30	407.10
1990	1,343.9	131,574.40	4,876.81
1991	84.0	242,079.70	9,541.48
1992	17.5	284,554.70	Pesos[c] 0.9915
1993	7.4	305,512.10	0.9945
1994	3.9	317,287.70	0.9975
1995[d]	1.7	320,000.00	0.9980
1996[e]	2.0	325,000.00	1.00

[a] The Consumer Price Index measures price changes in the Greater Buenos Aires metropolitan area for a specific group of goods and services represented by the consumption of the population for the period July 1985 to June 1986.

[b] Annual average exchange rate to buy one US dollar. Exchange rate 1980-1985 has been converted to Australes for comparison.

[c] Changes in Argentina's monetary unit relative to the 1995 Peso:

    Until December 31, 1969 M$N 10,000,000,000,000 = 1 Peso

    Until May 31, 1983 $Ley   100,000,000,000 = 1 Peso

    Until June 14, 1985 $a   10,000,000 = 1 Peso

    Until December 31, 1991 $A   10,000 = 1 Peso

    Since January 1, 1992 $US1   = 1 Peso

[d] Preliminary Figures

[e] Projected Figures

Source: República Argentina (1994); *Latin American Weekly Report* (1995-1996); Ministry of the Economy (1996).

changed for Argentina. Inflation reached 20,266 percent for the month of March 1990, the national currency accelerated its freefall, and poverty continued to sap the energies of increasing numbers of Argentines.

President Menem's promise of a responsible economic policy oriented toward maintaining stability evaporated in the face of the changing realities of the new global economic order. In an abrupt conversion in mid-1990 to the tenets of economic liberalism, Menem withdrew Argentina from the Non-Aligned Movement and declared that the country now belonged to a "single world....a new juridical, political, social, and economic order" (Gills and Rocamora 1992:515). He rejected the working class Peronist ideologies that had carried his *Justicialista* party to electoral success, turned toward *los grupos económicos* (the economic and social elite), and began to woo foreign capital. The doors were thrown open to multinational corporations, foreign investors, and Argentina's economic exiles who, Menem believed, could change society's socioeconomic face for the better. Progressive economic reforms were abandoned in favor of free-market strategies based on privatization, deregulation, state disengagement from the domestic economy, monetary stability, and international integration. Menem, and his Harvard-trained finance minister Domingo Cavallo, embraced entrepreneurs and the business establishment unabashedly and moved quickly to endorse the foreign policy objectives of the United States. As Juan Corradi (1995:77) noted, after "decades of isolation, Argentina was poised to join the free world..." Globalization became the new economic buzzword in Argentina.

Argentina's insertion into the maelstrom of the world economy presents a host of development problems for government and citizens alike. Perhaps the most direct symptom of globalization is what Jeremy Brecher and Tim Costello (1994:22) have called the "race to the bottom"--a reduction in social, labor, accessibility, and environmental conditions as a consequence of global competition for jobs, capital, and resources. In Argentina, the struggle to become more competitive in the global marketplace has encouraged a downward spiral in wages and social overhead which, in turn, is leading to a deterioration in real incomes and social and material infrastructure. A focus on producing and exporting cheaper products can aggravate the downward spiral and contribute to the socioeconomic polarization of the haves and the have-nots.

Regional disparities in growth and change at both the substate and suprastate levels remain a substantial barrier to reshaping Argentina's economy and society. The ongoing dominance of Buenos Aires and the wealthier Pampeana provinces over the national economy could hinder the diffusion of the benefits of globalization to the interior. Inadequate accessibility and mobility for individuals and businesses could have long-term negative effects on the ability of interior provinces to participate in regional integration and socioeconomic restructuring. Moreover, socio-economic instability in neighboring countries could disrupt the integration of MERCOSUR's economies, encourage increased levels of migration to Argentina, and hinder the development of complementary relationships. A failure to address adequately the problems of inflation, currency devalua-tion, environmental deterioration, and megacephalous urban growth in Bolivia, Brazil, or Paraguay could have spill-over effects on Argentina. For example, inflation in all three of Argentina's MERCOSUR partners continues to run at unacceptable levels (Table 2.6). National geopolitical ambitions also pose a threat to regional stability and could limit the progress of social and economic cooperation.

Menem's globalization strategies raise some important questions about the social responsibilities of the Argentine State. Throughout the past half a century, social welfare programs in Argentina frequently have been seen as political instruments, not as mechanisms of socioeconomic moderniza-tion. Excessive expenditure on social programs arguably constrained growth, encouraged a level of dependency on the State, and retarded the accumulation of capital. However, an analysis of the most dynamic post-World War II economies in Asia, Europe, and Latin America suggests that rapid economic growth is inextricably intertwined with effective investment in social projects (Lewis 1993). Education, basic health care, public ser-vices, and transportation are crucial to the development of human capital, which itself is fundamental to economic efficiency and democratic stability within a society.

Conclusion

The preceding chapters have provided a historical context for growth and change in Argentina and have laid out the essence of the social, political, and economic policies embraced by the federal government since 1990. One of the more serious issues for the future of Argentina, however, is that while much attention has been focused on the statistics that quantify Argentina's macroeconomic success since 1990, little attention is being paid to the social costs of globalization. What is the collateral damage to Argentina and where is this damage evident? The second part of this study

TABLE 2.6   Consumer Price Changes in Argentina, Brazil, Paraguay, and
Uruguay, 1980-1996 (in percentages)

Year	Argentina	Brazil	Paraguay	Uruguay
1980	100.0	82.8	22.4	63.4
1981	104.5	105.6	14.0	34.0
1982	164.8	98.0	6.8	19.0
1983	343.8	142.0	13.4	49.2
1984	626.7	196.8	20.4	55.3
1985	672.2	226.9	25.2	72.2
1986	90.1	145.2	31.7	76.4
1987	174.8	394.6	32.0	57.3
1988	387.7	993.3	16.9	69.0
1989	4,923.0	1,863.6	28.5	89.2
1990	1,832.0	1,584.6	44.1	129.0
1991	84.0	475.8	11.8	81.3
1992	17.5	1,149.1	17.8	59.0
1993	7.4	2,489.1	20.4	52.9
1994	3.8	929.3	18.3	44.1
1995	1.8	22.0	10.4	36.8
1996[a]	2.0	25.0	11.0	40.0

[a] Projected rate.
Source: ECLAC (1994); *Latin American Weekly Report* (1994-1996).

study examines the policies and strategies that are driving the restructuring
of Argentina's pillars of development. Chapter three looks at the changing
demographic structure of the country and examines the relationship
between society and place. The impact of the international division of
labor on production and the intertwining of capital with the space economy
in Argentina are explored in chapter four. In the final chapter of part two,
the role of transport and communication in restructuring regions and places
is examined and questions are raised about the long-term implications of
privatization and deregulation strategies.

PART TWO

Restructuring Argentina's Pillars of Development

3

Society and Place

Throughout Latin American, governments are attempting to redefine the relationship between society and the State. Reform of the State and the creation of opportunities for democratic, pluralistic participation in government top the region's social agenda in the 1990s. Structural reform in Argentina is forming the backdrop for changes in social policy. However, circumstantial events based on the interaction among different social actors tend to take center stage. For example, riots, national strikes, marches, and other activities protesting the social implications of government reform usually have the highest visibility in the media. Few people disagree that economic instability severely impedes the development of social policies and priorities and the achievement of social goals.

Yet, in Argentina, the primacy given to meeting economic objectives, achieving financial stability, and reforming the role of the State in the economy has led to the subordination or postponement of many social goals. The problem stems from a widespread belief that social and economic objectives must be pursued alternatively not concomitantly (see ECLAC 1994). The purpose of this chapter is to provide an illustrative profile of trends in Argentina's social development in the early 1990s by analyzing key demographic data and key social indicators of uneven development. First, I examine the changing composition and structure of the national population, then I assess the major dimensions of population redistribution. Finally, the spatial impact of these changes on Argentina's geography is examined.

Key Demographic Trends

The recent demographic history of Argentina conveys a picture of dynamic population change. Between 1945 and 1996, the national population doubled from approximately 17 million to over 34 million inhabitants. Yet the average annual population growth rate stayed at or below the global level of growth during the four decades between 1950 and 1990 and remained consistently below the rate of growth experienced by the Latin American region in general (Table 3.1). For example, Argentina's share of Latin America's total population declined from 10.8 percent in 1950 to 7.3 percent in 1991 (Table 3.2). Demographic projections suggest that Argentina's population will grow steadily into the twenty-first century to reach about 48 million by 2025, although the country's share of Latin America's total population should remain around 7 percent (see República Argentina 1995a). Along with neighbors Chile and Uruguay, Argentina has a relatively well developed socioeconomic structure compared to most other countries within Latin America and has not experienced the type of explosive population growth seen in Mexico or Venezuela.

Nonetheless, in recent decades the country has experienced a widening of the population pyramid base in some regions, with nearly 40 percent of the total population in 1991 under 20 years of age. At the same time, Argentina has developed into an increasingly plural society, with steady increases in the size of non-European ethnic groups. Nearly 500,000 permanent residence permits were granted between 1980 and 1994, the majority to immigrants from Bolivia, Chile, Paraguay, and Uruguay. However, Asians represent a growing minority in Argentina, with nearly 30,000 granted permanent residence during the 1980s alone. The number of migrants from Europe declined steadily between 1980 and 1992, although growing numbers of Jews from the East European and former Soviet regions continue to emigrate to Argentina.

It is inconceivable that such dramatic changes in Argentina's demographic structure have occurred without a major impact on the geographical distribution of people, on population composition in different places, and on the role of labor and capital in reshaping the country. Certainly, the general Latin American trend of rural-urban migration continues in Argentina, although not with the same intensity in the 1990s as experienced during the 1950s and 1960s. For example, between 1947 and 1970 the Greater Buenos Aires Metropolitan Area (GBAMA) accounted for 50 percent of the entire national growth in population. During the 1980s, GBAMA absorbed approximately 25 percent of Argentina's population growth, whereas many interior provinces doubled and even tripled their share of the nation's growth compared to previous decades. This coincides with the general perception by potential migrants that the comparative

TABLE 3.1   Average Annual Population Growth Rate Percentages by World Region, 1950-1990

Region	1950-60	1960-70	1970-80	1980-90
World	1.8	2.0	1.8	1.7
Argentina	1.8	1.6	1.8	1.5
Africa	2.3	2.5	2.8	3.0
Asia	1.9	2.3	2.1	1.8
Europe	0.8	0.8	0.5	0.5
Latin America	2.8	2.7	2.4	2.1
North America	1.8	1.3	1.1	0.9
Oceania	2.3	2.0	1.7	1.5
Post-Soviet	1.7	1.3	0.9	0.8

Source: República Argentina (1991).

TABLE 3.2   Percent Distribution of the Population in Latin America by Country, 1950-1991

Region/Country	1950	1960	1970	1980	1991
Latin America	100.0	100.0	100.0	100.0	100.0
Argentina	10.8	9.8	8.7	8.0	7.3
Bolivia	1.7	1.6	1.6	1.6	1.7
Brazil	33.5	34.5	34.6	34.4	34.4
Colombia	7.5	7.5	7.7	7.6	7.5
Chile	3.8	3.6	3.4	3.2	3.0
México	17.6	18.0	19.1	20.0	20.3
Paraguay	0.8	0.8	0.8	0.9	1.0
Perú	4.8	4.7	4.8	4.9	4.9
Uruguay	1.4	1.2	1.0	0.8	0.7
Venezuela	3.1	3.6	3.8	4.3	4.5
Rest of Region	15.0	14.7	14.5	14.3	14.7

Source: República Argentina (1991).

advantages provided by GBAMA in past decades, whether real or perceived, are not as available in the 1990s (Ainstein 1992). Nonetheless, Argentina's megacity continues to attract substantial flows of migrants.

Shifts in population distribution are closely associated with changes in demographic structure, but the relationship is not always unambiguous. Migration patterns, for example, are influenced by trends in employment, housing opportunities, perceptions of urban attractiveness, and mobility. However, structural and spatial changes in Argentina's population in recent decades have helped to reshape the sociodemographic profiles of most provinces and cities. Census data are available only up to 1991, barely two years into the Menem government's first administration. Thus, an analysis of globalization's impact on society and place since 1990 must rely on past demographic trends for evidence of change. While the absence of up-to-the-minute data presents some analytical problems, the 1991 census is recent enough to provide a solid statistical base from which to extrapolate some important shifts in population occurring in the 1990s.

Basic Demographic Data

Argentina's 1991 national census revealed a population of 32.6 million, an absolute increase of 4.7 million people or 16.7 percent since the 1980 census (Table 3.3). Population densities ranged from a high of 14,827 inhabitants per square kilometer in the Federal Capital to a low of 0.7 in the Patagonian province of Santa Cruz, with the national average at 11.7 people per square kilometer. The masculinity ratio averaged 95.6 males for every 100 females. Tierra del Fuego, Argentina's most remote province and the focus of government strategies to create a tax-free zone, recorded the highest number of males per 100 females (112.2), while the Federal Capital recorded the lowest (82.9). Most Patagonian provinces plus several northern provinces also have more males than females. During the 1980s, the country experienced a reduction in the proportion of infants (0-4 years) to the total population, as well as an increase in the number of older people. These data suggest a slight fall in the general birth rate and an increase in the number of people surviving to pensionable age, a trend usually found in Western, urbanized, industrial societies. Life expectancy at birth for the average Argentino born in the 1980s is approximately 73 years for females and 66 years for men, although these figures are much lower in the poorer interior provinces. The national infant mortality rate is 23.6 per 1,000 live births, again with much higher figures recorded outside the Pampeana region, especially in the Northwest.

TABLE 3.3   Argentina's Population by Region and Political Division, 1960-1991

Political Division	1960	1970	1980	1991
Metropolitan[a]	7,679,184	9,632,922	11,344,180	12,846,400
Federal District	2,966,634	2,972,453	2,922,829	2,965,403
Inner Suburbs	3,772,411	5,380,447	6,843,201	7,969,324
Outer Suburbs	940,139	1,280,022	1,578,150	1,911,673
Pampeana	6,656,419	7,293,428	8,433,930	9,559,335
B.A. Province	2,053,558	2,114,060	2,444,057	2,713,977
Córdoba	1,753,840	2,060,065	2,407,754	2,766,683
Entre Ríos	805,357	811,691	908,313	1,020,257
La Pampa	158,746	172,029	208,260	259,996
Santa Fé	1,884,918	2,135,583	2,465,546	2,798,422
Cuyo	1,350,739	1,540,819	1,876,620	2,227,530
Mendoza	824,036	973,075	1,196,228	1,412,481
San Juan	352,387	384,284	465,976	528,715
San Luis	174,316	183,460	214,416	286,334
Northeast	1,616,498	1,807,855	2,247,710	2,822,599
Corrientes	533,201	564,147	661,454	795,594
Chaco	543,331	566,613	701,392	839,677
Formosa	178,526	234,075	295,887	398,413
Misiones	361,440	443,020	588,977	788,915
Northwest	2,201,242	2,382,180	3,012,387	3,677,538
Catamarca	168,231	172,323	207,717	264,234
Jujuy	241,462	302,436	410,008	512,329
La Rioja	128,220	136,237	164,217	220,729
Salta	412,854	509,803	662,870	866,153
Santiago Estero	476,503	495,419	594,920	671,988
Tucumán	773,972	765,962	972,655	1,142,105
Patagonia	506,457	705,000	1,032,619	1,482,002
Chubut	142,412	189,920	263,116	357,189
Neuquén	109,890	154,570	243,850	388,833
Río Negro	193,292	262,622	383,354	506,772
Santa Cruz	52,908	84,457	114,941	159,839

(*continues*)

TABLE 3.3 (*continued*)

Political Division	1960	1970	1980	1991
Tierra del Fuego	7,955	13,431	27,358	69,369
Country Total:	20,010,539	23,362,204	27,947,446	32,615,404

[a]The Metropolitan Region includes the Federal District of Buenos Aires, the 19 *Partidos* (Counties) of the Suburban Inner Ring, and the 32 *Partidos* of the Outer Suburbs including Greater La Plata.
Source: República Argentina (1994).

Spatial Dynamics of Demographic Change

An analysis of average annual population growth rates by region and by political division reveals some interesting trends. Growth in the original 19 counties of the Greater Buenos Aires Metropolitan Area has continued to decline since 1947, in part because these suburbs are almost totally urbanized (Table 3.4). During the 1980s, the highest levels of growth in GBAMA were recorded in seven of the counties that comprise the city's Middle Ring, which includes the capital of the province of Buenos Aires, La Plata (Figure 3.1). Overall growth in the Pampeana provinces has remained steady since 1947, although Entre Ríos grew rapidly during the 1970s compared to the 1950s and 1960s. Part of this growth can be attributed to the recent construction of the Brazo Largo bridge complex across the Río Paraná delta providing direct road and rail access from the outer suburbs of Buenos Aires to Entre Ríos and beyond to Uruguay and Brazil. La Pampa province has experienced the most dynamic change of population in the Pampeana region since 1947. Although only 260,000 people lived in the province in 1991, growth is being spurred by land availability, better environmental conditions, and an improving economic base.

In the Cuyo region, both Mendoza and San Juan provinces are experiencing a slowdown in annual growth rates. The northwestern and northeastern regions continue to show above average rates of growth, with many provinces recovering from the outmigration caused by severe economic recession during the 1950s and 1960s. These regions also have attracted numerous migrants from neighboring countries in recent decades.

TABLE 3.4   Average Intercensus Population Growth Rate Percentages in Argentina by Political Division, 1947-1991

Region/ Political Division[a]	1947- 1960	1960- 1970	1970- 1980	1980- 1991
Argentina	17.4	15.6	18.0	14.7
Metropolitan				
Federal District	- 0.4	0.2	- 1.7	1.2
GBA Inner Suburbs	59.4	36.1	24.2	14.3
Pampeana				
Entre Ríos	1.7	0.8	11.2	11.3
Santa Fé	7.6	12.6	14.4	12.0
Córdoba	11.8	16.2	15.6	13.2
BA Province	12.6	12.6	17.0	13.4
La Pampa	- 4.9	8.1	19.2	21.2
Cuyo				
San Juan	22.6	8.7	19.3	12.2
Mendoza	25.5	16.8	20.7	16.0
San Luis	3.9	5.1	15.6	27.8
Northeast				
Chaco	17.5	4.2	21.4	17.0
Corrientes	1.1	5.7	15.9	17.6
Misiones	29.0	20.6	28.7	28.1
Formosa	34.2	27.5	23.6	30.0
Northwest				
Santiago del Estero	- 0.5	3.9	18.4	11.6
Tucumán	20.0	- 1.0	24.0	15.3
Jujuy	28.1	22.8	30.7	21.6
Catamarca	10.0	2.4	18.7	23.5
Salta	26.5	21.3	26.4	25.7
La Rioja	11.0	6.1	18.7	28.4
Patagonia				
Río Negro	27.5	31.1	38.3	26.8
Chubut	32.8	29.2	32.9	29.2
Santa Cruz	15.8	47.9	31.1	31.8
Neuquén	17.7	34.7	46.4	45.2
Tierra del Fuego	34.8	53.8	73.3	91.9

[a] Ranked low to high during the 1980-1991 period in each region by province.
Source: República Argentina (1991).

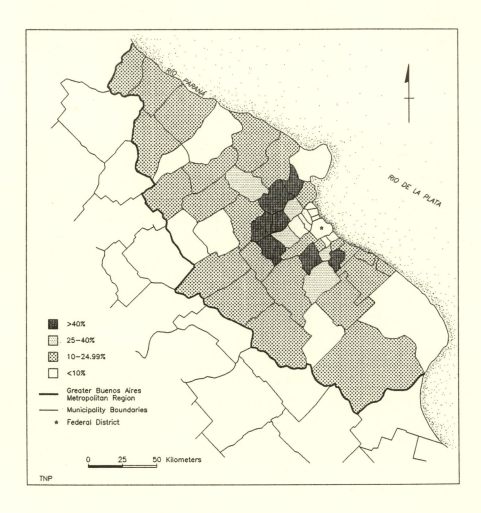

FIGURE 3.1   Population Growth Rates in the Greater Buenos Aires Metropolitan
Area, 1980-1991. *Source*: República Argentina (1991).

Patagonia consistently has recorded the highest rates of growth since 1947,
driven by the federal government's regional development strategies to open
up this frontier region and by the discovery of valuable natural resources.
Neuquén and Tierra del Fuego grew the most rapidly during the 1980s, and
this growth shows no sign of abating during the 1990s.

Urban Dominance

Disequilibrium in the distribution of population at the national level effectively divides Argentina into two demographic realms: the Pampeana, including Buenos Aires, and the rest of the country. With only 30 percent of the national territory, the Pampeana region contains 70 percent of the country's population. Conversely, the remaining 30 percent of Argentina's inhabitants are scattered across 70 percent of the country. Moreover, in many provinces, the most important urban center--generally the capital--contains over 30 percent of the province's population usually on less than 10 percent of the land area (Table 3.5). Some important exceptions include Buenos Aires province. Here, La Plata is the provincial capital but it is functionally part of the Greater Buenos Aires Metropolitan Area. The largest urban area outside GBAMA in Buenos Aires province is Mar del Plata, which contains 20 percent of the provincial population on less than one percent of the land area. Similarly, in the province of Santa Fé, Rosario is the largest city with approximately 40 percent of the province's inhabitants located on 1.42 percent of the land area. In many provinces, urban growth in recent decades has extended the capital city's functional area into surrounding counties. In Mendoza, for example, the five counties surrounding the capital contain nearly 50 percent of the provincial population on less than two percent of the land area. Other exceptions include the county of General Roca in Río Negro province that borders the city of Neuquén to the east. Over 52 percent of Río Negro's provincial population is located in this county.

The pattern of capital city dominance found at the national level is replicated at the provincial level, with the major city in each province growing much faster than its hinterland. Rural-urban migration in Argentina continues to occur primarily at two scales: hinterland to major provincial center, and thence to the Greater Buenos Aires Metropolitan Area. In 1947, 37.5 percent of the national population was considered rural. During the immediate post-World War Two period, the total number of rural inhabitants in Argentina peaked at 6 million. Since then, the number of rural residents has declined every year to reach a post-World War Two low in 1991 of just under 4.3 million. Conversely, the number of urbanites in Argentina has tripled since the 1940s. From just under 10 million in 1947--62.5 percent of the national population--the number of urban residents has tripled to just under 30 million, or 87 percent of the total population. In 1991, Argentina had 17 cities with populations exceeding 200,000 that together contained approximately 65 percent of the country's inhabitants

TABLE 3.5   Percent Share of the Provincial Population of the County that Contains the Provincial Capital, 1947-1991

Region/ Provincial Capital	Percent of Provincial Territory	1947	1960	1970	1980	1991
Pampeana						
Córdoba	0.34	25.8	33.4	38.7	41.2	42.7
La Plata	0.31	7.1	5.0	4.6	4.4	4.3
Paraná	6.31	18.8	21.7	23.3	24.9	27.1
Santa Fé	2.30	12.1	14.0	14.6	15.5	15.8
Santa Rosa	1.76	11.1	17.5	22.0	26.2	30.0
Cuyo						
Mendoza	0.03	16.6	13.2	12.2	10.0	8.6
San Juan	0.03	31.5	30.3	29.3	25.3	22.5
San Luis	17.09	22.5	28.0	32.2	37.4	42.3
Northeast						
Corrientes	0.57	13.7	19.9	24.4	28.4	33.7
Formosa	8.60	27.6	26.8	30.1	35.4	41.0
Posadas	3.10	19.7	21.5	23.5	25.6	27.8
Resistencia	3.50	N/A	22.1	27.6	33.0	35.5
Northwest						
Catamarca	0.67	22.1	29.2	33.8	37.9	41.6
Jujuy	4.48	25.2	29.8	35.8	40.8	44.7
La Rioja	15.21	25.0	30.9	35.5	42.3	48.1
Salta	1.11	26.3	29.8	35.8	40.1	43.1
Santiago	1.55	17.0	21.6	24.0	27.7	30.0
Tucumán	0.40	34.3	37.2	42.6	40.6	41.4
Patagonia						
Neuquén	7.81	29.4	46.3	58.2	64.0	68.1
Rawson	1.75	10.4	12.0	18.1	25.8	28.1
Río Gallegos	13.87	22.6	40.1	44.5	48.8	49.4
Viedma	4.34	6.2	4.9	6.0	7.4	8.8
Ushuaia	43.53	43.2	43.4	42.3	41.6	42.8

Source: República Argentina (1991).

TABLE 3.6   Argentina's Cities with Metropolitan Populations Greater than 200,000 Inhabitants, 1991

Rank	Metropolitan Area	Population
1	Greater Buenos Aires[a]	12,846,400
2	Greater Córdoba	1,179,067
3	Greater Rosario	1,067,738
4	Greater Mendoza	981,070
5	Greater Tucumán	622,348
6	Mar del Plata	530,664
7	Greater Santa Fé	440,581
8	Greater Salta	373,859
9	Greater San Juan	353,476
10	Greater Paraná	273,210
11	Greater Resistencia	266,134
12	Greater Santiago del Estero	264,272
13	Greater Neuquén	262,168
14	Corrientes	257,876
15	Bahía Blanca	255,145
16	Greater Jujuy	229,284
17	Greater Posadas	217,877
	Total:	20,421,169

[a] Includes the city of Greater La Plata with approximately 640,000 inhabitants.
Source: República Argentina (1991).

(Table 3.6).   Figure 3.2 illustrates the various urban regions in Argentina with their respective zones of urban influence. Although Buenos Aires is shown as dominating much of the Pampeana region, in reality its economic, social, political, and culture influences extend across the entire country.

Urban growth historically has been driven by four important processes: (1) the mechanization of agriculture during the nineteenth and twentieth centuries, which reduced the need for manual labor; (2) the lack of access to land ownership by immigrants; (3) the development of industry primarily in the major cities; and (4) a tendency to focus transport and communication services and infrastructure on and between the major urban centers, with little attention paid to mobility in the rural hinterland. A

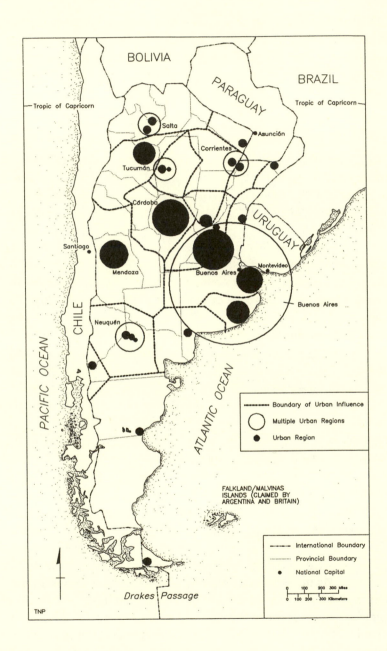

FIGURE 3.2   Argentina's Urban Regions with Boundaries of Influence, 1991.
Source: After Roccatagliata (1992b).

fifth more insidious but less understood process involves the embedded attitudes in Argentine culture that value urban life as sophisticated and civilized and that discount rural life as backward, underdeveloped, and barbaric. The siren call of urban life in Argentine society is powerful and extremely successful in attracting migrants.

Rural Depopulation

Rural depopulation shows no sign of abating during the 1990s. The provinces with the smallest percentage of rural inhabitants include Buenos Aires and Córdoba in the Pampeana, and Santa Cruz, Tierra del Fuego, Chubut, and Neuquén in Patagonia (Table 3.7). Most Patagonian provinces are dominated by vast tracts of land that do not support intensive, commercial agriculture; carrying capacities are low and excess rural population tends to gravitate to the urban centers. On the pampas, agriculture is highly mechanized and focused on export production, while agricultural processing plants and manufacturing facilities are concentrated in the major cities. Provinces with over 30 percent of the population considered rural (in Argentina, urban is defined as those locations with 2,000 or more inhabitants) are found only in the North. Santiago del Estero, for example, remains just under 40 percent rural in population composition. Many of the interior provinces still are relatively isolated in the 1990s, several are dominated by one major crop (cotton, sugar, or wine), and most have relatively low levels of industry and manufacturing. Subsistence agriculture remains important in both the Northwest and the Northeast. Except Formosa, every province in Argentina has fewer rural inhabitants in the 1990s than in the 1960s, despite the addition of over 12 million people to the national population between 1960 and 1991.

Ethnic and Gender Composition

Unlike many Latin American countries that have substantial mestizo and indigenous populations, Argentina is dominated by direct European descendants, primarily Italians and Spaniards. Barely 3/10th of one percent of the country's population in the 1960s claimed mestizo or indigenous descent, with 7/10th of one percent claiming Black or Asian descent (República Argentina 1960). Data on ethnic composition from Argentina's censuses have not been published since 1960, but indirect evidence (migration statistics, residence permits granted, etc.) suggests that the

TABLE 3.7 A Comparison of Urban and Rural Population by Region and Political Division, 1960 and 1991

Region/Political Division	1960 Urban	Rural	Percent Rural	1991 Urban	Rural	Percent Rural
	(thousands)			(thousands)		
Pampeana						
Buenos Aires	8,668	1,063	10.9	14,952	608	3.9
Córdoba	1,208	546	31.1	2,380	387	14.0
Entre Ríos	403	403	50.0	792	229	22.4
La Pampa	63	96	60.4	193	67	25.8
Santa Fé	1,347	538	28.5	2,429	369	13.2
Subtotal:	11,689	2,646	18.5	20,746	1,660	7.4
Cuyo						
Mendoza	497	327	39.7	1,100	313	22.2
San Juan	188	164	46.6	424	104	19.7
San Luis	90	84	48.3	232	54	18.9
Subtotal:	775	575	42.6	1,756	471	21.1
Northwest						
Catamarca	73	95	56.5	184	80	30.3
Jujuy	117	125	51.7	418	94	18.3
La Rioja	53	75	58.6	167	54	24.4
Salta	212	201	48.7	684	182	21.0
Santiago del Estero	175	301	63.2	408	264	39.3
Tucumán	424	350	45.2	875	267	23.4
Subtotal:	1,054	1,147	52.1	2,736	941	25.6
Northeast						
Chaco	215	328	60.4	576	264	31.4
Corrientes	259	274	51.4	590	206	25.9
Formosa	51	127	71.3	270	128	32.2
Misiones	125	236	65.4	493	295	37.4
Subtotal:	650	965	59.8	1,929	893	31.6
Patagonia						
Chubut	79	64	44.8	314	43	12.0
Neuquén	40	69	63.3	336	53	13.6
Río Negro	85	108	56.0	405	102	20.1
Santa Cruz	27	22	44.9	146	14	8.7
Tierra del Fuego	8	3	27.3	067	2	2.9
Subtotal:	239	266	52.7	1,268	214	14.4
Argentina	14,407	5,599	28.0	28,435	4,179	12.8

Source: República Argentina (1994).

ethnic complexity of the country is changing dramatically in the 1990s. Five percent of the population, or 1.63 million people, reported a birthplace outside Argentina in the 1991 census. Of that figure, half of the non-natives came from countries contiguous to Argentina, while the other 50 percent came from other countries. The latinamericanization of Argentina proceeds at a steady pace in the 1990s, particularly in the Buenos Aires area, in the cities of the Northwest, and in Patagonia. Sixty-eight percent of all non-native born residents in 1991 were concentrated in the Greater Buenos Aires Metropolitan Area (60%) and in the province of Buenos Aires (8%). The remaining 32 percent were scattered across the interior. Growth rates between 1947 and 1991 in the Pampeana, Cuyo, and Patagonia regions in the number of non-natives from contiguous countries were close to, or exceeded, 300 percent (Table 3.8).

Fourteen percent of the provincial population in Santa Cruz and Tierra del Fuego, for example, are non-natives from neighboring countries (particularly Chile). As mentioned earlier, 81.6 percent of all permanent residence permits granted to foreigners between 1981 and 1992 were to residents of the five countries contiguous to Argentina: Bolivia, Brazil, Chile, Paraguay, and Uruguay. Over the past decade, Argentina regularly has received the highest number of *undocumentados* (illegal immigrants) of any Southern Cone country (Caviedes and Knapp 1995). Paraguayans tend to seek rural employment in the northern sugar cane, cotton, and vegetable areas and urban employment in Buenos Aires as taxi drivers and construction workers. Bolivians also seek manual labor in Buenos Aires, but they are most prominent as seasonal laborers in the sugar cane fields of the Northwest and in the fruit fields of Catamarca, San Juan, and Mendoza. Uruguayans tend more toward the urban clerical and professional jobs found in Buenos Aires, while Chileans work as miners, shepherds, and fruit pickers in the Andean region provinces. Asians (especially Koreans) have become an important ethnic minority in Argentina during the 1990s, although as a group they tend to concentrate in the city of Buenos Aires. Levantines also make up a sizeable ethnic minority in Argentina, President Carlos Menem being the most notable individual of Levantine extraction. The Federal District of Buenos Aires also is home to one of the largest urban Jewish communities in Latin America.

An interesting change in the gender composition of Argentina's population is the ongoing decline in the index of masculinity. From a peak of 115.5 to 100 in 1914, the number of males per 100 females has declined steadily ever since. In 1991, it stood at 95.6 per 100 females. The

TABLE 3.8   Distribution by Region of Non-Native Residents from Countries Contiguous to Argentina, 1947-1991

Region/ Political Division	1947	1970	1991	Growth Rate (%) 1947-1991
Argentina	311,617	578,200	817,144	162.23
Pampeana	121,313	302,050	491,603	305.24
Federal District	52,015	97,800	115,605	122.25
Buenos Aires	39,319	180,200	344,721	776.73
Córdoba	5,954	8,350	11,552	94.02
Entre Ríos	12,496	5,800	5,578	- 55.36
La Pampa	1,227	1,200	1,564	27.47
Santa Fé	10,302	8,700	12,583	22.14
Cuyo	11,117	21,700	45,877	312.67
Mendoza	7,758	17,800	39,804	413.07
San Juan	3,114	3,400	3,643	16.99
San Luis	245	500	2,430	891.84
Northwest	46,457	54,700	59,008	27.02
Catamarca	340	150	517	52.06
Jujuy	27,198	33,200	30,173	10.94
La Rioja	223	300	910	308.07
Salta	16,839	18,750	23,436	39.18
Santiago del Estero	435	450	630	44.83
Tucumán	1,422	1,850	3,342	135.02
Northeast	98,377	113,650	84,690	- 13.91
Chaco	16,219	10,150	6,727	- 58.52
Corrientes	6,444	4,950	6,006	- 6.80
Formosa	31,203	35,050	25,030	- 19.78
Misiones	44,511	63,500	46,927	5.43
Patagonia	34,353	86,100	135,966	295.79
Chubut	7,208	19,500	24,975	246.49
Neuquén	8,057	12,300	31,913	296.09
Río Negro	7,876	29,150	47,284	500.36
Santa Cruz	8,985	20,300	22,172	146.77
Tierra del Fuego	2,227	4,850	9,622	332.06

Source: After Sassone (1989); República Argentina (1994).

masculinity index in Patagonia historically has remained high, in part because of the type of economic activity dominant in the region (resource extraction), the harsh climate, and the in-migration of single men attracted by higher salaries. Moreover, the masculinity index in rural areas continues to be higher than in urban centers because more women still migrate to the cities in search of employment (particularly domestic service).

Demographic Pyramids

An analysis of demographic pyramids in Argentina reveals the presence of all three major types. Type "A" is typical of regions or countries considered underdeveloped or predominantly rural and generally it is shaped liked the Eiffel Tower. Many interior provinces, for example, have a broad base of people aged 0-20 and very few inhabitants over 75 years of age. Demographic pyramid "B" is characteristic of relatively new countries with extensive agriculture and industrial development (for example, Argentina, Australia, and Canada). This bell-shaped pyramid describes the contemporary population of Argentina and the Pampeana provinces, where the share of each 5-year bracket decreases relatively evenly in step fashion from the teenage to the elderly groups. Finally, type "C," often described as a funeral urn, represents the population profile of big cities or highly industrialized regions. The Federal District of Buenos Aires has a type "C" demographic pyramid, with approximately equal numbers of people found in every age bracket from 0 to over 80 years.

Increasing numbers of elderly people in the major cities are having an important social and economic impact on Argentine society, especially during the current globalization period. In 1993, about two-thirds of Argentina's 3.2 million pensioners collected only the minimum pension of US$150 a month, whereas the basic food basket in Buenos Aires cost nearly US$400 a month (*Latin American Weekly Report* 1993). Nearly one million elderly people have no retirement benefits at all. Economic problems have triggered higher incidences of suicide among the elderly in Buenos Aires and elsewhere in recent years, capturing media attention outside Argentina (Nash 1992). Images of grandmothers driven by economic despair to leap off high-rise buildings or to hang themselves in public places are a serious blow to the Menem government's efforts to trumpet the social successes of globalization. Nélida Redondo, a sociologist in Buenos Aires, estimated recently that nearly 30 percent of Argentina's elderly population now fall into a category called the "new poor" (Nash 1992).

Social Indicators of Uneven Development

Raw demographic statistics do not portray accurately the human condition. Age, sex, nationality, and annual growth rates all are important indicators of change in a country, but they do not help us to understand in any detail the problems of uneven social development. The concept of uneven development grew out of political economy and Marxist discourse and was popularized in the 1960s by Samir Amin's writings on imperialism (Amin 1976). Amin's work focused on the production and exchange relationships between center and periphery economies that gave rise to, and reinforced, unequal development. Classic theories on imperialism have been superceded in recent years by ideas about the process of the internationalization of capital, a process which further reinforced development inequalities not only between national entities but also within them. Since the 1970s, debate over uneven social development within countries has come to dominate planning and policy making agendas throughout Latin America. In Argentina, the development debate has been primarily national in nature, framed by dependency versus modernization theories, top-down versus bottom-up strategies, and growth-pole ideologies. Little attention has been paid to the role of national culture and regional sociocultural uniqueness in the development process.

The term "development" is extremely ambiguous and exhaustive attempts have been made since 1945 to define it more precisely. In essence, development is a multifaceted process whereby a society moves toward achieving a certain quality of life which, ideally, should be determined by the society itself. Quality of life encompasses social, political, environmental, economic, and cultural facets, both qualitative and quantitative, of societies and is extremely difficult to measure accurately. It cannot and should not be equated solely with economic growth (Simon 1990). The goals of regional development, as discussed in the mainstream literature, are to reduce unemployment, poverty, and socioeconomic disparities among individuals and communities within a defined geographic area (Keeling 1994). In this section, I focus on five major indicators of uneven socioeconomic development: general poverty, unsatisfied basic needs, education, health, and housing.

Poverty in Argentina

Structural inequalities inherent in the capitalist free-market system play a significant role in the creation of poverty and a low quality of life. Critics blame capitalism for rewarding greed, exploiting the vast majority of humans, repressing dissenters, and for concentrating enormous wealth in the hands of the few. Capitalism frequently is viewed as inherently unjust and at the very root of poverty. Indeed, global capitalism in the 1990s has been described as nothing more than the "pillage" of the global community (Brecher and Costello 1994). Approximately one-third of the developing world's population--1.3 billion people--live in absolute poverty, often too poor to provide even the minimum caloric intake necessary for basic human functions (United Nations 1993). Poverty, economic insecurity, and the resulting social disruption continue to undermine human relationships, social values, and traditional ways of life in societies around the world.

In Argentina, global economic forces have combined with internal state policies and development strategies to create a crisis of poverty. Yet Argentina's poverty crisis is not a new phenomenon; poverty has been endemic in the country since the arrival of the Spanish in the sixteenth century. However, what makes the crisis such a major development issue in contemporary Argentina is the widespread nature of poverty and the almost overwhelming numbers of people suffering from inadequate basic needs. The current poverty crisis has its roots in the post-World War Two development of Argentina. Juan Domingo Perón's policies of social justice during the late 1940s and early 1950s led to a significant improvement in the material conditions of the urban poor, with the imposition of a minimum wage, fixed rents, price controls on basic commodities, employment protection, and retirement pensions (Waldmann 1993). Unfortunately, a culture of dependency on the welfare state became embedded in the Argentine social, economic, and political systems, where economic growth and national wealth were taken for granted. Throughout the 1960s and 1970s, state-controlled and directed programs absorbed an ever-increasing share of the national income, even though economic conditions continued to deteriorate. As Peter Waldmann (1993:92) argued, for Menem and the current generation, "the golden future predicted in the 1940s has not materialised. Instead, they witnessed the 'Latinamericanisation' of their country which became prey to debt, poverty and inflation." In 1990, as Menem's globalization policies were about to be introduced, over 10 million people in Argentina lived on or below the poverty line. Under Menem, the poor no longer can look to the State for protection. Thus, the poverty crisis could continue to pose a very serious threat to the socio-economic restructuring of the country, at least for the foreseeable future.

This is not to suggest that Argentina has enjoyed little success in attack-ing poverty. Since 1980, the country has made substantial improvements in satisfying the basic needs of the population, with most indicators showing that progress on all fronts is occurring. In 1992, for example, Menem's government established two anti-poverty programs--the Argentine Social Investment Fund (FAIS) and the Federal Solidarity Program--designed to lay a solid foundation of basic social services. It is too early to tell if these programs are having any significant impact on poverty. Unfortunately, according to a 1990 CEPAL report, Argentina is the only Latin American country during the past two decades to demonstrate systematic and persistent increases in the general level of poverty (CEPAL report cited in Carlevari and Carlevari 1994). Eight percent of Argentina's population in 1970 could be considered in poverty; by 1986 the percentage had increased to 13. Moreover, according to a report prepared by Argentine economist Gustavo Márquez for SELA, Argentina has been slow to reduce overall disparities since 1970, despite ranking 2nd out of 18 countries in Latin America on the Index of Human Development (IHD) (Table 3.9). The IHD is used to measure quality of life and the level of disparity between social groups. Included in IHD measurement are life expectancy, income per capita, literacy, and the degree of education achieved by at least half the population.

An important difference about poverty in Argentina compared to many other countries is that it is primarily an urban not a rural phenomenon. Most of the country's poor are located in the major provincial cities and in the capital. Land ownership patterns, industrial concentration practices, and transport networks, among other processes, have acted as push-pull fac-tors in Argentina, encouraging both national and foreign migrants to seek opportunities in the major urban centers. However, infrastructure and jobs to support the increasing numbers of urban dwellers have been totally in-adequate, and thousands of people annually become mired in poverty. For example, the number of people living below the official poverty line in the city of Buenos Aires in October 1992 exceeded two million (Carlevari and Carlevari 1994). In addition, the gap between rich and poor in urban Argentina continues to widen. The richest 10 percent of Argentina's popu-lation in 1993 controlled a 35.3 percent share of the national income, an in-crease over its 1980 share of 30 percent (Table 3.10). Yet both the poor and the middle class were worse off in 1993 compared to 1980. Although the poorest 20 percent of Argentina's population has recovered the most since the economic crisis of 1989, they also have fallen the furthest behind since 1980, with incomes in real terms only 58 percent of the 1980 level.

TABLE 3.9 A Comparison of Social and Economic Disparity Reduction Rates in Latin America, 1970-1990[a]

1970-1990	1980-1990	IHD Rank 1991[b]
RAPID RATE OF REDUCTION		
Chile	Bolivia	17
México	Chile	3
Costa Rica	Colombia	9
Uruguay	México	7
Honduras	Honduras	16
Brazil	El Salvador	15
MEDIUM RATE OF REDUCTION		
Panamá	Perú	12
Ecuador	Paraguay	8
Colombia	Dominican Republic	13
Venezuela	Brazil	10
Bolivia	Ecuador	11
Nicaragua	Venezuela	5
SLOW RATE OF REDUCTION		
Paraguay	Panamá	6
Perú	Argentina	2
Argentina	Costa Rica	4
El Salvador	Nicaragua	14
Dominican Republic	Uruguay	1
Guatemala	Guatemala	18

[a] Countries listed in descending order within each of the three categories.
[b] Corresponds to the countries listed in the column for 1980-1990. IHD is the Index of Human Development with 1 the highest rank.
Source: *Latin American Weekly Report* (1994).

Although Argentina enjoyed continued macroeconomic success during 1994 and 1995, this success made little impact on the pattern of income distribution. A survey of 25 districts in late 1995 by INDEC, the national statistical institute, suggests that economic expansion since 1991 has helped to worsen an already highly skewed national income distribution pattern (*Latin American Weekly Report* 1996:47). Fifty percent of Argentina's

TABLE 3.10   Income Distribution in Argentina, 1980-1993

Percentages	1980	1989	1993
Share of Income %			
Poorest 10 %	1.9	1.2	1.7
Middle 80 %	68.1	58.1	63.0
Richest 10 %	30.0	40.7	35.3

Real Incomes by Groups, 1980=100

Year	Poorest Quintile	Second Quintile	Third Quintile	Fourth Quintile	Richest Quintile	Total
1980	100	100	100	100	100	100
1986	89	94	89	95	86	91
1989	25	37	40	48	60	49
1991	41	53	58	62	68	61
1993	58	62	66	75	73	70

Source: Internal World Bank Report (1994) "Un perfil de la emergencia de los pobres en Argentina," in *Latin American Weekly Report* (1994:450-1); *The Economist*, Argentina Survey, November 26, 1994, p. 14.

population, or about 17 million people, earned approximately 18 percent of the total income, whereas the wealthiest 15 percent of the population (5 million) took about 50 percent of total income. In the port city of Bahía Blanca in the southern corner of Buenos Aires province, the share of total income earned by the poorest 50 percent of the population fell by 15.8 points. And in an embarrassment to President Carlos Menem, income in his home province of La Rioja, in the Northwest region, fell by 11.3 points for the poorest 50 percent of the population. In the dominant northwestern city of Tucumán, a region wracked by unemployment problems in recent years, the upper segment of society accounted for approximately 52 percent of total income.

In Greater Buenos Aires, the poorest 50 percent of the population received only 14.2 percent of the total urban income. Perhaps reflective of the government's Patagonian development efforts in recent years, the largest share of total income received by the poorest 50 percent of the population was in Ushuaia, capital of Tierra del Fuego, with 18 percent, and in the capital of Santa Cruz province, Río Gallegos, with 17 percent (*Latin American Weekly Report* 1996:47).

Evidence clearly indicates that globalization of the domestic economy certainly has exacerbated incidences of urban and rural poverty. In 1995, urban unemployment had reached record highs, Buenos Aires had the distinction of being the most expensive city in Latin America, increased numbers of urbanites worked in the informal economy, and a staggering 5 million or more urban dwellers lived in abominable conditions. In Greater Buenos Aires alone, according to government statistics, approximately 3.3 million people or nearly one-quarter of the urban population now live below the poverty line (*Latin American Weekly Report* 1996:249).

Unsatisfied Basic Needs

Analyses of unsatisfied basic needs in Argentina are a recent phenomenon. In 1984, the National Institute of Statistics and Census (INDEC) published a landmark study on poverty in Argentina based on data collected for the 1980 census (República Argentina 1984). INDEC followed this study in 1990 with an in-depth analysis of urban poverty in Argentina based on household surveys in the 19 counties of GBAMA's inner suburbs and in four interior cities--General Roca, Neuquén, Posadas, and Santiago del Estero (República Argentina 1990). These studies defined unsatisfied basic needs (UBN) as the existence of one or more of five conditions: (1) overcrowding (more than 3 persons per room), (2) unsuitable dwellings (rented rooms, slum construction, etc.), (3) poor sanitary conditions (homes without toilets), (4) inadequate school attendance (homes with school-aged children not attending school), and (5) poor subsistence capacity (households with four or more persons per working member, with a head of household who has a low level of education). Another method of measuring UBN involves the establishment of a "poverty line." In 1995, this line was roughly 400 pesos (US$400) per month for a family of four. Households whose per capita income falls below this line are considered in poverty. The "indigence line" is defined as those households unable to supply the minimum daily food requirements. From a strictly nutritional perspective, a poor urban family in Argentina requires an average of 11,650 calories per day to be fed adequately (Aguirre 1994).

The total number of people suffering from UBN in 1991 declined to 6.4 million (20 percent of the population) from 7.6 million in 1980 (28 percent). Several interior provinces experienced major reductions (Figure 3.3).

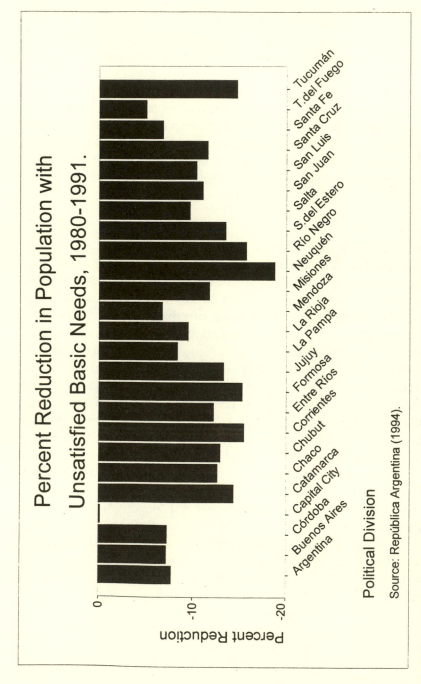

FIGURE 3.3 Percent Reduction in Argentina's Population with Unsatisfied Basic Needs, 1980-1991.
Source: República Argentina (1994).

However, Patagonia, the Northeast, and the Northwest regions all recorded increases in their absolute share of Argentina's total population with UBN (Table 3.11). La Rioja, Salta, and Tierra del Fuego also experienced a net increase in the total number of people suffering from UBN in 1991 compared to 1980, as did the Federal District of Buenos Aires. In the Northeast, 35.3 percent of the population lack basic needs and in the Northwest 32.7 percent have unsatisfied basic needs. Ten provinces have UBN rates between 27 and 40 percent, all of which are in the interior (Figure 3.4). The suburban counties of Greater Buenos Aires have the highest absolute number of people living with UBN, more than 2 million in the early 1990s. The second highest absolute numbers of people with UBN are found in the Pampeana cities of Rosario and Córdoba.

Other indicators of poverty include dwellings without access to running water. Almost all dwellings in the Federal District of Buenos Aires were served with running water in 1991, whereas nearly 60 percent of the dwellings in Misiones province had no water access. Other interior provinces with high rates of non-access to water include Santiago del Estero (42.8%), Formosa (41.1%), and Chaco (38.1%). The 19 counties that comprise GBAMA's inner suburbs also recorded a high rate of 43.6 percent. Most of the people with poor water access live in the myriad *villas miserias* (shantytowns) that are found along the banks of major streams or on vacant ground around the urban perimeter.

Except for La Rioja (27.5%), all the interior northern provinces recorded a rate in excess of 30 percent for the total number of dwellings without basic plumbing. Some of the worst affected provinces are Chaco (52.5%), Santiago del Estero (54%), Misiones (57%), and Formosa (58.6%). The same pattern is repeated for dwellings without proper flooring, without water discharge, and without access to running water or a well. Interior northern provinces, particularly Santiago del Estero and Formosa, suffer from the highest rates of unsatisfied basic needs across all categories. By any criteria, the Pampeana region is much better served by basic needs than the interior, although pockets of serious poverty persist in the major Pampeana cities, particularly among the shantytown residents of the capital. Overall, the reduction of unsatisfied basic need rates is proceeding more rapidly in the Pampeana region than in the interior.

Education and Illiteracy

A society's ability to develop and to participate in the regional and world economies is shaped directly and indirectly by a country's level of

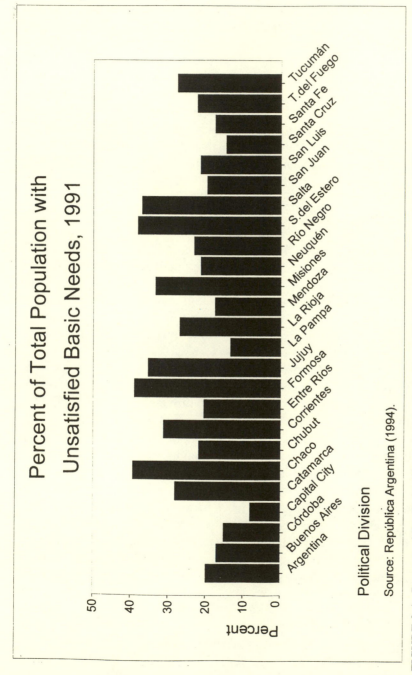

FIGURE 3.4 Percent of the Total Population in Argentina with Unsatisfied Basic Needs, 1991.
Source: República Argentina (1994).

TABLE 3.11   Argentina's Total Population with Unsatisfied Basic Needs by Region, 1980-1991

Region	1980	Percent	1991	Percent
Pampeana	4,302,144	56.6	3,506,865	54.6
Cuyo	496,499	6.5	411,711	6.4
Northwest	1,358,360	17.9	1,201,470	18.7
Northeast	1,086,171	14.3	995,167	15.5
Patagonia	360,158	4.7	312,044	4.8
Argentina	7,603,332	100.0	6,427,257	100.0

Source: República Argentina (1994).

education. An educated and literate workforce theoretically is better able to shape the interactions between labor, capital, and place for maximum community and individual benefit. A recent study by the Economic Commission for Latin America and the Caribbean (ECLAC 1994) on the social panorama of the region pointed out that completion of secondary school is a prerequisite for opening up major opportunities for social advancement. In other words, 10 or more years of basic education translate into a probability of avoiding poverty that ranges from 82 to 97 percent. Moreover, the cultural development of a society in terms of the arts, entertainment, media, information, and literature depends heavily on the reading and writing skills of the populace.

In spite of its status as a relatively new country, Argentina has made impressive strides this century in developing a highly literate and educated society. Compared to other Latin American countries, Argentina enjoys one of the lowest overall rates of illiteracy (Table 3.12). At the global level, it also enjoys one of the highest proportions of students enrolled in full-time education, one of the highest student matriculation rates, and one of the lowest student-teacher ratios (Table 3.13). Nonetheless, in recent years Argentina's education system has been plagued by ideological purges, declining infrastructure, poorly compensated teachers, and inadequate capital investment. Several northern provinces, for example, suffer from illiteracy rates that are double the national average and thirteen times the rate recorded in the Federal District. Santiago del Estero, Corrientes, Chaco, Formosa, and Misiones all have illiteracy rates exceeding eight percent of the national population aged 10 years and over (Figure 3.5).

TABLE 3.12 Absolute Illiteracy Rates in Selected Latin American Countries, 1990

Country	Percent Illiterate
Uruguay	4
Argentina	5
Chile	7
Costa Rica	7
Paraguay	10
Panamá	12
Venezuela	12
Colombia	13
México	13
Ecuador	14
Perú	15
Dominican Republic	17
Brazil	19
Bolivia	23
El Salvador	27
Honduras	27
Guatemala	45
Haití	47

Source: World Bank (1993).

Exacerbating the problem of underdevelopment in the interior is the fact that far more females than males are illiterate. Female illiteracy has a direct impact on birth rates and labor participation rates, and also helps to perpetuate male dominance in many aspects of Argentine society. In Jujuy province, for example, nearly 18,000 women were considered illiterate in 1991 compared to 7,420 men.

A distinction needs to be made here between those people considered absolutely illiterate--individuals who never attended school and cannot read or write--and those described as functionally illiterate--individuals who attended school for some period of time but who since have lost many of the rudimentary skills of reading and writing and who can only function at the simplest level. In Argentina, as in most countries, few statistics exist on functional illiteracy. A 1992 survey of 1,000 students in Buenos Aires revealed that 82 percent earned less than a passing grade in mathematics and 22 percent earned zero (*Economist* November 26, 1994); these were

TABLE 3.13   The Ratio of Students to Teachers at the Primary Level in Selected
Countries, 1989

Country	Students Per Teacher
Italy	12
France	16
Germany	18
Argentina	19
New Zealand	19
United Kingdom	20
Japan	21
Brazil	23
Uruguay	23
Bolivia	25
Paraguay	25
Spain	25
Perú	29
Chile	29
Colombia	30
Ecuador	31
México	31

Source: World Bank (1993).

among the best educated students in Argentina! Unofficial estimates
suggest that functional illiteracy rates in the interior provinces exceed 25
percent of the population. My own limited experience talking to students,
workers, officials, and others in the Northwest in 1988 and 1991 supports
this estimate. Both absolute and functional illiteracy rates remain the highest among rural and foreign females.

Although during the 1980s tremendous improvements were made in
overall accessibility and attendance rates for school-age children in most
areas of Argentina, several interior provinces have experienced setbacks.
Between 1980 and 1991, the percentage of children aged 10-14 who no
longer attend school increased from 10.8 to 12.4 percent in Misiones, from
10.5 to 12 percent in Santiago del Estero, and from 9 to 9.4 percent in
Tucumán province. The general rate of schooling for children aged 5 to 17
also improved during the 1980s, but the interior provinces continued to
record levels well below the Federal Capital. In the 13-17 age group,
schooling rates for Misiones (49.8%), Chaco (51.3%), Santiago del Estero

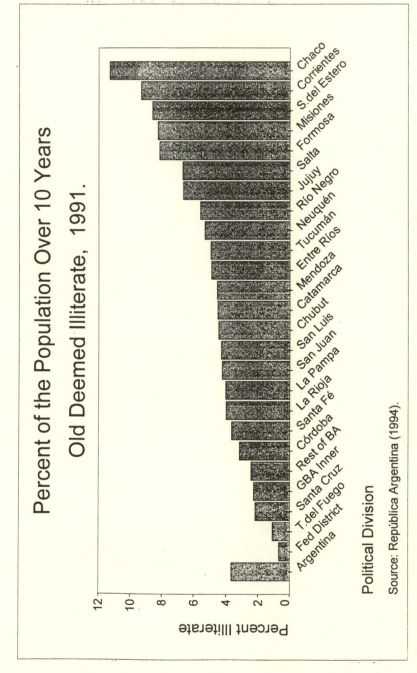

FIGURE 3.5 Percent of the Population over 10 Years Old in Argentina Deemed Illiterate, 1991.
Source: República Argentina (1994).

(52.2%), and Corrientes (57.2%) remained below the national average (66.7%) and substantially below the Federal Capital's rate of 86.5 percent. Barely 20 percent of the population aged 18-22 in many interior provinces attended school in 1991, compared to nearly 50 percent in the Federal Capital (República Argentina 1994). Moreover, despite Argentina's impressive ratio of students to teachers compared to other countries, most of the interior provinces have ratios 50 to 100 percent higher than those experienced in Buenos Aires (Sanmarchi 1989). Better quality schools and the promise of more employment opportunities in the Buenos Aires area act as a powerful force of attraction, especially among teenage males in the Northwest and Northeast regions.

Indicators of Health and Welfare

Statistics on the health and welfare of Argentina's society provide further evidence of disparities between provinces and regions in the quality of life. Access to basic health care, protection from criminal activities, and the provision of benefits after retirement are essential components of social development. In this regard, Argentina is closer to the levels of health and welfare enjoyed in the industrial North Atlantic countries than in most Latin American countries. Indeed, Argentinos take considerable pride in pointing out to visitors that the water generally is safe to drink, fresh fruits and salads can be consumed without risk of stomach ailments and, should the need arise, physicians and dentists are accessible (at least in Buenos Aires) and well trained. Moreover, until the end of the 1980s, individuals could move about the urban or rural landscape with little risk of personal assault or harassment. However, in recent years sporadic outbreaks of cholera and other ailments caused by contaminated water have become more common, particularly in the North. Increases in the rate of delinquency since 1990, especially murders and robberies, also have tarnished Argentina's reputation as a safe, visitor-friendly, and healthy country.

Infant mortality rates remain the highest in the northern provinces of Argentina, where deaths per 1,000 live births are typically twice as high as those recorded in the Federal District of Buenos Aires (Table 3.14). Diseases contracted in the perinatal period are the leading causes of death in infants under 1 year old. Despite significant improvements made during the 1980s in reducing the rate of infant mortality throughout Argentina, several northern provinces suffered slightly higher mortality rates in 1992 than in 1989, when Argentina experienced its most profound period of

TABLE 3.14   Infant Mortality Rates per 1,000 Live Births by Region and Political Division in Argentina, 1980-1991

Region/ Political Division	1980	1985	1989	1992
Argentina	33.2	26.2	25.7	23.6
Pampeana				
Federal District	18.5	15.3	15.9	14.9
Buenos Aires	28.4	23.8	23.9	22.4
Córdoba	24.2	22.6	21.1	19.6
Entre Ríos	35.8	25.8	23.9	22.1
La Pampa	30.3	24.7	23.5	21.3
Santa Fé	34.3	28.7	28.3	20.8
Cuyo				
Mendoza	31.8	25.2	25.2	22.1
San Juan	30.1	27.6	27.9	23.7
San Luis	37.2	32.8	33.8	23.7
Northwest				
Catamarca	41.9	46.0	24.6	28.1
Jujuy	51.4	32.8	35.4	32.5
La Rioja	45.8	30.2	34.7	26.0
Salta	52.1	34.0	32.3	32.8
Santiago del Estero	35.1	25.3	28.6	28.7
Tucumán	42.0	29.2	28.4	28.8
Northeast				
Chaco	54.2	39.4	37.9	33.5
Corrientes	44.6	32.5	33.7	27.7
Formosa	38.1	30.9	32.0	32.3
Misiones	51.9	33.6	30.0	27.0
Patagonia				
Chubut	34.8	26.3	22.9	19.8
Neuquén	31.7	23.6	21.9	16.1
Río Negro	35.7	26.3	25.5	22.7
Santa Cruz	34.4	22.0	21.8	20.4
Tierra del Fuego	20.3	9.4	18.0	11.2

Source: República Argentina (1994).

economic and social decline. The quality of access to health care facilities generally decreases the further away one gets from the Federal Capital. However, compared to the national average, many interior provinces fared reasonably well in the number of beds available at health-care establishments per 1,000 people in 1992 (Figure 3.6). Yet an analysis of changes in the number of beds available at health-care establishments revealed that many interior provinces actually had fewer beds available in 1992 compared to 1980 (Figure 3.7). Several provinces showed little improvement during the period despite overall increases in population. The Federal District, Buenos Aires province, Córdoba, and Santa Fé were the main recipients of increases in available beds, whereas Tucumán and Mendoza suffered from the greatest reduction.

More than one third of Argentina's population, a staggering 12 million people, lives without health care coverage. An estimated 3.5 million residents in the Greater Buenos Aires Metropolitan Area alone have no medical plan or welfare fund. In several interior provinces, more than half the population has no health coverage (Figure 3.8). Children under the age of 19 comprise 45.26 percent of the total population without coverage, and approximately 35 percent of all children in Argentina aged 0-14 have no health coverage. Compounding the health-care problem is the astonishing amount of corruption that permeates the health system. Moreover, 34.7 percent of Argentina's employees, 2.8 million people, have no social security deduction from their wages and thus are not covered by state programs. In the public sector, 94 percent of all employees have a social security deduction, whereas only 63 percent have coverage in the private sector. Those employed in domestic service rarely have social security coverage; 93 percent of such employees pay no social security contribution (República Argentina 1994).

Crime rates are intimately related to socioeconomic problems. The number of criminal offences in Argentina reached an all-time high in 1989 during the country's most serious period of economic crisis in recent memory. Economic restructuring in the 1990s also is having an impact on delinquency rates. Rising urban unemployment and underemployment, coupled with an overvalued currency, are viewed as causal factors in Argentina's rising crime rates. Narcotics offenses have increased exponentially since 1980. The historic colonial trunk route from Peru and Bolivia to Buenos Aires has become a major pipeline in the 1990s for the movement of cocaine on its way to the North Atlantic markets. Murder rates are the highest in decades and crimes against individuals have more than

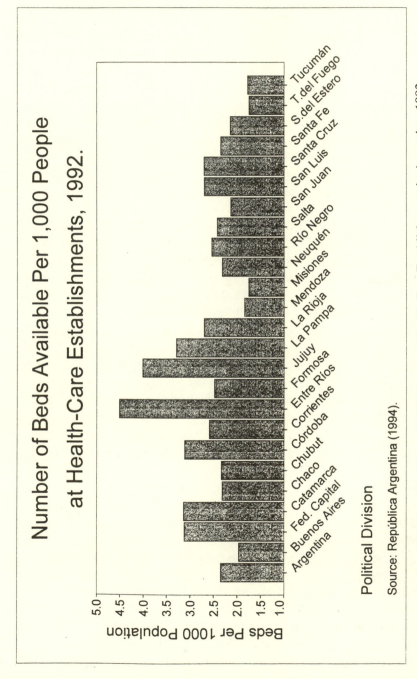

FIGURE 3.6 Number of Beds Available per 1,000 People at Health-Care Establishments in Argentina, 1992.
Source: República Argentina (1994).

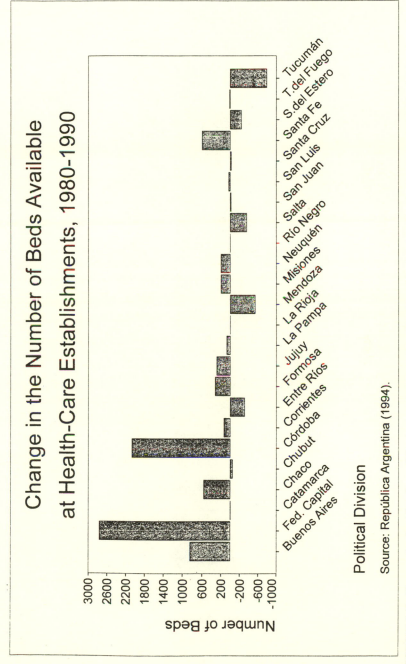

FIGURE 3.7 Change in the Number of Beds Available at Health-Care Establishments in Argentina, 1980-1990.
Source: República Argentina (1994).

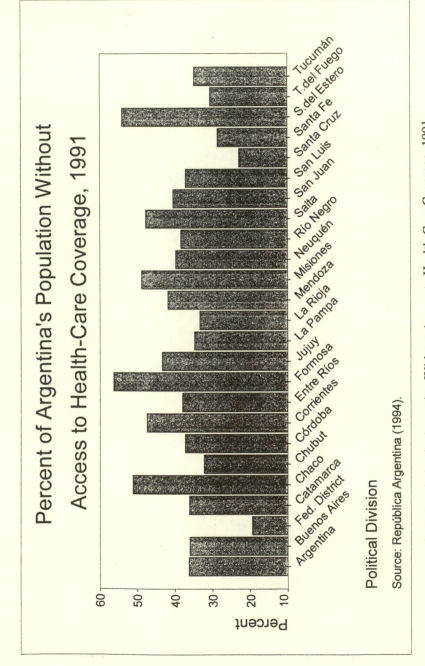

FIGURE 3.8 Percent of the Population in Argentina Without Access to Health-Care Coverage, 1991.
Source: República Argentina (1994).

doubled since 1980. Surprisingly, many interior provinces considered very safe during the 1970s and 1980s suffered very high increases in delinquency rates between 1980 and 1992 (Table 3.15). A variety of government and private individuals in Buenos Aires suggested to me during off-the-record discussions that rising crime rates in the interior are a direct result of immigration from neighboring countries, yet I could find no evidence to prove or disprove this theory. During a visit to a police station in the Federal District after having my camera stolen in one of the city parks, several police officials told me that the perpetrators probably were *cabeceras negritas* (greasers or little blackheads), which is the racist and derogatory term frequently used to describe immigrants from Bolivia, Peru, and Paraguay. There do appear to be statistical links, however, between poverty and crime rates in the major urban centers of the country as well as in the interior provinces.

Housing and Habitat

The final indicator of uneven development addressed in this chapter is the provision of housing and habitat. Housing deficits are one of the most acute problems affecting the social order in countries around the world. A major issue for governments, institutions, and individuals in Argentina over the past few decades has been a lack of sufficient and adequate housing, especially in the major urban centers. In 1960, according to a report by the Regional Office of Metropolitan Area Development, only 1.6 million residential units were available in the Greater Buenos Aires Metropolitan Area to accommodate 2 million families (República Argentina 1969). At the national level, the housing deficit rose from 2.5 million units in 1980 to 3.2 million units in 1991 (Carlevari and Carlevari 1994). Moreover, deficient construction, the lack of electricity, water, and sewer, overcrowding, and inadequate police and fire protection combine to leave millions of Argentinos living in substandard housing conditions. Over 30 percent of the occupied housing in Santiago del Estero, Misiones, and Formosa had no access to electricity in 1991 (Figure 3.9). Nearly 60 percent of all houses in Misiones province had no access to running water in 1991 (República Argentina (1994). The housing situation in many interior provinces remains critical.

The most visible and oft-discussed aspect of housing problems in Latin America is the existence of urban shantytowns or self-help settlements known variously as *villas de emergencia, villas miserias, favelas,* or

TABLE 3.15   Delinquency Rates per 1000 Inhabitants by Region and Political
Division in Argentina, 1980-1992

Region/ Political Division	1980	1989	1992	Change % 1992/1980
Argentina	81.5	203.5	156.8	92.4
Pampeana				
Federal District	87.7	327.8	104.5	19.2
Buenos Aires	39.7	107.6	115.8	191.8
Córdoba	125.2	304.6	203.4	62.5
Entre Ríos	67.5	151.3	129.1	91.3
La Pampa	193.9	294.5	218.2	12.5
Santa Fé	127.0	265.9	203.9	60.5
Cuyo				
Mendoza	104.8	209.0	192.5	83.7
San Juan	114.2	299.2	195.5	71.2
San Luis	42.7	147.1	124.0	190.5
Northwest				
Catamarca	124.9	205.6	184.9	48.1
Jujuy	153.8	310.2	271.3	76.4
La Rioja	86.1	195.2	153.3	78.0
Salta	96.3	479.0	368.4	282.5
Santiago del Estero	165.7	257.2	181.3	9.4
Tucumán	104.1	188.9	141.2	35.7
Northeast				
Chaco	144.1	325.5	224.2	55.6
Corrientes	58.5	162.1	127.9	118.6
Formosa	106.5	134.5	91.2	- 14.3
Misiones	45.4	174.0	125.7	176.9
Patagonia				
Chubut	65.1	187.0	151.4	132.6
Neuquén	112.5	211.0	382.5	240.0
Río Negro	108.5	228.0	162.1	49.4
Santa Cruz	96.3	218.3	186.8	94.0
Tierra del Fuego	105.6	212.1	100.7	- 4.6

Source: República Argentina (1994).

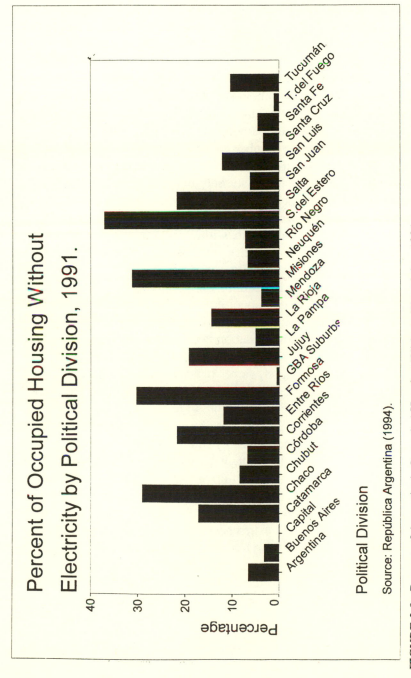

Percent of Occupied Housing Without
Electricity by Political Division, 1991.

FIGURE 3.9 Percent of Argentina's Occupied Housing Without Electricity, 1991.
Source: República Argentina (1994).

barriadas. Although governments and planners debate the terminology used to describe self-help housing and about the actual living conditions and time of tenure in these settlements, most agree that the distinguishing characteristic of self-help housing is that it "always begins as a rudimentary form of shelter lacking all kinds of services and is developed on land which either lacks planning permission or which has been invaded" (Gilbert 1994: 80). A popular misconception about self-help housing is that it exists only in the peripheral zones of Latin American urban centers. While most large self-help settlements are found around the outer perimeter of many Latin American cities, a growing number also are located in the inner city. In Argentina, self-help housing ranging from isolated squatter settlements to larger *villas_miserias* can be found not only in the inner suburbs and on the fringes of the major cities along low-lying areas, but also near the city center. In 1995, for example, several self-help settlements were located in the downtown area of the Federal District within walking distance of the Plaza de Mayo. Of the 200,000 hectares that comprise the Federal District, some 250 hectares are occupied by 15 *villas miserias* that contain over 100,000 people. Self-help housing has proliferated in Argentina's cities since the 1940s quite simply because the poor have had no alternative. Any available piece of unoccupied land, vacant building, or suitable structure that can be used for temporary accommodation is sought out by the poor. Shacks on vacant land are constructed with whatever material is available: corrugated metal, cardboard, wood, stone, masonry rubble, and rubber tires. Most of these dwellings lack any type of basic public service, such as water, sewage, electricity, transportation, or telephone.

As Alan Gilbert (1994) pointed out, the spatial dispersion of self-help housing in cities has been encouraged by improvements in suburban public transport, the benign attitude of many governments toward informal land occupation, and the spreading net of urban services and infrastructure. In Argentina's major cities, self-help housing can be found in multiple jurisdictions, diffused over a broad expanse of urban territory. This makes coordination and management extremely complicated. Property speculation in the major cities since 1990 also has complicated the problem of adequate housing provision. As the commercial-bureaucratic role of Argentina's cities expands to meet the needs of the new world economy, pressure to convert dwelling units to office buildings is increasing, particularly in Buenos Aires. Moreover, increased rates of urban unemployment and underemployment are forcing thousands of people from formal into informal housing, as they no longer can pay the monthly rent or mortgage.

Informal housing also continues to be the dominant means of shelter for migrants from rural areas to the city. The immediate future for housing in Argentina remains uncertain. In August, 1992, the federal government signed an agreement with the provincial governments to transfer funds automatically for the construction of houses in the interior. Unfortunately, both the National Housing Fund (FONAVI) and many government agencies that deal with housing are riddled with bureaucratic ineptitude, inefficiencies, and rampant corruption.

Conclusion

Despite the moderate growth of Argentina's population by Latin American or world standards since the 1940s, the past two decades have constituted a period of major change in the country's demographic patterns. The overall composition of the population has shifted toward older average ages, more nuclear households, rising labor force participation, and increased numbers of urbanites. The most distinctive features of post-1940s Argentina--increased Latin American and Asian migration, the baby boom, and megacephalous urban growth--have become embedded deeply in the national population profile. Arguably, these features could produce further socioeconomic upheavals in the coming decade. More important, however, is that demographic changes have altered considerably the character of most places and regions in Argentina.

Solutions to Argentina's uneven development problems require strategies that address the spatial component of demographic change. Contemporary government policies in this regard appear to have four primary objectives, the first of which is to reshape the patterns of immigration to Argentina. In recent months, the federal government has raised the issue of stricter immigration controls, especially from Bolivia and Paraguay. The second is to create the conditions needed to contain the out-migration from the interior provinces of the Northwest, Northeast, and the Cuyo. A third objective is the promotion of external and internal migration to Patagonia. Growth pole strategies are playing a significant role in this regard (see Chapter 8). Finally, from a geopolitical perspective, the government sees a need to populate the frontier zones preferably with native-born Argentinos. Tremendous concern exists about the possible dilution of the demographic weight of Argentine natives in frontier zones, especially if foreign immigration continues at the current level and pace.

In addition to specific demographic objectives, several emerging issues that interconnect cultural, economic, political, and social realms in unique ways are shaping Argentina's contemporary social policy initiatives. These issues cut across local, regional, and national boundaries, with impacts on the social actors involved in these realms as well as on the realms themselves (ECLAC 1994). Although these issues are examined in detail in the third part of the study, a brief overview provides context for the following chapter's analysis of the capital-labor-production nexus.

Rural conflicts ranging from ethnic to environmental issues have become increasingly important, especially in Bolivia, Brazil, and Paraguay. Agrarian reform programs, for example, have resulted in rural violence throughout the region in recent years, and spillover effects are felt in Argentina. A failure to address rural social problems seriously in Argentina could lead to more direct conflict over the short-term between governments and *campesinos*. Changes in social values are at the forefront of concerns about family, religion, and the legal order. The recent International Conference on Population and Development has fueled debate about divorce, abortion, birth control, and the family at all levels of Argentine society. Concerns over AIDS, drug use, pornography, homosexuality, domestic violence, and the role of the Catholic church are shaping legislation that could have profound and far-reaching implications for Argentina's society well into the next century. Ongoing environmental degradation in Buenos Aires and other big cities is raising serious concern about the social costs of economic restructuring. Especially at risk from air pollution and contaminated water are children and the elderly. Political corruption remains high on the list of people's concerns in Argentina about the management of public funds. Bureaucratic fiscal ineptitude, rampant tax evasion, and bribery of public and private officials continue to retard the country's ability to make more substantial progress with social reforms. The role of the military in Argentine society has been reshaped since 1990, with President Menem eliminating compulsory military service in favor of a voluntary system. His government has reduced military spending drastically, but will these savings be translated into social expenditure? Finally, and perhaps most serious of all Argentina's current social issues, is the growing concern over urban crime, increased drug trafficking and use, and white-collar fraud. Some critics of Menem's policies argue that a clear causal link exists between globalization and a variety of social ills. In a scathing commentary on the government's policies, Joe Schneider (1994:10) lambasted the "sham and shame of democracy-by-decree, with quasi-stability camouflaging growing unemployment, a monumental trade deficit, proliferation of school-age dunces, chronic deterioration in health conditions, and unchecked hooliganism in the Boca-River gangs."

Varying degrees of demographic and socioeconomic polarization at regional, subregional, and local scales lie at the core of the myriad changes which have reshaped the geography of Argentina over the past decade, and which continue to shape Argentina today. The following chapter examines the economic forces that are inextricably intertwined with shifts in demographic patterns, as well as the impact that the demography-labor nexus has had on the spatial organization of capital circulation, labor activity, and patterns of production and trade. The exacerbation of place differentiation in Argentina also provides the rationale for the more locally focused analyses in part three of the study.

4

Capital, Labor, and Production

Argentina's economic map has changed more dramatically and fundamentally than its sociodemographic map since 1990. Privatization, industrial restructuring, service sector growth, and agricultural change are reshaping the capital-labor-production nexus in a variety of ways in different places. The country's rearticulation with the world economy has been described as the "Argentine miracle" (Corradi 1995:78). During the first five years of Menemism, the economy grew by over 30 percent, third in the world growth rankings behind China and Thailand. Argentina's 6.2 percent growth in real gross domestic product (GDP) during 1994 outpaced every other Latin American country except Peru (11%) and Guyana (8%). Adjusted GDP for 1994 probably will have exceeded 270 billion pesos, approximately 8,180 pesos (US$8,200) for each inhabitant (*Economist* November 26, 1994). Although Argentina's GDP for 1995 recorded a decline of 2.5 percent, a poor performance compared to neighboring Chile's 8 percent growth rate for the year, government estimates forecast a favorable 2 percent or more growth rate for 1996. While this does not compare favorably overall with countries such as Australia, Canada, Spain, or the United States, it does represent a substantial recovery from the economically devastating years of the 1980s (Table 4.1). Moreover, Argentina has raced ahead of its regional neighbors in GDP growth since 1990. Economic indicators show that Argentina has recovered the ground it lost during the 1980s and now stands poised to experience solid growth over the coming decade.

The country's macroeconomic success, however, is tempered by the pain of microeconomic adjustments. Increased unemployment, bankruptcies, poverty, and regional inequalities present serious challenges to the Menem

TABLE 4.1   The Evolution of Gross Domestic Product in Argentina, 1980-1996

Year	GDP in Millions of Current US$	GDP Per Capita (US$/Year)
1980	208,606	7,388
1981	168,779	5,888
1982	99,602	3,424
1983	103,642	3,513
1984	116,504	3,894
1985	88,240	2,909
1986	105,764	3,441
1987	108,544	3,486
1988	122,725	3,892
1989	82,281	2,577
1990	141,598	4,521
1991	189,540	5,794
1992	228,745	6,911
1993[a]	250,000	7,500
1994[a]	271,000	8,180
1995[a]	265,000	8,000
1996[b]	275,000	8,200

[a] Estimated figures subject to final adjustment.
[b] Projected figure.
Source: After Carlevari and Carlevari (1994); República Argentina (1994); *Latin American Weekly Report* (1995-96).

government reelected in May 1995 for a new four-year term. Many interior provinces, for example, traditionally have relied on a closed national econ-omy, with state subsidies, inflation, tax avoidance, and corruption often necessary for economic survival (Corradi 1995). Reengagement with the world economy has caused many provincial economies to contract and un-employment rates to soar. Moreover, the financial windfall from the sale of Argentina's public assets between 1990 and 1995 is unlikely to be re-peated. With privatization having run its course, Argentina now must look toward new sources of capital and foreign investment if it is to maintain the recent pace of growth. This chapter examines the changes in capital, labor, and production that are shaping the socioeconomic map of Argentina.

First, I discuss the process of capital restructuring and provide an over-view of the privatization policies that serve as the foundation for the reorganization of Argentina's capital-labor-production nexus. Next, the structure of the country's labor force is analyzed for evidence of recent change, with a specific focus on transformations in Argentina's cost of living compared to other Latin American countries. An analysis of the spatial dynamics of modifications to patterns of production and trade follows, with a focus on primary and secondary sector restructuring, growth pole strategies, and service sector growth. The role of MERCOSUR and other trade blocs in reshaping Argentina's regional and global trade relationships also is examined. Finally, I discuss Argentina's economic competitiveness in the contemporary global economy and I argue that the Achilles heel of economic restructuring in Argentina is the government's failure to plan for an integrated, multimodal transport and communication system.

Recapitalizing Argentina

One of the key pillars in the regional development of a country is the circulation of capital, both intangible and tangible, within the state. Capital can encourage the production and circulation of commodities, it can increase the productivity of labor, and it can be invested in physical infra-structure that, in turn, can provide new opportunities for the creation and turnover of capital. Spatial dichotomies in capital circulation and invest-ment within a country contribute to uneven patterns of development and help to create situations whereby the capital-labor-production nexus has different impacts in different places.

Historically, the city of Buenos Aires has dominated Argentina's circuits of capital and the pampas hinterland has contained much of the country's industrial and agricultural means of production. As Michael Johns (1992) pointed out, during the "golden years" of Argentina's development (1880-1920), most of the enormous capital surplus generated by the pampas flowed into Buenos Aires. Here, the elite families engaged in the conspicu-ous consumption of services and commodities (often imported), invested in urban real estate, and established many of the city's banks and import houses. Yet little domestic capital found its way back into infrastructural development projects, especially in the interior provinces. Foreign capital provided the impetus for much of the infrastructure constructed in the Pampeana region, most notably British and French capital for railroad construction. Indeed, foreign investors controlled approximately 48 percent of Argentina's total fixed capital during the first decades of the 20th century (Diaz-Alejandro 1970). Unfortunately, little of this foreign capital circulated into the interior provinces, many of which remained impoverished, underdeveloped, and capital-deprived well into the 1950s and 1960s.

New influxes of foreign capital in the 1960s favored the petroleum and automotive sectors and had a substantial impact on the interior of Argentina. For example, natural gas and oil pipelines from the Campo Durán fields in the northwest province of Salta supplemented energy resource development projects in Patagonia and the Cuyo and helped to create new jobs and urban growth in the interior. However, industrial and manufacturing investment remained firmly focused on Buenos Aires and the Pampeana, encouraging a flood of migrants from rural to urban environments and from interior provinces to Buenos Aires. A lack of capital for housing, public service infrastructure, transportation, industry, and agriculture continued to plague interior regions. Moreover, whenever political and economic crises threatened order and stability in Argentina--and crises occurred frequently between the 1960s and 1980s--domestic capital fled overseas. During periods of high inflation and weak currency rates, both local and international capital tended to seek more profitable investment arenas. For example, in 1989 alone an estimated US$4.3 billion in private capital left Argentina for more stable areas. Official estimates put the total amount of Argentina's private capital circulating offshore at over US$60 billion in 1989. The country's lack of entrepreneurial and investment capital throughout the 1980s had extremely negative effects on the government's ability to develop infrastructural projects, to maintain a stable economy, and to tackle the issue of uneven regional development.

Throughout the 1970s and 1980s, the United States and seven European countries (in order of importance: Italy, France, Germany, The Netherlands, Switzerland, Spain, and Sweden) together provided 92 percent of direct foreign investment (DFI) in Argentina. Approximately half of all foreign capital received went directly into industrial manufacturing, particularly automobiles, petrochemicals, and food processing. The gas and petroleum (21.4 percent) and financial sectors (15.3 percent) absorbed a little over one third of invested foreign capital during this period (CEPAL 1995). In the 1980s, Argentina received only US$6 billion in DFI compared to Brazil's US$16 billion and Mexico's US$13 billion. However, 74 percent of all profits generated by DFI during this period was reinvested in Argentina. In contrast, only 42 percent of the profits in Brazil and 58 percent of the profits in Mexico were reinvested back into the domestic economy.

Moreover, a comparison between the first and second halves of the 1980s reveals a dramatic change in reinvestment strategies. Between 1980 and 1984 only half of the profits generated by DFI in Argentina were reinvested, whereas Brazil and Mexico both recorded higher percentages. However, between 1985 and 1989, 94.4 percent of profits in Argentina generated by DFI remained in the country, while only 32 percent in Brazil and 53 percent in Mexico were reinvested (CEPAL 1995). Although DFI in Argentina reached its highest level in over two decades at the end of the 1980s, increased economic instability began to threaten the inflow of foreign capital and to force domestic capital overseas.

In 1990, the Menem government introduced policies to restructure the circuits of capital in Argentina. Menem viewed taming inflation and arresting the collapse of the national currency as critical to the recapitalization of the country. Absent a guarantee of stability in the local capital markets, argued Menem, the federal government would continue to struggle in its attempts to lure capital investment to Argentina. The key to Argentina's monetary stability has been the April, 1991, implementation of the Convertibility Law that requires the Central Bank to back 100 percent of Argentina's monetary base with gold, currency, or other foreign currency assets. With the introduction of the new Argentine Peso in January 1992, the sale of national currency became pegged at a 1:1 basis with the U.S. dollar (see Table 2.5). Although in 1996 the Peso remained overvalued by at least 30 percent against the U.S. dollar, currency stability, substantial overall GDP growth, and low inflation have resulted in macroeconomic success for Argentina. Between 1991 and 1994, the country experienced dramatic increases in economic growth. Gross domestic product rose by 33 percent, capital investments soared by 120 percent, and domestic consumption grew by 37 percent.

Changes in the value of Argentina's currency and the annual inflation rate reflect the stability of the domestic economy. Economic restructuring policies have stabilized both currency and consumer prices since 1990 (see Table 2.5). Inflation fell to single digits for the first time in over 13 years, consumer prices leveled off, and the peso remained stable against the U.S. dollar. Stability in Argentina's financial market is crucial if the country is to attract the global capital needed to fund major infrastructural improvements. Financial stability and liberalization of the capital markets since 1990 have encouraged a net inflow of private funds into Argentina, reversing the negative trends of the 1980s. In 1991, US$2.3 billion in private capital returned to Argentina, nearly US$8 billion was repatriated in 1992, and over US$5 billion returned in 1993. Much of this capital has been invested in real estate development projects in and around the capital, Buenos Aires. In partnership with multinational companies, local capital has helped to fund the construction of international hotels in the capital such as the Hyatt complex near Retiro station, major shopping malls like the Bullrich Center, and urban rehabilitation projects such as Puerto Madero. Stability in both currency and inflation rates also has driven the expansion of the country's stock market. Barely US$300 million in shares traded on the stock exchange in 1986. By 1992, this figure had exploded to US$32 billion, an indication of a renewed level of confidence in the domestic economy. Transactions in government securities grew from US$13.6 billion in 1989 to over US$94 billion in 1992, with market capitalization exceeding 12 percent. Privatization policies and more efficient tax collection methods also have stimulated an increase in government revenues, enabling vital capital to be redirected from inefficient, loss-making activities to more productive social infrastructure programs.

Since 1994, the stock market has exhibited much greater volatility, with negative changes in equity a more common trend. Argentina's capital markets suffered seriously from the Mexican financial crisis of 1994-1995, the so-called "Tequila effect," and recovery proved extremely slow through the latter half of 1995. In November 1995, the stock market stood at 92 percent of its December 1994 value and at only 69 percent of its December 1993 value (CEPAL 1995). Moreover, Argentina's public debt of US$87.6 billion at the end of 1995 (the third highest in Latin America behind Brazil (US$170 billion) and Mexico (US$153 billion)), coupled with private sector debt of over US$7 billion, has caused concern about the country's long-term financial future and its ability to maintain capital stability. Public debt accounted for approximately 29 percent of GDP in January 1996, not an unmanageable ratio compared to Ecuador with 85 percent of its GDP in public debt (*Latin American Weekly Report* February 29, 1996). However, Argentina's total debt is 4.5 times its exports. In addition, at the end of 1995 the country suffered from the second-highest debt interest-to-exports ratio in South America at 23.5 percent (Peru recorded the highest ratio at 32.1 percent).

Foreign capital inflows slowed down during 1995, with Argentina receiving only US$2 billion in direct foreign investments (DFI) compared to Mexico's US$6 billion and Brazil's US$3.2 billion. Subtle geographic shifts in the flow of capital to Argentina from other countries also are underway. Western European countries, for example, contributed 52 percent of DFI in Argentina in 1993, while North America's share fell to 30 percent. European countries in particular have participated heavily in Argentina's privatization program. Telefónica de España and Stet-France Cable et Radio have invested in the country's new telecommunications companies; Iberia Airlines of Spain owns a portion of Aerolíneas Argentinas, the national airline; Societa Italiana per il Gas y Camuzzi Gasometri is involved in Argentina's privatized Gas del Estado company; and Repsol de España, Total Austral de Francia, and Electricité de France all have invested in Argentina's energy sector (CEPAL 1995). Between 1990 and 1993, 50.1 percent of the Argentine government's total privatiza- tion proceeds from foreign sources emanated from European countries: Spain (23.2%), Italy (13.3%), France (10.3%), and the United Kingdom (3.3%). The United States (26.6%), Canada (3.9%), and Chile (11.3%) were the other three major overseas sources of privatization funds. In the mid-1990s, 28 major multinational corporations controlled 438 companies in Argentina, with nearly two-thirds of these companies of European origin (Table 4.2).

Early indicators from the first few months of 1996 suggested that Argentina may have recovered from the "Tequila" effect and that economic recovery once again is underway (*Latin American Weekly Report* 1996: 248). Volumes on the Buenos Aires Stock Exchange have returned to 1992 levels, with approximately US$40 million in daily trading. Foreign invest- ment, particularly into private-sector securities, had increased by US$1 billion during the first three months of 1996 compared to 1995, and more Argentinos were holding their bank deposits in pesos rather than in dollars offshore. High world grain prices also were expected to boost Argentina's export earnings and to generate a positive trade balance for 1996. How- ever, despite real macroeconomic successes in Argentina, historical inertia in the development and circulation of capital has retarded the ability of Menem's globalization policies to reshape the socioeconomic landscape in a spatially balanced manner.

Just as in the late nineteenth century, when Argentinos shied away from investing in what were perceived as speculative technologies (railroads, tramways, and ports), particularly in the interior, domestic capital in the 1990s is not flowing into projects that could have important forward and backward linkages in the national economy. Weak circuits of capital in interior provinces directly impact the reshaping of the socioeconomic land- scape by restricting the availability of funds for infrastructural development projects. Few improvements in educational facilities, transportation, public

TABLE 4.2   Multinational Corporations in Argentina, 1994

Corporation	Country of Origin	Number of Companies Controlled
Fiat/Macri	Italy/Argentina	63
Enterprises Quilmes	Luxembourg	47
Techint	Italy/Argentina	46
Renault	France	45
Brown Boveri	Switzerland	35
Coca Cola	United States	17
Soldati Brown Boveri	Switzerland/Argentina	15
Siemens	Germany	12
Masalin	Germany	11
Camea	Canada	11
Johnson and Johnson	United States	10
Indupa	France/Argentina	9
La Vascongada	United Kingdom	9
Lepetit-Dow	United States	9
André	Switzerland	9
Nobleza Piccardo	United Kingdom	9
Pirelli	Italy	8
Minera Aguilar	United States	8
Bayer	Germany	8
Duperial	United Kingdom	8
Hoechst	Germany	7
Ford	United States	7
La Oxígena	France	7
Philips	Netherlands	6
Deutz	Germany	6
Chiclet's Adams	United States	6
Rhodia	France	5
Royal Dutch Shell	Netherlands	5
Total:		438

Source: Durán et al. (1995).

service infrastructure, or resource development projects have been forth-coming beyond Buenos Aires and its immediate hinterland. Capital invested in the construction of luxury boutiques, glitzy shopping malls, sports facilities, and high-rise condominiums in and around Buenos Aires, and in land speculation and the consumption of luxury imported goods, has done little to broaden the economic base of Argentina, to encourage the investment of capital in public infrastructure, or to facilitate regional development in the interior.

Concomitant with the Menem government's policies to bring financial stability to Argentina came new ideas about what role the state should play in the national economy. Most of the country's state-run industries and public services had been plagued for decades by corruption, management and labor inefficiencies, a lack of capital investment, and a loss of public confidence. Argentina's desperate need for a major infusion of investment capital to rehabilitate collapsing public infrastructure in the interior and to cope with the demands of participation in the increasingly competitive global economy prompted the government to turn toward privatization and deregulation policies. Under the rubric of "globalization," these policies were designed to open up the national economy to global competition and to attract investment capital to Argentina. The Menem government argued that state disengagement from all aspects of the economy would generate a cascading or "trickle-down" effect that would have positive implications for socioeconomic development throughout Argentina's interior provinces.

State Disengagement from the Economy

From the 1940s onwards, with a few exceptions, successive governments in Argentina trumpeted the values of industrialization and devalued the agro-exporting model of development. Policy makers believed state engagement in the national economy to be the best instrument for liberating the country from the clutches of an exploitive world economy. A stable, more balanced, state-directed economy, driven by decreased imports and increased exports of consumer goods, could articulate Argentina more favorably with world markets. However, protectionism and state intervention became excessive and Argentina did not integrate fully into the world economy (Saútu 1993). Critics of Argentina's post-World War Two development suggest that the country could have participated in the international economic boom of 1950-1970 had it not pursued unrestricted import substitution industrialization and state intervention (see Lewis 1990; Erro 1993). By the end of the 1980s, the State's role in the economy increasingly was seem as a source of inefficiency, bureaucratic ineptitude, and rampant corruption.

In a swift and unorthodox change of policy in 1990, the newly elected administration of Carlos Saúl Menem abandoned the Peronist ideals of state intervention and protectionism. Menem's logic for embracing the new ideology of globalization seemed simple: only by opening Argentina's economy to global competition and reducing the role of the public sector could the country rectify its past mistakes, restructure its society and economy, and rejoin the global community of nations (*U.S. News and World Report* May 7, 1990; *New York Times* September 22, 1992). According to Menem, capital circulated under no flag, and he saw no distinction between national and foreign capital (*Business Week* September 24, 1990). Thus, the doors of Argentina should be opened to the world economy and global capital embraced.

Argentina For Sale. Key to the federal government's globalization strategies was the plan to extricate itself from the public services arena. Redefining the role of the State in the national economy required the privatization of most state-owned companies. In 1990, over 120 state-run entities in Argentina controlled a sizeable portion of the domestic economy. By 1994, only eight public companies remained in operation (República Argentina 1994). In Buenos Aires, for example, the subways, suburban railroads, water and sewage networks, electricity systems, telephone networks, and other public services quickly were sold off to private investors (Keeling 1996). Argentina's railroads, state-run factories, ports, and national airline also were placed on the auction block. Privatization, argued the government, would reduce the burden of subsidizing public services and improve their management and efficiency. A long history of government financial and management ineptitude in the transport sector lends credence to the popular belief that privatization will provide an improved quality of service, while relieving the financially strapped federal, provincial, and local legislatures of fiscal responsibility for transport provision.

Many Argentines complained, however, that privatization simply was a "bargain sale of grandmother's jewelry," a reference to the nationalization of public enterprises by Perón in the late 1940s (Imai 1992:448). Adolfo Canitrot (1993:91) argued that the government's privatization policies were an "all-out effort targeted to eradicate public enterprises completely." For example, rather than broadening the ownership base of public enterprises through share sales to small investors, privatization has concentrated ownership and control in the hands of approximately ten large Argentine conglomerates headquartered in Buenos Aires (Canitrot 1993). Despite the use of Argentine as well as foreign capital to fund the purchase of these public enterprises, privatization policies have generated a great deal of nationalistic rhetoric. Graffiti messages such as *Patria sí, Colonia no* (country yes but colony no) have sprung up all over the country protesting privatization, a clear indication of public sentiment about increased foreign investment in Argentina's economy.

Privatization policies in Argentina are not a new phenomenon. They had been tried during the 1970s and early 1980s, but had targeted mostly small enterprises with little impact on the national economy. The ideology of a state-controlled and directed national economy had become embedded in the culture, supported by unions and workers alike who benefitted from inefficiencies and job protection programs. Unfortunately, state involvement in transport, industry, and public services had created a culture of waste, featherbedding, corruption, and non-competitiveness. Indeed, Argentina's state-driven employment and production structure had many parallels to the Soviet system: multiple employees for a single position, poor quality production, physical deterioration of infrastructure, serious pollution problems, and underutilized capacities.

Since 1990, most state-controlled enterprises and services have been transferred to private ownership either through outright sale or via the granting of long-term operating concessions. Since 1990, 121 state-owned or controlled companies have been sold off to the private sector (ECLAC 1995). For example, 85 percent of Aerolíneas Argentinas, the national airline company, now is controlled by a private consortium that includes Iberia Airlines of Spain. Several North American companies have invested in Argentina's freight railroads, as well as in the suburban rail services of Buenos Aires. Approximately US$18.4 billion in cash flowed into the national treasury between January 1990 and December 1995, in addition to several billion dollars in debt securities, as a result of these privatizations. However, in the government's haste to divest itself of the public enterprises, maximize the proceeds, and achieve its political goals, very little attention has been paid to regulation, competition, or loss of service. The successful privatization of public utilities especially requires the prior development of a regulatory framework to safeguard public assets and to ensure the provision of needed services (Abdala 1994). This has not happened in Argentina. Moreover, during the entire privatization process, the government consistently has ignored the issue of who would be affected negatively by state disengagement from the provision of public services. Also consistently ignored by the government has been the geographical impact of privatizing public services. The benefits of privatization have been proclaimed loudly and frequently from the high altar of Menemism, but the social costs remain hidden in flowery rhetoric and the slogan of "economic surgery without anesthesia."

Privatization of state-run services had an immediate impact on the labor market in Argentina. Downsizing and the shedding of surplus labor swelled the ranks of the unemployed in many of the major Pampeana cities. For example, Argentina's state petroleum company has reduced its work-force since 1990 from 52,000 to 6,000 people. More dramatically, the railroad companies reduced their workforce from a peak of 87,000 employees prior to privatization in 1991 to 5,230 in 1995 (Richter 1996). As a result, unemployment rates exploded, particularly in many interior provinces, as surplus labor generated by privatization downsizing could not be absorbed into other sectors of the economy. Provincial governments in many interior provinces traditionally controlled unemployment rates by creating bloated bureaucracies supported, in part, by funds remitted from the federal government. In La Rioja province, the state once governed by President Carlos Menem, nearly 75 percent of the economically active population during the 1980s was directly or indirectly supported by the provincial government. The most corrupt strategy involved the hiring of "phantom" employees or *ñoquis* who turned up at work once a week simply to collect a paycheck. Critics of Menem argue that many of his friends, acquaintances, and relatives, at one time or another, have been on the pro-vincial payroll without actually working. This type of subsidized employ-ment (or unemployment) still permeates the political-economic culture of Argentina, with serious consequences for the economic future of interior provinces such as La Rioja.

Although the recapitalization of Argentina has proved successful in a number of areas, industry and agriculture still remain woefully short of in-vestment capital, particularly in the northern provinces. Moreover, despite the privatization of many public services, most Argentinos outside the Pampeana region have yet to experience any significant improvements in basic infrastructure. In the interior regions of Patagonia, the North, and the Cuyo, it could be argued that the circulation of investment capital has actually deteriorated since 1990. Little solid evidence on the landscape exists of infrastructural improvements. In 1996, Argentina's foreign debt remained high (nearly US$90 billion), less than 40 percent of the stock market was tradable because of elite control of shares, and the domestic savings rate hovered around a miserable 18 percent of GDP. Moreover, the record number of business failures in 1995 (nearly 900 companies filed for bankruptcy, up 57 percent over 1994), coupled with a doubling of the number of labor disputes between 1992 and 1995 (from 700 to 1,370), suggest that Argentina's capital restructuring policies are having a serious impact on the structure of the labor market.

Restructuring the Labor Market

Economic restructuring in Argentina has replaced the traditional statist system with a free-market environment driven by deregulation and privatization. As a consequence, the labor market is experiencing a period of dynamic reorganization at all scales and in every sector of the economy. Throughout Latin America, workers generally have born the brunt of the social debt of economic restructuring. As labor markets are restructured and labor relations deregulated, decreased employment stability, an increase in temporary employment, the growth of the informal sector, and an increase in subcontracting all act to reshape the region's labor patterns (Munck 1994). Moreover, with declining minimum wages and the erosion of purchasing power, workers face a future of severe inequity and social differentiation. Not surprisingly, the reaction by trade unions to structural adjustment policies, particularly in Argentina, has been defensive and reactive. Yet as Ronaldo Munck (1994:92) pointed out, labor (and organized labor specifically) has little to gain over the long-term from defending a "now superseded model of capitalist accumulation centered around the state sector and oriented toward a protected internal market." Notwithstanding the ongoing debate about the relative merits of structural adjustment, the reality in Argentina is that the entire labor market is being reconstituted as the state disengages from the economy.

Changes in the Employment Structure

The most noticeable social impact of Argentina's privatization strategies has been an increase in the level of open unemployment and a restructuring of the employment mix. During the first half of 1995, Argentina's open unemployment rate surpassed 18 percent, second only to Nicaragua (23%) in Latin America. At the beginning of 1996, nearly 2.2 million Argentines officially were out of work, with a further 1.3 million underemployed and working less than 35 hours per week. Yet from 1991 to 1994, the initial period of socioeconomic restructuring, over 515,000 new jobs were created. Why, then, has unemployment become such a major problem for

Argentina? Part of the answer lies with the fact that the economically active population grew by 1.3 million between 1991 and 1994, far outpacing the supply of new jobs. Both President Menem and Gerardo Martínez, the secretary-general of the labor group Confederación General del Trabajo (CGT), have blamed the influx of foreign workers for the country's high rate of unemployment (*Latin American Weekly Report* 1995:326). However, labor statistics refute this argument by suggesting that the overall rate of unemployment would shrink by only 0.2 percent if all immigrant workers were replaced by Argentinos. Another part of the unemployment puzzle is that, before the introduction of privatization policies, many state-run enterprises engaged in featherbedding practices. This created an over-employment problem and kept real unemployment rates artificially low. State and local governments were especially over-staffed. For example, the Federal District of Buenos Aires had ten municipal workers for each city block in 1993, and two-thirds of the US$180 million collected by the municipality each month went directly to pay salaries (*Buenos Aires Herald* April 24, 1993).

Many interior provinces continue to suffer from labor inefficiencies. Nearly 60 percent of all employees in Catamarca and La Rioja provinces worked in the public sector in 1991, compared to less than 25 percent in Buenos Aires. The number of civil servants officially employed in the Federal administration has been reduced dramatically, from a high of 874,000 positions in 1989 to approximately 200,000 in 1994. However, many of these jobs simply have been transferred to municipal and provincial governments. Some government agencies headquartered in the Federal District have grown since 1989. The Presidencia de la Nación department, which oversees national strategic planning, grew from 13,000 to over 20,000 employees between 1989 and 1994. Similarly, the Ministry of the Interior has expanded its employee base by 10 percent, while the Ministry of the Economy has expanded by 50 percent (República Argentina 1994).

Changes in the structure of non-governmental employment in Argentina reveal several distinct patterns. The type of employment restructuring occurring in Buenos Aires is quite different from that experienced by the interior provinces. Unemployment growth in the Greater Buenos Aires Metropolitan Area is the result of the pace of new job creation lagging behind the rate of workforce expansion. Conversely, unemployment in the interior reflects a net loss of jobs, as the size of the economically active population in 24 provincial cities changed little between 1991 and 1994 (*Latin American Weekly Report* 1995). In the city of Tucumán, the employment rate (total population divided by the economically active population actually employed) declined from 33.8 percent in April 1983 to 31.5 percent during May 1994. Interior cities such as Jujuy, Corrientes, Posadas, and Santiago del Estero also experienced reductions in the general employment rate during this period (República Argentina 1994).

In the rural areas of many interior provinces, unofficial statistics suggest that unemployment and underemployment rates have exploded to between 50 and 75 percent of the economically active population. These rates could further encourage rural-to-urban migration, exacerbating the already desperate conditions for millions in the country's major urban centers. Unemployment growth has been more severe in the larger urban centers as a consequence of deindustrialization and privatization (Table 4.3). Layoffs, worker suspensions, and corporate downsizing have been particularly severe since 1994 in Greater Buenos Aires, Córdoba, and Rosario. All of the Pampeana cities, with the exception of Santa Rosa, recorded double-digit unemployment rates in May 1995. Santa Fé, Rosario, Bahía Blanca, and the suburbs of Greater Buenos Aires experienced unemployment rates over 20 percent, with underemployment rates equal to and, in many cases, higher than these numbers. Real unemployment rates in many interior cities are actually higher than reported because of the bloated bureaucracies that afflict the economies of these provinces.

Employment demand indicators show that the supply of new jobs in Argentina fell by nearly 35 percent between April 1994 and April 1995 (*Latin American Weekly Report* 1995). Based on classified advertisements in the major cities, the National Institute of Statistics and Census (INDEC) noted that job offers in the commerce sector were down by 50 percent during the first quarter of 1995 compared to the same period in 1994. Commerce and services had provided the majority of the new urban jobs created during 1992 and 1993. A comparison of employment demand indicators in Buenos Aires using 1974 as a benchmark highlights the collapse of construction and domestic service employment and the growth of job opportunities for salespeople, brokers, and managers (Table 4.4).

Using similar methodology, the same pattern of employment demand changes could be found in other Pampeana cities. An analysis of the distribution of the total employed population between 1980 and 1994, using Buenos Aires as a benchmark, reinforces the importance of major changes in the employment mix. Employment opportunities in the commercial, social, and personal services sectors continued to expand at the expense of jobs in construction and industry (Table 4.5). As with the pattern of

TABLE 4.3   Official Open Unemployment Rate in Argentina's Main Urban Centers, 1984-1995[a]

Region/ Main Urban Center	October 1984	May 1989	October 1992	May 1994	May 1995
Argentina	4.4	8.1	7.0	10.7	18.4
Pampeana					
Federal District	1.2	5.2	4.8	9.0	14.3
GBAMA Urban Centers	3.8	8.7	7.5	11.9	22.6
Bahía Blanca	6.2	10.6	10.7	15.8	20.2
Córdoba	5.1	8.8	5.3	7.8	15.2
La Plata	6.2	7.0	6.5	8.9	15.4
Paraná	4.2	10.5	7.1	8.8	13.3
Rosario	6.2	7.5	8.5	13.1	20.9
Santa Rosa and Toay	4.1	6.2	2.4	5.7	8.5
Santa Fé	8.6	15.2	12.3	16.9	20.9
Cuyo					
Mendoza	3.7	4.4	4.4	6.0	6.8
San Juan	7.1	11.6	9.3	9.4	16.8
San Luis	4.3	7.1	6.7	7.6	20.3
Northwest					
Catamarca	5.7	10.4	5.9	8.1	12.4
Jujuy	6.3	7.1	6.6	8.5	12.7
La Rioja	5.6	6.5	8.7	6.0	11.7
Salta	9.2	8.1	9.8	10.7	18.7
Santiago del Estero	3.3	8.6	2.3	2.7	8.6
Tucumán	10.6	12.6	12.5	14.8	19.9
Northeast					
Resistencia	4.5	8.4	5.4	7.2	12.5
Corrientes	6.3	8.1	3.6	9.6	15.3
Formosa	5.3	9.2	8.9	7.7	5.4
Posadas	5.3	6.2	5.8	11.2	9.7
Patagonia					
Comodoro Rivadavia	2.9	11.4	13.9	10.9	14.0
Neuquén	3.3	8.6	8.9	10.7	16.7
Alto Valle	5.8	3.2	6.8	13.0	6.9
Río Gallegos	2.9	5.0	3.7	6.1	7.4
Ushuaia/Río Grande	NA	9.2	9.1	5.7	9.0

[a] Total unemployment as a percentage of the economically active population.
Source: República Argentina (1994); Ministry of the Economy (1996).

TABLE 4.4   Employment Demand Indicators in Buenos Aires, 1974-1993

Sector	1974	1980	1985	1989	1993
Professional	100	73.3	48.4	70.7	90.7
Managers	100	238.0	155.4	104.2	185.0
Administrative	100	176.7	104.6	90.4	84.2
Sales and Brokers	100	124.3	246.2	177.8	172.9
Domestic Service	100	62.0	94.4	38.8	16.1
Industry	100	128.2	52.7	93.7	124.3
Construction	100	1,648.5	10.3	24.9	15.7
Personal Services	100	112.4	35.1	45.1	19.4
Overall Level	100	179.2	82.3	87.2	102.6

Note: The indicators are based on help wanted advertisements published daily in newspapers in the Federal District. They measure labor demand determined from the press and not hiring actually taking place.
Source: República Argentina (1994).

of employment demand, the same general trend in employment distribution by sector is found in other Pampeana cities as well as in the major interior urban centers. However, far fewer financial, commercial, and service sector jobs are being created in the interior cities compared to Buenos Aires, even though primary and secondary sector jobs continue to be lost. Changes in the structure of employment in Argentina reflect trends evident at the global level. Between 1965 and 1990, most countries in the three basic development categories (low, medium, and high income) experienced reductions in the contribution of agriculture to their gross domestic product, with a resultant decline in primary sector jobs. The average increase in the contribution of the service sector to gross domestic product in all low, medium, and high income countries was four percent over the same period. In Argentina, however, services jumped from 42 percent of gross domestic product in 1965 to 57 percent in 1990, an indication of this sector's importance in creating new jobs. This trend toward the creation of tertiary and quaternary sector employment has been evident in the more mature economies of Britain, Japan, the United States, and Canada throughout the 1980s and early 1990s. Industrial sector contribution to gross domestic product also increased on average about four percent in those countries ranked in the medium and high income categories, although several of the traditionally more industrialized countries such as Britain and the United

TABLE 4.5 The Percentage Distribution of the Employed Population in Buenos Aires by Activity Category, 1980-1994

Period	Industry[a]	Construction	Commerce[b]	Services[c]	Other[d]	Total
April 1980	29.5	9.0	18.0	28.5	15.0	100
April 1981	28.2	9.0	19.3	28.6	14.9	100
April 1982	26.1	8.0	19.9	30.7	15.3	100
April 1983	24.9	6.4	19.2	34.2	15.3	100
April 1984	26.2	5.7	17.1	35.0	16.0	100
May 1985	25.4	7.3	17.3	29.1	20.9	100
April 1987	25.8	6.6	19.0	33.7	14.9	100
May 1988	25.1	7.5	19.0	32.2	16.2	100
May 1989	25.0	6.5	18.7	33.3	16.5	100
May 1990	23.3	6.2	19.8	33.5	17.2	100
May 1991	23.8	6.4	20.4	33.4	16.0	100
Oct 1992	23.6	5.7	21.2	33.3	16.2	100
May 1994[e]	22.0	5.0	22.0	35.0	16.0	100

[a] Industrial and manufacturing employment.
[b] Retail trade, restaurants, and hotels.
[c] Agriculture, quarrying, public services, transportation, and financial services.
[d] Social and Personal Services.
[e] Preliminary figures from unpublished working documents at the National Institute of Statistics and Census (INDEC) in Buenos Aires.
Source: República Argentina (1991, 1994).

States have continued to lose industrial and manufacturing jobs since the late 1970s. In many developing countries (low income ranking), industrial and manufacturing employment has grown steadily since the 1970s as the industrial sector's contribution to gross domestic product increased on average between 1965 and 1990 from 26 to 36 percent.

In contrast, Argentina suffered tremendous declines in manufacturing and industrial employment during this same period, with the industrial sector's contribution to gross domestic product declining from 41 percent in 1965 to 22 percent in 1992. Although a slight recovery in some manufacturing employment has occurred since 1992, especially in the food, beverage, and tobacco sector and in wood products, overall trends suggest that the declines are continuing (República Argentina 1994). Using a base index of 100 percent in 1990 to represent the total number of workers employed in manufacturing, during the first quarter of 1994 the textile sector registered 74.4 percent employment, basic metal industries recorded 65.3 percent, and chemical products logged 91.8 percent. Similar declines are evident in the total number of hours worked in manufacturing. Total manufacturing hours worked declined from a base of 100 in 1990 to 88.4 during the first quarter of 1994. Particularly hard hit have been textiles, footwear, plastics, chemical products, and basic metal industries.

Labor productivity also continues to change rapidly as a consequence of economic restructuring. For example, at the national level, Argentina remained well below the Latin American average in 1992 for labor productivity in steel, retail banking, and telecommunications (Table 4.6). Only food processing, the traditional base of Argentina's manufacturing economy, registered a productivity rate higher than the regional average in 1992. Moreover, based on a United States productivity index of 100, Argentina remains woefully underproductive in all four selected industries. Recent private sector investment in manufacturing, industry, and services, however, has begun to have an impact on the dynamics of labor productivity in Argentina. Since 1992, Argentina has shown encouraging signs of an overall increase in industrial output, with some factories working at full capacity. Yet the labor market remains volatile, in part because workers' real wages have failed to keep pace with living costs.

Wages and the Cost of Living

At the national level, average real wages have not shown much improvement since 1990 and they continue to remain below the figure for 1980. Based on an index of 100 for 1990, average real wages in Argentina during 1995 were 100.9, compared to 130.0 in 1980. This compared unfavorably with Chile, where average real wages have improved to 123.3 in 1995 based on an index of 100 in 1990. Peru, Mexico, Uruguay, Bolivia, and Costa Rica all have experienced positive rates of real wage improvement since 1990. Within Argentina's industrial sector, standard real average monthly wages per worker hovered around 87 percent for 1995 based on an index of 100 for 1983 (ECLAC 1995). Low inflation in Argentina has not allowed any large wage adjustments in recent years. The chief measures used to control labor costs have been a reduction in working hours, the suspension of overtime, and public sector cuts in employment. Yet despite nominal wage stability, the labor market remains volatile. Recent research on strike activity in Argentina between 1984 and 1993 illustrates the spatial

TABLE 4.6   A Comparison of Argentina's Labor Productivity in Selected Industries, 1992

| | | USA = 100 | | |
Country	Steel	Food Processing	Retail Banking	Telecoms[a]
Argentina	30	52	19	55
Brazil	44	29	31	89
Colombia	15	36	30	101
México	32	27	28	67
Venezuela	29	29	25	85
Latin America Average[b]	37	34	29	80

[a] Unadjusted for differences in quality.
[b] Weighted by employment.
Source: *Latin American Weekly Report* (1994).

dynamics of labor unrest. James McGuire (1996) analyzed strike records in Argentina and found that a disproportionate amount of labor unrest has occurred in the impoverished interior provinces. Moreover, contrary to general perception, strike activity has been highest among public sector employees in the interior and not among industrial workers in the major Pampeana cities of Buenos Aires, Rosario, and Córdoba. As Table 4.7 highlights, nine of the 11 provinces with double-digit strike volume rates (SVR) are in the interior, primarily in the Northwest region. In these provinces between 1984 and 1993, teachers and civil servants accounted for over half of all strikes, 90 percent of all strikers, and 93 percent of the total number of working days lost.

Argentina's labor market showed its volatility during June and July, 1995, when riots erupted in several interior cities. In San Juan, 1300 kilometers west of Buenos Aires in the shadow of the Andes Mountains, government employees rioted in protest over plans to cut wages. San Juan's provincial government had amassed a US$2.7 billion deficit and desperately needed to cut its expenditures. All wages above US$400 per month, announced Governor Jorge Escobar, would be cut by 20 to 30 percent immediately. This action would prevent the loss of thousands of government positions, he argued, and would help San Juan cope with its current financial crisis (*Latin American Weekly Report* 1995:358). The day

Table 4.7   Strike Activity in Argentina By Province, 1984-1993

Province	Economically Active Population[a]	Strike Volume Rate[b]	Number of Strikes
Northwest			
La Rioja	67,370	55.6	43
Salta	229,845	46.2	111
Jujuy	135,505	46.0	80
Tucumán	350,917	27.3	141
Catamarca	75,955	12.3	30
Santiago del Estero	198,400	11.4	38
Patagonia			
Santa Cruz	56,677	28.7	27
Chubut	117,812	14.4	59
Tierra del Fuego	22,063	8.6	11
Río Negro	178,184	6.6	35
Neuquén	128,949	4.7	35
Pampeana			
La Pampa	94,496	13.6	9
Santa Fé	876,109	11.1	153
Córdoba	932,435	7.4	156
Federal District	1,217,254	4.9	434
Buenos Aires	5,170,051	1.7	279
Entre Ríos	282,917	1.6	31
Greater Buenos Aires	3,259,454	0.7	213
Cuyo			
San Juan	148,716	5.2	49
Mendoza	417,102	5.1	46
San Luis	96,110	2.7	23
Northeast			
Chaco	226,568	13.5	84
Corrientes	214,397	3.6	43
Formosa	102,127	2.7	8
Misiones	228,951	1.4	18

[a] As of 1991.
[b] Working days lost to strikes divided by Economically Active Population.
Source: McGuire (1996:142-143).

before the riots broke out in San Juan, the Unión Industrial Argentina (UIA) called on the federal government to introduce emergency plans to help ameliorate the impact of unemployment and wage cuts. Policy changes suggested by the UIA included the elimination of social security contributions by employers for all newly created jobs, an emergency salary for unemployed heads of household over 50 years of age in exchange for their work on projects deemed in the public interest, and the creation of special lines of credit to help fund new job-creating activities. Riots in Salta and Santiago del Estero in Argentina's Northwest region, in Córdoba, and in the suburbs of Greater Buenos Aires also placed the level of discontent over the effects of economic restructuring in the national and international spotlight (see Manzetti 1994).

Recent social unrest over wages and living costs suggests that Argentina's "economic miracle" has bypassed completely the interior regions and the social classes that most need help in the new economic climate. The impoverished Northwest region, for example, has suffered tremendously from the federal government's economic restructuring policies. In Jujuy, a large steel plant once run by the military has been privatized and nearly 70 percent of its workforce made redundant. Sugar farmers have invested in huge sugar-harvesting machines to compete more efficiently with Brazil. This has reduced the demand for seasonal labor, increased local rates of agricultural unemployment, and encouraged more migration to the industrialized Pampeana cities. Recent studies indicate that there are rural areas of Jujuy province where unemployment affects nearly 80 percent of the population. Although wages and costs of living traditionally are lower outside the main urban areas of the Pampeana, interior residents have fewer official and unofficial safety nets to fall back on when economic crises erupt. At the national level only 6.4 percent of the nearly 1.7 million workers unemployed, or 110,000 people, were receiving unemployment benefits during the first half of 1995, and most of those lived in the Pampeana region. Compared to an average monthly wage of US$550, unemployment benefits only provide between US$150 and $300 a month, are limited to six months, and are available to only one recipient per household. Moreover, short-term informal employment opportunities are much less readily available in the interior provinces than in and around the major Pampeana cities.

At the regional level, Argentina has fared poorly recently in comparisons of monthly costs of living, minimum wages, and economic hardship indices. Figure 4.1 shows Argentina with the highest average monthly cost of living during 1994 among the 17 major countries of Latin America. A

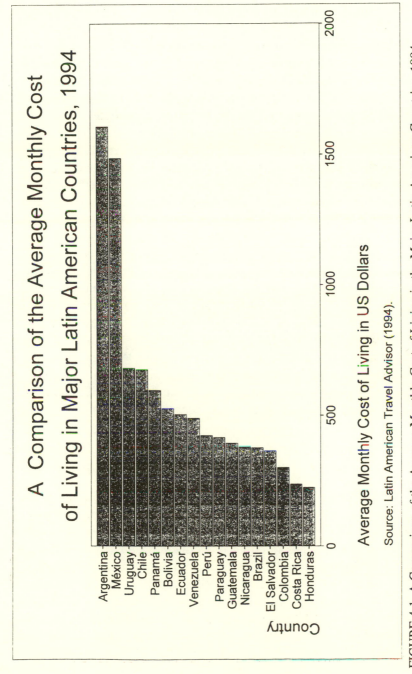

FIGURE 4.1 A Comparison of the Average Monthly Cost of Living in the Major Latin American Countries, 1994.
Source: Latin American Travel Advisor (1994).

comparison of the minimum monthly wage in each of these countries to the average cost of living further highlights the plight of Argentina's citizens (Figure 4.2). A gap of over US$1,300 monthly between the minimum wage and the cost of living in Argentina has fueled social unrest and a rising tide of criticism against President Menem's economic policies. Although Argentina falls in the middle of the group on the 1994 index of economic hardship (Figure 4.3), there is little doubt that Menem's redistribution of economic resources and ongoing austerity policies have further concentrated wealth in the hands of the elite and forced millions of people deeper into poverty. Yet President Menem has argued that Argentine workers are overpaid compared to other countries in Latin America. In an interview with *Business Week* (August 28, 1995:45), Menem contended that workers in Argentina have "the highest salaries on the continent.... That's why Paraguayans, Bolivians--even Brazilians and Chileans--come to work" in Argentina. Downward pressure on wages, especially in the major cities of the interior provinces, is seen as an essential component of economic restructuring and a key to making Argentine more competitive in the regional and world economy. However, wages in Argentina continue to lag behind the pace of inflation, with the once large and prosperous middle class bearing the brunt of social change. Buenos Aires has become the Western Hemisphere's second most expensive city behind New York for businesses, tourists, and residents alike. Yet despite the short-term problems of rising costs of living, unemployment, and a declining quality of live, Argentina's government continues to insist that economic and monetary stability are crucial to the long-term success of the country's restructuring strategies.

Restructuring Patterns of Production and Trade

The third major component of Argentina's economic globalization strategies involves the reorganization of domestic and international patterns of production and trade. Historically, the primary sector of the economy (agriculture and minerals) has dominated production and trade patterns in Argentina. The country's wealth stemmed from the agricultural production of the Pampeana region's farms and ranches and by the 1920s its exports had grown to represent 3.1 percent of the total value of global trade. Argentina ranked first among global exporters of primary produce and sixth in total world trade. By the 1980s, Argentina's share of total global trade had dropped to below 0.4 percent and its role in the global economy had

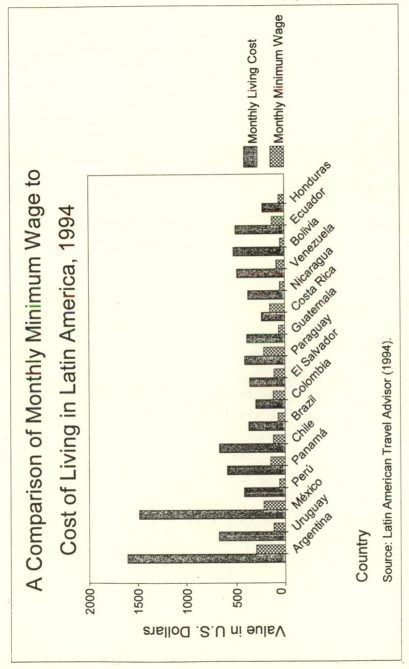

FIGURE 4.2 A Comparison of Monthly Minimum Wage to Cost of Living in Latin America, 1994.
Source: Latin American Travel Advisor (1994).

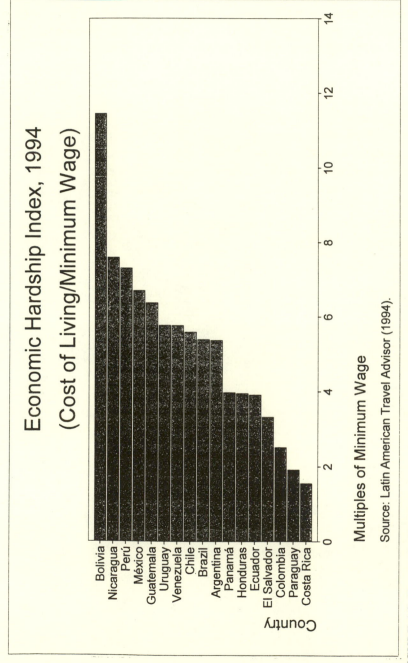

FIGURE 4.3 Economic Hardship Index in Selected Latin American Countries, 1994.
Source: Latin American Travel Advisor (1994).

changed considerably (Bortagaray 1992). Primary production continued to decline as a percentage of total gross national production, while the secondary and quaternary sectors grew. Moreover, regional development policies introduced in the 1960s and 1970s began to shift the focus of production away from the Greater Buenos Aires region. Minerals from Patagonia and the Northwest, rice and cotton from the Northeast, sugar from the Tucumán area of the Northwest, wines and fruits from the Cuyo, and manufactures from a number of interior cities began to reshape Argentina's geographic patterns of production. Although Buenos Aires and the Pampeana still overwhelmingly dominated production and trade, interior regions began to play a more important role in the structure of Argentina's economic patterns and trade relationships. The introduction of globalization strategies in 1990, however, may have refocused the development process more sharply on Buenos Aires and the Pampeana region to the detriment of the interior.

Patterns of Production

Three key processes have helped to reshape Argentina's patterns of production in recent years. First, the agricultural sector's contribution to the country's total exports has experienced a slight resurgence after decades of neglect by the federal government. Second, a clustering of industrial activity in and around the major Pampeana cities appears evident once again, despite several decades of industrial promotion and decentralization schemes designed to shift production to interior provinces. Third, planners and policy makers in Argentina have identified a number of development axes and growth pole centers across the country as they attempt to spread the benefits of regional integration and economic liberalization to all regions. Moreover, growth in the service sector as a consequence of economic restructuring strategies is changing the spatial dynamics of urban development and focusing greater attention on tourism opportunities in the interior provinces.

Primary Sector Resurgence. Throughout Latin America, the economic crisis of the 1980s and the growth of externally oriented development strategies helped to focus greater attention on the promotion of agricultural exports. Export strategies in particular have dominated recent discussions on primary sector growth and development (Carter et al. 1996). In Argentina, since 1990 the primary sector has enjoyed a modest renaissance of sorts, although agriculture's contribution to total GNP and to the export market generally has declined in significance over the past several decades. Agriculture represented barely eight percent of total economic activity in Argentina in 1992 (República Argentina 1994). Agribusiness is becoming increasingly more integrated with Argentina's industrial sector. A significant amount of agricultural land now is controlled by industrial companies who have integrated products from the land vertically with later products. For example, the huge Argentine multinational, Bunge y Born, has begun to package and process agricultural goods produced from corporate-owned farms. Argentina still maintains a significant presence in the international agricultural commodity market, even though global demand for the country's produce has weakened considerably in recent decades. In 1994, the country ranked 10th among the world's leading commodity exports in cereals, 3rd in vegetable oilseeds and oil, and 9th in tobacco (República Argentina 1994). Exports of agricultural products reached US$9.7 billion in 1995 and were expected to increase by 17 percent in 1996 to US$11.35 billion. Grain exports alone were projected to exceed US$7 billion in 1996, despite a severe drought that affected significant portions of the pampas growing area. Exports of wine rose by 900 percent in 1995 over the previous year to nearly 225 million liters, a result of stronger marketing efforts in the United States and Europe. Meat exports grew by 36 percent in 1995 and the export of hides increased by 15 percent over the previous year. Short-term opportunities for increased European sales of Argentine beef developed in early 1996 as a result of Britain's problem with "mad cow" disease and the European Union's ban on the importation of British meat products. However, some long-term instability is inherent in the country's export-driven agricultural sector because, over the short-term, farm profits are almost solely contingent on global commodity prices. Global price fluctuations are an extraneous factor for the individual farmer, who has little control over commodity price manipulation.

At the beginning of the 1990s, 50 percent of Argentina's farms were under 50 hectares in size and accounted for only 1.7 percent of the total land surface in agricultural use. In contrast, 50 percent of Argentina's total land surface in agricultural production (approximately 88 million hectares) was controlled by 1.6 percent of the total number of farming establishments. Most of the farms over 5,000 hectares in size are located either in the Pampeana region or in Patagonia, where large sheep *estancias* are the norm. Half of all the productive farms in Argentina are located in the Pampeana region and they accounted for 40 percent of the total land area in agricultural use. The major portion of Argentina's export production comes from the Pampeana region, which has become increasingly more agroindustrial in nature. Although many interior regions are producing agricultural products for the regional and global export markets in the 1990s, they remain hampered by poor technology, undercapitalization, environmental deterioration, marginal product quality, and inferior transportation linkages to domestic and external consumers.

Renewed Industrial Concentration. Throughout the 1960s, 1970s, and 1980s, Argentina's governments pursued a variety of programs designed to alleviate the concentration of industrial activity in the Greater Buenos Aires region. Tax incentives, subsidies, the development of industrial estates and, at times, coercion succeeded in reducing the number of industrial establishments dramatically in both the Federal District and the inner suburbs of Greater Buenos Aires. In 1954, for example, over 40,000 factories were located inside the Federal District. By 1984, this number had been reduced to just under 16,000 (Table 4.8). Overall, however, the Pampeana's share of the total number of industrial establishments in Argentina fell only from 82.8 percent in 1954 to 77.6 percent in 1984. The interior regions had garnered a larger share of the country's industrial activity, but these gains proved to be minimal.

Inadequate transport and communication infrastructure, a small internal consumer market, corruption, and gross inefficiencies combined to stymie the deconcentration of industrial activities to the interior. By the late 1980s, indicators suggested that a reconcentration of manufacturing in the major Pampeana cities was underway. Privatization policies also began to encourage a renewed focus of industrial activities on the Pampeana region. Private investors realized that the major market for their products lay in the triangle between Rosario, Córdoba, and Greater Buenos Aires. Moreover, linkages to the regional, hemispheric, and global economies were the strongest in the Pampeana region and the weakest in the interior. Preliminary results from the 1994 national economic census revealed that the Pampeana's share of Argentina's industrial establishments has increased for the first time in over 25 years (see Table 4.8). Patagonia was the only interior region to show an increase, while the Cuyo, Northeast, and Northwest regions all showed overall declines. Several provinces in the Northwest, however, did experience a slight increase in the total number of industrial establishments between 1985 and 1994, most notably Catamarca, Jujuy, and Salta. The Pampeana region once again contains nearly 80 percent of the total industrial capacity of Argentina. Both the Federal

TABLE 4.8   The Distribution of Argentina's Industrial Establishments by Region and Political Division, 1954-1994

Province/ Region	1954	1964	1974	1985	1994
Federal District	40,075	30,651	23,838	15,864	17,348
GBA Suburbs	33,250	31,878	30,033	27,904	28,244
Buenos Aires	13,521	22,428	16,567	12,787	12,958
Córdoba	13,987	13,756	13,441	10,602	9,734
Entre Ríos	3,714	3,313	3,151	3,471	2,524
La Pampa	1,193	1,266	1,185	1,112	863
Santa Fé	17,144	17,302	15,103	13,123	11,732
Pampeana	122,884	120,594	103,318	84,863	83,403
Mendoza	5,554	6,244	5,330	5,297	4,723
San Juan	1,802	1,669	1,027	1,512	1,192
San Luis	1,899	767	888	805	959
Cuyo	9,255	8,680	7,245	7,614	6,874
Chaco	2,453	1,876	2,141	2,317	1,867
Corrientes	1,401	1,220	1,333	1,418	1,068
Formosa	476	479	758	935	849
Misiones	1,812	2,026	2,688	3,158	1,666
Northeast	6,142	5,601	6,920	7,828	5,450
Catamarca	607	417	522	395	515
Jujuy	707	541	707	769	894
La Rioja	654	414	403	523	432
Salta	1,773	1,258	1,436	1,381	1,426
Santiago	1,658	802	1,152	1,053	867
Tucumán	2,020	1,952	2,307	2,101	1,430
Northwest	7,419	5,384	6,527	6,222	5,564
Chubut	784	755	630	691	899
Neuquén	327	376	390	549	973
Río Negro	1,330	1,347	1,100	1,227	1,209
Santa Cruz	158	258	198	226	333
Tierra del Fuego	72	62	60	153	265
Patagonia	2,671	2,798	2,378	2,846	3,679
Total:	148,371	143,047	126,388	109,373	104,970

Source: República Argentina (1994, 1995).

Capital and the 19 municipalities of Greater Buenos Aires' inner suburbs gained industrial establishments between 1985 and 1994 after decades of declines. The other four Pampeana provinces all continued to lose industrial activity. Moreover, the Pampeana still contains 54 percent of the country's designated industrial sites, despite efforts to develop new estates and zones in the interior provinces (Table 4.9). Only San Luis province in the Cuyo region has benefitted from the creation of special industrial zones over the past few decades. The Northwest and the Northeast regions still remain underindustrialized, with few businesses taking advantage of the government's industrial parks.

Growth Pole Strategies. Policy makers in Argentina long have favored the growth-pole approach to spatial development. Ideas of polarized growth originated in France during the 1950s and 1960s (Perroux 1955). In theory, the dynamism and extensive linkages of selected urban centers, or growth poles, should function as stimulators for a region and promote regional growth and modernization. Growth poles were implemented in Argentina during the early 1970s, when certain industries were linked with cities designated as development poles (Morris 1972, 1975). Unfortunately, the regional multiplier effects of new industries proved extremely weak because forward and backward linkages focused on Buenos Aires, not on the surrounding growth-pole hinterlands. As a result, the strategies only exacerbated urban primacy and widened the gap between the growth pole and its rural hinterland.

New strategies developed in the early 1990s against the backdrop of Argentina's national restructuring policies have focused renewed attention on key urban centers throughout the interior. Planners and policy makers have identified a number of strategic urban centers linked together by a network of six major development axes (Figure 4.4). The most important axis runs north from the Greater Buenos Aires Metropolitan region along the Río Paraná to the cities of Rosario and Santa Fé. Much of Argentina's industrial capacity presently is located along this corridor (see Chapter 7). The axis continues north toward Resistencia and Formosa and eventually to Asunción, Paraguay. An eastern branch of this dominant axis runs through Entre Ríos province to the Northeast region and into Brazil, Paraguay, and Uruguay. The second major axis runs south from Buenos Aires and incorporates Mar del Plata and the port city of Bahía Blanca. An extension of this axis continues down the Patagonian coast to Comodoro Rivadavia, the country's most southerly growth pole, and on to Tierra del Fuego.

TABLE 4.9   Argentina's Industrial Sites by Type and by Political Division, 1993

Province/ Region	Type of Site			Number of Establishments		
	Estates	*Zones*	*Areas*	*Estates*	*Zones*	*Areas*
Buenos Aires	22	3	13	205	10	15
Córdoba	4	4	4	21	13	18
Entre Ríos	4	-	7	11	-	95
La Pampa	3	2	1	14	12	-
Santa Fé	6	-	2	43	-	28
Pampeana:	39	9	27	294	35	156
Mendoza	1	6	2	8	29	-
San Juan	1	-	-	11	-	-
San Luis	1	4	1	52	304	29
Cuyo:	3	10	3	71	333	29
Chaco	1	-	1	16	-	10
Corrientes	-	-	-	-	-	-
Formosa	1	-	-	10	-	-
Misiones	-	-	-	-	-	-
Northeast:	2	-	1	26	-	10
Catamarca	-	-	3	-	-	32
Jujuy	-	6	-	-	16	-
La Rioja	3	-	-	107	-	-
Salta	2	-	-	21	-	-
Santiago d. Estero	1	-	-	11	-	-
Tucumán	-	-	-	-	-	-
Northwest:	6	6	3	139	16	32
Chubut	8	5	2	52	1	45
Neuquén	4	1	2	41	3	13
Río Negro	6	-	-	59	-	-
Santa Cruz	-	-	-	-	-	-
Tierra del Fuego	-	-	3	-	-	90
Patagonia:	18	6	7	152	4	148
Total:	68	31	41	682	388	375

Note: Industrial estates, zones, and areas all are locations designated by the federal government specifically for industrial use.
Source: República Argentina (1994).

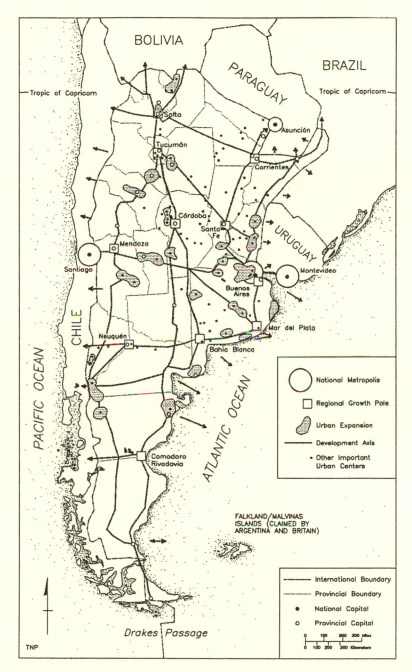

FIGURE 4.4   Regional Growth Pole and Urban Expansion Sites in Argentina, 1995. *Source*: After Roccatagliata (1994).

Argentina's third major development axis runs due west from Buenos Aires and incorporates the major cities of the Cuyo region. Mendoza functions as the dominant growth pole for the central Andean zone. Along the eastern slopes of the Andes runs the fourth axis of potential development, which links the growth poles of Salta and Tucumán in the Northwest region to Neuquén and the entire eastern Patagonian region via Mendoza. A fifth development axis traverses the heart of Argentina from Bahía Blanca on the Atlantic coast through the growth pole of Córdoba and on to Tucumán and Salta in the Northwest. The final axis of potential development links the Northwest and Northeast regions together and remains dependent on the route of the planned bi-oceanic corridor between Brazil and Chile. Crucial to the successful implementation of growth pole strategies, of course, is the development of adequate transport and communication services and infrastructure along the growth axes. Previous growth pole and industrial deconcentration policies have proved to be dismal failures in part because planners and policy makers consistently ignored the vital role of transport and communication in the regional development process. In mid-1996, Argentina's government had yet to articulate a clear and comprehensive plan to achieve national economic integration. The government's enthusiastic embrace of privatization policies, for example, essentially has abrogated national and regional infrastructural planning to private companies.

The development of growth poles and urban expansion zones also has implications for patterns of change in Argentina's service sector. The rapid growth of financial, personal, social, and business services since the 1970s is typical of many urbanized, industrial countries. In Argentina, quaternary economic activity increased from 31 percent of total GDP in 1980 to nearly 45 percent in 1995. Most service-oriented jobs are located in the primary cities of each province, with Buenos Aires dominating the spatial distribution of service activities in Argentina. This concentration pattern further encourages rural-to-urban migration flows and argues for closer attention by planners and policy makers to the distribution hierarchy of service provision.

Patterns of Trade

Argentina's national and international trading and investment relationships are strongly influenced by patterns of transportation and communication. Historically, trade between Argentina and its regional neighbors has not been a priority. Indeed, during the colonial period, Spanish laws severely restricted trade between countries within Spain's Latin American empire. From the mid-1800s to the mid-1900s, Europe absorbed most of Argentina's exports, while providing the majority of its imports. Although hemispheric trade relationships are improving, only four percent of Argentina's total imports in 1993 came from non-contiguous countries in the hemisphere other than the United States. Just under 11 percent of the country's exports in 1993 went to non-contiguous countries besides the United States.

With the introduction of import-substitution industrialization policies in the 1930s, Argentina became a highly protected economy somewhat isolated from the global trade networks. Trade tariffs and import quotas dominated the country's manufacturing and industrial sectors. Manufacturing costs remained high, product quality was poor, products often were obsolete compared to other countries, and domestic investment in capital goods remained low (Dornbusch 1995). Since the 1950s, but particularly since 1990, successive governments in Argentina have focused increasing resources on improving the country's position in the global export market. Primary products and agricultural-based manufactures, in general, continued to be the mainstay of Argentine exports up until the late 1980s, ranging from a high share of 82.3 percent of total exports in 1983 to a low of 63.1 percent in 1989. Only beginning in 1990 did manufactures of industrial origin begin to increase as a percentage of total exports. Industrial manufactures accounted for 27.2 percent of total exports in 1990, compared to barely 16 percent in 1981. Moreover, Argentina managed to maintain a trade surplus during most of the 1980s (Table 4.10). After Carlos Menem's government introduced its economic liberalization and globalization policies in 1991, however, Argentina's trade balance reverted to a negative figure, as cheap manufactured goods flooded into the country. Preliminary trade figures for 1995 show a strong export performance once again and the government argues that this is a clear sign that economic restructuring policies are beginning to work.

One of the consequences of economic restructuring in Argentina has been a rapid growth in imports, especially in luxury consumer goods. Domestic industries are unable to compete effectively with cheap textiles and shoes from Asia, automobiles from Brazil, and machinery from the North Atlantic economies. As a result, many small manufacturing operations in urban centers around the country have been squeezed out of business by cheap imports. This has had a tremendous impact on the retail trade. According to Argentina's Federation of Business and Commerce (Fedecámaras),

TABLE 4.10   Argentina's Exports and Imports, 1980-1995

| Year | (Millions of Current Dollars) | | |
	Exports	Imports	Trade Balance
1980	8,021	10,541	- 2,520
1981	9,143	9,430	- 287
1982	7,625	5,337	2,288
1983	7,836	4,504	3,332
1984	8,107	4,585	3,522
1985	8,396	3,814	4,582
1986	6,852	4,724	2,128
1987	6,360	5,818	542
1988	9,135	5,322	3,813
1989	9,579	4,203	5,376
1990	12,353	4,077	8,276
1991	11,978	8,276	3,702
1992	12,236	14,872	- 2,636
1993	13,117	15,545	- 2,428
1994	15,839	19,880	- 4,041
1995[a]	20,600	17,900	2,700

[a] Preliminary estimates.

Source: República Argentina (1993b); *Latin American Weekly Report* (1994-96).

during the first quarter of 1995 approximately 30,000 retailers were driven into bankruptcy following a 30 to 40 percent decline in retail sales during 1994 (*Latin American Weekly Report* 1995:159). In the city of Buenos Aires alone, nearly 7,000 retailers were driven out of business, with another 10,000 businesses bankrupt in Buenos Aires province.

Direct evidence of Argentina's changing patterns of regional and global economic linkages from the provincial perspective is not readily obtainable. Reliable statistics, for example, on the proportion of Argentina's exports that have value added within each development region do not exist. Neither is it possible to calculate with any degree of accuracy capital flows between major countries and individual cities and provinces within Argentina. However, ample secondary evidence exists to suggest that Argentina's trade patterns and relationships at the regional and global levels are undergoing realignment. Changing transportation and communication

routes and international tourism flows intimate an increased level of economic interaction with regional neighbors. In addition, the rapid growth of
foreign corporate and multinational activities in Argentina, spurred by
privatization and deregulation policies, has opened up the national economy
to regional and global capital circulation and has linked both the country
more strongly to the major financial centers of the global economy.

Global Trade Patterns. Perhaps the most useful indicators of Argentina's
changing external economic relationships are import and export data. North
America, Europe, and the Soviet Union absorbed most of Argentina's exports in the 1970s and provided the majority of the country's imports. In
1985, the United States took 12.2 percent of Argentina's exports, Europe
purchased 25.4 percent, and 22 percent of all exports went to other Latin
American countries. A similar pattern of trade could be found in the origin
of Argentina's imports in 1985. The United States provided 18.2 percent,
Europe 33.1 percent, and other Latin American countries 34.7 percent of
the country's total imports. Almost all of these imports came through
Buenos Aires, with the majority destined for the Pampeana's urban market
and the remainder for the much smaller interior market.

Although Brazil has become Argentina's primary trading partner, the
United States continues to play an important role in the domestic economy.
Eleven percent of Argentina's exports and 22.8 percent of its imports were
with the United States in 1994. The country's economy depends on electrical equipment, mechanical parts, precision instruments, and other advanced
technology products from the United States. The so-called "invisible" trade
with the United States, which includes professional services, consulting,
popular music, soft drink and food franchises, movies, and other aspects
of popular culture, is growing daily and it has had a powerful impact on the
economy and particularly on the urban landscape of Argentina in recent
years.

Despite the rhetoric of improving Pacific Rim trade and the possible key
role of Argentina in a Pacific-Atlantic Rim economic region, imports and
exports between Argentina and East Asia have shown little improvement
in recent years. East Asia provided less than 14 percent of Argentina's total
imports in 1993 and 1994, up only slightly from 12.6 percent in 1980, and
from taking 6.7 percent of Argentina's exports in 1980, East Asia purchased
just under 10 percent of the country's exports in 1993 and 1994 (Figures 4.5
and 4.6). Poor transport and financial links with Asian markets have hindered the development of the country's Pacific Rim relationships in recent

138

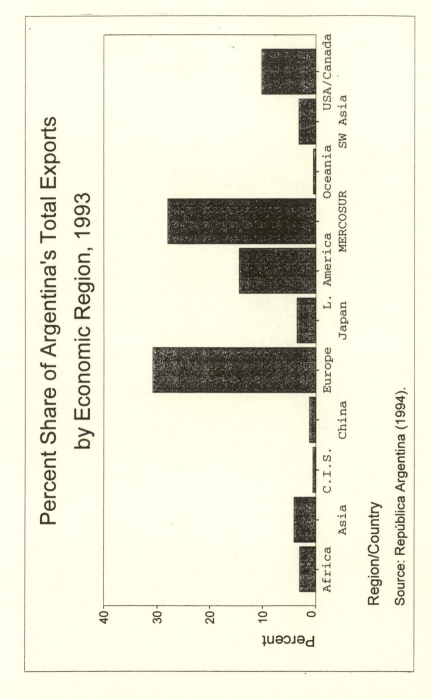

FIGURE 4.5 Percent Share of Argentina's Total Exports by Economic Region, 1993. *Source:* República Argentina (1994).

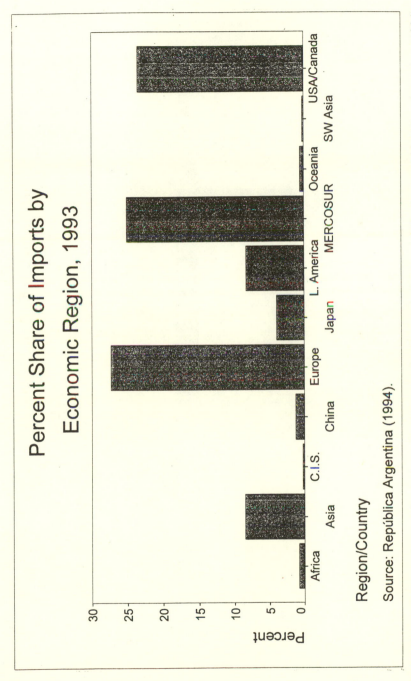

FIGURE 4.6 Percent Share of Argentina's Total Imports by Economic Region, 1993. *Source:* República Argentina (1994).

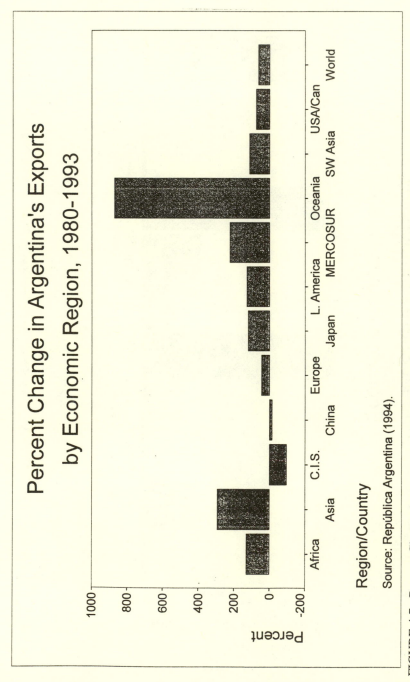

FIGURE 4.7 Percent Change in Argentina's Total Exports by Economic Region, 1980–1993.
Source: República Argentina (1994).

years. Moreover, Japanese, Hong Kong, and Singaporean investment capital has not been sought actively by Argentina's economic elite, who have preferred to rely on old established relationships with Europe and the United States. As Figures 4.5 and 4.6 illustrate, in 1993 Europe remained Argentina's dominant trading partner. Although the region of Oceania recorded the greatest overall increase in imports from Argentina between 1980 and 1993, its total share of Argentina's export trade remains less than one half of one percent (Figure 4.7).

Regional Trade Patterns. The boom in intraregional trade within Latin America during the first half of the 1990s continued to be a driving force shaping Argentina's external trade patterns. After decades (if not centuries) of isolation from its regional neighbors, Argentina's trade relationships with Brazil, Paraguay, Uruguay, Chile, and Bolivia are changing dramatically. For example, despite the problems between Brazil and Argentina over tariffs and protectionist measures, trade between these two neighbors has grown rapidly since 1990. Barely 11 percent of Argentina's total world trade in 1975 occurred with the countries that now are members of the newly established Common Market of the Southern Cone (MERCOSUR), Brazil, Paraguay, and Uruguay (Chile signed an agreement in 1996 to join the union in the near future). By 1994, traditional trading patterns had begun to show signs of realignment as Argentina's economic restructuring policies changed the dynamics of its global and regional economic links. The biggest realignment in trading links involved Argentina's new MERCOSUR partners. Although trade with Brazil particularly had improved steadily since the mid-1980s, rapid growth occurred only after 1990. From a paltry US$358 million in exports to Brazil during 1983, exports soared to US$3.7 billion in 1994. Imports from Brazil totaled only US$395 million in 1983, but by 1994 imports had reached US$4.3 billion (Ministry of the Economy 1996). Especially important in the Argentine domestic market are Brazilian automobiles and automotive parts, shoes, textiles, and machinery.

Trade with the three MERCOSUR members reached over 30 percent of Argentina's total exports and 21 percent of total imports in 1994, and this number is expected to show steady growth throughout the remainder of the 1990s. In 1995, for example, preliminary figures indicate that Brazil took about 27 percent of Argentina's total exports, mainly in manufactured goods. Exports of non-agricultural manufactures and fuels drove the strong growth in Argentina's exports during 1994 and 1995. Bilateral trade with

Chile, not yet a full member of MERCOSUR, exceeded $1.2 billion in 1993, up by 15 percent from 1992, and 12 times the average amount of trade during the 1980s. Improved economic relationships with Chile are forcing a reevaluation of transport and communication infrastructure between Argentina and its Pacific neighbor. Transport links traditionally have been relatively poor and they continue to hinder trade growth between the two neighbors.

Regional Integration Strategies

Current perceptions of the contemporary global economy are being shaped by the notion that aggressive competition between regional trade blocs is inevitable. Very persuasive arguments have been presented recently about the possibility of severe economic battles among individual states in these blocs and between the trade blocs themselves (see Cohen 1991; Friedman 1991; Garten 1992; Thurow 1992). The implications of interstate regional integration for international relations are indeed profound, not only for states within trade blocs but also for states without. With the emergence of an increasingly interconnected and competitive world economy, states or groups of states on the fringes of trade blocs are becoming more susceptible to the vagaries of the global marketplace. Many countries are realizing that protectionist and internally focused social, economic, and political policies are incompatible with the contemporary global system. As a result, pressures to liberalize national economies and to ally with one or more of the established regional trade blocs have encouraged the reorganization of traditional interstate relationships in countries such as Argentina.

The development of MERCOSUR, for example, is in part both a short-term response to the perceived threat of a tripolar economic bloc (the NAFTA, the European Union, and the APEC) and a long-term strategy for eventual hemispheric economic integration. Indeed, during the first six months of 1995, both Chile and Bolivia announced their intention to seek membership in MERCOSUR, and talks between officials of the Andean Pact countries and MERCOSUR have focused on the possibility of creating a unified South American Common Market before the end of the millennium. Many observers in the Southern Cone believe that states and regions left out of the regional integration process could become increasingly marginalized and could be more vulnerable to political and economic upheaval. Thus, attention is turning toward the development of regional integration strategies that can articulate the national economies of countries such as Argentina and Brazil not only with each other but also with regional and global economies. Such strategies are drawing heavily from the ideology of hemispheric and continental integration. The promise of future alliances with trade blocs such as the NAFTA and the European Union also figures prominently in the rhetoric of interstate regional integration reverberating throughout Latin America.

An accelerated process of integration with the international economy is a crucial component of Argentina's economic restructuring policies. Since 1990, the domestic economy has benefitted from a significant increase in the incorporation of new machinery, technology, and capital from overseas, all of which have spurred improvements in the quantity and quality of goods and services available to the population. Incorporation into the world economy, argued the Menem government, will enable Argentina to reap the benefits of one of the "most significant current world trends: the globalization of national economies" (República Argentina 1994:xxiii). Tariff and non-tariff barriers have been reduced to stimulate competitiveness and to decrease the gap between international and domestic prices. The most significant step toward integrating Argentina more fully into the world economy, however, has been the development of MERCOSUR, which had its genesis in the Foz de Iguazú Declaration signed in 1985 by the presidents of Brazil and Argentina. Paraguay and Uruguay joined the two giants in 1990, and MERCOSUR came into effect on January 1, 1995. These four neighbors have the potential of an expanded market of over 200 million people. As Table 4.11 highlights, Argentina's imports to, and exports from, its MERCOSUR partners have shown steady increases since 1986. Trade between MERCOSUR members represented 22 percent of the members' total world trade in 1995, up from 19 percent in 1994. By the turn of the century, MERCOSUR trade will dominate Argentina's economy.

Crossing the Rubicon

For Argentina, there is no turning back from the development path chosen by the Menem government in 1991. The capital-labor-production nexus has been altered irrevocably and, at least from a macroeconomic point of view, Argentina at last appears headed in the "right direction." However, as this chapter's analysis pointed out, several major problems remain embedded in the country's socioeconomic structures. Agriculture remains bedeviled by debt, inadequate technology, and an unbalanced

TABLE 4.11 The Volume of Trade Between Argentina and its MERCOSUR
Partners, 1980-1995

	Year	Brazil	Paraguay	Uruguay
ARGENTINA		(millions of current U.S. Dollars)		
Exports	1980	765	189	182
	1981	595	169	128
	1982	568	145	116
	1983	358	87	77
	1984	478	94	83
	1985	496	72	99
	1986	698	67	129
	1987	539	61	168
	1988	608	80	187
	1989	1,124	96	208
	1990	1,423	147	263
	1991	1,489	178	311
	1992	1,671	272	384
	1993	2,814	358	512
	1994	3,655	498	650
	1995[a]	4,800	650	600
Imports	1980	1,072	85	148
	1981	893	92	121
	1982	688	49	90
	1983	667	39	89
	1984	831	50	98
	1985	612	20	66
	1986	691	47	93
	1987	819	70	114
	1988	971	68	131
	1989	721	49	99
	1990	718	41	116
	1991	1,526	43	235
	1992	3,339	65	351
	1993	3,570	73	571
	1994	4,286	72	79
	1995[a]	4,200	95	500

[a] Estimated value.

Source: Direction of Trade Statistics Yearbook (1993); República Argentina
(1994); Ministry of the Economy (1996).

distribution of farm size and ownership. Industry is undercapitalized, highly concentrated in the Pampeana region, and hampered by an inflexible labor market. Transport and communication services and infrastructure are too inadequate for integrated, multimodal regional development strategies to have any real impact. And crushing poverty, underemployment, and deteriorating social service infrastructure continue to cripple the interior regional economies.

What is the prognosis for Argentina's future socioeconomic health in terms of capital, labor, and productivity? The 1996 edition of the *World Competitiveness Yearbook* published by the International Institute for Management Development (IMD 1996) sheds light on some of the important areas that Argentina's government, business leaders, and citizens must address if socioeconomic progress is to continue in the future. The IMD measures the competitiveness each year of 46 major urbanized and industrialized countries, including China, South Africa, and several Latin American states. According to Stephane Garelli (1996) of the IMD, competitiveness is a country's ability to generate added value and thus to increase its national wealth by managing successfully its assets, attractiveness, aggressiveness, globality, and proximity. Moreover, a country must integrate these myriad relationships successfully into an economic and social model. The IMD annual report summarizes a country's rank in eight major categories: the domestic economy, internationalization, government, finance, infrastructure, management, science and technology, and human resources. Within each of these eight categories are 225 subcategories that provide a more detailed analysis of a country's strengths and weaknesses relative to the other countries in the study.

According to the IMD report, Argentina's overall economic performance over the past year dropped the country from 30th to 32nd in the world competitiveness rankings. From a rank of 16th in 1994 in terms of internationalization, Argentina fell to 28th place. The country also fell in overall attractiveness by one place down to 31st, in aggressiveness five places down to 35th, and in terms of its overall domestic economy one rank down to 30th position. Infrastructural improvements over the past twelve months pushed Argentina up one rank in that category to 27th position. An examination of the subcategories revealed several weaknesses in Argentina's socioeconomic structures. In the category of internationalization, the country ranked last in trade-to-GDP ratio and in the export of goods and commercial services. On the positive side, however, Argentina ranked 1st in openness to foreign investors and 2nd in its terms of trade index.

In the government category, Argentina ranked 43rd in anti-trust laws and in the overall quality of justice, 39th in improper practices (corruption), and 35th in its hiring and firing practices. On the asset side of the competitiveness balance sheet, Argentina's government ranked in the top ten for its liberal tax structures and for its overall economic policies. The country did not fare well in the category of finance, ranking below the 40th position in short-term interest rates, factoring practices, the cost of capital, the efficiency of the banking sector, and access to credit. Access to local capital markets, ranked 2nd, was Argentina's only positive financial attribute.

Inadequate transport and communication infrastructure also continue to be a major barrier to national economic competitiveness. Argentina ranked 44th in international telephone costs, 42nd in the provision and quality of roads, and 35th in total connections to the Internet and in the number of cellular mobile phone subscribers. However, in terms of overall infrastructure, the country ranked 4th in arable area, 8th on the greenhouse index, 11th in total indigenous energy production, and 16th in its glass recycling rate. Argentina remains weak in science and technology, ranking last in research cooperation and 42nd in science and education. The country's management structures are hampered by industrial disputes (ranked 42nd), poor quality management (40th), a lack of customer orientation (42nd), and inadequate social responsibility (38th). Finally, in the human resources category, Argentina ranked 42nd in overall unemployment, 38th in the value of its educational system, 38th in the values of society, and 35th in worker motivation and in brain drain to other countries. On the plus side in human resources, the country ranked 3rd in its pupil-teacher ratio and 7th in higher education enrollment.

These statistics suggest that much work remains to be done in the socioeconomic restructuring of Argentina. There is little debate that the country has made spectacular progress in several areas. However, weaknesses continue in some key components of Argentina's national and regional development strategies. The most critical weakness remains in the very foundation of the socioeconomic restructuring process--transport and communication. In the final chapter of this section, I explore the role of transport and communication in the development of Argentina and I highlight the key areas that require immediate government and business attention.

5

Transport and Communication

As the foundation for the three major pillars of regional development and a crucial component of socioeconomic restructuring in Argentina, transport and communication are critical to growth and change over space and through time. Transport and communication services and infrastructure facilitate and condition interaction between people, institutions, labor, capital, and the regional environments. However, since the nineteenth century, transport routes in Argentina have been dendritic in nature, geared to carry export products from the interior to the ports. In the more remote areas of the Northeast, the Northwest, and Patagonia, transport provision historically has been poor and inadequate for regional development (Roccatagliata 1992a). Moreover, successive transport policies have failed to address the lack of connectivity with neighboring countries and have reinforced Buenos Aires' dominant position within Argentina (Keeling 1993). Privatization of the transport and communication sector since 1990 has caused a realignment of internal spatial arrangements, with important consequences for the locational utility of regions and places.

Loss of critical public transport services to rural communities proved to be one of the immediate spatial impacts of privatization. For example, foreign investors to date have shown little interest in purchasing and operating Argentina's loss-making interior passenger trains. This situation seems reminiscent of Britain's failure to invest in Argentina's interior railroads between the late-nineteenth and early twentieth century. Although several provinces have attempted to maintain current rail passenger service, the financial cost is beyond the ability of most provincial governments. Airline services to some remote communities also have been curtailed, and road maintenance on essential highways remains inadequate for existing and potential future traffic.

The level of connectivity experienced by Argentina along the local-global continuum plays a crucial role in shaping relationships between the country, its neighbors, and regional urban centers and also between various socioeconomic spaces within the country. Transport and communication also help to shape the response of individuals and institutions to the forces of change. The long-term success of globalization forces in Argentina and the country's incorporation more fully into the world economy depend, in large part, on the government's response to increased demands for transport and communication services and infrastructure. In this chapter, I examine recent changes in Argentina's transport and communication infrastructure and services at three different scales. First, the country's transoceanic links to the global economy are analyzed, with a specific focus on Buenos Aires' position on the global airline network. Second, I explore changes in Argentina's connectivity within the Western Hemisphere by examining links first to non-contiguous countries and then to countries contiguous to Argentina. Particularly important are transport relationships within the framework of the MERCOSUR regional trade alliance. Third, national transport and communication facilities are examined, with a specific focus on inadequacies inherent in the national networks. The chapter concludes with an analysis of the likely impact of infrastructural improvements that is based on an economic potential model. Regional economic potential analysis can provide good data and a spatial rationale to support government and private transport investment strategies for future development. A critique of contemporary transport policies and strategies in Argentina puts future development prospects in perspective and provides a transition to the local and regional development issues addressed in part three of the study.

Global Links to Global Cities

Within the context of the emerging global economy, certain regions and major urban areas have evolved in recent years to become command and control centers of power, capital, labor, and communication. "World cities" in particular are conceptually and practically linked to the restructuring of the global economy, to the spatial reorganization of the international division of labor, and to the strategies of multinational corporations (Friedmann and Wolff 1982). World cities are linked together by increasingly complex and sophisticated networks of airlines, telecommunications circuits, and data transfer systems. Airline linkages, however, provide the best evidence of transport's role in facilitating local-global connections. Air networks and their associated infrastructure are highly visible and air transport remains the preferred mode of global mobility for the transnational capitalist class, migrants, tourists, and high-value, low-bulk goods (Keeling 1995). Moreover, airline links to the major cities that dominate the global economy are an important component of a country's aspirations to enhanced status in the global system.

Air Connectivity

Direct air connections to world cities represent both the globalization of trade and society and the emergence of an information- and producer services-based economy. These connections have, in fact, become a metaphor for economic success (Abbott 1993). The perception exists that improving a country's level of global connectivity endows certain competitive advantages. In Argentina, government bureaucrats, planners, and policy makers have begun to recognize the importance of international trunk routes in the articulation of the country with the global economy. The aggressive airline privatization and deregulation program introduced in 1990 is designed to stimulate route development and to enhance customer service.

Argentina's links to the global economy are dominated by Buenos Aires. The capital long has functioned as Argentina's gateway to the world and as the world's doorway to Argentina. Almost all airline traffic between the outside world and Argentina flows through Buenos Aires, with the exception of a few flights that connect a handful of interior cities with cities in neighboring countries. However, an examination of the city's position on, and accessibility to, the global airline network illustrates how poorly connected Buenos Aires is at the global level. Although factors such as government regulation, airline hubbing practices, supply and demand, and historical inertia all exert strong influence over city-pair relationships on the global airline network, by any measure Buenos Aires has yet to extend its global reach beyond a few key cities (for example, Miami and Madrid). Figure 5.1 illustrates Buenos Aires' position on the global airline network. An analysis of 266 cities whose populations exceeded one million revealed twenty cities that dominated their respective national and regional hinterlands in 1992, each serving as major hubs in the global airline network (Keeling 1995). Within this functional hierarchy, Buenos Aires occupied the penultimate position (Table 5.1). Only 52 non-stop transoceanic flights per week served Argentina, and Buenos Aires had direct connections to

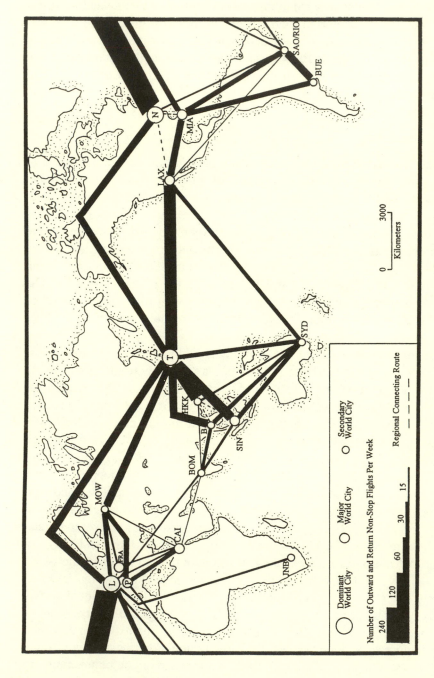

FIGURE 5.1   Argentina's Position on the Global Airline Network, 1992. *Source:* Official Airline Guide (1992).

TABLE 5.1 A Comparison of World City Connectivity on the Global Airline
Network, 1992

Global Hub	Non-Stop Flights[a]			Cities Served[b]		
	Global	Regional	Domestic	Global	Regional	Domestic
London	775	3,239	1,063	126	116	17
New York	644	634	8,837	86	45	126
Paris	565	2,264	1,436	140	93	53
Tokyo	538	401	1,814	62	18	38
Frankfurt	482	1,376	771	114	76	19
Miami	311	1,389	2,146	43	58	61
Cairo	277	34	114	62	16	9
Los Angeles	245	419	7,150	47	33	103
Bangkok	231	483	307	57	24	17
Amsterdam	229	1,593	0	94	86	0
Singapore	221	831	0	57	39	0
Hong Kong	154	713	0	33	36	0
Zurich	147	1,258	155	61	80	2
Sydney	144	89	1,541	35	14	53
Rio de Janeiro	93	44	933	28	12	41
Moscow	87	400	1,430	64	51	108
Bombay	64	111	313	30	20	31
São Paulo	64	97	1,418	27	13	63
Buenos Aires	52	336	414	21	19	41
Johannesburg	40	108	450	18	23	25

[a] Total number of flights per week to the hub city with no intermediate stops
between city pairs. Regional flights are those originating and terminating within
a hub city's geographical region (i.e. Europe for London, South America for
Buenos Aires).
[b] The number of cities served includes all cities with either non-stop or direct
flights (one or more intermediate stops between city pairs) to/from the major
global hubs.
Source: Official Airline Guide (1992).

only 21 cities on the global network. Unfortunately, the spatial dynamics
of Argentina's global connectivity have changed little since the 1970s
(Table 5.2). Between 1972 and 1996, the frequency of non-stop flights
from Buenos Aires rose from 14 to only 34 per week, with nine cities
served in 1996 compared to three in 1972. The volume of weekly direct
flights actually declined by over 50 percent over the 24-year period, with

TABLE 5.2   A Comparison of Transoceanic Airline Connections to and from Argentina, 1972, 1982, and 1996

Region/ City	Number of Flights Per Week					
	Non-Stop			Direct[a]		
	1972	1982	1996	1972	1982	1996
Europe						
Amsterdam	-	-	-	2	2	3
Brussels	-	-	-	2	-	-
Copenhagen	-	-	-	1	2	-
Frankfurt	-	-	3	8	6	3
Geneva	-	-	-	2	2	-
Lisbon	-	-	-	6	4	-
London	-	-	3	4	4	3
Madrid	4	5	13	10	5	1
Moscow	-	-	-	-	-	1
Nice	-	-	-	1	-	-
Paris	-	-	4	8	6	4
Rome	-	-	5	6	4	4
Stockholm	-	-	-	1	-	-
Zurich	-	-	-	7	5	3
Africa						
Cape Town	-	2	2	-	-	-
Casablanca	-	-	-	2	-	-
Dakar	9	2	-	3	2	-
Freetown	1	-	-	-	-	-
Gran Canary	-	-	1	-	-	-
Johannesburg	-	-	-	-	-	3
Las Palmas	-	1	-	2	-	-
Sal, Cape Verde	-	-	1	1	-	-
Pacific						
Auckland	-	-	2	-	-	-
Kuala Lumpur	-	-	-	-	-	2
Total:	14	13	34	65	42	27

[a] Flights that use the same plane but stop in an intermediate city before reaching the final destination.

Source: Official Airline Guides (1972, 1982, 1996).

six fewer cities served in 1996. Long-range, wide-bodied jets introduced after 1972 caused some cities that served primarily as fuel and service points to be dropped from the network (for example, Dakar and Las Palmas). Moreover, economies of scale that resulted from the increased use of wide-bodied jets altered service frequencies between many major hubs.

Privatization, deregulation, and route rationalization policies also have affected Argentina's position on the global airline network. However, Argentina's traditional European relationships continue to exert strong influence over connectivity patterns. Argentina had 13 non-stop flights per week to Madrid in 1996, with less frequent direct service to London, Rome, Paris, and Frankfurt. The link between Buenos Aires and Madrid not only reflects historic colonial ties but also the relationship with Iberia Airlines of Spain, which now owns a major financial interest in Argentina's national airline (Aerolíneas Argentinas). MERCOSUR's recent signing of trade and development agreements with the European Union could usher in a new period of strong ties between Argentina and Europe, especially if the Malvinas (Falkland) Islands issue is satisfactorily resolved with Britain and if other hemispheric trade groups fail to take advantage of developing regional economic relationships.

Economic growth in the Pacific Rim has yet to influence Argentina in any significant way in terms of transportation. In mid-1996, the country had no direct connections to East Asia's major urban centers: Hong Kong, Singapore, Seoul, Taipei, and Tokyo. Moreover, Argentina had only one direct connection to the African continent. Malaysian Airlines has introduced a new twice-weekly service between Buenos Aires and Kuala Lumpur via Cape Town and Johannesburg in South Africa. In addition, two weekly flights to New Zealand, with a special connecting flight to Australia, reflect the growing socioeconomic ties between Argentina and the Oceania region. Many Argentines migrated to Australia during the 1960s and 1970s, when the military ran the government.

Over the past decade, Argentina has experienced a rapid increase in the volume of air traffic, reflecting the importance of connectivity to the global airline network (Table 5.3). The total number of passengers transported on international flights grew from 1.7 million in 1983 to over 4 million in 1993, and freight tonnage transported by air more than doubled during the same period. Increased volumes of low-bulk, high-value goods shipped by air are a major indicator of a country's changing economic dynamism. Economies of scale in air freight movement have encouraged flexible production and just-in-time inventory practices in many high-technology

Table 5.3 International Airline Traffic, Argentina, 1983-1993[a]

Year	Total Number of Passengers Transported	Freight Transported (Tons)	Mail Transported (Tons)	Total Tons Transported[b]
1983	1,672,000	38,583	2,141	41,276
1984	1,998,000	43,963	2,428	46,895
1985	1,952,000	41,703	1,992	44,318
1986	2,546,000	51,838	2,165	54,921
1987	2,500,000	52,219	2,396	55,438
1988	2,628,000	50,773	2,178	53,125
1989	2,887,000	50,578	2,127	52,907
1990	3,280,000	54,871	2,431	57,302
1991	3,535,000	64,744	2,604	67,348
1992	4,054,000	85,258	2,985	88,243
1993	4,251,000	96,133	3,084	99,217

[a] Data refer to domestic and foreign companies providing regular services to Argentina. Although the data refer to Argentina, almost all international traffic flows through Buenos Aires.
[b] Rows do not sum because miscellaneous goods have been omitted.
Source: Repúblic Argentina (1994).

industries. This, in turn, has altered the dynamics of domestic economies. The movement of specialized products such as electronics, health supplies, scientific instruments, and telecommunications equipment to and from Argentina not only signifies a shift away from traditional industrial activities but also suggests changes in domestic consumption habits. In 1993, for example, electrical equipment and precision instruments accounted for nearly 20 percent of Argentina's total imports, up from 13 percent in 1980 (República Argentina 1994). These high-value products most frequently are shipped by air.

Telecommunication Links

The provision of telecommunications services is an equally important yet less visible aspect of Argentina's global connectivity. Fiber optic cable, satellite transmission systems, dedicated computer lines, and facsimile capabilities developed over the last decade have changed the space-time relationships of most countries. Theoretically, new telecommunications technology allows almost any individual or institution with the necessary equipment in Argentina to connect into the global information highway and to interact with other individuals and institutions across the globe. Geographic space between people in the 1990s has been compressed to such a degree by telecommunication technologies that individuals 8,000 kilometers apart are literally seconds apart in information space. Access to the Internet or World Wide Web allows documents and other data to be accessed almost instantaneously from anywhere in Argentina with the right equipment.

Argentina's telecommunications facilities continue to improve measurably, primarily through privatization strategies. Until 1989, the ENTEL company, an inefficient, overbureaucratized state monopoly, controlled the country's telecommunications sector. Stories of telephone usage problems in towns and cities across Argentina are of legendary proportions, and commercial growth particularly in the interior has been seriously retarded by inadequate telecommunications facilities. Between December 1991 and March 1992, the federal government split ENTEL into four companies and sold them to private consortia. Telefónica de Argentina now provides basic telephone services in southern Argentina and Telecom Argentina services the north. The line separating the service areas of these two companies runs right through the middle of Buenos Aires and on across the nation, effectively creating two service zones. A serious flaw in the territorial division of telecommunication services is that little allowance has been made for competition among the different operators. A state monopoly over the country's telephone systems effectively has been replaced with two private monopolies, with one company controlling the south and the other dominating the north. Two smaller private companies provide international, telex, ship-to-shore, and data transmission services. Macroeconomic indicators of change--such as increased numbers of telephones in service, higher volumes of voice and data traffic, and higher quality telecommunications service--argue that privatization is a success. Between 1990 and 1993, over 1.5 million new telephone lines were installed, the number of digital lines skyrocketed from 460,000 to nearly 2.3 million, and the number of public telephones more than doubled to 47,000 in service, while the number of personnel employed dropped from nearly 41,000 to under 34,000. However, local experiences suggest that tremendous imbalances in telecommunications provision still exist between the interior and the coast. Most of the gains in telecommunications improvement have been felt in Buenos Aires and in the major cities of the Pampeana region.

Modernization of the urban telephone network has facilitated an increase in the use of facsimile machines, telexes, and computers for international communication. Yet access to the evolving global information highway still is restricted to a select segment of society: certain government departments, universities, and multinational corporate offices. Over 65 percent of all installed computer and telecommunications equipment in Argentina is located in the Greater Buenos Aires metropolitan area, primarily within the Federal District (Carlevari and Carlevari 1994). For many urban residents, making an international telephone call still requires a personal visit to one of the several telecommunications offices scattered around the city. Calls to the major urban centers of North America, Western Europe, and the contiguous South American countries (Uruguay, Brazil, Paraguay, Bolivia, and Chile) dominate international telecommunications traffic to and from Buenos Aires (República Argentina 1994).

Maritime Links

The final component in Argentina's network of global connectivity is the international shipping sector. Maritime transport continues to play an important role in the articulation of Argentina with the world-economy, especially the movement of container traffic and high-bulk, low-value goods. Argentina's primary ports are Buenos Aires, La Plata, Rosario, and Bahía Blanca, with other important ports located along the Río Paraná and along the Patagonian coast. Approximately 75 percent of the country's global imports are received through Buenos Aires, a share relatively unchanged over the past two decades. In contrast, the shipment of Argentina's exports has become a little more geographically diverse, with only about 30 percent outgoing from Buenos Aires in 1993 compared to 54 percent in 1980. Privatization of the port system is encouraging more competition among the various Atlantic ports, and initial trends suggest a greater distribution of export tonnage away from Buenos Aires.

During the early 1970s, Buenos Aires ranked as one of the world's major seaports, second only to New York in the Western Hemisphere in volume handled. Although its global ranking has dropped since the 1970s, Buenos Aires still handles about 40 percent of Argentina's total international freight tonnage. A variety of international shipping companies maintain offices in the capital, providing service to most of the world's major ports. The country is served by biweekly container and general cargo service to and from South and West Asia, and by more frequent connections to North America and Europe. However, despite the privatization process,

Argentina's ports continue to suffer serious infrastructural and management problems (Roccatagliata 1993b). Massive inefficiencies in the port system stem from a lack of adequate long-term policies, intermittent planning, continued infrastructural disinvestment, bureaucratization of port management, jurisdictional conflicts, corruption, and labor disputes. For example, it cost approximately US$12 to US$14 to move one ton of cargo through the port of Buenos Aires in 1992, compared to under US$6 a ton at Brazilian ports (Roccatagliata 1993b). Moreover, Argentina does not have a well-developed deep-water port fully linked to the national transport network that can comfortably accommodate large ocean-going vessels, particularly container ships. A port facility at least 15 meters (45 feet) deep is necessary if Argentina is to take advantage of the economies of scale provided by bulk carriers and giant container ships. At present, port capacity in Buenos Aires is limited to ships with less than 10 meters (32 feet) of draught and no more than 170,000 displacement tons.

Another problem for Argentina is the rapid worldwide growth in container traffic. Only two operational cranes for container transhipment were available at the country's major port of Buenos Aires in 1994, and the port lacked sufficient storage and loading space near the docks for efficient container management. Moreover, Argentina's railroads lack the infrastructure needed to ship and distribute containers rapidly and efficiently from port to customer. The newly privatized rail companies recognize the importance of the global containerization movement and have taken steps to modify flat cars for container transport and to invest in special handling equipment (Richter 1996). Yet the country's continuing inability to participate fully and competitively in the global maritime network remains a major issue for the future of Argentina's connection to the global economy. Some planners envisage central Argentina as a major corridor for a future South American land-bridge between the Atlantic and Pacific economies. However, absent adequate port infrastructure, massive harbor improvements, and development of the transportation corridor between Buenos Aires and Santiago-Valparaíso in Chile, Argentina could lose this land-bridge opportunity to a Brazil-Bolivia-Chile-Peru corridor currently in the planning stage.

Hemispheric Connectivity

Argentina's government officials, academics, business people, planners, and policy makers clearly appreciate the importance of connectivity to the global economy. One of the principal objectives of Argentina's economic and social restructuring program is an "intensification of trade, [and the] financial and technological integration of the Argentine economy in world markets" (República Argentina 1993b:63). The efficient, rapid, and inexpensive movement of people, goods, and information is central to the achievement of a more dynamic role for the country in the emerging global economy. A major component of Argentina's economic restructuring program is the realignment of links within the hemisphere. These links can be divided into two areas of importance: non-contiguous and contiguous countries.

Transport Links to Non-Contiguous Countries

The United States dominates transport and communication links between Argentina and non-contiguous countries in the hemisphere. Economic ties between the two countries have strengthened dramatically since the 1950s, when the United States began to replace European countries as the primary source of Argentina's investment capital. Twenty-three percent of Argentina's total imports in 1993 were from, and 10 percent of all exports were to, the United States (República Argentina 1994). Although this import-export relationship has experienced considerable volatility over the years, with market share shifting gradually to the MERCOSUR countries and back to Europe, the United States still plays an important role in Argentina's hemispheric transport links.

Airline flights to cities in North America dominate Argentina's links to non-contiguous countries in the hemisphere. Nearly 75 percent of all non-stop and direct flights from Buenos Aires to non-contiguous countries are to North American cities, particularly Miami and New York. Miami has become the dominant gateway city between North and South America since the 1980s, and Buenos Aires has four daily non-stop flights to this major regional hub (Table 5.4). With the exception of New York, all the other connections to North American cities were via an intermediate point. Few Middle American or Caribbean countries have major air links to Argentina; only two cities enjoyed direct air connections to Buenos Aires in 1996. For example, Mexico City, the largest North American urban center in population size, had no non-stop or direct flights to Argentina. This lack of connectivity reflects Mexico's orientation toward the north and the historically poor trade relationships between Middle and South America. Connectivity to non-contiguous countries within South America also is extremely poor. In most cases, only the dominant urban center within a country (Caracas,

TABLE 5.4   A Comparison of Hemispheric Airline Connections to Buenos Aires, 1972, 1982, and 1996

| Buenos Aires | Number of Weekly Flights | | | | | |
| | Non-Stop | | | Direct[a] | | |
To/From	1972	1982	1996	1972	1982	1996
North America						
Dallas-Fort Worth	-	-	-	-	-	7
Los Angeles	-	-	-	7	8	7
Miami	-	4	28	15	16	7
Montréal	-	-	-	1	1	-
New York City	5	-	16	22	17	6
San Francisco	-	-	-	3	6	-
Toronto	-	-	-	1	1	-
Vancouver	-	-	-	1	1	-
Washington D.C.	-	-	-	2	1	-
Middle America						
Cancún	-	-	-	-	-	4
Curacao	-	1	-	-	-	-
Havana	-	-	1	-	-	1
Mexico City	-	-	-	5	5	-
Panamá City	2	-	-	7	3	-
South America **Non-Contiguous**						
Bogotá	-	-	6	6	4	1
Cali	-	-	-	1	-	-
Caracas	2	2	4	-	2	1
Guayaquil	-	1	-	3	4	-
Lima	5	3	10	19	8	-
Quito	-	-	-	3	3	-
South America **Contiguous**						
Antofagasta	-	-	-	2	-	-
Arica	-	-	-	1	-	-
Asunción	9	6	21	8	5	-
Belo Horizonte	-	-	-	-	-	2
Brasilia	-	-	-	-	-	14
Cochabamba	-	-	-	1	-	-
Colonia	-	-	8	-	-	-
Curitiba	-	-	7	-	-	7

(Continues)

TABLE 5.4   (*Continued*)

| Buenos Aires | Number of Weekly Flights | | | | | |
| | Non-Stop | | | Direct[a] | | |
To/From	1972	1982	1996	1972	1982	1996
Florianopolis	-	-	9	-	-	7
Fortaleza	-	-	-	-	-	7
Iguassu, Brazil	-	8	-	-	-	-
La Paz	2	1	-	4	4	5
Montevideo	148	115	87	-	-	-
Porto Alegre	10	3	21	-	7	-
Punta Arenas	-	-	-	2	-	-
Punta del Este	12	51	4	-	-	-
Recife	-	-	-	-	1	7
Rio de Janeiro	18	18	27	32	42	41
Salvador	-	-	-	-	-	7
Santa Cruz	2	4	7	-	2	1
Santiago	29	36	70	6	5	-
São Paulo	21	23	71	11	23	36
Total:	266	276	397	163	169	168

[a] Flights that use the same plane but stop in an intermediate city before reaching the final destination.
Source: Official Airline Guide (1972, 1982, 1996).

Lima, Quito, etc.) is connected to Argentina, with less than daily service the norm. Within the hemisphere, almost all goods and people move via the maritime or airline networks, as surface transportation to non-contiguous countries is nearly impossible given the vast distances, difficult physical terrain, and absence of infrastructure.

One of the long-term goals of countries in the Western hemisphere has been to develop an Inter-American highway system, with an all-weather, paved route linking Alaska to Tierra del Fuego. In South America, several countries have made some progress in constructing this intrahemispheric link. Brazil, for example, invested heavily in a Trans-Amazon highway network after the 1960s, and Peru began work on its Carratera Marginal project designed to open up the area along the eastern slopes of the Andes mountains. Yet despite some of these more high-profile projects, progress on a truly inter-American terrestrial network has proved extremely disappointing. Little evidence exists of any significant surface cargo movement between Argentina and non-contiguous countries in South America and there are no direct passenger services between Argentina and cities in non-contiguous countries.

It is possible to reach cities in Peru, Ecuador, Colombia, and Venezuela by bus from Argentina, but the journey would be excruciatingly long and would require several changes of bus enroute. For example, Thomas Cook's 1995 international timetable listed a regular bus service from Buenos Aires to La Paz, Bolivia, which covered the 2,770 kilometers in 55 hours. From La Paz, another bus covered the 1,500 kilometers to Lima, Peru, in approximately 50 hours. In Lima, another bus change would have enabled a traveler to cover the 2,020 kilometers to Quito, Ecuador, in 40 hours. From Quito, a 30-hour, 1,110-kilometer bus ride to Bogotá, Colombia, was possible, with a change of buses necessary at the international frontier. Finally, bus service to Caracas, Venezuela, covered the 1,370 kilometers between the two capitals in 35 hours, again with a change of bus at the international frontier. As this example illustrates, nearly 10 days of traveling would be required to cover the 8,800 kilometers between Buenos Aires and Caracas, Venezuela. Obviously, for those who can afford the ticket price, airline travel between Argentina and the major urban centers of other Southern American countries is the preferred mode of travel. The railroad network in South America also is highly fragmented, with connections between the major urban centers of neighboring countries almost nonexistent. Such patterns of transport isolation have seriously impeded the process of suprastate regional development and integration throughout modern history.

Transport Links with Contiguous Countries

Until the late 1980s, connectivity between Argentina and neighboring countries was at best superficial. Historical links to Europe and, more recently, to North America combined with poor regional economic and social complementarity to keep Argentina relatively disconnected from its neighbors throughout most of the twentieth century. Incompatible railroad gauges, high levels of distrust between neighbors, unpaved roads in border regions, and no political-economic context for regional interaction also acted to isolate Argentina, Bolivia, Brazil, Chile, Paraguay, and Uruguay from each other. In addition, each country developed a national trade and transport network concerned more with shipping exports products to port than with fostering cross-border connections and regional interaction.

Since the 1980s, however, political rapprochement and regional economic integration strategies have encouraged greater levels of interaction between Argentina and its neighbors. Increased levels of trade with Argentina's three MERCOSUR partners--Brazil, Paraguay, and Uruguay--as well as stronger commercial links to Chile, have focused renewed attention on the importance of transport and communication networks in the Southern Cone.

Changes in the level of airline connections between Argentina and Brazil reflect the growing importance of bilateral trade between the two countries. In 1972, Argentina had airline service to only 3 Brazilian cities; by 1996, ten cities had direct connections to Argentina (see Table 5.4). Moreover, weekly flight frequencies between the major cities have increased substantially, with ten non-stop flights each day between Buenos Aires and São Paulo. Airline service to Santiago, Chile, also has increased since the 1980s, a reflection of the quickening pace of trade between the two countries. Flight frequencies to Montevideo in Uruguay have declined steadily since the 1970s, in part because of stiff competition from long-distance buses and from the very competitive hydrofoil and ferry services in the Río de la Plata estuary. At the national level, Buenos Aires dominates Argentina's airline linkages to contiguous countries, and few interior cities have direct air links to neighboring countries. Mendoza does have daily air service across the Andes to Santiago, Chile, Córdoba enjoys a weekly service to São Paulo, Brazil, and a weekly service links the Northwest to Bolivia. However, most air travelers from Argentina's interior provinces to neighboring countries are required to transit Buenos Aires.

A comparison of the four MERCOSUR countries and their respective regional and global linkages revealed that few major network changes occurred between 1972 and 1993 (Table 5.5). Only Brazil experienced any significant increase in the total number of cities served in neighboring countries. Although the volume of weekly flights between Argentina and contiguous countries rose by 120 over the 21-year period, the number of cities served only increased by one. As the table illustrates, North America and Europe continue to exert strong influences over the Southern Cone countries. One of the real structural barriers to spreading the benefits of regional integration and economic globalization to the interiors of Argentina and its regional neighbors is the continued dominance of each country's major urban center. Most regional urban centers remain isolated from hemispheric and global transportation networks.

Inadequate surface links between Argentina and contiguous countries long have frustrated regional development strategists and planners (Basco

TABLE 5.5   A Comparison of the MERCOSUR Countries' Regional and Global Airline Connectivity, 1972-1993

From/To Year	Contiguous Countries		Other South American Countries		North America		Europe		Rest of the World	
	A	B	A	B	A	B	A	B	A	B
Argentina										
1972	276	14	7	6	7	10	4	13	10	4
1993	396	15	10	5	29	11	19	8	2	3
Brazil										
1972	98	13	1	2	24	7	37	12	12	7
1993	199	20	14	3	133	14	81	13	5	9
Paraguay										
1972	30	9	4	4	0	3	0	3	0	1
1993	43	8	11	4	4	2	0	3	0	0
Uruguay										
1972	184	6	7	5	0	2	0	9	0	3
1993	218	5	5	4	0	4	0	5	1	1

A The number of non-stop scheduled airline flights per week from the MERCOSUR country to other regions of the world.

B The number of cities served by scheduled airline flights from the MERCOSUR country to other regions of the world.

Source: Official Airline Guides (1972, 1993).

et al. 1988; Padula 1993). Indeed, the federal government of Argentina has stated that poor cross-border infrastructure is a significant barrier to regional integration and it places a high priority on the development of stronger ties to neighboring countries (República Argentina 1993a). Yet despite the rhetoric and the myriad proposals for upgrading regional transport networks, few improvements have been forthcoming since 1990. Suprastate regional railroad links now are almost nonexistent and the quality of roads across Argentina's borders remains dismal. Despite poor infrastructure and a lack of basic maintenance on the major international routes, much of Argentina's cross-border goods and passenger traffic is carried by trucks and buses. However, a new railroad freight link between

São Paulo and Buenos Aires did begin operation in 1996 and it is scheduled to provide full daily service between the two cities. Other cross-border railroad link improvements are scheduled over the next decade, and hope remains high among many transport specialists that MERCOSUR will encourage futher infrastructural development. Bus connections between Buenos Aires and the major cities of neigh-boring countries maintain average journey times comparable to long-distance bus service in the United States. For example, deluxe motor-coaches cover the 2,757 kilometers between Argentina's capital and São Paulo in 36 hours at an average speed of 77 kilometers per hour (Table 5.6). Competition between bus companies and the airlines have kept ticket prices for cross-border journeys affordable, at least for the middle class; a one-way ticket between Buenos Aires and São Paulo cost approximately US$120 in 1995. Freight rates between Brazil and Argentina have declined by nearly 50 percent since 1990 as a consequence of improved operating efficiencies and the elimination of many cross-border restrictions. Im-proved delivery speeds, lower shipment costs, and less bureaucratic red tape are crucial to many retailers and manufacturers in Argentina who rely on just-in-time inventory methods to remain competitive and to reduce operating costs.

The long-term success or failure of regional integration strategies in the Southern Cone depends heavily on how well Argentina and its neighbors address the problem of transport and communication. Government bureau-crats, planners, business people, and local boosters throughout the region have identified a number of projects designed to link the Atlantic and Pacific coasts via highly developed corridors. For example, Jorge Soría Quiroga (1995), the mayor of Iquique, a northern port city in Chile, has developed a series of maps and plans to illustrate how his city could benefit as a nodal point along several bi-oceanic corridors linking Chile, Argentina, Brazil, Bolivia, and Paraguay. The concept is that Brazil's soya farmers in the Mato Grosso and Argentina's wheat farmers on the pampas could save time and money by shipping their products from Chile's Pacific ports to North America and Asia. In return, Japanese cars, Korean electronics, and Chinese textiles could be shipped back over the Andes to the major east coast urban centers (*Economist* 1995). For many agricultural producers in central Argentina and in the Mato Grosso of Brazil, the Chilean ports are as close as the ports in Buenos Aires or Santos.

Four transborder corridors have been identified for the region, three of which run through Argentina. The first corridor would link Rio de Janeiro, São Paulo-Santos, Porto Alegre, Montevideo, Buenos Aires, and Santiago

TABLE 5.6 Bus Connections From Buenos Aires to Major Urban Centers in Contiguous Countries, 1995

City	Distance (Kms)	Frequency Of Buses Per Week	Journey Time in Hours	Index of Connectivity[a]
Asunción	1,375	44	21	0.92
Ciudad del Este	1,255	5	18	0.86
Curitiba	2,392	15	34.5	0.86
Florianopolis	2,122	15	26	0.74
La Paz	2,770	4	55	1.19
Montevideo	715	28	8.5	0.71
Porto Alegre	1,692	8	22.5	0.80
Potosí	2,196	2	50	1.37
Rio de Janeiro	2,870	15	42	0.88
Santa Cruz	2,463	3	47	1.14
Santiago	1,540	14	24	0.94
São Paulo	2,757	15	36	0.78
Uruguaiana	1,001	8	16	0.96
Valparaíso	1,550	3	24	0.93

[a] The index of connectivity is calculated by dividing journey time by total kilometers. A connectivity index of 0.71 represents an average speed of 84 kilometers per hour.

Source: Thomas Cook (1995); Various company timetables.

and Valparaíso along a Southern Cone superhighway. Although designed primarily as a major road corridor, the link between Argentina and Chile lends itself to development as a high-speed rail freight route. To support this particular link and to provide international connections to several of Argentina's major interior cities, a spur would run from Mendoza across to Córdoba, Santa Fé, into Misiones province, and on to Paranagua in Brazil. A second corridor is envisioned to follow the path of the original colonial trunk route north from Buenos Aires (see Figure 2.1). This corridor would provide bi-oceanic links for Argentina's northern provinces with a direct line connecting Peru's port city of Mollendo near Arequipa to Buenos Aires via Bolivia and the Northwest. A third plan called the *Capricorn Project* would link Porto Alegre on Brazil's southeast coast to the Chilean ports of Iquique and Antofagasta via Corrientes, Salta, and the Sisco Pass in Northwest Argentina. The fourth corridor would follow the existing railroad line from Santos in Brazil to Corumba on the Brazil-Bolivia border, and then run through Bolivia via Santa Cruz and Cochabamba to the Chilean port of Iquique or Arica.

Despite the dreams, plans, and lofty ideas of people interested in developing these important transportation corridors, international rivalries and national bureaucracies present formidable obstacles to any real progress on the projects. Nonetheless, in 1996 several pilot studies either were underway or had been recently completed. For example, Louis Berger International, a Washington D.C. consulting company, produced a feasibility study financed by the World Bank on the construction of a 30-mile bridge across the Río de la Plata estuary from Buenos Aires to Colonia, Uruguay (Green 1993). Work also continues on the Hidrovía project designed to develop the Río Paraná corridor and to open up the central western section of Brazil (Durán et al. 1995).

Argentina currently maintains 21 major operational cross-border links to neighboring states, several of which are slated for immediate improvement. Three other major transborder projects are in the planning stage. Of these 24 total operational or planned links, four are with Uruguay, four with Brazil, three each with Paraguay and Bolivia, and ten links are across the Andes with Chile. Ferries and hydrofoils run regularly across the Río de la Plata estuary from Buenos Aires to Colonia and Montevideo in Uruguay. As mentioned above, a 30-mile long bridge is planned for this important corridor. Three other bridges, all in Entre Ríos province, span the Río Uruguay: the Puente San Martín links Gualeguaychú to Fray Bentos in southwestern Uruguay; Puente Artigas connects Colón to Paysandú; and an international bridge joins Concordia to Salto in northwestern Uruguay. The latter bridge provides both road and railroad access.

In Corrientes province, the Vargas-Justo bridge provides both road and rail links between Paso de los Libres and the Brazilian city of Uruguaiana. A new road and rail bridge across the Río Uruguay is planned between Santo Tomé and São Borja in Brazil as one component of the bi-oceanic corridor project. Misiones province has only one cross-border link to Brazil, the international bridge across the Río Iguazú between Puerto Iguazú and Foz de Iguaçú, although the Hidrovía project will create a navigable fluvial route along the Río Paraná into Brazil. A new bridge is planned between Puerto Iguazú and Paraguay across the Río Paraná. The only existing cross-border link between Misiones province and Paraguay is the newly constructed road and rail bridge between Posadas and Encarnación. In Formosa province, the Loyola International Bridge across the Río Pilcomayo connects Clorinda to Asunción and is the only other access to Paraguay. Salta province in the extreme northwest has two transborder routes to Bolivia. Both a road and a railroad link Pocitos to Yacuiba in southeastern Bolivia, while the Aguas Blancas international bridge carries a road across the Río Bermejo into south-central Bolivia. In northern Jujuy province, both a road and a railroad cross the border between La Quiaca and Villazón. This route forms part of the *Corridor Libertador*, designed to link Buenos Aires to Peru and its Pacific Ocean ports.

Ten important transport routes breach the Andes that separate Argentina from Chile. These routes are in regular use, although all of them require massive infrastructural improvements, and one new route remains in the planning stage. Jujuy province began work in 1983 on a road project designed to connect the province's capital with the Chilean ports of Antofagasta, Iquique, and Tocopilla via the Paso de Jama (*Economic Information* 1983). Similarly, the government of Salta has developed plans to improve the dirt road across the Paso de Sisco in the province's northwestern corner to encourage economic interaction with northern Chile. An existing road and rail link across the Paso de Socompa in Salta province also is targeted for major infrastructural improvements. In Catamarca, the San Francisco pass provides a route across the Andes to the Chilean port of Caldera, as does the Peñas Negras pass in La Rioja province. Improvements to the Paso de Peñas Negras are problematic, however, because there is no existing road infrastructure in this remote corner of the province. The Paso del Inca route, some 80 kilometers to the south in northern San Juan province is a more likely candidate for infrastructural improvements, but this would defeat the objective of La Rioja province to have its own Andean crossing and corridor to the Pacific Ocean.

San Juan's major Andean route is the Agua Negra pass linking the northwestern corner of the province to the Chilean port of Coquimbo. Although other potential Andean crossings exist in southern San Juan, their development is unlikely because little economic potential exists in this remote area of the province. Mendoza's Uspallata Pass currently is the major corridor between Argentina and Chile (see Chapter 8). Almost all traffic between the two neighbors utilizes this route. Plans are on the drawing board for a new, 25-mile long road tunnel under the Andes that would provide a fully surfaced, year-round route between the two countries. These plans also call for the rehabilitation of the one-meter-gauge railroad that runs through the pass from Mendoza to Valparaíso. In the southern corner of Mendoza province, the Paso de Pehuenche provides an alternate route to the fertile valleys south of Santiago, Chile.

Neuquén province in northern Patagonia has the final two important routes across the Andes to Chile, although the region of Patagonia does contain a number of other very minor and rarely used Andean passes. Regional development plans for Patagonia call for the extension of the broad-gauge railroad line from Zapala across the Andes to Temuco and the southern Chilean ports. Planners argue that this route would provide the fruit and vegetable growers of the Río Negro valley more rapid access to the Pacific Rim markets via Chile's ports. In the southwestern corner of Neuquén province, the Puyehue pass links Argentina's lake district and the resort region of San Carlos de Bariloche to southern Chile. South of the Puyehue pass, there are no other important routes across the Andes, perhaps with the exception of the road between the coal mines of Río Turbio in extreme southwestern Santa Cruz and the Chilean town of Puerto Natales, which supplies labor for the coal mines.

Each one of these important cross-border routes described above has distinct advantages and disadvantages in terms of the regional integration process. One major consideration for Argentina's national integration strategies is the role of provincial governments in the development of transborder links. Failure to involve provincial and local governments in the planning process could hinder the forward and backward economic linkages that result from transport infrastructure improvements and could further isolate many interior regions. Other considerations include the investment cost of new infrastructure and the long-term operating cost of the cross-border links. Cost-benefit analyses of specific corridor development projects must be undertaken to determine the optimum social, economic, political, and environmental benefits. Finally, Argentina's planners and policy makers must address the inefficiencies and inadequacies inherent in the country's existing national transport and communication networks before any benefits could be gained from cross-border improvements.

National Transport Networks

Argentina's system of transport and communication networks functions as an essential component of the national geoeconomic structure and it has served as one of the most significant elements in the organization of national territory. Without a doubt, since the nineteenth century Argentina has enjoyed a level of transport and communication infrastructure and service unparalleled in Latin America. No other country in the region boasts a railroad system as geographically widespread or a road network as encompassing as Argentina. However, Argentina's transport and communication networks were designed primarily to ship export products from the interior to the Atlantic ports and out into the global economy, not to encourage regional development, integration, or cross-border interaction. Moreover, after the 1950s, investment in transport and communication infrastructure as a percentage of GDP began to decline significantly. The state-owned railroad system, for example, collapsed into disrepair, plagued by chronic inefficiencies, poor management practices, and brutal competition from road-based services. In addition, the railroads were hampered by a geographic coverage designed for the nineteenth century and not for a contemporary state that needed to integrate its interior regions and to interact more forcefully with neighboring states.

Buenos Aires dominates the national transport and communication system, with most airline routes, passenger trains, and long-distance buses focused on the metropolis. This dendritic pattern makes some sense when you consider that Buenos Aires contains 40 percent of the national population, a substantial portion of Argentina's financial power, all federal government functions, and much of the country's industrial and manufacturing capacity. However, thus dendritic network encourages a concentration of flows to the Pampeana region from the interior and acts as a substantial barrier to the diffusion of socioeconomic restructuring benefits to interior provinces. A lack of transverse interprovincial links and poor cross-border connectivity has hindered the national development of Argentina and encouraged the country's socioeconomic bifurcation.

To address these and other transport and communication problems, the federal government since 1991 has embarked on a program to privatize, deregulate, and restructure national transport networks and services. Forming the backbone of the government's restructuring policies are the five major transport and communication modes: railroads, highways, airlines, shipping, and telecommunications. Each of these modes has undergone profound reorganization and restructuring over the past five years, with both short- and long-term implications for Argentina's future.

Railroads

At its height, the national railroad system of Argentina extended over 47,000 kilometers, with 21 of the country's 23 provinces enjoying direct connections into the network. Only Santa Cruz and Tierra del Fuego in Patagonia remained isolated from the national system. National network integration remained illusive, however, because the system evolved using four different track gauges. East of the Río Paraná, a standard-gauge network (1.435 meters) connected the provinces of Misiones, Corrientes, and Entre Ríos to Buenos Aires. West of the Río Paraná, a narrow-gauge system (one meter) extended from Buenos Aires to San Juan, Catamarca, La Rioja, and Tucumán provinces via Córdoba. From the city of Tucumán, extensions ran northward toward Bolivia through Salta and Jujuy, and eastward into Formosa and Chaco provinces. A branch line on the meter-gauge system also ran northward along the western side of the Río Paraná to service northern Santa Fé and southern Chaco provinces.

The backbone of the national railroad system was the broad-gauge system (1.676 meters) that blanketed the Pampeana agricultural zone and extended westward to La Pampa, San Luis, Mendoza, and San Juan. Lines radiating from Buenos Aires also served the Atlantic coast cities of Mar del Plata, Bahía Blanca, and Viedma, with extensions westward to the provinces of Neuquén and Río Negro. The final component of the national network was a 402-kilometer, narrow-gauge (0.75 meters) line that linked the city of Esquel in northwestern Chubut to the broad-gauge line that ran through Río Negro province.

Beginning in 1991, the federal government embarked on an ambitious railroad privatization program. Ferrocarriles Argentinas, the federal railroad entity, was divided into nine distinct companies, with long-term operating concessions to six of the nine new entities granted to consortiums of national and international investors. The final three components of the national network are undergoing reorganization in preparation for privatization. In 1996, approximately 32,000 kilometers of railroad line remained in operation providing basic freight service to every provincial capital except Catamarca, Rawson, and Ushuaia. Figure 5.2 generalizes the main routes of Argentina's existing railroad system. For clarity, several minor lines have been omitted from the map, as have a number of lines that had been abandoned but that now are undergoing rehabilitation.

Ferroexpreso Pampeano operates the rehabilitated transverse route linking Rosario and the Atlantic port city of Bahía Blanca. The majority of the company's lines service the western third of Buenos Aires province and the northeastern corner of La Pampa. Two-thirds of Ferroexpreso's cargo in 1995 comprised grain products from the pampas farms. East of the Río Paraná, freight service is provided by Ferrocarril Mesopotámico. In

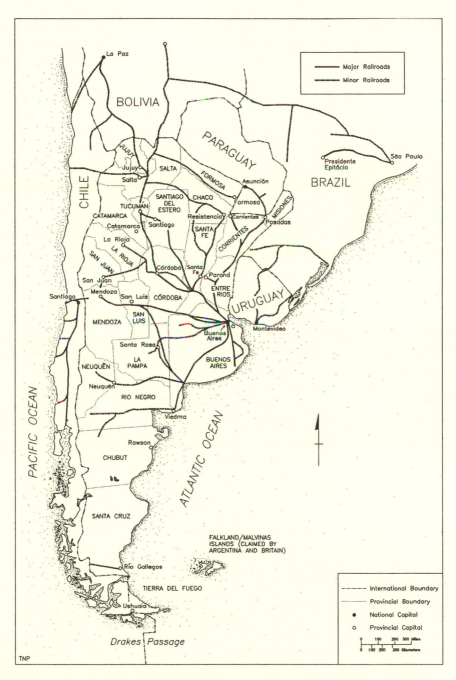

FIGURE 5.2   Argentina's Railroad Network, 1996.

1994, stone (28%), sugar (13%), soya (11%), and rice (10%) were the principal products transported by rail from Misiones, Corrientes, and Entre Ríos provinces. Southern Córdoba, San Luis, Mendoza, and San Juan are serviced by the Buenos Aires al Pacífico company. Cereals, petroleum products, and stone make up the bulk of this company's cargo. Much of Buenos Aires province, as well as the route from Bahía Blanca into northern Patagonia, is served by Ferrosur Roca, whose major cargo in 1994 was cement (23%) and stone (42%). Nuevo Central Argentino operates rail service in the northern section of Buenos Aires province and links the three major industrial centers of Rosario, Córdoba, and Greater Buenos Aires. Nuevo Central also operates the broad-gauge route from Rosario through Santiago del Estero to the northwestern city of Tucumán. Agricultural products are the backbone of this company's freight business. The sixth component of the national network to be privatized, the intraurban commuter system of Greater Buenos Aires, has been divided into four major concessions, each operated by private consortiums.

Early results from the privatized companies have been encouraging. In 1995, the overall freight tonnage carried and the total ton-kilometers run by the five private freight railroads showed significant improvement over 1994 (Table 5.7). Even the state-owned Belgrano system experienced a reversal of its three-decade decline in freight tonnage, registering a 20 percent increase in overall freight tonnage during 1995. The private railroad operators have invested in new technologies and rolling stock, and have begun to address the problem of deteriorating infrastructure. However, in terms of national network integration, the issue of fragmented networks still remains unaddressed. Little economic incentive exists at present to encourage the freight railroads to plan and develop an integrated, intermodal network. Moreover, the federal government has no long-term strategy to use the railroad network as a regional development tool. Once again, this planning failure is reminiscent of the British railroad companies' nineteenth-century strategy of only building and maintaining railroads where an economic incentive existed. As a result, Argentina's interior provinces remained poorly served by railroad technologies throughout much of the past century. Is history about to repeat itself?

A final concern related to the privatization and restructuring of Argentina's national railroad network is the issue of intra- and interurban passenger service. Suburban commuter trains and inner city subway services in the Greater Buenos Aires Metropolitan Region now are operated by four private companies. Burlington Northern from the United States and

TABLE 5.7   Performance Statistics for Argentina's Six Freight Railroads, 1994-1995

Railroad	Network Kilometers	Tons (in millions) 1994	1995	Ton-Kms 1994	1995
Ferrosur Roca	3,342	2.47	3.32	958	1,263
Nuevo Central Argentino	4,512	3.48	3.53	1,190	1,166
Ferroexpreso Pampeana	5,238	2.48	2.91	1,014	1,163
Buenos Aires al Pacifico	5,254	2.44	2.85	2,066	2,310
FC Mesopotámico	2,739	1.17	1.22	620	690
FC Belgrano	10,451	1.13	1.36	747	1,021
Total:	31,536	13.17	15.19	6,612	7,613

Source: Richter (1996).

Transurb of Belgium are the two major foreign investors in partnership with Argentine companies. After decades of traffic declines, ridership on the commuter network increased by approximately 20 percent in 1995, while the subway system experienced a 30-percent increase in ridership (Richter 1996). Stations and terminals are being remodeled and renovated, as are passenger cars and engines, and extensions of both the subway and commuter systems are in the advanced planning stages. No other intra-urban passenger railroad system operates outside of Buenos Aires.

The interurban passenger railroad network remained in limbo during 1995. Only the Buenos Aires to Mar del Plata corridor has attracted any serious attention from private operators, as this is the most heavily traveled route in Argentina. Most of the country's other interurban passenger services either have been abandoned completely or turned over to the provincial governments, few of whom have the financial resources needed to run passenger railroads. Networks of interurban railroads, however, are critical proximate influences shaping the growth of national urban systems and individual cities. Indeed, the development of high-speed rail systems in Europe and Japan over the past decade has provided an alternate mode of transport for interactions over short to medium distances (150-650 kilometers). Studies of the impact on urban connectivity of France's high-speed rail system (TGV), for example, suggest that new railroad links accentuate and strengthen the dominant nodes of national and supraregional transport networks (Benoit et al. 1993). High-speed railroads also are playing instrumental roles in spreading the development impetus of involvement in the global economy to national and regional hinterlands. Heightened levels of interurban, intraregional, and interregional connectivity serve to stimulate socioeconomic interaction and can provide new dimensions to stagnant local economies.

A brief comparison of interurban railroad links for selected cities in 1995 highlights the important role played by high-speed rail service in national and supraregional connectivity (Table 5.8). Major urban centers such as London, Tokyo, Melbourne, New York, Paris, and Madrid now enjoy high levels of interurban railroad connectivity. For example, a 400-kilometer journey from Paris to Nante takes just under two hours, whereas the journey from Mar del Plata to Buenos Aires, a similar distance, takes over 5 hours. It takes four hours to cover the 632 kilometers between London and Edinburgh, giving the two cities a 0.38 connectivity index. Contrast the 680-kilometer journey between Buenos Aires and Bahía Blanca, which takes over 11 hours and has a connectivity index near 1.0. The index of connectivity is an excellent indicator of comparative levels of development in high-speed rail transport and it illustrates how many urban centers have become much closer in time-space to important secondary and tertiary cities. Argentina's failure to address seriously the issue of interurban passenger networks could have extremely negative consequences for future regional development and economic interaction, especially in interior provinces.

Highways

Major paved roads in Argentina were few and far between prior to the 1960s. The few major roads that did exist generally followed existing railroad routes and served to move agricultural products from the farms to the nearest railhead. Investment from the United States during the 1960s in truck and automobile factories, coupled with the rapid deterioration of the railroad system, encouraged an explosion in both automobile use and road construction. Between 1965 and 1980, the length of paved roads in Argentina rose from 21,400 to over 51,000 kilometers, although most of the new road construction was concentrated in the Pampeana. The total number of automobiles in the country increased at an annual rate of 8.5 percent from 1965 to 1980, and the use of trucks and buses for cargo and passenger movements began to dominate transport flows.

Argentina's national and provincial interurban highway network in 1995 exceeded 200,000 kilometers, 30 percent of which was paved. Every

TABLE 5.8   A Comparison of Interurban Railroad Connectivity Between
Selected Urban Centers, 1995

Origin	Destination	Distance (Kms)	Journey (Time)	Index of Connectivity[a]
0-499 Kilometers				
Paris	Lille	227	1 hr	0.26
Lyon	Paris	427	2 hrs	0.28
Tokyo	Sendai	351	1 hr 46 m	0.30
Paris	Nantes	396	1 hr 58 m	0.30
London	Manchester	304	2 hrs 25 m	0.48
New York	Washington	362	2 hrs 55 m	0.48
New York	Boston	373	4 hrs 10 m	0.67
Mar del Plata	Buenos Aires	400	5 hrs 10 m	0.77
Rojas	Buenos Aires	220	4 hrs 14 m	1.16
São Paulo	Qurinhos	450	9 hrs 12 m	1.23
500-999 Kms				
Tokyo	Osaka	553	2 hrs 30 m	0.27
Madrid	Seville	574	2 hrs 45 m	0.29
Bordeaux	Paris	568	2 hrs 56 m	0.31
London	Edinburgh	632	4 hrs	0.38
Sydney	Melbourne	961	10 hrs 23 m	0.65
Istanbul	Ankara	578	7 hrs 20 m	0.76
Santiago	Concepción	577	8 hrs 40 m	0.90
Buenos Aires	Bahía Blanca	680	11 hrs 15 m	0.99
Mexico City	Guadalajara	613	11 hrs 25 m	1.12
Buenos Aires	Santa Rosa	606	11 hrs 45 m	1.16
Necochea	Buenos Aires	503	9 hrs 55 m	1.18
Buenos Aires	General Pico	524	11 hrs 25 m	1.31
1000+ Kms				
Paris	Madrid	1,489	12 hrs 32 m	0.51
Edinburgh	Penzance	1,007	10 hrs 42 m	0.64
Mexico City	Monterrey	1,022	14 hrs 10 m	0.83
Los Angeles	Seattle	2,233	34 hrs 15 m	0.92
Johannesburg	Cape Town	1,530	25 hrs 25 m	1.00
Tucumán	Buenos Aires	1,170	20 hrs 30 m	1.05
Santiago	Puerto Montt	1,088	20 hrs 20 m	1.12
Buenos Aires	Bariloche	1,741	36 hrs	1.24

[a] The index of connectivity is calculated by dividing journey time by total kilometers. A connectivity index of 0.26 represents an average speed of 227 kilometers per hour. *Source*: Thomas Cook (1995).

provincial capital and most secondary urban centers are linked to the national road grid (Figure 5.3). However, an analysis of the 37,000-kilometer national highway system revealed that many interior provinces still suffer from a lack of paved roads (Table 5.9). In the Northeast, Chaco, Formosa, and Misiones are below the national average, and four of the six Northwest provinces also suffer from a lower-than-average paved road percentage. Approximately 70 percent of the national highways in the North are paved, compared to over 94 percent in the Pampeana and Cuyo regions. As a region, Patagonia recorded the lowest percentage of paved national highways with 53 percent. A comparison of the ratio of road kilometers to the size of each province and to the total population of each province revealed some interesting statistics. As expected, the larger Patagonian provinces have the highest ratio of land area in square kilometers per kilometer of paved road. Much of the western portions of these provinces are sparsely populated. The Pampeana provinces contain 42 percent of the country's paved national roads, thus geographic coverage here is much denser than in the northern provinces. Each kilometer of paved road also served the highest number of people in Buenos Aires province because it contains nearly 50 percent of Argentina's total population. Tucumán recorded the second highest ratio of people per kilometer of paved road because it is the second smallest province in Argentina but the fifth most populated.

Despite an extensive road-building program over the past three decades, traffic flows on Argentina's national highway network still are dendritic in nature and dominated by Buenos Aires (Figure 5.4). The location of the country's major industrial facilities along the Río Paraná and in the three largest urban centers--Buenos Aires, Córdoba, and Rosario--helps to concentrate traffic flows in the Pampeana region. Beyond the Greater Buenos Aires region, few freeways exist and many of the national routes remain narrow, poorly maintained, and unsuitable for heavy volumes of commercial traffic. To address this problem, contemporary federal government transport plans call for the privatization of Argentina's major highways. Private investors have received concessions to approximately 15,000 kilometers of roads, and toll highways are slowly being introduced across the country, although critics have argued that the only real infrastructural improvements to date have been the construction of toll booths.

There are lessons to be learned in Argentina from Mexico's current experiment with privatized roads. A network of major toll roads now fans out from Mexico City linking the capital region to Veracruz, Guadalajara,

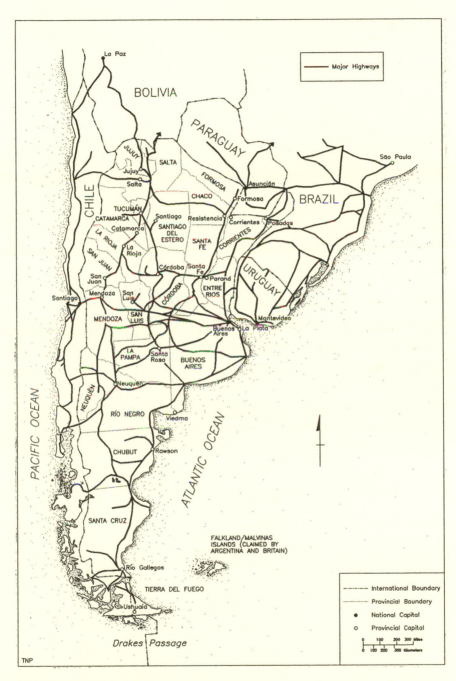

FIGURE 5.3 Major Highways in Argentina, 1995.

TABLE 5.9   Argentina's Interurban Highway Network, 1993

Region/ Province	Total Kms	Paved Kms	Percent Paved	Coverage Ratio[a]	Persons Per Km[b]
Pampeana					
Buenos Aires	4,661	4,661	100	66.03	3,338
Córdoba	2,373	2,360	99	70.05	1,172
Entre Ríos	1,448	1,295	89	60.83	788
La Pampa	1,569	1,251	80	114.66	208
Santa Fé	2,463	2,238	91	59.43	1,250
Cuyo					
Mendoza	1,505	1,348	90	110.41	1,048
San Juan	767	727	95	123.22	727
San Luis	1,284	1,284	100	59.77	223
Northeast					
Chaco	1,089	759	70	131.27	1,106
Corrientes	1,633	1,601	98	55.09	497
Formosa	1,273	519	41	138.86	768
Misiones	874	568	65	52.47	1,389
Northwest					
Catamarca	886	649	73	158.09	407
Jujuy	755	396	52	134.39	1,294
La Rioja	1,281	887	69	101.10	249
Salta	1,769	1,008	57	154.25	859
Santiago del Estero	1,436	1,226	85	111.22	548
Tucumán	480	399	83	56.45	2,862
Patagonia					
Chubut	2,193	1,379	63	162.93	259
Neuquén	1,477	1,061	72	88.67	366
Río Negro	2,358	1,487	63	136.53	341
Santa Cruz	2,382	942	39	258.96	170
Tierra del Fuego	881	62	7	342.95	1,119
Total:	36,837	28,107	76	98.91	1,160

[a] Coverage Ratio is the total land area in square kilometers for each kilometer of paved national highway.
[b] Persons Per Km. represents the total population served by each kilometer of paved national highway.
Source: República Argentina (1994).

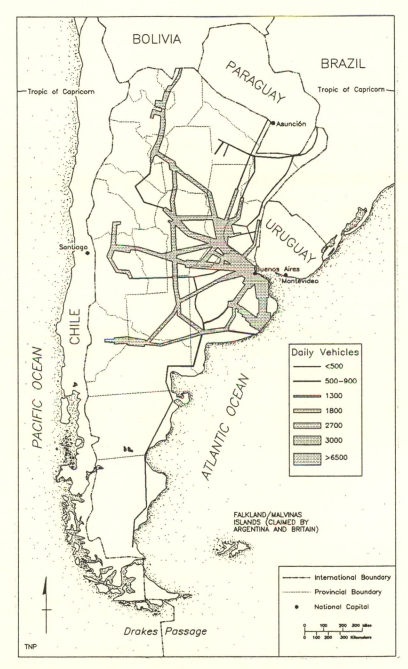

FIGURE 5.4   Traffic Flow Patterns in Argentina, 1990.
Source: After Roccatagliata (1992a).

Oaxaca, Acapulco, San Luis Potosí, and other major urban centers. For example, tolls on the 450-kilometer route between the capital and Veracruz cost over US$10 for an automobile and four to six times more for a truck, depending on its size. From Monterrey to Nuevo Laredo on the Mexico-U.S. border, a journey of about 250 kilometers on the toll road cost approximately 100 pesos (US$13) in June 1996 for a passenger car. Because toll prices are so high, most truckers in Mexico use the poorly maintained free roads. Lack of traffic on the toll roads thus forces the Mexican government to raise tolls to cover costs, which discourages even more drivers from using them. This vicious cycle creates a serious dilemma for Mexican planners and traffic analysts. It is likely that Argentina's planners and transport officials will face the same problem as increasing numbers of toll roads are introduced across the country in the coming years.

Other Transport and Communication Networks

From humble beginnings in the 1950s, Argentina's national airline network has evolved a dendritic pattern, with most flights originating and terminating in Buenos Aires and linking provincial capitals and other important urban centers to the federal capital. Few interprovincial corridors exist and connections between interior regions remain negligible. Privatization has affected the domestic network by reducing the volume of flights to many cities in the interior, particularly Patagonia. Competition with long-distance buses has kept airline ticket prices at a reasonable level since 1991, but many interior towns and cities are no longer served by scheduled passenger airlines.

The fluvio-maritime network in Argentina is focused almost exclusively on the Pampeana region. With the exception of some navigation on the upper Río Paraná in the Northeast region and a handful of Atlantic ports in Patagonia, the bulk of Argentina's imports and exports is handled by five major ports: Rosario on the lower Paraná, Buenos Aires, Quequén, Mar del Plata, and Bahía Blanca. Historically, Argentina's ports have been ill-equipped to cope with the demands of an export-oriented economy. A lack of adequate investment, coupled with poor planning, labor conflicts, overbureaucratization, and interjurisdictional friction, brought the national port system to the verge of collapse at the end of the 1980s. Since 1991, privatization policies have been applied to the fluvio-maritime system and many of the port complexes either have been returned to provincial government control or sold outright to private consortiums. Improvements in port infrastructure, along with new investment in freight railroads, could rein-vigorate the fluvio-maritime network and position Argentina to participate more efficiently in the regional and global economies.

Finally, until recently other transport and communication networks at the national level have focused almost exclusively on Buenos Aires and the Pampeana region, especially telecommunications systems. Planners hope that privatization of the national telephone network will encourage the development of transverse networks to link interior cities and towns with their neighbors. However, in 1995 the Pampeana region still contained the major share of the country's telecommunications infrastructure. Other transport projects underway as a result of privatization strategies include several gas and oil pipeline projects across the Andes from Argentina to Chile. For example, the Gasoducto Gas-Andes company began construc-tion in March 1996 on a 500-kilometer gas pipeline linking La Mora in Argentina with Santiago, Chile (*Oil and Gas Journal* 1996). Further to the south in Patagonia, Gasoducto Transandino was poised to begin construc-tion on a 1,250-kilometer pipeline from Neuquén province to Concepción, Chile, with completion scheduled for December 1997.

Future Transport and Communication Strategies

A key element of the Argentine government's territorial, economic, and social reorganization policies is the restructuring of transport flow patterns within the country and between neighboring states. A recent report prepared by a special government task force on the formulation of policies for territorial reorganization in Argentina highlighted transport and com-munication as fundamental instruments of territorial development. The report stated that the government should consider it necessary and oppor-tune "to integrate and complement the different modes of transport, to improve network infrastructure with the aim of developing axes of development to achieve internal and external territorial integration, and to improve accessibility, mobility, and interaction between cities and regions" (República Argentina 1993a:56). Absent strategies and policies designed to achieve these goals, argued the report, Argentina could face severe diffi-culties in development, it could be further geographically bifurcated, and it could become increasingly isolated from the global economy.

The difficulty for planners and policy makers, of course, is determining which regions need the greatest attention and what levels of transport and communication infrastructure and service are required. There is little disagreement that Buenos Aires exerts an undue influence over the country and that transport and communication are deficient in the areas beyond the Pampeana core. As a result, policies in Argentina are being formulated that focus on the development of axes of articulation and interaction. A series of strategic regional capitals and intermediate urban agglomerations around the country have been identified and development axes linking these areas to each other and to Buenos Aires have been proposed (see Figure 4.4). However, while these links make sense intuitively, the policies lack a sound theoretical and statistical basis for implementation. Certainly, any improvements in transport and communication in the interior provinces are welcome. However, given the economic, geopolitical, social, and regional development goals espoused by the Argentine government, coupled with the scarcity of funds to achieve many of these goals, a much clearer implementation timetable and project rationale is needed. One useful methodology for examining the potential impact of transport infrastructure improvements is an economic potential analysis.

Economic Potential Analysis

Economic potential measures the nearness or accessibility of a specific volume of economic activity to a particular point or region. Its genesis lies in the concept of regional potential and was first used in an analysis of population distribution (Stewart 1947). Between the 1950s and the 1980s, researchers such as Harris (1954), Clark (1966), and Rich (1980) refined the regional potential concept in analyses of industrial location, focusing specifically on the market or economic potential of regions. Most recently, Gibb and Smith (1994) used economic potential analysis to challenge the generally accepted belief that the benefits generated by the Channel Tunnel linking England and France would be confined to the southeast region of the United Kingdom.

The formula for measuring a region's accessibility to economic activity, as given by Rich (1980), is:

$$P_i = \sum_{j=1}^{n} M_j/D_{ij}^{\propto} \tag{1.1}$$

where P_i = the potential of region "i"
M_j = a measure of the volume of activity activity in region "j"
D_{ij} = the measure of the journey distance/time or transport cost between regions "i" and "j"
$\propto$ = the distance/time/cost exponent.

Summing all the "n" regions in the study area yields the potential value for region "i" in units of economic activity per unit of distance, time, or cost. Regions with the highest potential values theoretically have access to more economic activity within a specified distance than regions with lower values. High relative accessibility confers comparative advantages within the region concerned by reducing the time and distance costs associated with moving products, people, inputs, and information. In contrast, more inaccessible regions are handicapped by comparative disadvantages in the form of higher time and distance costs, which include the perception of regional inaccessibility. Economic potential analysis, therefore, can provide useful evidence of how and where transport improvements potentially might be the most effective.

Methodology. The major methodological issues presented by economic potential analysis include scale of analysis, the definition and measurement of economic activity, the distance matrix, the problem of tariff barriers, and the estimation of a region's self-potential. The area of study comprises 24 regions, which include the 23 provinces of Argentina and the Federal District of Buenos Aires. In each region, a major town or city was chosen as the nodal point, with the volume of economic activity in that region allocated to that location. Gross Domestic Product (GDP) values for 1993, based on regional distribution percentages derived from Argentina's 1994 national economic census, were used to approximate the mass M_j term (expressed in millions of Argentine pesos at current prices) (República Argentina 1994, 1995). GDP values are regarded widely as the best available accurate measure of the volume of economic activity in regions.

All nodes in the study area were connected by "links" to neighboring nodes, including, where necessary, links to nodes in non-contiguous regions. The nodal matrix for Argentina comprised 59 primary links, with a mean distance between each node in the matrix of 638 kilometers. The nodal matrix had a standard deviation of 369 kilometers, and 38 percent of the 59 primary links had distances between nodes above the mean distance for the study area. The shortest link between two nodes (Corrientes and Resistencia) was 25 kilometers across the Río Paraná, with the longest link 1,831 kilometers between Buenos Aires and Comodoro Rivadavia in Patagonia.

The major empirical work in calculating potential economic values centers on the calculation of the distance, time, or transport cost between nodes. This involves selecting appropriate cost or distance measures and calculating the necessary transport time, cost, or distance exponents. Meaningful transport cost data for Argentina are extremely difficult to obtain and the considerable time and problems involved in gathering such data could not be justified in terms of providing any appreciable difference in the final potential results. Therefore, the present study used the most direct road or rail distances between the regional nodes. A Thomas Cook *Overseas Timetable* (1995) and an Argentine road atlas provided the base data required to build a distance matrix. The distance term D_{ij} represents potential interregional rail freight journey times. Manufacturers are concerned primarily with the time needed to ship their goods, especially in the contemporary world of just-in-time inventory practices, not with the distance over which those goods have to travel. Moreover, in most urbanized, industrialized countries, transport costs have become a relatively minor component of the final cost of delivered goods and services. However, the importance to regional socioeconomic development of the accessibility and mobility of people should not be overlooked. Efficient, cheap, rapid, and high-quality passenger services and infrastructure are fundamental to Argentina's regional development and are a major component of the present study.

A further consideration in operationalizing the economic potential model is the issue of a region's self-potential, the contribution to the potential of region " i " of its own mass value. In other words, how can the special case of D_{ii} in the array D_{ij} be quantified? Various approaches to this problem have been tried in past research. Rich (1980) has argued that the clustering of economic activity around the major urban center of most officially-defined regions supports the use of the following formula to calculate D_{ii}:

$$D_{ii} = (0.5) \sqrt{\frac{\text{area of the region}}{\Pi}} \qquad (1.2)$$

Finally, four time scenarios were incorporated into the economic potential calculations. The base scenario assumed an average node-to-node journey time of 60 kilometers per hour. This scenario recognizes existing road and rail conditions in Argentina, accounts for the police checkpoints located around many cities and provincial boundaries, and draws on field experience of internal journey times. Scenario two assumes an overall improvement in the operating condition of Argentina's major roadways, with an average node-to-node journey time of 110 kilometers per hour. In the third scenario, average node-to-node journey times are calculated at 160 kilometers per hour. These times would result from the introduction of an integrated, multimodal national road and rail network between Argentina's major cities, allowing for rail running speeds up to 200 kilometers per hour along rehabilitated intercity pathways. The final scenario assumes a high-speed rail network similar to that under construction in Europe, which would allow for node-to-node average journey times of 225 kilometers per hour.

Results. The original hypothesis posited that the more peripheral regions of Argentina could experience higher gains than the core areas in absolute and relative accessibility with basic improvements in transport services and infrastructure. The initial results for scenario one (60 kph) show that the smallest potential increases in economic potential are experienced by the four dominant industrial areas: Buenos Aires province (1.67%), the Greater Buenos Aires Metropolitan Area (3.2%), Córdoba (2.73%), and Santa Fé (3.1%) (Table 5.10). The largest potential increases are found in the northern interior provinces of Catamarca (14.25%), Chaco (14.98%), Formosa (15.15%), La Rioja (16.88%), and Santiago del Estero (12.73%). These provinces traditionally have lagged behind socially and economically and long have been considered the most underdeveloped of Argentina's interior provinces. Curiously, La Pampa province, traditionally incorporated into the coastal, and thus wealthier, region showed a potential gain of 11.23 percent. This is a function of the province's extremely low self-potential (12.51%), the lack of an industrial base, and its relatively central location within Argentina.

As expected, provinces with above-average rates of GDP also experienced the highest percentage of self-potential increase. In other words, the Greater Buenos Aires Metropolitan Area (GBAMA) gained only 16.54 percent of its potential increase from other provinces; 83.46 percent of the GBAMA's total potential increase came from its own self-potential. In contrast, provinces with below-average rates of GDP experienced the lowest percentage of self-potential increase. La Rioja, for example, one of Argentina's poorest provinces, gained nearly 90 percent of its total potential increase from other provinces. Tierra del Fuego, however, the most isolated province in Argentina with an average distance to every other node in the matrix of 3,244 kilometers, showed a high rate of self-potential (61.49%). Transport time and distance are so high for Tierra del Fuego that it experienced lower benefits from overall improved connectivity than other interior areas. Overall, the country would experience only a 4.49 percent

TABLE 5.10   Absolute and Relative Economic Potential Values for Argentina: Scenario One--60 Kilometers Per Hour

Political Division	1993 GDP (millions of pesos)	Self Potential	Percent Self	Total Potential (millions)	Percent Increase
GBAMA	61,679	1,648	83.46	1,975	3.20
Buenos Aires	44,664	459	61.55	745	1.67
Catamarca	2,145	36	11.65	306	14.25
Chaco	3,753	63	11.25	562	14.98
Chubut	6,153	69	33.96	203	3.30
Córdoba	22,801	298	47.84	623	2.73
Corrientes	6,230	112	21.95	508	8.16
Entre Ríos	8,707	165	26.53	622	7.14
Formosa	1,864	37	13.08	282	15.15
Jujuy	3,651	84	27.90	302	8.26
La Pampa	3,396	48	12.51	381	11.23
La Rioja	1,915	34	10.52	323	16.88
Mendoza	10,545	145	36.46	399	3.78
Misiones	4,392	135	38.37	353	8.03
Neuquén	7,047	122	36.08	339	4.81
Río Negro	5,464	64	21.32	302	5.54
Salta	5,234	71	23.83	296	5.66
San Juan	3,472	62	17.12	360	10.38
San Luis	6,945	133	28.66	465	6.70
Santa Cruz	2,987	32	23.29	138	4.62
Santa Fé	27,626	403	46.97	858	3.10
Santiago del Estero	2,706	39	11.31	345	12.73
Tierra del Fuego	3,983	145	61.49	236	5.93
Tucumán	7,967	282	52.45	538	6.76
Total:	255,326	4,686	40.89	11,461	4.49

Note: GBAMA refers to the Greater Buenos Aires Metropolitan Area, which contains the Federal Capital, Provincial Capital (La Plata), and the suburban counties.

average increase in GDP per kilometer based on the existing transport network, and 45 percent of the total increase would be absorbed by the Pampeana provinces and the Buenos Aires megalopolis. In the interior, only the northern provinces of Chaco and Tucumán would gain anywhere near a 5 percent share of the overall improvement in GDP.

Scenario two, based on an overall improvement of travel times to 110 kilometers per hour, revealed that the four northeastern provinces of Chaco (27.45%), Corrientes (14.96%), Formosa (27.76%), and Misiones (14.72%) achieved the largest combined average increase in economic potential at 19.25 percent. The six northwestern provinces followed with a combined average increase in potential of 16.37 percent. The lowest potential increases were experienced by the most economically active Pampeana provinces, but overall they captured 45 percent of the total potential increase (Table 5.11). Potential increases in millions of pesos were fairly uniform for the majority of interior provinces.

In terms of potential increase relative to the GBAMA, which recorded the highest potential increase across the board, the major industrialized provinces within the Pampeana planning region showed the highest percentage increases. Santa Fé recorded a 43.43 percent increase in potential relative to the GBAMA, while Buenos Aires province showed a 37.74 percent increase. However, many of the interior provinces fared extremely well when compared to the maximum increase in total economic potential. Chaco, Corrientes, Mendoza, San Luis, and Tucumán all experienced increases relative to the GBAMA of over 20 percent. The lowest percentage increases relative to the GBAMA were recorded by the more remote Patagonian provinces of Chubut (10.29%), Santa Cruz (6.99%), and Tierra del Fuego (11.97%).

Scenarios three and four are based on an improved railroad network and presume average point-to-point journey speeds of 160 and 225 kilometers per hour respectively (Tables 5.12 and 5.13). At 225 kilometers per hour, many of the northern interior provinces experienced increases in their own economic potential of over 40 percent. La Rioja (63.31 percent) showed the highest potential gain, while Formosa (56.79%), Chaco (56.15%), Catamarca (53.44%), and Santiago del Estero (47.73%) also experienced substantial gains. The low overall potential increase in millions of pesos per kilometer in Patagonia suggests that investment in railroad infrastructure might not be economically feasible at the present time. With the exception of a major line from Bahía Blanca in Buenos Aires province across to Neuquén in northern Patagonia, little railroad infrastructure presently exists in Patagonia. In contrast, a basic, although extremely dilapidated, railroad network already exists in the western and northern provinces. As Tables 5.12 and 5.13 suggest, improvements in this network to attain the running speeds used in the analysis could generate acceptable economic returns and would provide a strong boost to the depressed

TABLE 5.11   Absolute and Relative Economic Potential Values for Argentina: Scenario Two--110 Kilometers Per Hour

Political Division	Increase in Own Potential Millions of Pesos	Percent	Percent Increase Relative to GBAMA
GBAMA	3,623	5.86	-
Buenos Aires	1,366	3.06	37.74
Catamarca	560	26.13	15.48
Chaco	1,030	27.45	28.47
Chubut	373	6.06	10.29
Córdoba	1,143	5.01	31.57
Corrientes	932	14.96	25.74
Entre Ríos	1,140	13.09	31.49
Formosa	517	27.76	14.30
Jujuy	553	15.14	15.28
La Pampa	699	20.58	19.31
La Rioja	593	30.95	16.37
Mendoza	731	6.93	20.19
Misiones	646	14.72	17.86
Neuquén	621	8.81	17.15
Río Negro	554	10.15	15.32
Salta	543	10.38	15.00
San Juan	660	19.02	18.25
San Luis	853	12.28	23.56
Santa Cruz	253	8.48	6.99
Santa Fé	1,572	5.69	43.43
Santiago del Estero	632	23.34	17.45
Tierra del Fuego	433	10.87	11.97
Tucumán	987	12.38	27.26
Total:	21,014	8.23	

Note: GBAMA recorded the maximum increase in total economic potential.

economies of the interior. Economic potential analysis does have several theoretical and practical weaknesses, and a number of other inputs to the model could have been considered: for example, population dynamics, levels of industrialization, existing external trade links, decentralization policies, and land-bridge policies. Nonetheless, at the very general level, the results suggest a strategy of spatial development that should focus more on the northern than on the southern interior provinces. Certainly, the

TABLE 5.12   Absolute and Relative Economic Potential Values for Argentina: Scenario Three--160 Kilometers Per Hour

Political Division	Increase in Own Potential Millions of Pesos	Percent	Percent Increase Relative to GBAMA
GBAMA	5,265	8.54	-
Buenos Aires	1,987	4.45	37.74
Catamarca	815	38.01	15.48
Chaco	1,499	39.94	28.47
Chubut	542	8.81	10.29
Córdoba	1,662	7.29	31.57
Corrientes	1,356	21.76	25.74
Entre Ríos	1,658	19.04	31.49
Formosa	753	40.39	14.30
Jujuy	804	22.03	15.28
La Pampa	1,017	29.94	19.31
La Rioja	862	45.02	16.37
Mendoza	1,063	10.08	20.19
Misiones	940	21.41	17.86
Neuquén	903	12.82	17.15
Río Negro	807	14.76	15.32
Salta	790	15.09	15.00
San Juan	961	27.67	18.25
San Luis	1,241	17.86	23.56
Santa Cruz	368	12.33	6.99
Santa Fé	2,287	8.28	43.43
Santiago del Estero	919	33.95	17.45
Tierra del Fuego	630	15.82	11.97
Tucumán	1,435	18.02	27.26
Total:	30,564	11.97	

Note: GBAMA recorded the maximum increase in total economic potential.

northern and western regions have a greater potential to capture economic activity across their respective international boundaries.

A further benefit to Argentina's development that goes beyond pure economic growth lies in the ability of transport improvements to reshape individual and community perceptions about place and region. Buenos Aires, for example, is perceived by many as the sophisticated, Europeanized, and civilized heart of the nation, whereas interior provinces are

TABLE 5.13   Absolute and Relative Economic Potential Values for Argentina: Scenario Four--225 Kilometers Per Hour

Political Division	Increase in Own Potential Millions of Pesos	Percent	Percent Increase Relative to GBAMA
GBAMA	7,403	12.00	
Buenos Aires	2,794	6.26	37.74
Catamarca	1,146	53.44	15.48
Chaco	2,108	56.15	28.47
Chubut	762	12.39	10.29
Córdoba	2,337	10.25	31.57
Corrientes	1,906	30.59	25.74
Entre Ríos	2,331	26.77	31.49
Formosa	1,058	56.79	14.30
Jujuy	1,131	30.98	15.28
La Pampa	1,430	42.10	19.31
La Rioja	1,212	63.31	16.37
Mendoza	1,495	14.18	20.19
Misiones	1,322	30.10	17.86
Neuquén	1,270	18.02	17.15
Río Negro	1,134	20.76	15.32
Salta	1,111	21.22	15.00
San Juan	1,351	38.91	18.25
San Luis	1,744	25.11	23.56
Santa Cruz	518	17.33	6.99
Santa Fé	3,216	11.64	43.43
Santiago del Estero	1,292	47.73	17.45
Tierra del Fuego	886	22.24	11.97
Tucumán	2,018	25.33	27.26
Total:	42,975	16.83	

Note: GBAMA recorded the maximum increase in total economic potential.

viewed as isolated, backward, uncivilized, and barbaric. Rural-urban migration patterns over the past fifty years have been driven, in part, by this perception of the capital's attractiveness and also by the location of major industries in and around the relatively well-connected Pampeana cities. Growth pole strategies in Argentina designed to encourage development in interior provinces have been mostly a miserable failure, in part because little attention was paid to the practical and perceptual issues of mobility and accessibility. Transport improvements, then, could not only revitalize the stagnant and depressed interior economies, but also they could help to reshape traditional perceptions about the quality of life in the interior and to improve individual mobility.

For example, the city of Tucumán is approximately 1,200 kilometers northwest of the federal capital. Present surface journey times average about 22 hours between cities. Basic road improvements could reduce the journey time to about 12 hours, while the introduction of high-speed rail services could further reduce intercity journey times to under 6 hours. Although initially some demographic and economic backwash might occur, as access to the dominant city becomes quicker, more affordable, and easier, over the long-term a "spread effect" (to use Gunnar Myrdal's (1957) terminology) should counteract the initial depletion of human and financial resources in the interior. In Argentina, however, backwash is unlikely to have any serious negative consequences, as the human and financial resources of the interior provinces already have been severely depleted. As Truman Hartshorn (1971:269) observed, "growing markets, new technology and friction of distance, combined with congestion, pollution, and diseconomies of scale in the heartland and the amenities of the hinterland, [should] make outlying areas more attractive to development (over time)."

Another important potential benefit from transport improvements in Argentina's hinterland stems from the country's growing trade and social links with its neighbors. Argentina's increased socioeconomic activity with its Common Market (MERCOSUR) partners has focused renewed attention on the inadequate nature of surface transportation between the partners. Particularly problematic are the cross-border links. If Argentina is to take advantage of the socioeconomic development impetus provided by MERCOSUR, and if the potential benefits of regional economic integration are to "trickle down" to the interior provinces, then much closer attention must be paid by Argentina's planners and policy makers to the role of transport and communication in the integration process.

A Critique of Transport Policies in Argentina

The results of the economic potential analysis for Argentina demonstrate that the advantages offered by transport improvements are not necessarily confined to the already dominant Pampeana provinces. However, inadequate supporting transport infrastructure and services are likely to limit any potential benefits from transport improvements and to have some serious repercussions for Argentina's more isolated regions. In light of Argentina's recent move toward neoliberal economic restructuring policies, what is the potential for meaningful transport improvements in the near future?

Transport policies since 1945 have been driven by two major factors: the development of regional planning strategies designed to deconcentrate industrial and manufacturing activities, and the management of transport first through nationalization strategies and recently through privatization policies. The Perón government of the late 1940s nationalized much of the transport sector, yet designed and implemented few policies aimed at the national, regional, or local development of the transport system. Transport languished between the 1960s and the 1980s and, in many ways, proved to be the Achilles heel of successive government regional development policies. Interior industries and manufacturers could not compete with the coastal cities in national and global markets because inadequate transport facilities placed many interior provinces at a competitive disadvantage.

Transport policies in Argentina have not responded to current theories and practices concerning the role of transport in regional development. The idea that transport's role is merely to facilitate economic interaction at the global and interregional levels has become embedded in transport policy planning. Present regional development and integration strategies in Argentina make the same mistake as past policies in focusing solely on global and interregional links. Little attention has been paid in these policies to intraregional and local connectivity. Furthermore, transport planners and policy makers have elected to address transport issues and problems on a modal basis or from a modal perspective. The development of an integrated, multimodal national approach has not been forthcoming. The potential cost and service benefits from focusing on the coordination of multimodal transport have been largely ignored. Throughout the interior provinces of Argentina, for example, air, rail, bus, and road freight networks operate independent of each other, with no spatial or temporal coordination at any level of the system. Vertical or horizontal integration in the transport and communication networks of the interior provinces is unknown.

In addition, Argentina's transport policies have responded to a conception of the interior that emanated from regional development policies formulated in Buenos Aires. These policies have treated the interior provinces as functional regions with homogeneous characteristics rather than as historically defined regions with spatially and temporally complex characteristics. Policy priorities have been driven by an emphasis on state and corporate action rather than by considerations of distinctive regional economic, social, and cultural characteristics. Thus, policies are reactive rather than proactive, and Argentina's federal government has had to respond to regional inequalities after the fact rather than prevent them from occurring. Conceptualizations of the Northwest and other regions also have been driven by the implicit assumption that these regions should be like Buenos Aires, rather than by the realities of spatial conflict and struggle within the regions themselves.

Transport's role in Argentina's global, hemispheric, and regional development should include an explicit acknowledgment of the relationship between transport, people, and places. Transport networks cannot be planned without an understanding of the cultural inputs that help to define the network. Why do people choose to travel to a particular location? Where are needed services located? What are the time and cost relationships between communities, individuals, and the needed services? And what are the ideologies that drive the provision of the infrastructure needed to facilitate interaction? The role of transport in regional development, however, cannot be measured by transport mode and provision analyses alone. Applying a gravity model, for example, to the cities of Salta and Tucumán in Northwest Argentina may indicate that a certain amount of interaction is likely to occur between them. Yet without a detailed analysis of the economic, social, political, and environmental circumstances of each city (in other words, the cultural factors), such models have little value.

Argentina's transport policies in the mid-1990s are aimed at privatizing and deregulating the transport arena. Airline, railroad, and telephone networks have been sold piecemeal to private concerns without any overarching national development plan. The government believes that supply and demand mechanisms will act as a development agent and thus, beyond the privatization strategies, no federally driven national, integrated, multimodal transport policies are needed. A long history of government financial and management ineptitude in the transport sector lends credence to the popular believe that private enterprise will provide a better quality of service, while relieving the financially strapped federal and provincial governments of fiscal responsibility for transport provision. Although short-term benefits are beginning to be felt from the transport privatization process, the long-term consequences may be disastrous for Argentina's goal of creating a dynamic, unified, national economy and society able to compete at the regional and global levels. Moreover, changes in transport provision can have a differential effect on Argentina's different socioeconomic spaces. Indeed, since 1990, four dominant socioeconomic spaces have emerged in Argentina, each experiencing different impacts from the country's restructuring policies.

The following section of the study examines local and regional development issues by focusing on these four specific types of geographic space. First, the megacity as a distinct spatial environment is examined, with a specific focus on how Buenos Aires is responding to the changes in Argentina's pillars of development. Second, I analyze Argentina's prosperous agricultural provinces, which have functioned as the country's economic backbone for over a century. Transition areas are the third type of geographic space examined in part three of this study. The Cuyo and Patagonian provinces face an uncertain future as a consequence of Argentina's economic liberalization policies. The key issue is whether these transition areas can achieve a higher level of development as a result of national restructuring or whether they will slip into the abyss of poverty and underdevelopment. Finally, I explore the problems of Argentina's submerging northern rural areas. Already mired in poverty and maldevelopment, and long dependent on the prosperous core for financial and economic survival, these poorest of Argentina's provinces face a bleak future within the context of neoliberal economic restructuring.

PART THREE

The Geographical Impact:
Local and Regional Development Issues

6

The Megacity

A distinctive characteristic of urban evolution in developing countries during the twentieth century has been the phenomenon of megacephalous growth. In countries as diverse as South Korea, Nigeria, and Argentina, the growth of the dominant city, particularly since 1945, has outpaced the ability of the government to plan for and provide basic human needs. By the year 2010, more than half of the world's population will live in cities, and demographic projections suggest that 25 of these cities will be "megacities" with over 10 million people each. Little wonder, then, that megacities around the world have captured the attention and imagination of planners, researchers, politicians, the media, and potential migrants. Media stories about Mexico City's horrendous pollution, Bangkok's traffic gridlock, or violence and corruption in Lagos often create a negative image about life in the megacities of the developing world and suggest that these cities are ungovernable and out of control. On the positive side, many cities are attempting to maximize the potential their size and resources give them by learning from the successes and failures of other urban centers. For example, the Mega-Cities Project based in New York has developed a network of urban leaders from around the world in order to coordinate the myriad approaches to solving urban problems and to foster the transfer of these approaches from one megacity to another.

Megacities are playing an increasingly important role in the evolution and function of our global society, not only in terms of their contribution to the world economy but also in terms of the challenges they present to planners, managers, and residents at a variety of geographic scales. This chapter examines the role of Buenos Aires, Argentina's megacity, in the national urban, social, and economic systems. The analysis focuses on four elements critical to the city's future development: planning, housing, accessibility and mobility, and environmental management. Weaknesses in these four arenas pose serious short- and long-term challenges to Argentina's government and citizens as the country proceeds down the path of globalization and socioeconomic restructuring.

Megacephalous Urban Growth

Latin America is the most urbanized region of the developing world, with over 75 percent of the region's people residing in an urban environment. Today's urban population is greater in number than the entire population of Latin America in 1980! (Griffin and Ford 1993). Since the late 1950s, countries such as Argentina have experienced an urban population explosion, primarily in the dominant city but also in many of the major provincial centers. Although the dominance of one city over a country long has been a characteristic of Latin America, the growth of large secondary cities over the past 40 years has been phenomenal. In 1950, 66 cities in the region had populations over 100,000, yet none exceeded 5 million. In 1996, nearly 40 cities surpassed the one million mark and four cities-- Mexico City, Rio de Janeiro, São Paulo, and Buenos Aires--each have over 10 million people and merit megacity status. In addition, these four megacities have developed, or are developing, "world city" characteristics, an increasing concentration of business command and control functions that distinguish their role as regional centers in the global economy (Keeling 1995). John Friedmann (1995) has identified those world cities which function as major nodes in the global economy, and Buenos Aires is identified as an important secondary city within the world hierarchy (Figure 6.1).

Argentina's megacity dominates the country demographically. The urban agglomeration of Buenos Aires contained over 13 million people in 1996, approximately 40 percent of the country's total population (see Table 3.3). Three million people reside within the 200 square kilometers of the Federal District, 8 million inhabit the 19 *partidos* (counties) of the inner suburbs, and over 2 million people live in the 32 *partidos* than comprise the outer suburbs. Argentina's fifth largest urban agglomeration, Greater La Plata, with nearly 650,000 people, is included in the outer suburbs of the Greater Buenos Aires Metropolitan Area. La Plata is the capital of the province of Buenos Aires. Megacephalous urban growth since the 1950s also has been evident in many of Argentina's 23 provinces, especially in the provincial

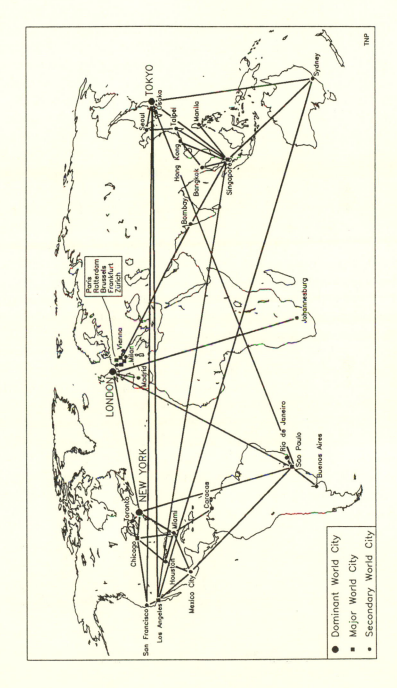

FIGURE 6.1 Buenos Aires' Position in the Network of World Cities. *Source:* After Friedmann (1995).

capitals. Greater Córdoba, the capital and dominant city of Córdoba province, has over 1.2 million inhabitants and accounts for approximately 43 percent of the province's total population. Argentina's third largest city, Greater Rosario in the province of Santa Fé, recorded nearly 1.1 million inhabitants in the 1991 census. The cities of Greater Rosario and Santa Fé together accounted for 54 percent of the total population of Santa Fé province.

As discussed in chapter three, high urban primacy rates also are evident in provinces beyond the Pampeana region. Argentina's fourth largest city, Greater Mendoza, which had just under 800,000 inhabitants in 1996, represented 53 percent of the province's total population. Nearly 60 percent of Tucumán province's population is concentrated in Greater San Miguel de Tucumán, and the city of Salta contains approximately 45 percent of Salta province's total population. Similar urban dominance rates are found throughout the Northeast and in Patagonia (see Table 3.5). Demographers in Argentina argue that high primacy rates will persevere well into the twenty-first century if rural conditions deteriorate further, transport services outside the core remain extremely poor, land division through inheritance continues, and the process of globalization bypasses the interior provinces. In 1950, 53.3 percent (9 million) of Argentina's 17 million people lived in small rural communities and in towns of less than 50,000 inhabitants. By 1991, barely 11 million (33 percent) of the country's 33 million people lived in towns and dispersed villages of less than 50,000 inhabitants. In contrast, only 16 percent of the total population lived in intermediate-sized urban areas (between 50,000 and 1 million) in 1950, compared to over 30 percent in 1991 (Erbiti 1993; República Argentina 1991). Rural to urban migration continues unabated in Argentina, with sophisticated, cosmopolitan, and Europeanized Buenos Aires the ultimate destination of many migrants.

The Evolution of Argentina's Megacity

Buenos Aires' history spans over 400 years and incorporates myriad events, personalities, and spatial changes, some more important than others in shaping the city. This capsule review of the city's evolution focuses on three important periods. It sets the stage for a more detailed examination of the four elements critical to the contemporary restructuring process detailed at the beginning of the chapter.

From Genesis to the Railroad (1580-1880). Buenos Aires' first genesis in 1536 proved short-lived. The expedition of Pedro de Mendoza from Spain to the Río de la Plata estuary was motivated by the Spanish Crown's desire to establish a strategic foothold in the southern regions of the New World. By 1541 the tiny settlement on the right bank of the estuary had been abandoned in favor of a more secure location inland at present-day Asunción. Four decades later, an expedition led by Juan de Garay arrived back in the estuary from Asunción and reestablished the settlement. Buenos Aires took shape slowly on the only stretch of high ground along the estuary's right bank that allowed protection from flooding, a deep anchorage for ocean-going vessels, and a source of fresh water.

Spanish rules on town construction, specifically the Laws of the Indies promulgated in 1573, guided the initial form of Buenos Aires. Juan de Garay and his followers laid out a rectangular grid of 15 blocks by 9 blocks and proceeded to construct a fort, church, jail, and *cabildo* (municipal council chamber). By 1600, the settlement held approximately 1,100 people, although it occupied a relatively insignificant position in Spain's South American empire. Commercial power in the New World centered on Lima, Mexico City, and the Caribbean ports, and all trade with the Southern Cone had to proceed along a highly circuitous route via the Pacific Coast and the Caribbean (see Figure 2.1). Although Buenos Aires offered a shorter route via the South Atlantic to the rich silver mines of Potosí, the Spanish Crown argued it could not provide adequate protection during the long land and sea voyage.

Buenos Aires' isolated location at the end of the long trunk route from Peru gave the growing town some measure of autonomy and economic self-sufficiency. However, when the Portuguese founded the trading center of Côlonia dô Sacramento across the Plata estuary from Buenos Aires in 1680, the significance of the fledgling city changed dramatically. Against the backdrop of an emerging European world economy and political rivalry between European states, Buenos Aires grew in importance as a regional entrepôt, a defensive site against Portuguese and English economic and territorial incursions, and as a gateway city to the exportable resources of the interior. Slave trading and silver smuggling provided the economic foundation for Buenos Aires' growth during the early eighteenth century. Later in the century, the ideal habitat of the pampas grasslands provided a new foundation for growth and change. With the rapid multiplication of horses and cattle on the flat, open pampas, animal hides and fats became the backbone of the urban economy.

As Buenos Aires grew in importance toward the end of the eighteenth century, an antagonistic relationship with the interior towns of the West and Northwest regions began to develop. Commercial interests in the interior controlled much of the region's trade and were linked symbiotically to the economic fortunes of the Potosí silver mines and of Peru. Any economic gain by Buenos Aires was viewed as a loss by the interior merchants and vice versa. Moreover, urban development proceeded more rapidly in Buenos Aires than in the interior settlements, in part because of the port city's strategic location, its access to the pampas, and both legal and illegal trade with other European powers.

The entire spatial dynamic of Spain's South American empire underwent dramatic restructuring in 1776 as part of the Spanish Crown's attempts to reap greater bounty from its colonies. The Crown created a new administrative region called the Viceroyalty of the Río de la Plata centered on Buenos Aires, which would control territory that included present-day Bolivia, Paraguay, Uruguay, most of Argentina, and parts of northern Chile. Buenos Aires now dominated all economic, political, and military activities for thousands of miles. This territorial reorganization had tragic consequences for the northwestern settlements, as trade and social links with Bolivia and Peru were gradually replaced by stronger links to the Buenos Aires and the Atlantic coast.

Conflict between the interior and Buenos Aires over control of the region accelerated with the collapse of Spain's empire and the independence movements of the early nineteenth century. Political clashes between Federalists, who tried to preserve regional autonomy and protect interior economies, and Unitarists, who favored a strong central government in Buenos Aires, plagued the emerging nation for over 60 years. During this period, Buenos Aires and its immediate hinterland grew by leaps and bounds, while the interior regions stagnated and sank slowly into a morass of poverty, isolation, and economic underdevelopment. By the 1860s, the population of Buenos Aires had surpassed 160,000, nearly 10 percent of the country's total population. New technologies began to reshape the urban landscape as British investment capital spurred the construction of trolleys, railroads, and port facilities.

Railroads and Urban Expansion (1880-1930). Buenos Aires emerged in 1880 as Argentina's federal capital with the creation of a 200-square-kilometer Federal District. Propelled by urban transport improvements and an agricultural revolution on the pampas, both Buenos Aires and Argentina became incorporated more fully into the world economy. During this golden age of Argentina's development, two powerful mythologies arose that have shaped development ideologies and policies to this day: the myth of Europeanness, which argued that Buenos Aires represented the civilized, modernized European world while the interior remained barbaric and backward, and the myth of that which is good for Buenos Aires is good for Argentina. In other words, the entire country should aspire to develop in the image of the sophisticated, cosmopolitan, Europeanized capital.

Paris provided a template for urban planners and managers in the late-nineteenth and early-twentieth centuries as they attempted to provide Hispanic colonial Buenos Aires with a more Parisian feel. Colonial buildings and narrow streets were replaced by broad, paved avenues reminiscent of the Champs d'Elysées (Figure 6.2). European architectural styles influenced heavily the construction of new public and private buildings in the downtown core (Figure 6.3), and the British modeled the city's transportation infrastructure after their own. European immigrants flooded into the city and changed its ethnic, linguistic, and class structures. Most of Argentina's proto-industrial activities were concentrated in and around the city, providing jobs and social advancement to the thousands of migrants (Walter 1982).

More than any other technology in the nineteenth century, railroads changed the face of Buenos Aires. Charles Sargent (1974) illustrated how innovations in transportation, real estate development, and population growth coalesced between 1880 and 1930 to transform the city into a modern and dynamic urban center. By 1900, the Federal District boasted a dense network of tramways that linked the major neighborhoods to the commercial-bureaucratic downtown core. A series of railroad lines that linked more distant areas to five major downtown terminals supplemented the tram network The first subway line constructed in Latin America entered service in Buenos Aires during December 1913 and became another important symbol of the city's sophistication and development. City managers proudly boasted that accessibility and mobility in the city rivaled Paris, London, or New York. By contrast, most people in the interior towns still moved around by horse and cart or on foot, a century removed from the dynamic capital of Buenos Aires.

Over the 50-year period of Argentina's Golden Age, the population of Buenos Aires grew 14-fold. By 1930, the capital held over three million people and it had become the largest city in Latin America. Internally, the city had evolved spatially into three clearly demarcated zones. To the

FIGURE 6.2   Avenida 9 de Julio in Central Buenos Aires.

FIGURE 6.3   Parisian-Style Architecture in Central Buenos Aires.

north, the wealthier urbanites inhabited the mansions and *quintas* (suburban estates) of Barrio Norte, Palermo and Belgrano. Near the city center and west of the Plaza Congreso could be found the middle-class neighborhoods of Flores, Almagro, and Caballito. The industrial and manufacturing *barrios* (neighborhoods) of Avellaneda, Barracas, and La Boca to the south housed the bulk of Buenos Aires' working class. Land speculation encouraged by railroad expansion pushed the boundaries of the city ever outward as new *barrios* sprang up along the suburban railroad lines that splayed out from the Federal District. As few zoning or planning regulations existed, subdivisions frequently were created with few basic facilities. Developers did not view the provision of street lights, water pipes, paved roads, and sewer lines as part of their mission. Lack of planning during the initial stages of Buenos Aires' urban expansion thus laid the foundation for the crisis of inadequate basic public services that currently plagues the city.

Automobiles and the Middle-Class City (1930-1990). During the 1930s, political crises in Argentina, combined with a global economic depression and, later, the outbreak of World War II, brought to an end the golden age of development. Import substitution industrialization (ISI) policies were introduced to allow Argentina more national economic flexibility in a changing world. These policies favored the Buenos Aires metropolitan area. Moreover, after 1945, the government of Juan Domingo Perón began to reshape Buenos Aires society by improving worker benefits, housing, and jobs in the public sector. A strong and broad-based middle-class sector developed in the city. However, as industry grew and agricultural production declined, jobs and a better standard of living became available only in the major urban centers and primarily in Buenos Aires.

Coupled with deteriorating transport infrastructure in the interior and development strategies that favored the capital, Perón's urban policies encouraged massive rural-urban migration. Between 1947 and 1951, for example, 200,000 people annually migrated to Greater Buenos Aires from interior provinces. With little housing available in the Federal District, most migrants ended up moving to the rapidly expanding suburban *partidos* to find temporary shelter in *villas miserias* (shantytowns). During the next four decades, the population of Buenos Aires exploded from under five million to nearly 13 million, with almost all of this growth occurring beyond the boundaries of the Federal District. Moreover, the spatial dynamics of mobility in the city changed as the metropolitan area grew, and automobiles, roads, and freeways slowly replaced the tramways, trolley buses, and railroads as the primary means of transportation (Figure 6.4).

The adaptation of megacities to new socioeconomic functions through the rearrangement of transport supply is a widespread phenomenon of the twentieth century. Wolfgang Schivelbusch (1986) traced the process back to the transformation of Paris in the late-nineteenth century by Baron Georges Haussmann. Los Angeles, in the United States, stands out as a classic example of profound urban restructuring in order to accommodate large roadway systems and the automobile (Barret 1983). Here, transit policies considered public transportation a private business, and automobiles quickly replaced Los Angeles' extensive streetcar system. Recent changes in the world economy have helped to redefine the role of megacities, and many are turning anew toward public transport solutions to accessibility and mobility problems. In Buenos Aires, automobiles and freeways became a central part of urban planning ideologies from the 1950s onwards, as the United States exerted more economic and cultural influence on Argentina and as the domestic automobile industry expanded. Ownership and use of an automobile were promoted as the "Holy Grail" of an urban, middle-class lifestyle and as a metaphor for class status, economic power, and development progress. During the 1970s, automobiles became the most important form of consumption for the middle class, and their increased use influenced the construction of several major freeways in the downtown core.

In the 1980s and early 1990s, changes to the urban form and function of Buenos Aires were driven primarily by internal forces. However, immigrants from Europe, Asia, and Latin America continued to have a significant impact on the built environment by influencing the style of homes, businesses, and religious structures (Figure 6.5). Increasing numbers of squatters and shantytown dwellers, mostly from the interior and contiguous countries, crowded into any available space in the city, especially into areas close to the downtown commercial center. A concentration of service, financial, and tourist activities within the Federal District encouraged the densification and northward expansion of the commercial-bureaucratic core. On the fringes of the metropolitan area, country clubs and middle-class estates developed as improved road conditions made commuting easier and quicker. Few major infrastructural changes occurred within the city, except for some property speculation, facilities for the elite, or private projects such as tourist hotels. Public service infrastructure remained neglected and continued to deteriorate rapidly. By 1990, Argentina had sunk again into an economic crisis of epic proportions. Spurred by this crisis and by

FIGURE 6.4 Traffic Flow Near Retiro in Central Buenos Aires.

FIGURE 6.5 Eastern Orthodox Church in San Telmo, Buenos Aires.

profound changes in the global political and economic order, the newly elected government of Carlos Menem looked for fresh solutions to the problems of both city and nation.

Contemporary Buenos Aires

During the early 1990s, Buenos Aires started to emerge from the shadows of Argentina's long-term instability to reassert itself in the regional and global urban network. Globalization strategies in the form of free-market economic policies, regional economic alliances, state disengagement from most aspects of industry and service, and rapprochement with neighboring states now are reshaping the socioeconomic fabric of the city. Buenos Aires is changing in profound and fundamental ways as the federal government charts what it hopes is a new, more productive course through the stormy waters of the world economy. However, juxtaposed against the optimism and successes of economic restructuring are the realities of managing a megacity. Environmental degradation, rising unemployment, declining health and social welfare, social polarization, deindustrialization, collapsing infrastructure, and grinding poverty for increasing numbers of people are posing serious challenges to city managers and residents alike.

Debate rages in Argentina over whether globalization of the economy is responsible for declines in the national quality of life. Some argue that the Menemization (the term frequently used to describe President Menem's policies) of the country has destroyed the urban middle class and has accelerated the latinamericanization of Argentina. Buenos Aires and Argentina now must address problems more typical of other developing Latin American countries rather than problems typical of developed European states. Others point out that these policies are the only acceptable medicine for a country suffering from decades of social, political, and economic malaise. Stability in the national currency has been achieved by pegging the peso to the U.S. dollar on a one-for-one basis and annual inflation rates have been reduced to low single digits. Business has become more efficient, tax revenues have increased, foreign investment is flowing into the country, and infrastructural needs are being addressed through privatization. Yet Buenos Aires has become the most expensive city in Latin America and second only to New York in the hemisphere (Table 6.1). Moreover, as detailed in the preceding chapters, unemployment rates are high, industrial jobs have disappeared, and hundreds of thousands of people have fallen into poverty.

TABLE 6.1 The Cost of Living in the Major Cities of Latin America Compared to New York, 1994

City	Country	Cost of Living Index
New York	United States	100
Buenos Aires	Argentina	92
Rio de Janeiro	Brazil	85
São Paulo	Brazil	83
México City	México	81
Panamá City	Panamá	76
Montevideo	Uruguay	75
Guatemala City	Guatemala	74
Bogotá	Colombia	71
Lima	Perú	70
San José	Costa Rica	68
Santiago	Chile	68
Quito	Ecuador	67
Asunción	Paraguay	64
Caracas	Venezuela	47

Source: *Latin American Weekly Report* (1995).

Potential changes in the social, economic, and spatial environments of Buenos Aires over the coming decade will depend greatly on how well government and residents address the following critical issues. First, can the various political jurisdictions of the Buenos Aires metropolitan region coordinate policies and goals to plan and manage effectively this growing megacity? Second, can the city meet the growing demand for adequate housing and basic public services? This issue is particularly critical given that migration to Buenos Aires from the interior provinces and from poorer neighboring states is unlikely to abate dramatically in the coming years. Third, how will levels of accessibility and mobility change in the city as a consequence of privatization and deregulation strategies? Finally, what strategies are under development to address the environmental deterioration of the city? Some of the more obvious byproducts of megacephalous urban growth are air pollution, water contamination, excessive solid waste, and unprocessed human wastes. Buenos Aires must contend with all of these problems and more as it tries to balance socioeconomic restructuring with improvements in the quality of life.

Planning and Managing a Megacity

Defining the exact areal extent of contemporary Buenos Aires is an important first step in discussing the planning and urban management process. What are the formal, functional, and even perceptual boundaries of the metropolitan area? Historically, metropolitan Buenos Aires comprised the Federal District and the nineteen *partidos* surrounding the core. Argentina's National Census Institute (INDEC) long has relied on this definition when publishing data about the city. Megacephalous growth during the 1960s and 1970s, however, led planners and others to incorporate Greater La Plata and six other *partidos* (the middle suburbs) into their definitions of Greater Buenos Aires. In addition, strategies outlined in 1978 by the Department of Planning and Development (SEPLADE) for the modernization of Buenos Aires included the 23 counties of the outer suburbs in definitions of the metropolitan axis (SEPLADE 1978) (Figure 6.6). SEPLADE's boundary around the city's urbanized and semi-urbanized territory coincides generally with the northwest to southeast course of the Río Salado, west of Buenos Aires, and with the Río Paraná and its delta to the north. Moreover, discussions with residents of the outer suburbs and with geographers and planners in Buenos Aires suggest that there is a strong perception in the urban periphery of "attachment" to the city of Buenos Aires. Throughout the twentieth century, Buenos Aires has been a mecca for migrants from the interior and from neighboring countries. Most of these migrants believe that they are an integral part of the functional city, despite the physical distance that separates them from the downtown core.

In the 1990s, many geographers, planners, and urban managers agree that the framework for planning and managing urban growth and change in Buenos Aires should incorporate the territory defined by SEPLADE. This definition of Buenos Aires makes sense for a number of reasons. It acknowledges that the dynamics of development in the city have spatial implications that reach beyond the boundaries of the Federal District and the original 19 *partidos*. Incorporating the middle and outer suburbs provides a sound basis for integrated strategies designed to address the spatial distribution of growth in the metropolitan region. SEPLADE's definition also recognizes the urban interdependencies, transportation patterns, and interlinked associations of establishments that help to shape functional relationships in the entire Greater Buenos Aires region. Finally, it lays the foundation for a coordinated approach to confronting the political, economic, and social tensions that result from the involvement of

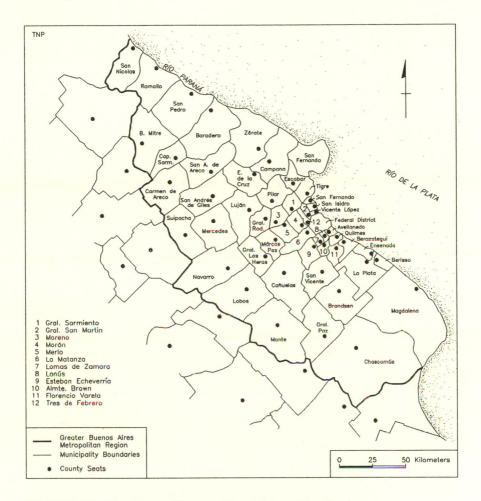

FIGURE 6.6   The Greater Buenos Aires Metropolitan Region.
Source: SEPLADE (1978).

Argentina's megacity in the world economy and in the system of world cities (Keeling 1996).

Management of the Greater Buenos Aires metropolitan area is fragmented between national, provincial, and local bureaucracies, an interjurisdictional body, and several quasi-governmental organizations. Herein lies the root of Buenos Aires' urban management problems. The Federal government maintains jurisdiction over the Federal District and has operational power over interjurisdictional matters. The District's legislative body is elected directly by city residents, but is controlled politically by the national legislature. Situations have arisen whereby the mayor, a Presidential appointee, often comes from a political party different from the controlling group in the legislature. Such a situation can seriously complicate the administrative process within the Federal District. Buenos Aires' urban management problem is exacerbated by the absence of any functional administrative territorial subdivisions, zones, or regions to govern the three million people who live within the Federal District.

Forty-seven very distinct *barrios* (neighborhoods) comprise the 200-square kilometer Federal District (Figure 6.7). Within these official neighborhoods, dozens of other smaller *barrios*, essentially clusters of high-rise government apartments, have clearly defined identities. Population levels within these 47 *barrios* have remained mostly stable since the 1950s, although depopulation has become evident in the poorer southern areas. The Constitution of 1949 granted to the president of Argentina all power over the Federal District, with no provision for input from the electorate over the appointment of the *intendente* (mayor). However, as part of the Menem government's political restructuring program, direct elections for the office of mayor took place for the first time in June 1996. The incumbent *intendente*, a Menem political appointee, campaigned hard during the first half of the year, cleaning up city streets, beautifying parks, and pledging to restore some of Buenos Aires' former splendor. However, in a close race, Fernando de la Rua from the opposition Radical party won the election to become the first elected mayor of Buenos Aires (Sims 1996). Menem's restructuring program also intends to reduce the Federal District's bureaucracy from 100,000 to 70,000 by the end of the decade. In the early 1990s, approximately 90 percent of the Buenos Aires City Council budget went to provide salaries and allowances for councillors (*Buenos Aires Herald* April 24, 1993).

The government of the Province of Buenos Aires headquartered in La Plata administers the 51 *partidos* that comprise Greater Buenos Aires. Each of the municipalities that constitute Greater Buenos Aires has an elected mayor and a legislative body. Similar problems occur in the suburban *partidos* as in the Federal District, with clashes between mayors and legislative bodies from opposing political parties frequently frustrating the planning and management process. In addition, the policy goals of the Buenos Aires provincial government are not always in accord with the goals of the Federal District or with the unique needs of the entire metropolitan region. The National Environmental Commission of the Buenos

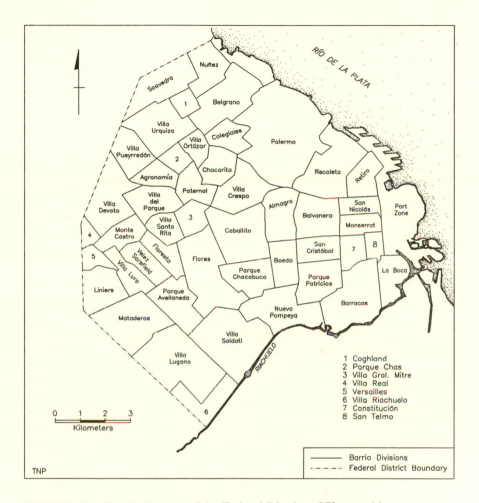

FIGURE 6.7   The 47 *Barrios* of the Federal District of Buenos Aires.
Source: República Argentina (1991).

Aires Metropolitan Area (CONAMBA), established in 1987, has attempted to coordinate interjurisdictional relationships between the Province of Buenos Aires and the City of Buenos Aires. Unfortunately, CONAMBA lacks any real political power and it has failed to promote any meaningful policy dialogue between the myriad bureaucracies involved in managing the megacity. For example, historically the federal government has controlled the public enterprises that provide infrastructural services (energy, transportation, sanitation, water, etc.) in the metropolitan region, although both provincial and local governments have input into the process. Yet the physical and contextual jurisdictions of these enterprises rarely have corresponded, and massive operating inefficiencies and inequities have been the inevitable result. Beginning in 1991, Menem's privatization program began to replace uncoordinated government-run public services with privately run public services, which now are experiencing the same coordination problems. Thus, although ownership has changed, service inefficiencies and infrastructural inadequacies remain for huge sections of the city's population. In addition, even though privatization and deregulation policies have created new and clearly defined operating arenas for public services, regulatory power still rests with a combination of federal, provincial, and local authorities, none of whom have any clearly enunciated or coordinated regulatory policies.

In contemporary Buenos Aires, no clear, integrated, urban management plans or strategies exist. Bureaucratic relationships between the city's different territorial units are fraught with territorial rivalries, petty jealousies, ideological differences, rampant corruption, and a lack of long-term urban planning and management goals. Most planners and policy makers agree that a megacity of 13 million people should not be managed in such a piecemeal and fragmented manner. Buenos Aires desperately needs a management plan that treats the entire metropolitan region as a single, integrated functional unit. Unfortunately, the science of city and regional planning is not well developed in Argentina and little progress has been made in recent decades toward the development of sound, long-term, coordinated urban management policies.

Public officials and private citizens alike in Buenos Aires often consider the term "urban management" an oxymoron, and they long have bemoaned the ills of unrestrained development, bureaucratic corruption, the lack of land-use controls, air pollution, shantytown growth, and inadequate public services. Yet despite these urban management weaknesses, megacities like Buenos Aires, as Alan Gilbert (1994) argued so persuasively, have absorbed millions of people since 1945 without suffering a major disaster or social revolution. Buenos Aires continues to suffer, of course, from incredible waste and inefficiencies, unacceptable levels of corruption, and often total incompetence in the urban management arena. Overall though, Buenos Aires' urban managers and planners have coped reasonably well with growth and change in recent decades. The real problem for the metropolitan area is the political, economic, and social context within which urban planning and management takes place. Management and planning policies consistently are stymied by a lack of political will, resources, training and, most importantly, funding to contain and manage urban growth. Moreover, the failure to define clearly the megacity's spatial limits and components has encouraged a fragmented and haphazard approach to urban management issues.

Jorge Hardoy (1972) argued over two decades ago that the structured growth of Buenos Aires was a national problem that required planning and policy making within a broad national context. The capital has such a major impact over the entire country that careful planning for Buenos Aires is critical to Argentina's national development. However, a lack of planning for orderly urban growth in Buenos Aires has plagued both city and nation ever since the 1880s. City plans have been around since the 1900s, but they generally have been unconnected, ineffective, and frequently ignored. Zoning or land-use planning laws are either non-existent or extremely weak, resulting in a veritable hodgepodge of buildings, functions, and activities across all parts of the city. There exists a lack of continuity in planning and policy matters, which is further exacerbated by public disinterest in urban management issues. Coupled with the jurisdictional problems described previously, the unbridled expansion of Buenos Aires since the 1940s has resulted in an urban management crisis of astounding proportions.

Housing. A lack of sufficient and adequate housing has plagued planners and city managers in Buenos Aires for much of the twentieth century. Inadequate housing, however, started to become a serious problem after the 1950s, when industrial concentration in the Pampeana and poor investment strategies in the interior encouraged tremendous rural to urban migration flows. According to a report by the Regional Office of Metropolitan Area Development, in 1960 only 1.6 million residential units were available in Greater Buenos Aires to accommodate 2 million families (República Argentina 1969). To address the chronic shortage of housing in the city, the federal government created the National Housing Fund (FONAVI) in 1972 under the supervision of the Ministry of Social Welfare. A special tax of between 2.5 and 5 percent on gross wages paid in the city would provide funding for FONAVI housing projects. These funds were designated for the construction of low-rent apartments for the urban poor, although preferential treatment on the apartment waiting lists is not guaranteed by low-income status. In addition, FONAVI has struggled to maintain compliance of the wage-tax payment since its inception. Many employers, including the federal government, fail to collect or remit the wage tax; thus FONAVI remains constantly short of capital. Coupled with FONAVI's ongoing problems, inflation, land speculation, a land shortage in the inner suburbs, and government ineptitude continue to affect public housing construction programs negatively, forcing migrants and others to seek alternate housing solutions.

In the inner city *barrios* of La Boca and San Telmo, and in the industrial suburbs of Avellaneda, Lanús, La Matanza, Tres de Febrero, and General San Martín, much of the housing stock is old, dilapidated, deteriorating, and without adequate services. Jorge Mochkowsky (1991) argued that the failure of Argentina's government to address deteriorating housing conditions is part of the new free-market economic philosophy. As the economy of Buenos Aires opens up to global forces, property speculation and increased land-rent values are playing key roles in restructuring the city's landscape. Government officials theorize that economic liberalization forces will encourage land and property speculation around the city, thus raising the value of land. In turn, increased land values will encourage new privately funded office, shopping, and apartment complexes. *Barrios* such as San Telmo and Montserrat that are close to the financial and institutional center of Buenos Aires have become prime targets for property speculation and urban renewal, with neighborhoods such as Balvanera, Constitución, and Retiro a close second. Expulsion of the poor and the working class from the downtown core thus becomes a key component of the successful restructuring and modification of land use in Buenos Aires.

Liberalization of Argentina's economy also is helping to create a situation in the urban housing market of Buenos Aires whereby several conflicting forces are coming into play. Economically disadvantaged residents of the inner city are forced to move out to the suburbs through increasing rents, property speculation, restrictions on illegal building occupation (squatting), and a lack of low-income housing construction. Yet in the suburbs, the loss of industrial employment and continued inefficiencies in public transport have forced many lower income residents to seek jobs and housing in the inner city. Service, financial, and administrative jobs are more readily available in the downtown core than in the suburbs. The economically disadvantaged, therefore, are caught in a vicious circle. Moreover, many wealthier middle-class urbanites are buying property and joining country clubs in the outer suburbs because cheaper automobiles and better urban highways allow for rapid commuting to the city center. At the same time, a lack of basic public services, rising crime rates, and massive traffic jams are encouraging other suburbanites to purchase or rent one of the many new luxury apartments under construction in the northern *barrios* of the Federal District. Thus, two circular patterns of movement are at work within the Greater Buenos Aires metropolitan area, each creating friction with the other. Many wealthier suburbanites are moving back to the inner city while their potential neighbors are moving out to exclusive neighborhoods in the suburbs, and the inner city poor are being forced out to the suburbs but need to be close to the Federal District to find suitable employment. As a result, throughout Buenos Aires luxury high-rise apartments and suburban estates are juxtaposed against rudimentary forms of shelter lacking any basic services and clusters of low-income housing.

Sixty-nine percent of the population within the Federal District resides in apartments and 25.3 percent resides in single-family houses. This concentration of people in high-rise apartments accounts for the high overall density rate of 14,805 people per square kilometer in the inner city. Housing type occupation statistics for the 19 *partidos* (counties) of the inner suburbs show a very different picture (República Argentina 1991). Only 12.7 percent of the total population in the nineteen inner suburbs of Buenos Aires lived in apartments in 1991. Seventy-five percent lived in single-family homes, while another 10 percent lived in farms and cabins. Population densities per housing unit are much higher in the suburbs than in the inner city, although overall population density in the inner suburbs was only 2,160 people per square kilometer. Housing shortages continue to be a problem. Argentina's 1991 census recorded that the total number of households in the Federal District of Buenos Aires exceeded the number of available housing units by over 45,000, while in the inner suburbs of the city there were 89,000 more households than available housing units.

A clear spatial imbalance exists between the provision of basic services in the Federal District and in the inner suburbs. For example, over 95 percent of the houses in the Federal District have running water and direct sewer connections (Table 6.2). In contrast, barely 25 percent of the population in the 19 inner suburbs have direct access to both running water and a sewer. A staggering 3.5 million people in the suburbs are without sewer service or running water. To address the problem of inadequate water facilities in Buenos Aires, the government has privatized the city's water system. A consortium led by France's Lyonnaise des Eaux now operates Aguas Argentinas and it plans to provide potable water to every Buenos Aires resident by the year 2023. The private company already has constructed two water filtration plants, 77 kilometers of underground pipelines,

TABLE 6.2. Availability of Services in the Home in Buenos Aires, 1991

Political Division	Total	Running Water and Sewer	Only Running Water		Sewer Only	No Running Water or Sewer	Unknown
			With Toilet	Without Toilet			
Federal District							
Houses	978,330	936,251	5,183	15,306	635	156	20,799
Households	1,023,464	970,969	5,748	18,981	659	182	26,925
Population	2,871,519	2,714,532	20,224	64,725	1,734	555	69,749
Percentage	100	94.54	0.70	2.25	0.06	0.02	2.43
19 Inner Suburbs							
Houses	2,083,676	588,178	484,723	40,863	41,366	824,189	104,357
Households	2,172,716	606,928	506,606	42,511	42,819	858,065	115,787
Population	7,924,424	1,975,000	1,821,574	172,433	155,648	3,397,037	402,732
Percentage	100	24.92	22.99	2.18	1.96	42.87	5.08

Source: República Argentina (1994).

and nine pumping stations (Wright 1996). Moreover, plans have been formulated to establish a network of wastewater treatment facilities around the Greater Buenos Aires to solve the problem of water pollution and raw sewage dumping in the cities streams and rivers.

Lack of access to basic services such as sewer facilities and potable water is most acute in the *villas miserias* that lie along the banks of Buenos Aire's streams and rivers. Here, disease is a constant problem and water pollution adds to the misery that the residents of these shantytowns must endure on a daily basis. Urban shantytowns have become the archetypal symbol of modern Latin American housing, yet few of these settlements existed in Buenos Aires before 1950 (Gilbert 1994). Those that did exist generally were small and located relatively close to the downtown core. Between the 1950s and the 1990s, the population living in *villas miserias* in Buenos Aires exploded from less than 100,000 to over one million as rural migrants flooded into the capital. In the mid-1990s, approximately ten percent of the city's population lived in some form of self-help housing. Inside the Federal District, for example, over 51,000 people lived in *villas miserias* in 1994, occupying some 12,000 houses that covered about 1.38 square kilometers. The exact number of people living in substandard housing conditions across the entire Greater Buenos Aires Metropolitan Area is unknown, but estimates from government officials and private researchers put the number in excess of one million.

Most of the *villas miserias* are clustered along the banks of the Río de la Reconquista and the Río de la Matanza, and in the *partido* of Quilmes (see Figure 6.8). Riparian land often is the primary target of self-help settlers because it is almost always undeveloped, it often has little commercial value, and because the various government bodies in Buenos Aires have little motivation to enforce land use controls (Keeling 1996). Within the Federal District, *villas miserias* are found in the poorer southern neighborhoods and near the city's major transportation center of Retiro. The area around Retiro is an attractive location from squatters and shantytown dwellers alike because of its proximity to major transportation centers, the docks area, and surrounding businesses and upscale residences (Figure 6.9). Moreover, one of the pull factors encouraging the growth of *villas miserias* in the city center over the past decade has been the ongoing deterioration of public transport services.

Accessibility and Mobility. Since the late nineteenth century, Buenos Aires has been endowed with one of the best urban transport networks in

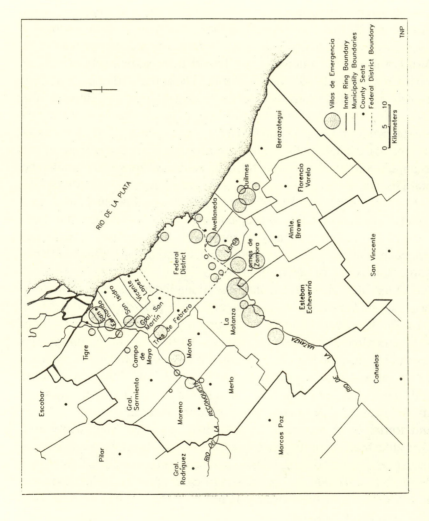

FIGURE 6.8 Location of *Villas Miserias* in Greater Buenos Aires, 1994. *Source:* After Torres (1993).

FIGURE 6.9 Retiro Transportation Complex and the Buenos Aires Skyline.
Source: Courtesy of Juan A. Roccatagliata.

Latin America, despite the chronic inefficiencies and poor infrastructure that plague the system. Suburban railroads particularly encouraged the type of urban sprawl experienced by the industrialized countries of Europe and by the United States. A dendritic urban network developed that splayed out from terminals in the Federal District to the growing inner, and later outer, suburbs (Figure 6.10). Moreover, railroads helped a property-owning, mobile urban middle class to develop in Buenos Aires (Sargent 1974). Electric trams in the city center facilitated high levels of accessibility and mobility during the early decades of the twentieth century and encouraged population densification in many of the inner-city *barrios*. Subways and an expanded urban bus network also improved the interaction of people, goods, and information throughout the Greater Buenos Aires Metropolitan Area. However, investment in urban public transport declined rapidly after the 1950s. Increased levels of private automobile use linked to a growing middle-class sector, along with service inefficiencies, chronic labor problems, bureaucratic ineptitude, and rampant fare evasion in public transit, all contributed to steady declines in ridership.

In 1982, 75 percent of all passenger traffic in the Greater Buenos Aires

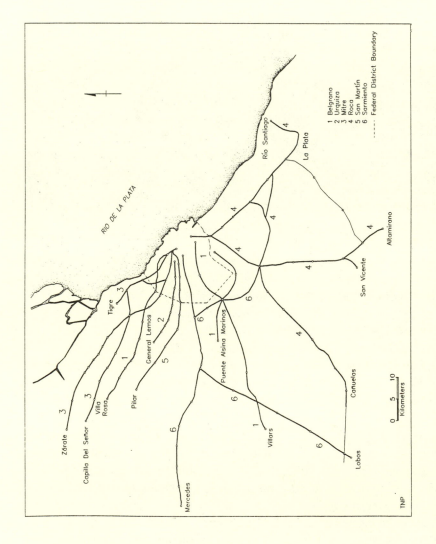

FIGURE 6.10 Suburban Railroad Network in Buenos Aires, 1993. *Source: After Stoetzel (1993).*

Metropolitan Region moved by road, with suburban railroads handling 16 percent, and subways 8 percent of the remaining traffic. A decade later, the suburban railroads' share of urban traffic movements had fallen to 8 percent, while road traffic had increased its share to 84 percent. Despite the considerable change in modal split during the 1980s, about the same number of passengers, 2.6 billion, were transported within the Greater Buenos Aires metropolitan region in 1993 compared to 1980 (República Argentina 1994). The most staggering growth in urban traffic over the past 15 years has been in the number of private automobiles used for daily commuting. Few concrete statistics exist on the total number of daily trips generated by private automobiles in Buenos Aires, but local newspapers and city planners suggest that over one million cars move in and out of the inner city each weekday (*Buenos Aires Herald* May 1994). Add to this figure another one million buses, trucks, and taxis each weekday that vie for precious space on the city's roads and conditions are ripe for congestion, pollution, and accidents.

Poor urban planning and development since the 1950s, coupled with a deterioration in the city's public transport system, have compounded contemporary traffic problems in Buenos Aires. Modern urban traffic does not mix well with the many narrow, colonial-era streets of the city center, in part because pedestrian sidewalks along these streets are extremely narrow and crowded much of the day. According to a scathing editorial in the May 13, 1994, issue of the *Buenos Aires Herald*, traffic congestion in the city must be blamed on engineers who have been:

> allowed to carry out all sorts of preposterous plans which have gouged out the living cores of many parts of the city, draining off the population into the suburbs so as to give way to the tyranny of the car. Whole chunks of the city have been demolished to build interchanges, flyovers, parking-lots and far from improving inner city traffic, such a policy has simply aggravated the matter further by pouring more vehicles into an ever-congested area.

The federal government responded to the growing congestion by passing the Traffic Emergency Law in May, 1994, which banned cars from the Federal District one day per week. This type of traffic calming has already been tried in other megacities, most notably Mexico City, but it has yet to have a significant impact on air quality, noise, or congestion. Government officials argued that the law would keep approximately 500,000 vehicles off the city's streets each weekday. Once again, however, planners demonstrated a piecemeal approach to problem solving. No long-term traffic management plans have been forthcoming to address the other 1.5 million vehicles that clog the Federal District's roads daily. Automobile circulation in the Federal District was restricted once before, between March 1974 and May 1976 in response to the global oil crisis, but the policy had little long-term effect on calming the city's traffic growth.

Accessibility and mobility problems in Buenos Aires are related closely to the spatial distribution of people within the city. As in most Latin American cities, the poor tend to live around the periphery and must rely heavily on public transport to reach jobs mostly found in the inner city. Until recently, wealthier *porteños* lived primarily within the boundaries ot the Federal District and relied almost exclusively on public transport. Since the 1980s, middle-class and wealthier suburbs have expanded into the urban periphery and automobile commuting from these suburbs has become the preferred method of reaching employment in the downtown area. Freeway construction and the improvement of major arterials throughout the city also has encouraged a shift away from public transit and into private automobiles.

Contributing to the mobility problem in Buenos Aires is the way that automobiles are mythologized and packaged for urban consumption. Private automobile ownership is portrayed as the pinnacle of middle-class achievement in Buenos Aires and is the dream of every poor immigrant and factory worker. Automobile ownership has become the metaphor for urban success. Argentina's government loudly proclaims the latest increases in automobile production at the Ford, Mercedes, or Volkswagen plants and supports the industry through a bewildering array of subsidies, tax incentives, and public infrastructure. In contrast, public transport has been starved of capital and left to fend for itself. Yet little mention is ever made of the billions of dollars spent on road construction and maintenance, which is a direct subsidy to the automobile sector. Railroads and subways must build and maintain their own rights of way at a substantial capital cost to that sector. Privatization of the city's subways and railroads since 1991 essentially has relieved the government from having to address the public transport problem. At stake for Buenos Aires from a transport-environment perspective, however, is the very essence of life in the megacity. Will the inner city become like Caracas, dissected by urban freeways and no longer with a definable historic urban core? Is Buenos Aires on the road to becoming choked daily with traffic and pollution, the Southern Cone's equivalent of México City? Unfortunately, absent a clear strategy for urban traffic calming and the revitalization of public transport facilities, these scenarios appear inevitable.

In many of the world's megacities, traffic planners are beginning to realize that growing demands for road space created by increased automobile use can never be met adequately. One of the automobile's greatest advantages in an urban environment--spatial flexibility--creates a monumental problem for transport planners. Roads and freeways tend to spread mobility and transport demand over a wide area, whereas public transport helps to concentrate movement along specific corridors. In addition, the enormous economic, social, and environmental costs of freeway construction have stimulated planners to reappraise the role of both freeways and public transport. New investment in light rail, traditional rail, buses, and bikeways in megacities like Buenos Aires could revitalize urban centers and redress the imbalance between public transport supply and demand (Keeling 1996). The current crisis of accessibility and mobility in Buenos Aires has reinforced the fact that monomodal solutions to transport problems are doomed to failure. Megacities such as Buenos Aires can only progress in an environmentally sustainable manner by engaging multimodal solutions to urban transport problems, solutions that address the problems of mobility for all segments of urban society.

Environmental Management. For much of the twentieth century, management of the physical environment in Buenos Aires has been piecemeal. Responsibilities typically have been divided among a number of government institutions and agencies. Difficulties in managing the city's environment are exacerbated because no "environmental problem" ever has been defined. There also is institutional confusion about how to address environmental issues and implement policies and about who should have responsibility for particular problems. As a result, the various components of environmental management in Buenos Aires are split between multiple jurisdictions and among multiple institutions, with little coordination between them (Pace 1992). Megacephalous growth over the past 50 years in Buenos Aires has occurred with few concerns for its environmental implications. Although laws frequently were passed to address garbage disposal, human waste, industrial effluents, air pollution, and other by-products of urbanization, enforcement remained negligible and sporadic. To make matters worse, constant political and economic turmoil between 1930 and 1990 pushed environmental concerns to the very bottom of the government's urban management agenda. In the contemporary climate of economic liberalization and privatization policies, environmental concerns are being subordinated to the overwhelming desire of individuals, institutions, and bureaucrats to incorporate both city and nation rapidly into the world economy. Economic growth in an expanding free-market global system is seen as critical to the future of Argentina. As a result, governments and planners merely pay lip-service to environmental issues. One of the more serious problems has been the reluctance of public, private, and foreign enterprises to invest in pollution awareness and reduction campaigns. Illegal toxic waste dumping, industrial effluent discharge into the urban waterways, exhaust emissions into the local atmosphere, and perhaps irreversible damage to the city's flora and fauna all continue to contribute to the environmental degradation of Buenos Aires.

In the Río Matanza-Riachuelo basin, for example, pollution has reached unheard of levels as a consequence of uncontrolled industrial and household wastes. The watershed covers 2,300 square kilometers and contains over 3.5 million people. Only 17 percent of the population that lives in the suburban *partidos* within the river basin has sewer service and only 55 percent has piped potable water. Studies have shown that high quantities of both illegal and legal untreated household and industrial wastes are discharged daily into the river system. Much of the daily discharge is water in a complete state of putrefaction (Brailovsky and Foguelman 1992). Analyses of the levels of dissolved oxygen in the Río Matanza have highlighted the serious nature of water pollution in Buenos Aires (Berón 1981). In the area around Dock Sud near the river's union with the Río de la Plata estuary, measurements revealed a ration of 0.0 mg of oxygen per 2 liters of water; a ratio of 2.5 mg per liter is the minimum level required for fish to survive. In other words, the river was essentially dead in its lower reaches. Moreover, since the 1980s pollution has worsened in this watershed!

The Menem government responded to concerns about the city's deteriorating environment in 1991 by creating the National Secretariat on Natural Resources and the Human Environment. To date, little evidence has emerged of the Secretariat articulating a comprehensive environmental strategy. At the non-governmental level, the environmental or ecological movement has grown since the return to democratic government in 1983. Unfortunately, a lack of previous experience and the absence of coordinated social organizations have limited the political role of the environmental movement in Buenos Aires. About 100 Non-Government Organizations (NGOs) are active on a continuous basis in the environmental arena, with activities that range from broader development issues to more focused habitat and ecological issues (Pace 1992). Compounding the problem for government and NGOs alike is that environmental issues rarely have been at the forefront of *porteño* concerns about the city. In 1993, Mansilla, Delich and Associates surveyed 600 city residents and found that the economy, political corruption, and rising unemployment were the most pressing urban concerns; environmental issues barely rated a mention *(Buenos Aires Herald* May 6, 1993, p. 11). Overcoming general apathy toward the state of Buenos Aires' environment remains a major challenge to the city's urban planners, managers, and environmental advocates.

The Future of the Megacity

The realities of contemporary global economic restructuring argue for a redefinition of development strategies for the world's megacities. As governments struggle to carve out a niche for both megacity and nation in the global system, they must be cognizant of the negative, neutral, and positive impacts of socioeconomic restructuring on people's lives. In Buenos Aires, planning and policy making should not occur in a vacuum, because the city plays a very important role in Argentina's spatial articulation at the national, regional, hemispheric, and global levels. If planners and policy makers ignore the centrifugal and centripetal implications of economic restructuring in Argentina for relationships along the local-global continuum, they invite the potential for serious urban crises in the immediate future. Argentina's democracy remains in a fragile condition and any major social upheavals in the nation's megacity could trigger serious challenges to the democratic process.

Perhaps the most sensitive issue to arise from Argentina's economic liberalization experiences to date is the ongoing marginalization of distinct segments of society and of certain neighborhoods in Buenos Aires. Social polarization in Buenos Aires is a reality, with increased numbers of people living in poverty, racism and crime on the increase, too many children dying from disease and starvation, suicides among the elderly at epidemic levels, and the once expansive middle-class sector squeezed by rising costs and declining incomes. Although the contemporary liberalization of Argentina's economy is having a differential impact on the class structure in Buenos Aires, any type of restructuring at the national, regional, or hemispheric level is likely to have similar effects. Some argue that capitalism in its current globalized form is the primary mechanism of social polarization within the world's megacities (Sassen 1991). There are bound to be winners and losers within the free-market capitalist system if governments pursue a *laissez faire* approach to social service provision. The problems of urban social polarization in a city the size of Buenos Aires can be addressed, however, only by instituting strong social services that mitigate potential damage to quality of life at the lower end of the capitalist spectrum. Economic liberalization strategies do not have neutral spatial impacts; the outcomes often are territorially and sectorally concentrated. Although Buenos Aires has managed to avoid some of the more serious social problems that characterize contemporary Lima, Mexico City, or Rio de Janeiro, current economic restructuring policies seem to be propelling the city down a development path from which there might be no easy or rapid return (Keeling 1996).

Argentina's political system poses real barriers to change in Buenos Aires. Federal, provincial, and municipal governments remain characterized by rampant corruption, personal power struggles, unethical corporate lobbying, and an almost messianic trust in the benefits of economic liberalization policies. Economic elites and administrative bureaucrats seem paralyzed by the recent economic success of liberalization policies and have yet to articulate a clear set of policies to address Buenos Aires' myriad problems. Although the long-term implications of Argentina's restructuring strategies are uncertain, there are some specific concerns that should be addressed immediately if both city and nation are to grow and change in a humanly and environmentally sustainable manner. First and foremost is the need for enhanced circulation and mobility for all sectors of Buenos Aires' society. Patterns of spatial bifurcation in Argentina will only be exacerbated absent an integrated, multimodal transport and communication system that binds both city and nation together. Buenos Aires could become fragmented even further between wealthy enclaves of globally connected urbanites and a turbulent sea of the poor and disenfranchised. In addition, the city could become increasingly disarticulated from the interior and from neighboring countries as global forces encourage the centralization of socioeconomic activities in Buenos Aires.

Second, a major focus on rehabilitating social infrastructure in Buenos Aires is needed. Public utilities, housing, access to educational facilities, and employment opportunities are fundamental to the ongoing development of the city. If basic social services continue to deteriorate in Buenos Aires, or at least fail to keep pace with demographic growth and change, a real potential exists for future social upheaval. Third, Buenos Aires desperately needs jurisdictional reform to allow for more holistic approaches to urban planning and management. Relying on a system of territorial management created a century ago makes little sense and only serves to highlight the inability of institutions and governments to adjust to the changing spatial dynamics of life in Argentina's megacity. Planners and policy makers must reevaluate the functional spatial boundaries of Buenos Aires within the context of local, regional, and national development problems. Finally, a partnership of trust is desperately needed in Buenos Aires between local, provincial, and federal governments, the business community, and city residents. Until the city's 13 million residents come to believe that elected officials and community leaders are striving to achieve a better quality of life for all segments of urban society, urban management in Buenos Aires will remain a zero sum game.

Throughout the twentieth century, Buenos Aires has evolved into the exclusive domain of privileged business interests, with an urban planning emphasis on industrial profits and a stable, protected economic environment. Since 1990, political, social, and economic ideologies have focused on the critically important goal of reshaping both Argentina and Buenos Aires into a competitive, free-market environment for the conduct of global commerce. Unfortunately, little attention has been paid to the short- and long-term social implications of economic liberalization policies. The development of broad-based, integrated social reform programs has been subordinated to the desire for economic order and progress in a free-market environment. Argentina's megacity continues to be wracked by severe social and environmental problems.

7

Prosperous Agroindustrial Provinces

Beyond the suburbs of Argentina's megacity lie the flat grasslands of the pampas and the prosperous agricultural provinces. The country's industrial, demographic, agricultural, and urban core extends approximately 750 kilometers from Buenos Aires to the north, west, and south, and can be divided into two important subregions: the Paraná-Plata urban-industrial corridor that extends from Greater La Plata to San Lorenzo just north of Rosario, and the agricultural-livestock zone of the Pampeana (Durán et al. 1995). Since the middle of the nineteenth century, the Pampeana has developed from what Larry Sawers (1996:17) termed "the useless pampas" into the socioeconomic heart and soul of Argentina. Within the limits of the Pampeana today reside nearly 70 percent of Argentina's total population, the majority of whom live in urban environments. Approximately 70 percent of the country's agricultural productivity emanates from the Pampeana, and the region contains nearly 80 percent of Argentina's industrial establishments and industrial workers. The bulk of Argentina's transportation infrastructure is located on the pampas and over three-quarters of the national gross domestic product is generated here (Daus and Yeannes 1992).

Globalization forces are changing the role of Argentina's prosperous agricultural provinces. This chapter examines the evolution of the Pampeana region from isolated frontier to economic heartland and addresses the major problems facing the region in the context of Argentina's global restructuring. Of particular importance are declining demands for the agricultural products of the pampas, a lack of alternate resource opportunities, and the problems of industrial and urban deconcentration.

The Pampeana Region

Government agencies typically include the provinces of Buenos Aires, Córdoba, La Pampa, Santa Fé, and Entre Ríos in descriptions of the Pampeana region (Figure 7.1). However, certain physical and economic characteristics help to define the limits of this prosperous agricultural area more sharply by excluding portions of these provinces. A narrow strip of Buenos Aires province that extends southward below the port city of Bahía Blanca lies beyond the climatic boundaries of the temperate pampas and is more properly included in the drier Patagonian region. This section lies between the 39th and 41st parallels and includes the delta of the Río Colorado.

The division between the Pampeana and the western interior provinces is quite arbitrary. A portion of San Luis province east of 65.5 degrees longitude and south of the 33rd parallel, including the two towns of Villa Mercedes and Buena Esperanza, should be included in definitions of the Pampeana. Although much drier than the central pampas, this area is dominated by cattle raising, grain production, and some oasis agriculture. In La Pampa province, only a small section of the northeast corner above the provincial capital of Santa Rosa receives more than 600 mm. of annual rainfall. West of the 65th meridian and south of the 37th parallel, rainfall is considered inadequate for the type of crops grown on the pampas (República Argentina 1994). Including all of La Pampa in the Pampeana statistical region thus presents some analytical problems because much of the province is desert-like, poor, and underdeveloped compared to the prosperous economic and agricultural core. Thus only the northeast corner is included.

The extreme northwestern corner of Córdoba province should be excluded from descriptions of the Pampeana core. The Sierras Pampeanas, with peaks ranging between 2000 and 2800 meters, lie west of the city of Córdoba and typically mark the end of the humid pampas. Finally, the northern sections of Entre Ríos and Santa Fé provinces above 31.5 degrees latitude also should be excluded from definitions of the Pampeana core. The land here is less fertile and more undulating, with a pronounced subtropical climate. Moreover, the major ports, industrial centers, and cities of these two provinces lie along the Río Paraná to the south, below the 31st parallel. In summary, the Pampeana region is characterized physically by a temperate climate, flat grasslands, fine-grained depositional (molisols) and wind-blown (loess) soils, an absence of mineral resources, and barely adequate drainage. Culturally and economically, the Pampeana contains

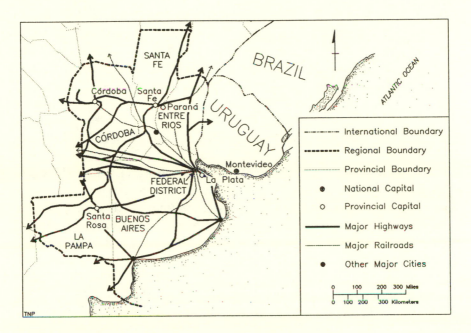

FIGURE 7.1   Provinces of the Pampeana Planning Region.

the bulk of Argentina's population, urban settlements, industrial centers, ports, and globally oriented commercial agricultural activities. Yet less than 140 years ago, in the early 1860s, the pampas remained a frontier or peripheral region of early post-colonial Argentina, largely undeveloped by Europeans.

From Colonial Backwater to Economic Core of Argentina

Throughout the colonial period, the pampas functioned as a physical barrier that separated the northwest and Andean settlements from the Atlantic coast. The region's major transportation route followed the Río Paraná north to present-day Rosario and then sliced across the flat landscape to Córdoba and on toward the northwest towns. A minor branch of this trunk route cut across the central pampas toward San Luis and Mendoza at the Andean foothills (see Figure 2.1). Small groups of semi-sedentary indigenous peoples inhabited much of the eastern pampas, hunting small deer, guanaco, and rhea. The Querandí, for example, occupied the right bank of the Río Paraná and resisted Spanish attempts to engage them in agricultural pursuits. Along the western and southwestern edges of the pampas lived the more advanced and aggressive relatives of the Chilean Araucanian peoples. These groups had adopted the horse and posed a substantial threat to Spanish expansion from the northwestern core (Scobie 1971). As late as 1780, Spanish control of the pampas extended barely 150 kilometers inland west from Buenos Aires and a few kilometers south of the secondary road that linked the Atlantic coast to San Luis and Mendoza.

Technology and a brutal military campaign against the indigenous peoples combined toward the end of the nineteenth century to turn the pampas from an isolated frontier to the economic backbone and core of Argentina. Technology transformed the pampas landscape and helped to incorporate Argentina fully into the world economy. Barbed wire for fences, windmills and tubemills for water, railroads for transportation, and new techniques for cattle raising and grain production created an export-oriented agricultural region that generated vast sums of capital surplus for the country's landed elite. Moreover, technology in the form of the repeating carbine and the railroad enabled the military to address seriously the "problem" of hostile indigenous groups. General Julio A. Roca's 1879 "Conquest of the Desert" eradicated the pampas of its indigenous groups by forcing them on to reservations or by killing them. Subsequent European colonization of the pampas between the 1880s and the 1910s dramatically changed the spatial dynamics of Argentina by shifting the country's political, economic, and demographic focus from the interior to the littoral.

The Pampeana and Buenos Aires Metropolitan regions accounted for less than 50 percent of Argentina's total population at the first national census in 1869. By 1914, over 70 percent of the national population resided in the Pampeana and Metropolitan regions. The interior cities of the Northwest and Northeast fell on hard times and remained firmly ensconced in a development time-warp, a century removed from the rapidly developing pampas. Agricultural processing industries sprang up in and around Buenos Aires and the port cities of Rosario, San Nicolás, and Bahía Blanca. A dense network of British-financed railroads snaked out across the flat pampas grasslands from terminals in Buenos Aires to capture the pampas' agricultural bounty. Foreign investment capital funded the infrastructure that helped to reconstruct the urban and rural landscapes of the pampas, and European migrants transformed the region's ethnic, social, political, economic, and cultural environments. Between 1900 and 1914, for example,

110,000 immigrants annually arrived in Argentina and almost all of them settled on the pampas in the major urban centers (Rock 1985). Agricultural exports from the pampas to a voracious world economy fueled the golden age of Argentina's growth and change and, by 1929, the country counted among the world's ten most affluent nations. Indeed, per capita income in the prosperous agricultural provinces probably ranked as high as in Canada and Australia (Waisman 1987; Sawers 1996).

Agriculture accounted for 27.1 percent of Argentina's gross domestic product between 1925 and 1929, but its overall share has continued to decline ever since. By the 1980s, agriculture had stabilized between 6 and 10 percent of GDP and currently it stands at approximately 7 percent (República Argentina 1994). The area of improved pampas land rose from 7.3 million to 27.2 million hectares between 1900 and 1930, but increased by only 200,000 hectares over the next 30 years as agriculture expanded into the interior provinces. Nonetheless, the Pampeana provinces in 1960 accounted for 90 percent of the 27.4 million hectares of improved land in Argentina (Crossley 1983). Nearly 90 percent of all the farms on the pampas were classified as smallholdings or family farms with less than 5 workers, and these farms accounted for approximately 45 percent of the total farm area. Pastoral activities and crops such as wheat, maize, and sunflower were the major components of the Pampeana's agricultural system.

Industrialization of the Pampeana

Global economic depression from 1929 to 1933, followed by six years of global conflict between 1939 and 1945, collapsed the demand for Argentina's agricultural exports. Successive governments in Argentina adopted import-substitution industrialization (ISI) policies as a response to changing world economic conditions. New factories and warehouses sprang up in and around the major pampas cities, particularly in Buenos Aires, to produce textiles, beer, furniture, and other similar non-capital intensive consumer goods. This does not mean, however, that industrial activities were unknown in the pampas cities prior to ISI. Proto-industrial development in Buenos Aires particularly had been underway since the end of the eighteenth century. ISI policies simply accelerated the development of the industrial sector and focused attention on the production of a broader range of consumer goods so as to be less reliant on imports. In the early stages of Argentina's ISI program, capital intensive goods such as automobiles, machinery, and electronics were not produced in any great quantities.

Argentina had little surplus industrial capital, a small pool of skilled labor, and no real access to required industrial technologies. Even the agricultural sector suffered tremendously from a lack of investment in new technologies. Throughout the 1940s and 1950s, agriculture remained inefficient, with high domestic prices, poor quality, and inadequate investment the norm. The agricultural sector collapsed from contributing 27.1 percent of Argentina's GDP during the period from 1925 to 1929 to barely 15 percent between 1965 and 1969 (Crossley 1983). Moreover, agricultural export earnings declined as an increasingly higher proportion of agricultural production was absorbed by the fast-growing Pampeana cities in order to feed well-paid urbanites.

Juan Domingo Perón intensified ISI policies after 1945 and nationalized Argentina's railroads, ports, major industries, and many other public services. Successive development policies in Argentina focused new industrial activities almost exclusively on the Greater Buenos Aires Metropolitan Area and along the Paraná-Plata corridor. Between 1943 and 1954, the number of industrial establishments in the Pampeana increased by 124 percent, with over 40 percent of Argentina's total industrial capacity located in the Greater Buenos Aires region. Industrialization of the Pampeana reached its peak in the 1950s and then started to decline during the late 1960s (see Table 4.6). Uncontrolled growth in Buenos Aires and other pampas cities, coupled with the economic plight of Argentina's interior provinces, led to the development in 1966 of the government's *Plan Esquema 2000*. As part of the Plan, a concerted effort was made to relocate industrial production out of the Federal Capital to designated industrial sites in the suburbs of Greater Buenos Aires and to other industrial areas around the country. However, many industrial companies retained administrative offices in the center of Buenos Aires, which served only to reinforce the commercial-bureaucratic nature of the capital.

At the same time, the discrediting of Peronist ideologies about economic nationalism encouraged an inflow of U.S. capital into Argentina. New factories financed by North American investment to produce pharmaceutical, automotive, and other more specialized manufactured products sprang up outside the Federal District of Buenos Aires. Between 1954 and 1974, industrial output in both Greater Buenos Aires and the Pampeana cities more than doubled. Smaller non-capital-intensive factories were replaced with larger capital-intensive factories, often funded by multinational corporate investment. Industrial development intensified along the Paraná-Plata corridor during the 1970s and 1980s. Steel mills in San Nicolás near the port of Rosario and in Ensenada near La Plata, the capital of Buenos Aires province, fed the automobile factories, shipyards, petrochemical plants, heavy equipment manufacturers, and transportation industries that lined the banks of the Río Paraná (Figure 7.2). Over 80 percent of the country's oil refining capacity is located between Ensenada and San Lorenzo, equally accessible to imported, coastal, and interior domestic supplies of crude oil.

A thermonuclear power station at Atucha near Zárate, 100 kilometers northwest of Buenos Aires, supplies energy to this important industrial corridor. Atucha was the first commercial nuclear power plant in Latin America and is an important symbol of Argentina's contemporary development efforts. A second plant called Atucha II is under construction near the original plant and is scheduled to begin energy production in 1997. Approximately 110 kilometers south of Córdoba sits Argentina's second functioning nuclear power station, the Embalse Río Tercero. Inaugurated in May 1983, the Tercero plant has a potential of 600,000 kw and it provides crucial energy for the major industries located in the city of Córdoba. Heavy industry in the Pampeana also relies heavily on hydroelectric power generated at a number of plants in the Northeast.

Other important industrial development zones in the Pampeana include Córdoba, Argentina's second largest city with 1.1 million people, where automotive, railroad, aeronautic, chemical, and metal-based industries took over from agricultural processing as the major employment sector. Córdoba has evolved since the 1940s as an important gateway city, situated midway between the Atlantic coast and the western interior provinces. Industrial activities also are located around Villa María and Río Cuarto in Córdoba province, in Santa Rosa, the capital of La Pampa province, around the southern port city of Bahía Blanca, and in Entre Ríos province at Gualeguaychú on the border with Uruguay. In the province of Buenos Aires, the Azul-Olavarría-Tandil triangle has developed as an important source of cement and a production center for agricultural machinery.

Industrial Deconcentration. Until the mid-1950s, almost of all Argentina's industrial capacity was located within the Pampeana region. Since that time, successive governments have implemented industrial promotion schemes designed to deconcentrate industry from the littoral to the interior provinces and to foster regional development. These schemes' immediate impact was felt by Buenos Aires and the larger Pampeana cities. More long-term effects have been felt by the interior provinces and these effects

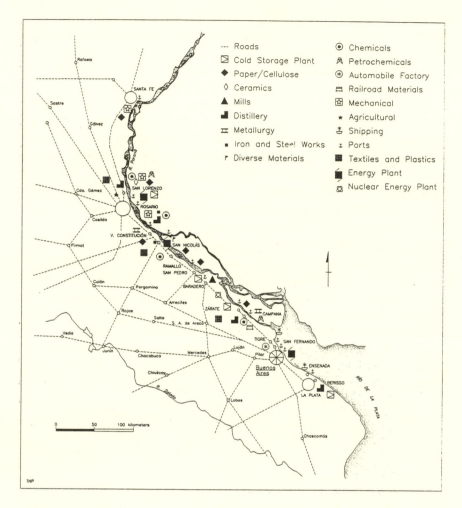

FIGURE 7.2 The Paraná-Plata Industrial Corridor. *Source*: After Daus and Yeannes (1992).

are explored in more detail in chapters 8 and 9. The first step in the decon-centration process occurred in 1972, when the government enacted laws designed to discourage new industries in the city of Buenos Aires (Schvarzer 1990). New factories were forbidden in the Federal Capital, and a tax proportional to the distance from the center of Buenos Aires was levied on new factories constructed within a sixty kilometer radius of the Plaza Congreso. Not surprisingly, a new industrial belt developed in the

Buenos Aires suburbs beyond the sixty kilometer limit (Keeling 1996). New factories in Córdoba and Rosario, Argentina's second and third largest cities respectively, also were prohibited.

From a regional development perspective, industrial deconcentration from Buenos Aires and the Pampeana region made some theoretical sense. Unfortunately, industrial deconcentration policies alone cannot and do not bring about regional development. In the interior provinces, inadequate transport infrastructure, inferior educational opportunities, poor social infrastructure, an extremely weak consumer sector, and almost non-existent cross-order economic relationships presented serious obstacles to industrial deconcentration. The major industrial centers of the Pampeana offer economies of agglomeration and scale, easier access to external markets, a trained and disciplined workforce, and specialized support services for industry (Sawers 1996). In addition, past development patterns have reinforced the practical and perceptual power that Buenos Aires and the other major Pampeana cities hold over the interior. These cities are more sophisticated and offer many more amenities than the provincial capitals of the interior. Historical inertia also plays a powerful role in restricting the process of industrial deconcentration. Many entrepreneurs, managers, technical personnel, and investors simply refuse to relocate away from the Pampeana cities to the interior.

Deindustrialization. The deceleration of the world economy during the 1970s and into the 1980s changed the environment within which Argentina functioned. Increased competition and reduced demand in the world economy encouraged the reorganization of production facilities and spurred the introduction of more sophisticated technologies. Large corporations merged with other corporations and became more multinational in form and function. Capital became more centralized and internationalized, seeking new arenas of greater return. The "Fordist" era of mass production began to evolve into what many have called the era of "flexible accumulation." The more successful manufacturing regions in the new global economy, argued Murray (1988:11), are those which "have linked flexible manufacturing systems with innovative organization and an emphasis on 'customization', design and quality."

As the bipolar political world fragmented and eventually collapsed, regional economic alliances such as the European Community began to play a more powerful role in the global economy. Argentina responded slowly to changing world conditions during the 1980s, maintaining a wall of trade tariffs to protect industrial production. However, the lack of new technologies, poor investment strategies, uncompetitive products, and large-scale inefficiencies in industry began to take their toll on Argentina's manufacturing sector. By late 1990, Argentina's politicians and planners began to argue that the successful restructuring of the domestic economy and stronger linkages to the world economy had to be accompanied by state deregulation and greater industrial competitiveness. Privatization policies implemented since 1990 have forced many large-scale, previously state-owned industries to restructure and downsize in order to remain competitive in the global marketplace. Industrial employees by the hundreds of thousands in Buenos Aires, Rosario, and Córdoba lost their jobs, although many have been absorbed by the expanding service and financial sectors. The Greater Buenos Aires Metropolitan Region alone accounted for over 80 percent of the 300,000 industrial jobs lost between 1985 and 1994 *(Latin American Weekly Report* 1996). As chapter four pointed out, unemployment and underemployment in the major Pampeana cities have skyrocketed since 1990. However, despite the forces of deconcentration and deindustrialization, the most recent economic census in Argentina revealed that industrial activity in the Greater Buenos Aires region increased between 1985 and 1994, whereas the number of industrial plants in the Pampeana provinces continued to decline (see Table 4.6).

Urban Growth in the Pampeana

The spatial dynamics of the Pampeana's industrial development have had several implications for the process of urbanization in the region. Post-1945 industrial development in Argentina favored the Pampeana cities and encouraged massive rural-urban migration flows. Certainly, the relative success of ISI policies would not have been possible without this massive transfer of demographic resources from the interior to the Pampeana. Impoverished farmers and unemployed urbanites flocked to the Pampeana cities in search of industrial and service jobs. By 1960, 14.2 million of Argentina's 20 million people lived in the Pampeana region, with seven million alone in Greater Buenos Aires. Shantytowns or *villas miserias* sprang up around the peripheries of the major cities to accommodate the influx of humanity, helping to spread the poverty of the interior to the core.

In the 1970s, regional development and industrial restructuring policies encouraged substantial internal migration in favor of the Pampeana cities. For example, between 1975 and 1980, Buenos Aires province received

341,000 migrants, Santa Fé and Córdoba each gained around 12,000 migrants, and La Pampa received 5,400 new residents (Carlevari and Carlevari 1994). However, during this same time period, the Federal District of Buenos Aires lost 170,000 residents, in part because of the military government's attempt to rid the city of shantytown dwellers and to ban further industrial growth within the capital. Population losses were experienced by the Northwest (95,000), the Northeast (74,000), and the Cuyo (28,000), although Patagonia actually gained 25,000 new residents during this period. Surprisingly, Entre Ríos province, which is considered part of the Pampeana region, lost nearly 30,000 people between 1975 and 1980.

Argentina's statistical center of population has continued its steady shift to the southeast throughout the twentieth century. In 1778, at the time of the census ordered by Charles III for the entire Viceroyalty of the Río de la Plata, the Northwest marked the center of population and functioned as the most important region. By the late-nineteenth century, the population center had shifted to central Santa Fé province, and throughout the twentieth century the statistical center has crept southward close to the city of Rosario. With 30 percent of Argentina's total land area, the Pampeana in 1991 accounted for 69 percent of the country's total population. Over 22 million of Argentina's 32.6 million inhabitants are concentrated in and around the major urban centers of the Pampeana. The country's second and third largest cities (Córdoba and Rosario respectively) are situated in the Pampeana, and other major cities such as Mar del Plata, Río Cuarto, Paraná, Santa Fé, and Bahía Blanca have sizeable populations and have grown at a steady pace since 1945 (see Table 3.6). Current demographic projections suggest a slowdown in migration from the interior to the Pampeana, although every month thousands of migrants continue to arrive in Buenos Aires and the other important urban centers. Absent significant improvements in employment opportunities, living conditions, and mobility in the interior provinces, population flows from the periphery to the Pampeana and from rural areas to urban centers will continue to characterize demographic change into the next century.

One of the underlying forces in the global economy directly shaping Argentina's urban system in the 1990s is the shift away from natural resource-based industries to human brain-power industries (Thurow 1996). Electronics, information, biotechnology, and finance, among others, are replacing industries traditionally based on natural resource extraction and production. Increasingly, these human resource activities are concentrated in major metropolitan areas such as Buenos Aires, Córdoba, and Rosario.

John Friedmann's (1995) world city hypothesis argues that, as basing points for national and global socioeconomic activity, dominant cities will continue to attract the brightest people, the most investment capital, and the best social and physical infrastructure. This suggests that Argentina's major Pampeana cities will grow at the expense of other urban areas and will attract the socioeconomic infrastructure crucial to long-term development.

Future Problems and Prospects

The Pampeana provinces have enjoyed over a century of development, driven first by agriculture and, since the 1950s, by industry and manufacturing, to become the economic core of Argentina. Although pockets of rural and urban poverty could be found throughout the region, particularly in the *villas miserias* of the major cities, Pampeana residents overall enjoyed the highest standard of living in Argentina, had excellent accessibility and mobility, received better education and healthcare services, and weathered the cyclical economic crises better than the interior. However, changes in global, regional, and national economic forces over the past decade have created tensions over the future role of agriculture, industry, and service-based activities in the Pampeana. President Menem's privatization and liberalization policies have changed the face of Argentina's economy and have opened up the Pampeana's agricultural and industrial sectors to global competition.

Restructuring the Pampeana's Economic Base

Does the world no longer need the quantity of agricultural commodities that the pampas is capable of producing, as Larry Sawers (1996) suggested? If not, what alternatives exist in the region to drive economic growth? Has the industrial sector been restructured adequately enough to function competitively and profitably in the regional and global economy? What role can tourism play in the restructuring of the Pampeana's economic base?

Agriculture. Recent statistics suggest that agriculture in the Pampeana, including stock raising, cereals, fruits, and vegetables, has stabilized after several decades of decline, although major year-to-year fluctuations still are evident. In Córdoba province, for example, agriculture's share of provincial GDP rose slightly from 11.28 percent in 1980 to 13.32 percent in 1992, with a peak share during this time period of 15.18 percent in 1988 (Table

TABLE 7.1 Gross Domestic Product in Córdoba Province by Sector, 1980 and 1992

Sector	1980	Percent	1992	Percent
	(In thousands of pesos at constant 1986 prices)			
Agriculture	78,027	11.28	108,172	13.32
Resource Extraction	2,051	0.36	1,381	0.17
Manufacturing	179,922	26.01	192,517	23.71
Public Utilities	12,231	1.77	18,451	2.27
Construction	37,186	5.37	25,614	3.15
Commercial Services	126,241	18.25	129,589	15.96
Transportation	23,937	3.46	36,262	4.47
Financial Services	111,225	16.07	136,614	16.82
Personal Services	120,600	17.43	163,423	20.13
Total:	691,870	100.00	812,023	100.00

Source: República Argentina (1995).

7.1). Entre Ríos and Santa Fé provinces both experienced slight reductions in agriculture's share of provincial GDP between 1980 and 1992. Agriculture in Entre Ríos accounted for 23.4 percent of provincial GDP in 1992, and in Santa Fé agriculture accounted for 10.4 percent of GDP (República Argentina 1995). The Pampeana remains the agricultural powerhouse of Argentina's primary sector, with 40 percent of the country's total farm area and 50 percent of the operational farms. Moreover, 85 percent of the total cultivated land and 87 percent of the land dedicated to annual crops in Argentina are located in the Pampeana region. Pastoral activities also are heavily concentrated in the Pampeana. Seventy-seven percent of all cattle in 1993 was found in the Pampeana region, with Buenos Aires province alone accounting for 36 percent of all cattle (Republica Argentina 1994). Pampeana agriculture completely dominates Argentina's total production of agricultural commodities for export.

Ninety-three percent of all cereal production in Argentina is from the Pampeana, with Buenos Aires the dominant province. For example, 98 percent of all wheat and 94 percent of all maize, along with the majority of oats, barley, rye, millet, and sorghum produced in Argentina comes from the Pampeana. Cereal exports generally have accounted for around 13 percent of the value of Argentina's total exports. Despite the pampas' bounty, Pampeana agriculture remains undercapitalized, technologically poor, and relatively inefficient compared to other countries around the world who have benefitted from rapid technological advances in agricultural production. For example, in the early 1990s, Pampeana farmers were applying only six kilograms per hectare of fertilizers compared to 97 kg/ha in the United States, 280 kg/ha in China, and 384 kg/ha in Germany (Carlevari and Carlevari 1994). Although environmentalists argue that less reliance on chemical additives is a positive attribute of Argentina's agricultural sector, the quality, quantity, and cost of crops produced in the Pampeana are not adequate to combat strong competition from other producers in the global market. Moreover, a lack of storage infrastructure such as silos and chronic inefficiencies in grain transport remain serious barriers to growth and profitability. Coupled with these and other structural problems, Pampeana farmers are finding competition in the global commodity market increasingly more difficult.

The pampas grasslands still are famous for beef production and large *estancias* continue to dominate the region. However, throughout the twentieth century smaller land holdings have made significant inroads into the pattern of land ownership in the Pampeana (Figure 7.3). More than half of all the farms in the Pampeana region today are less than 50 hectares in size, although they account for barely 2 percent of the total land area under agriculture. Approximately three-quarters of all the farms in the Pampeana are owner-occupied, with less than 20 percent run by tenant farmers. Agricultural land has become a much more valuable commodity since 1995, especially with substantial increases in export prices for wheat, maize, and soya. Between October 1995 and May 1996, for example, monthly rents per hectare in the Pampeana shot up 50 percent from US$100 to US$150 (*Latin American Weekly Report* 1996:274). Prices per hectare of land for wheat production rose from US$1000 to US$1500 during the same period, and land used for maize and soya shot up 40 percent from US$2500 to US$3500 per hectare. Many cattle ranchers are crowding their herds onto smaller parcels of grazing land in order to free up land for more the profitable production of grains. However, concern is being expressed in agricultural circles that many farmers are overextending themselves financially to take advantage of the current boom in global grain prices. What happens when the prices drop again, and farmers find themselves unable to meet their financial obligations?

Natural Resources. The Pampeana's natural resource base for the supply of industry and manufacturing is extremely poor. Primary materials

FIGURE 7.3 Pampas Farms Near Mar del Plata. *Source*: Courtesy of Juan A. Roccatagliata.

generally are imported from overseas or must be shipped long distances from interior provinces and from neighboring countries. For example, a lack of rock suitable for paving stone and timber for railroad construction inhibited the development of transportation infrastructure in the late-nineteenth and early-twentieth centuries. Coal and timber particularly had to be imported by the British companies that constructed, owned, and operated most of Argentina's major railroads. The Pampeana's principal mining district is Olavarría, approximately midway between Bahía Blanca and Buenos Aires. Here, dolomite used in the production of cement is extracted from the Tandilia hills, which are of Precambrian age. Granite and sandstone also are mined from Tandilia. Limestone and red sandstone are found in small quantities south of Paraná in Entre Ríos, and Argentina's major supplies of sodium sulphate are produced at Alsina Lake north of Bahía Blanca.

Timber plantations are an important new addition to the Pampeana's natural resource base and have helped to supply the paper, furniture, and construction industries since the 1980s. Of Argentina's total land area in timber plantations, approximately 10 percent is located in Entre Ríos, 7.5 percent is found in the delta area of the Río Paraná, and a further 9 percent is located in the southern part of Buenos Aires province. The majority of the cellulose and paper plants are clustered along the Paraná-Plata corridor, with 88 plants located in Buenos Aires province, six in the Federal Capital, two in Entre Ríos, nine in Córdoba, and 21 in Santa Fé province (Bortagaray and Peláez 1993). Exports of Argentina's paper products have surged since the late-1980s, although an increase in the use of recycled paper, especially in Europe and the United States, may have a dampening effect over the next decade. The cellulose-paper industry also faces stiff competition from other producers in South America and elsewhere, as well as challenges from environmentalists concerned about the liquid effluent from paper plants.

Other Prospects and Problems

Although Argentina continues to experience a decline in the number of industrial plants, particularly factories employing 1,000 or more people, the short-term outlook for industry is positive. Better technology, more capital, and greater efficiencies in the labor force all augur well for the future of industry in the Pampeana. However, ongoing management restructuring, privatization, downsizing, and retooling will create some measure of instability in the industrial sector for the remainder of the 1990s. Beyond the expected growth in the service sector, tourism is viewed as the most promising sector for future development.

The Pampeana can be divided into three key tourist activity zones. First, the urban centers, primarily Buenos Aires, will continue to attract large numbers of tourists. They contain the majority of the region's tourist infrastructure, cultural sites and activities, and services. Second are the Atlantic coast resorts, with development centered on Mar del Plata (Figure 7.4). Since the 1960s, these resorts have become the principal vacation destinations for middle-class *porteños* and other urbanites, who outnumber local residents three to one during the height of the summer season. Classic over-development has occurred in Mar del Plata and other coastal towns as local governments ignored building codes and allowed the construction of high-rise apartment towers without regard to the physical environment. Now, many of the beautiful beaches are shaded much of the day by these modern urban stalagmites, and cities like Mar del Plata have lost their original charm and architectural elegance.

The third major tourist zone encompasses the rural environments of the pampas and the lower Mesopotamian region. Attractions in this zone include many national parks, the Sierras of Buenos Aires Province, and the

FIGURE 7.4   Central Mar del Plata. *Source*: Courtesy of Juan A. Roccatagliata.

agricultural zone along the Río Paraná.   Only a small percentage of
Argentina's international tourists venture beyond the first two zones into the
interior as transport is difficult, organized tours are few, and rental cars are
extremely expensive.   Moreover, away from the major resort and urban
centers, tourist infrastructure is less available.   For example, as Table 7.2
illustrates, the provinces of Entre Ríos, La Pampa, and Santa Fé have far
fewer hotel facilities compared to Córdoba and Buenos Aires.   Most of the
available facilities are located in the major urban centers.   Yet overall, the
Pampeana is well-endowed with hotel accommodations compared to the
interior of Argentina.   Approximately three-quarters of all hotels in Argentina are located in the Pampeana, primarily in the Greater Buenos Aires
Metropolitan Region, Córdoba, and along the Atlantic coast.   Tourism
development, however, does not occur without environmental consequences, as the uncontrolled growth of Mar del Plata has demonstrated.
Environmental degradation of the Pampeana from tourism development and
other socioeconomic activities remains a critical issue for the region's future
development.
     Pollution in Argentina is not confined to the large urban centers,
although it is here that the problem of environmental deterioration is most
evident. Much of the rural area of the Pampeana also suffers from

TABLE 7.2   The Distribution of Hotel Accommodations in Argentina by Province, 1992

Province/ Region	Hotels	Hotel Rooms	Number of Beds
Buenos Aires	1,241	42,211	94,286
Córdoba	1,127	17,249	41,172
Entre Ríos	39	1,768	4,028
La Pampa	62	913	1,998
Santa Fé	65	2,754	6,067
Pampeana	2,534	64,895	147,551
Mendoza	139	4,424	10,927
San Juan	19	637	1,357
San Luis	42	2,170	6,571
Cuyo	200	7,231	18,855
Chaco	27	843	1,456
Corrientes	38	1,551	3,198
Formosa	8	262	563
Misiones	35	1,689	3,808
Northeast	108	4,345	9,025
Catamarca	25	703	1,579
Jujuy	23	933	2,064
La Rioja	23	674	1,414
Salta	63	2,600	4,211
Santiago del Estero	130	4,300	11,582
Tucumán	24	1,471	3,058
Northwest	288	10,681	23,908
Chubut	73	1,988	4,471
Neuquén	50	1,648	3,918
Río Negro	118	4,536	11,490
Santa Cruz	33	943	2,103
Tierra del Fuego	12	474	999
Patagonia	286	9,589	22,981
Total:	3,416	96,741	222,320

Source: República Argentina (1994).

serious environmental degradation. Salinization, soil erosion, flooding, and chemical poisoning are the four major problems facing agriculturalists in the Pampeana. Loss of land to urbanization and industrialization also is a major issue that planners must confront as they devise and implement regional development strategies.

Conclusion

Despite profound changes underway in the Pampeana region, these prosperous agroindustrial provinces have the capacity to weather the storm of Argentina's structural adjustment programs. The Pampeana has served as the country's economic backbone for over a century and there is little indication that the region's dominance in the spatial structure of Argentina will diminish. Domestic and international migrants continue to flock to the Pampeana's major cities. Industry, manufacturing, and service-oriented activities still favor Buenos Aires, Córdoba, and Rosario. And Argentina's transport and communication networks continue to focus almost exclusively on Buenos Aires. Moreover, there is no indication from government policies or strategies that any serious attempt at spreading the benefits of socioeconomic restructuring to the interior is being contemplated. Argentina remains bifurcated between the prosperous agroindustrial provinces of the Pampeana and the poorly developed and impoverished interior.

8

The Challenge of Transition Areas

From a socioeconomic development perspective, two regions exist in Argentina that can be classified as neither prosperous nor submerging. The agroindustrial oases of the Cuyo and the underdeveloped frontier of Patagonia currently are in a state of socioeconomic transition. Few areas of these two regions have experienced the type of agricultural-industrial development that propelled the Pampeana to relative prosperity from the 1880s onwards. Yet neither have these two regions suffered the depth and breadth of crushing poverty and underdevelopment that have characterized the northern provinces since colonial times. Part of the reason for this, of course, is that the historical context for both the Cuyo and Patagonia is completely different. Patagonia really didn't exist as a functional component of the Argentine state until the late nineteenth century. Throughout the twentieth century, Patagonia has served an important strategic geopolitical role in Argentina's national development. Patagonia also contributes powerfully to the myth that Argentina is rich in natural resources. A perception exists among policy makers and citizens alike that Patagonia really is an underdeveloped frontier waiting to be exploited properly.

For many years during the colonial period, political administration and communication linked the Cuyo region principally to Chile rather than to the Northwest or to the Atlantic coast. Moreover, during the first half of the twentieth century, industrious and entrepreneurial European migrants displaced the rural *gauchos* and *criollo* cattle ranchers who dominated the Cuyo. As a result of these and other structural differences, extreme social polarization, government corruption, and land-use problems are far less evident in the Cuyo region compared to the northern provinces. Although the cliché is overused, the Cuyo and Patagonia regions really do stand at a development crossroads in the mid-1990s. The development impact of economic globalization policies on these two regions over the coming decade will determine whether they move toward greater prosperity or whether they slip into the abyss of poverty, environmental degradation, and underdevelopment. In the following analysis, I provide a framework for addressing the likely future direction of the Cuyo and Patagonia. The first part of the chapter examines the agroindustrial oases that comprise the Cuyo region and focuses on the importance of Pacific Rim linkages, while the second section ventures into the underdeveloped frontier of Patagonia and explores the natural resource, geopolitical, and industrial bases that define the contemporary region.

Agroindustrial Oases of the Cuyo

The statistical or development region known as the Cuyo (an Araucanian word meaning sandy land) includes the provinces of Mendoza, San Juan, and San Luis. A more functional definition includes the westernmost section of Córdoba or the Sierras Pampeanas and the southeastern corner of La Rioja province. It excludes the southeastern corner of San Luis province, more properly included in the Pampeana, and the southern section of Mendoza province below the oasis of San Rafael and the Río Atuel, which functionally is part of Patagonia. Physically, the Cuyo can be divided into four orographic systems. First, the Cordillera Principal is the high mountain range that divides Argentina from Chile. It contains the Western Hemisphere's highest peak, Aconcagua, at 6,959 meters or just under 23,000 feet. In the shadow of Aconcagua sits the principal route linking Chile and Argentina, the Uspallata Pass. This is the only paved Andean crossing along the entire Chile-Argentina frontier, an indication of the communication difficulties facing the extreme western provinces.

Second, the Cordillera Frontal or Front Range stretches about 800 kilometers across the western sections of Mendoza, San Juan, and La Rioja provinces. Tributary streams of the Desaguadero watershed cut west to east through the mountains forming a number of valleys. Few settlements exist in this section of the Cuyo, and there is less than one person per square kilometer overall in the Front Range. Third, the Precordillera extends from just north of Mendoza to the border between La Rioja and Catamarca provinces, and also is sparsely populated. All three ranges are extremely arid, with the exception of the highest peaks, and the area in general receives less than 300 mm. of rainfall annually. The final physical zone is the Piedmont, which contains almost all of the Cuyo's population, settlements, and economic activity. Population densities are highest around the two major oases of Mendoza and San Juan. Nearly one million people live in the Greater Mendoza urban area and 360,000 reside in the Greater San Juan urban area. Together with San Luis and San Rafael, these major oases contain about 60 percent of the Cuyo's population. As a region, the Cuyo is the second most important contributor to Argentina's total gross domestic product after the Pampeana.

Settlement History and Economic Development

Before the arrival of the Spanish in the sixteenth century, the eastern slopes of the Andes fell under the influence of the mighty Inca empire. One of two major north-south highways that linked the extremities of the empire to Cuzco, the Inca capital, ran through the highlands and foothills of the Cuyo. The Uspallata Pass provided what seems to have been the southernmost transverse road across the Andes in the Incan highway system, linking the area around Mendoza with the valley area of Santiago, Chile (Fifer 1994b). Spanish incursions into the Cuyo first occurred after Francisco de Villagrá traveled the eastern Inca highway from Peru to Santiago in 1550-51. Governor Mendoza of Chile extended control of the Captaincy General of Chile over the Cuyo region by founding Mendoza in 1561 and San Juan in 1562. A third oasis was established in San Luis in 1594. Over the next 200 years, the Cuyo remained tied administratively and economically to Chile. Foodstuffs and livestock moved primarily across the Uspallata Pass during the snow-free summer months, although stronger trade links started to develop during the eighteenth century with other settlements scattered along the eastern Andean foothill zone.

With the creation of the Viceroyalty of the Río de la Plata in 1776, administrative power over Mendoza, San Juan, and San Luis passed from Santiago to Buenos Aires. However, trade links between Mendoza and Santiago remained strong until the early nineteenth century, when the creation of permanent political boundaries between the emerging states began to turn the Cuyo more permanently toward the Pampeana and Buenos Aires. Cattle remained the foundation of the regional economy well into the 1860s. Livestock bred in Córdoba and Santa Fé was fattened in the Cuyo's irrigated alfalfa pastures before export across the mountains to Chile. An earthquake in 1861 destroyed Mendoza and killed two-thirds of the city's residents, producing severe economic hardship in the area. When the government banned any further cattle trade with Chile in the mid-1860s, the economy of the Cuyo collapsed into depression and isolation.

Railroads and Wine. After the arrival of the broad-gauge Andino railroad in Mendoza (1884), San Juan (1885), and in San Rafael (1903), the region experienced an economic revolution. Cattle were replaced by viticulture and wine manufacturing as the Cuyo's economic foundation. The railroad dramatically reduced costs and travel time between producer and market, which, coupled with tariff protection from imported European wine, enabled the wine industry to grow rapidly. In turn, growth in the wine industry, its relationship to external commerce, and its dependence on irrigation led to the development of an intensive pattern of land use in the core area of the Cuyo (Fleming 1987). By 1914, wine production in the Cuyo exceeded Chilean production and it continued to expand thereafter, both in terms of acreage under vine and volume of wine produced (Zamorano 1992). Viticulture and wine production throughout the region received tremendous support from local and provincial governments, especially in the areas of irrigation water rights, irrigation infrastructure, marketing campaigns, and tax concessions for new vineyards (Scobie 1988).

Two areas of the Cuyo emerged as the most favorable zones for vine cultivation: the central sections of Mendoza and San Juan provinces, and a pie-shaped wedge of land that included the southeastern corner of La Rioja, southeastern Catamarca, and the extreme northwest of Córdoba. Coupled with economic opportunities related to the fast-growing wine industry, the railroad also encouraged an influx of migrants from Buenos Aires and the Pampeana. Mendoza received nearly 160,000 immigrants between 1890 and 1930, primarily Spaniards, Italians, and French but also significant numbers of Russians, Poles, Yugoslavians, Romanians, Czechs, Slovaks, Germans, Portuguese, and British (Zamorano 1992). By 1914, the population of Mendoza province stood at 278,000 and San Juan province recorded 120,000 inhabitants. Government support of the wine industry through tariff protection and other subsidies, plus small-scale industrial development in the major oases, contributed to steady population growth in the Cuyo until the late 1960s, when annual growth rates began to slow down. Most of this growth occurred in and around the major urban centers of the region--Mendoza, San Luis, San Juan, and San Rafael. By the 1991 census, the Cuyo's population had grown to 2.2 million, although 64 percent of the region's people lived in the northern third of Mendoza province in settlements along the major railroad lines.

Contemporary Economic Change

Argentina in 1980 was the fifth largest producer of wine in the world, with over 300,000 hectares in vine and wine production of approximately 25 million hectoliters (660 million gallons) annually (Foster 1988; Carlevari and Carlevari 1994). Three-quarters of all agricultural production in Mendoza and San Juan, and a substantial portion of the Cuyo's gross domestic product, could be attributed to viticulture and wine production (Manzanal and Rofman 1989; Sawers 1996). Together, Mendoza and San Juan provinces account for 80 percent of Argentina's vineyards and 92 percent of the country's total land area under viticulture. *Minifundios* dominate wine growing in the Cuyo, with 83 percent of the farms having less than 10 hectares of land. Typical vineyards have around 5 hectares under vine (Figure 8.1). In Mendoza, for example, about 65 percent of all the farms have five or less hectares, with these farms accounting for 20 percent of the total vineyard acreage (Zamorano 1992). About 20,000 people are employed directly by the 2,000 wineries and 245 bottling plants in the Cuyo and thousands more are involved in the industry indirectly, through transportation, retail distribution, and the provision of wine-related services (Carlevari and Carlevari 1994).

Between 1954 and 1991, Mendoza's provincial government owned and operated the Giol winery, probably the largest of its kind in Argentina. Market stability and the protection of small and medium producers were the stated goals of this operation, but by the end of the 1980s Giol had become essentially bankrupt. Moreover, both grape production and wine consumption have continued to decline since the 1970s. Changing consumer tastes in Argentina have reduced the demand for wine. Beer, soft drink, and fruit juice consumption all have increased per capita since the 1970s, whereas wine consumption has declined by over 50 percent (Sawers 1996). In addition, the trade liberalization policies that are reshaping Argentina's economy have directly affected the Cuyo wine industry. Argentine wine is not competitive in the global marketplace and exports of wine from the Cuyo represent barely 4 percent of total domestic production (República Argentina 1994). Nonetheless, wine exported in 1992 exceeded US$22 million in value, the highest amount in the history of the wine industry, and 75 percent of all exports was classified as "fine" or "reserve" quality wine. The principal destinations of wine exports from the Cuyo are Paraguay, the United States, Switzerland, and Japan.

Competition in the international wine market from Algeria, Romania, France, Australia, Chile, and the United States is fierce, and each country

FIGURE 8.1   Vineyards in Mendoza.

seeks to protect its own producers. Many of these countries also have a reputation for producing much better quality table wines than Argentina and thus vintners from the Cuyo have a much harder marketing task than other countries in making their wines attractive and competitive to often fickle consumers. From a geographic standpoint, the Cuyo also is highly disadvantaged. No other major wine-producing region in the world lies nearly 1,100 kilometers from its largest market or from the principal port used to export its product. Therefore, speed, cost, and efficiency of transportation are critical components of the wine industry. One potential solution for the Cuyo would be to use the Uspallata Pass and Chile's major port of Valparaíso, which is closer to many major export markets than Buenos Aires. However, both countries compete aggressively in the international wine market and Chile is unlikely to permit easier passage of its competitor's product. Chile's recent decision to join the MERCOSUR trade alliance with Argentina could have a positive long-term impact on the Cuyo's transportation dilemma.

Other agricultural products in the Cuyo have been introduced in recent years to counterbalance the decline in viticulture. Orchard crops such as peaches, plums, olives, pears, cherries, and apricots are contributing to economic diversification in the Mendoza and San Rafael areas, but yields are much lower than in the Alto Valle region of Patagonia (Carlevari and Carlevari 1994). Also grown in Mendoza province are spinach, squash, melons, tomatoes, garlic, and celery (Zamorano 1992). However, environmental problems related to soil erosion, declining soil fertility, increased salinization from irrigation water, and inadequate annual precipitation continue to pose serious challenges to any major improvements in the Cuyo's agricultural production.

Only modest mineral resources are found in the Cuyo, although Mendoza does contain about 10 percent of the country's proven oil reserves. Twenty-five percent of Argentina's non-metalliferous minerals by value of production came from the Cuyo in 1993 (República Argentina 1994). Industrial promotion schemes and growth pole strategies have not had much impact on the Cuyo. San Luis, 840 kilometers from Buenos Aires and considered the gateway to the Cuyo, benefited more than any other Cuyo city during the 1970s and 1980s from industrial promotion and tax incentives. Yet most industrial activities have developed in support of the agricultural and natural resource sectors and few mainstream consumer goods are produced in the region. For example, petroleum refining at the Luján de Cuyo plant in Mendoza province generates over 20 percent of the total regional gross industrial product (Durán et al. 1995). Part of the problem, of course, is distance from the major domestic markets of the Pampeana and the higher transport costs both for raw materials and finished goods. Apart from the wine industry, the major employment opportunities in the Cuyo in the 1990s have been in service, retail, transportation, and tourism. Commercial and financial activities, as well as social and personal services, all have increased as a percentage of regional GDP since the 1980s. In Mendoza, for example, commercial activities accounted for about 20 percent of provincial GDP in 1993 and financial services accounted for 13.5 percent (Table 8.1). Nonetheless, although the Cuyo has weathered reasonably successfully the socioeconomic storms that have battered much of the interior during the twentieth century, the region remains in limbo in terms of future development prospects.

Future Development

The Cuyo faces an uncertain future as Argentina's economic restructuring policies change the trade and transportation relationships that, for so long, have shaped the region. Agriculture in the Cuyo will be forced to adjust to

TABLE 8.1 Gross Domestic Product in Mendoza Province by Sector, 1986 and 1993

Sector	1986	Percent	1993	Percent
	(In thousands of pesos at constant 1986 prices)			
Agriculture	14,662	5.48	16,436	5.53
Resource Extraction	52,646	19.67	15,602	5.25
Manufacturing	74,124	27.70	73,166	24.64
Public Utilities	4,799	1.79	9,489	3.20
Construction	12,996	4.86	13,508	4.55
Commercial Services	31,349	11.71	58,189	19.60
Transportation	10,527	3.94	12,717	4.28
Financial Services	28,061	10.48	40,070	13.49
Personal Services	38,446	14.37	57,788	19.46
Total:	267,610	100.00	296,965	100.00

Source: República Argentina (1995).

new global, regional, and national conditions and manufacturing must adapt to more flexible production and marketing environments. However, there are three areas of change most likely to have a major impact on the Cuyo over the coming years: its location as a possible gateway to the Pacific Rim, its position along a potential north-south development axis, and its potential as a regional and international tourist destination.

Gateway Region to the Pacific Rim

Since the 1950s, the global economy has experienced a steady shift away from a North Atlantic to a Pacific Rim focus. The growth of Asian economies over the past forty years has been spectacular and has encouraged new trade relationships between Latin American countries and the Orient. These new relationships have significance for the future development of the Cuyo region. Chile's proximity to Argentina's western provinces is important because Chile now occupies a "hinge" position between the Southern Cone countries and the Pacific Rim (Fifer 1994a). In recent years, Pacific Rim investment has stimulated growth in Chile's domestic and export-based economy and, in turn, this growth is stimulating new economic relationships between Chile and Argentina. Chile is the largest foreign investor in Argentina, with private investment of over US$500 million in Argentine enterprises. Bilateral trade has grown steadily during the 1990s, and Chile recently announced its intention to seek full participation in the Southern Cone Common Market (MERCOSUR).

Changes in the political and economic relationships between Chile and Argentina have tremendous import for the Cuyo. For example, from a strictly transportation perspective, Mendoza is closer to Los Angeles and New York via the Chilean port of Valparaíso than via Buenos Aires. Moreover, the Uspallata Pass linking Mendoza to Santiago and Valparaíso is the only major connection between Argentina and Chile. Approximately 95 percent of all Andean traffic between the two neighbors utilizes the Uspallata Pass (Fifer 1994b). Moreover, two-way traffic across the border at Los Libertadores has increased rapidly since 1990, placing great stress on the existing infrastructure. New bilateral agreements between the neighbors have focused particular attention on the infrastructure problem. A new multimodal transport corridor has been proposed that includes rehabilitation of the Andean railroad and a new 21-kilometer road tunnel under the Andes. Presently, the old Transandine Railroad tunnel carries the two-laned paved road under the crest of the Uspallata Pass (Figure 8.2). Other plans call for the paving and realignment of the Agua Negra Pass linking Rodeo in San Juan province to the Chilean port of Coquimbo. Two minor and rarely used Andean passes, the Inca in the extreme northwestern corner of San Juan province and the Pehuenche at the extreme southwestern corner of Mendoza province, also have been suggested as targets for possible future development (Roccatagliata 1993b). Transport infrastructure improvements in the Cuyo dovetail into proposals for a new growth corridor across the Southern Cone, including a superhighway that would link Rio de Janeiro to Santiago via Buenos Aires and Montevideo. A variety of proposals for transcontinental railroad systems designed to link Atlantic and Pacific ports also are in development.

A North-South Andean Axis

One scenario in the federal government's plans for the territorial reorganization of Argentina focuses renewed attention on strategies for regional integration at both the state and suprastate levels (República Argentina 1993a). An important component of such strategies is a north-south Andean axis that would tie together a series of intermediate urban centers and provincial capitals (see Figure 4.4). The Cuyo could function as a pivotal region along this development axis. At present, strong spatial

FIGURE 8.2   The Road Tunnel to Chile in the Uspallata Pass.

discontinuities exist in terms of the location of population clusters and economic production. Extensive areas of the Andean region from the Northwest to southern Patagonia are characterized by very dispersed populations,
low densities, and poorly articulated economic activities.

   National Route 40 serves as the primary north-south route, connecting
the Cuyo to the Northwest via Chilecito in La Rioja province and to southern Patagonia via Zapala, San Carlos de Bariloche, and Esquel. This two-
lane highway is paved for much of its length but it is in extremely poor
repair, especially in the more remote sections of the Andean provinces.
Major infrastructural improvements to this route could help to improve
socioeconomic interaction between the Cuyo, Patagonia, and the Northwest, as well as facilitate improved connectivity with Bolivia and Chile.
Plans for economic and infrastructural development along this axis, however, rest upon the assumption that some improvements in regional
economic complementarity will be forthcoming. From the Cuyo's perspective, the absence of markets along this axis for the consumption of manufactured goods, industry's problem of isolation from the country's major
export points, and a lack of investment capital for development projects all
argue against any real progress in this project for many years to come. A
real dilemma for both provincial and national planners is the conflict
between the forces of supply and demand. Should the infrastructure be

improved first, even though little demand exists along the Andean axis at present for socioeconomic interaction? If the north-south axis is improved, would it stimulate the demand side of the equation? Theory does suggest that transport infrastructure improvements alone cannot and do not stimulate increased regional economic integration. On the other hand, if demand for socioeconomic interaction along the axis could be stimulated first, would a supply of infrastructure sufficient to support the increase automatically follow? Unfortunately, within the context of Argentina's contemporary economic restructuring policies, such questions have not been debated at the federal level. As indicated in chapter 5, the Menem government seems to have abrogated responsibility for any type of long-range, multimodal, integrated transport and regional development planning by privatizing the national transport network. The implications for the Cuyo in terms of north-south linkages are not positive.

Tourism

Provincial and city managers consider tourism a potential growth industry for the Cuyo in the coming decades. Three areas of tourist potential exist: alpine activities, ecotourism in the remoter parts of the region, and urban-based activities. Skiing facilities are available at Vallecitos, Las Cuevas, and Puente del Inca in the high valley of the Río Mendoza along the main highway to the Uspallata Pass (Figure 8.3). Alpine hiking, camping, and mountain climbing on Aconcagua and on neighboring peaks are growing in popularity. Several businesses in Mendoza have developed since the 1980s to service the growing numbers of visitors interested in alpine activities. An international consortium recently constructed an alpine complex in the Valley of Las Leñas near the headwaters of the Río Atuel in west central Mendoza province. Provincial officials hope to attract European and North American tourists to the area by taking advantage of the reversal of seasons from the northern hemisphere. Vacationers from the northern hemisphere can ski in Argentina during July and August.

Ecotourism is a fast-growing sector of the global tourism industry and myriad opportunities exist in the more remote areas of the Cuyo. Unfortunately, the Cuyo is poorly endowed with national parks, protected natural monuments, or restricted natural reserves controlled by federal regulations. Only the restricted natural reserve of Los Manantiales in Mendoza province near the Chilean border currently receives federal protection. However, the region has many ecological areas under provincial protection. Straddling

FIGURE 8.3   Ski Facilities in the Uspallata Pass.

the San Juan-La Rioja border on federal highway 40 is the Ischigualasto-
Talampaya complex. Eons of sandstone erosion in this arid region,
combined with flora and fauna from the Mesozoic era, have created some
spectacular landscapes; the white sandstone of Ischigualasto, for example,
gives this reserve its popular name: Valley of the Moon. In the northwestern corner of San Juan province within the mountains of the Front
Range, the San Guillermo Provincial Reserve contains the majority of
Argentina's vicuñas and other cameloid species. Caranday palms and
various species of mountain trees are the principal attractions of the
Papagayos zone at the foot of the Sierras de Comechingones in northeastern
San Luis province. This zone is threatened by the expansion of grazing
activities, which has accelerated the process of deforestation and soil
erosion in recent years. Other ecotourism areas include hot springs at
Termas de Pisanta near Rodeo in San Juan province and at Baños del
Zonda just west of the city of San Juan.

The Cuyo's urban centers provide a third area of potential tourism
growth. Mendoza, San Juan, San Luis, and San Rafael all function as
tourist service centers for their respective hinterlands. Hotels, restaurants,
museums, parks, and other tourism-related services and activities accommodate the thousands of domestic and international tourists that visit the
Cuyo each year. Wine-related activities are one of the main attractions in

Mendoza, as in San Rafael and San Juan. A particular attraction of San Juan is the colonial house of Domingo Faustino Sarmiento, the first president of Argentina born in an interior province. Sarmiento played an instrumental role during the late nineteenth century in shaping attitudes about national identity and development. He argued that Unitarism embodied civilization in the European mold and heavily supported the role of a Europeanized Buenos Aires as the core from which the development of the country should proceed. In contrast, federalism, according to Sarmiento, represented unprincipled barbarism and backwardness as evidenced by the *caudillos* and *gauchos* who controlled much of the interior (Sarmiento 1868).

The successful development of tourism as a major contributor to the regional economy cannot occur without forward and backward linkages throughout the socioeconomic structure of the Cuyo. Poor quality tourist infrastructure and inadequate accessibility and mobility will deter all but the hardiest and most determined traveler. The Cuyo's governments and business leaders have yet to address seriously the type of investment needed to develop tourism more fully. Moreover, a lack of protection for the region's important ecological areas and ongoing environmental deterioration in many parts of the region could deter potential visitors. One of the more serious financial problems facing the Cuyo's tourism industry is the overvalued Argentine peso. As a consequence of federal economic restructuring policies, Argentina now is the most expensive country in Latin America for tourists. International tourism in the Cuyo has shown signs of a decline in recent years, although an increase in domestic tourism has partially countered this loss.

Patagonia: An Underdeveloped Frontier?

Officially, Patagonia occupies 786,983 square kilometers or 28.4 percent of Argentina's continental land surface, second only in size to the Pampeana region. It includes the provinces of Río Negro, Neuquén, Santa Cruz, Chubut, and Tierra del Fuego (Figure 8.4). Functional definitions of Patagonia include the southern third of Mendoza province below the Río Atuel, western and southern La Pampa, and the southeastern corner of Buenos Aires province that lies within the Río Colorado watershed. Throughout the twentieth century, Patagonia has played a dominant role in Argentina's national identity. The region has contributed to the myth that Argentina is rich in natural resources, it has been the focal point of

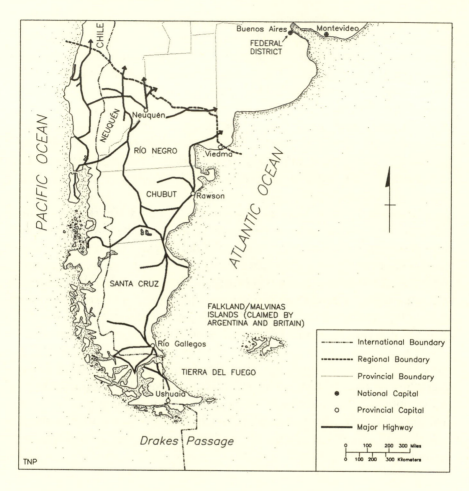

FIGURE 8.4   Provinces of the Patagonian Planning Region.

Argentina's post-1945 geopolitical strategies, and it continues to be seen by many as an underdeveloped frontier ripe for exploitation.

Physically, the entire region lies in the rain shadow of the Andes mountains, which block much of the precipitation from Pacific storms, although powerful westerly winds blow incessantly across the Patagonian plains. The eastern edge of Patagonia is very arid; for example, the Trelew-Rawson area in northeastern Chubut averaged 228 mm of rainfall annually (about 9 inches) between 1981 and 1993 (República Argentina 1994). Rainfall amounts increase along the central plateau, and sufficient precipitation is received along the Andean slopes to support extensive vegetation and even some rain forest (Sawers 1996). Tierra del Fuego receives greater rainfall, as well as ample amounts of snowfall to support a winter ski resort. Oceanic influences provide Patagonia a generally temperate climate for much of the year, although only northern Patagonia is warm enough for intensive agriculture.

Settlement History

Patagonia did not become a functional part of Argentina until the late nineteenth century. Prior to this, the region remained remote and inaccessible to all but the hardiest explorers. The origin of Patagonia's name is obscure, but it is often attributed to Magellan's encounter with the indigenous Telhuelche peoples. One story suggests that Magellan adopted the name in 1520 from the Spanish word for foot, *pata*, after observing the tall Telhuelche who wore large moccasins on their feet. Bruce Chatwin (1977) preferred a more romantic theory and speculated that Magellan took the word "Patagón" from a Spanish romance of the period that featured a fictional monster. Throughout the sixteenth century, rumors of Trapalanda, a South American El Dorado, were spread by gold-hungry Spaniards. However, with the exception of several Jesuit, and later Franciscan, missions in western Neuquén, few Europeans ventured very deeply into the region.

Charles Darwin's voyages in the early nineteenth century dispelled much of the early mystery of Patagonia. Darwin even predicted the disappearance or subjugation of the indigenous peoples as white Europeans began slowly to open up the region for settlement. Argentina's genesis as an independent political territorial unit focused renewed attention on Patagonia. The fledgling country's 1862 Constitution nationalized the territory of Patagonia and Law 1532 promulgated in 1884 divided the territory into the five provinces that exist today. Emerging geopolitical ideologies about the relationship between territory, national identity, and political strength, coupled with intense competition with Chile over boundaries and resources, spurred subsequent expansion into Patagonia.

Welsh Colonists. Many attempts were made to colonize Patagonia before the mid-nineteenth century, most of them unsuccessful. Colonists from Chile in 1843 settled in the extreme southwestern corner of Patagonia and founded present-day Punta Arenas. In 1856, the first group of

Welsh colonists, under the leadership of Captain Edmund Elsegood, arrived in Chubut but it abandoned its settlement attempts after only two years. Another group of Welsh colonists arrived in 1865 at Puerto Madryn. This group contained 153 people and it eventually settled in Rawson after the Argentine government granted land to the colonists (Williams 1991; Capitanelli 1992). The Welsh named their new town after the government minister who had organized the land grant. Despite hardships and a serious struggle to build irrigation canals, by the late 1880s over 1,200 people lived in the lower valley of the Río Chubut.

New groups of Welsh settlers continued to arrive between the 1880s and 1910, many pushing westward up the Chubut river valley to western Patagonia. By the late 1890s, eight Welsh colonies contained over 10,000 people, with approximately 320,000 hectares of land under intensive cultivation. Most of the region's land, however, disappeared into the hands of large landholders and speculators. After the Conquest of the Desert, for example, huge grants of land in Patagonia were given to military officers. An area the size of Switzerland, about 4.5 million hectares, was distributed among 541 soldiers. Many of these land grants became the large sheep *estancias* that still dominate most of Patagonia in the 1990s.

Railroad Development. Railroad construction into Patagonia began during the 1890s, as the federal government sought to extend its control over the more remote areas of the country. A threat of war with Chile over boundary disputes in Patagonia encouraged an extension of the British-owned Great Southern Railroad from the port city of Bahía Blanca to Neuquén in the shadow of the Andes. The railroad enabled the military to have rapid troop and matériel access to the western frontier. Construction reached the Río Colorado in 1897, Neuquén province in 1899, Zapala during 1901, and ended at Huincul in 1913. This line had been projected to link up with the Chilean railroad system across the Pino Hachado Pass, but tensions between the two countries and financial difficulties caused the abandonment of the project. Land grants to the Great Southern Railroad led the company in the 1920s to invest in an irrigation system along the Río Negro valley (Figure 8.5). Irrigation, argued the Southern's managers, would open up the valley to settlers and promote more business for the railroad. Fruit production, particularly pears, apples, and table grapes, quickly took hold, although the distance from major markets discouraged sustained development of the valley.

A second transverse line south of the Río Colorado initially extended

FIGURE 8.5   An Irrigation Canal in the Alto Valle, Neuquén. *Source*: Courtesy of Juan A. Roccatagliata.

west from Viedma and reached San Carlos de Bariloche, a resort town in western Río Negro province, during 1934. This line was extended north from Viedma to connect with the Pampeana network at Bahía Blanca, and south from Ingeniero Jacobacci using narrow-gauge track to reach the town of Esquel in northwestern Chubut. Although other extensions of the national railroad network were planned to open up the more southern areas of Patagonia, an integrated Patagonian railroad network never materialized (López del Amo 1990). Trelew near the delta of the Río Chubut was founded in 1880 as a railroad junction, designed to unite the upper Chubut valley with the Atlantic and with coastal settlements to the north and south. The line extended 17 kilometers westward to the Welsh settlement of Gaimán and eventually to Las Plumas and Rawson, but it never connected to the national network and was later abandoned. Other lines developed in isolation from the national network. From Comodoro Rivadavia, in the extreme southeast corner of Chubut province, the railroad ran west over 200 kilometers to Sarmiento. Plans called for the line to be extended north-westward to link up with the Viedma-Bariloche line and southwestward to reach the Andes near Lago Buenos Aires, but construction never continued. In northeastern Santa Cruz province, a railroad line ran along the northern banks of the Río Deseado from the small town of Las Heras to the port city of Puerto Deseado. Development plans called for this line to be extended into Comodoro Rivadia. This never happened.

Finally, a 230-kilometer narrow-gauge railroad was constructed between the port of Río Gallegos, in southeastern Santa Cruz, and the coal mines of Río Turbio on the Chilean-Argentine frontier. This line continues to transport coal from the mines to ships at Río Gallegos. Despite ambitious plans to use the railroad as a development tool during the first half of the twentieth century to open up Patagonia and to link it strongly to Buenos Aires and the Pampeana core, much of the region remained isolated. A lack of investment in transport infrastructure, and continuous political and economic crises at the national level, diverted attention away from Patagonia until the late 1950s. Nonetheless, the region's population grew steadily after 1900 to reach 150,000 by the 1920s, over 360,000 by 1947, and over half a million by the 1960 census (República Argentina 1994).

Contemporary Settlements Patterns

In the mid-1990s, approximately 1.5 million people live in Patagonia, the majority in the provinces of Río Negro and Neuquén within the basin of the Limay-Neuquén-Negro river system. Three axes of population define settlement patterns in contemporary Patagonia: the Atlantic coast, the Andean valleys, and the transverse river valleys. Cities along the Atlantic coast include Comodoro Rivadavia, Río Gallegos, Viedma, Rawson, and Ushuaia on Tierra del Fuego. Many of the coastal settlements have grown as export points for the region's natural resources: sheep, cattle, coal, petroleum, and natural gas. Development along the Andes axis has been limited to a 250-kilometer stretch between the 40th and 43rd parallel south. Here, only three important urban centers have developed in recent decades--San Martín de los Andes, San Carlos de Bariloche, and Esquel-- although none have populations exceeding 75,000. Development along this axis has been spurred by tourist activities and forestry, and several hydroelectric complexes provide power for the area.

The transverse fluvial valleys of the Ríos Negro and Chubut contain the major agricultural and urban centers of Patagonia. Greater Neuquén is the largest city in Patagonia with just over 250,000 inhabitants (Figure 8.6). Other Patagonian river valleys have neither adequate soils nor sufficient annual precipitation to sustain intensive agricultural activities. Thus, few urban areas are found in the interior of Santa Cruz or Chubut provinces. Growth-pole strategies and industrial promotion schemes attracted migrants

FIGURE 8.6   Neuquén City, Patagonia.   *Source*: Courtesy of Juan A. Roccatagliata.

from the Pampeana and Buenos Aires during the 1970s and 1980s, although rural-urban migration within and from Patagonia continues to dominate demographic change. The Patagonian region consistently has recorded Argentina's highest annual population growth rates since the 1950s (see Table 3.4). For example, Figure 8.7 details the percentage of population change in Argentina between 1980 and 1991 and highlights the high rates of increase recorded by all the Patagonian provinces.

Patagonia's Economic Foundation

In order of importance in terms of historical development, the region's economy today can be divided into four major sectors: agriculture, natural resource extraction, growth-pole industrialization, and tourism. Federal subsidies, first for irrigated agriculture and later for industrial activities, have created a dependency relationship between Patagonia and the core. Thus, within the context of Argentina's recent economic restructuring

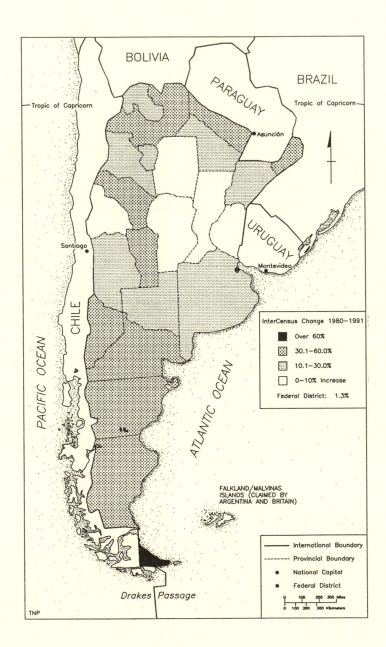

FIGURE 8.7 Intercensus Population Change in Argentina by Province, 1980-1991. *Source*: República Argentina (1991).

policies designed to make the country more competitive in the global marketplace, Patagonia has not fared well. Both domestic and international markets for Patagonian fruit have eroded in the face of cheaper and better quality produce from competitor countries. Chile in particular, along with South Africa, New Zealand, and Australia, present formidable export competition to Patagonia. Wool quality has declined since the 1950s, as has the quality of the sheep flocks, and meat from Patagonian sheep is not selling in the domestic market. Moreover, intense competition from Australia, the world's largest wool producer, has kept international wool prices deflated. The number of sheep slaughtered for export or for consumption in Argentina dropped precipitously from approximately 7 million head in 1980 to just over 3 million head in 1993 (República Argentina 1994). Many communities in Patagonia now rely heavily on tourism, especially ecotourism, as the mainstay of the local and provincial economy.

Agriculture. Patagonia contains 4 percent (about 15,000) of Argentina's total number of farms and approximately 31 percent of its total land area in agriculture. Of the region's 56 million hectares under development, less than 2 percent is controlled by 61 percent of the total number of farms in Patagonia, farms which have less than 1,000 hectares each. Less than 10 percent of the farms in Patagonia control 63 percent of the region's total arable land. *Megafundios*, or extremely large landholdings, are the norm for Patagonia, where sheep *estancias* (ranches) have been the only feasible use for the poor soil and grasses of the region. In the agricultural oases of the Alto Valle, land division is more favorable. In the county of General Roca, for example, 97 percent of the farms control 46 percent of the arable land (Capitanelli 1992). Nonetheless, throughout Patagonia agricultural productivity is hampered by an unequal distribution of land.

Agricultural production is further hindered by the fragmentation of land in *minifundios*, small farms typically under 25 hectares in size that usually are not very viable. Land fragmentation is exacerbated by Spanish inheritance laws that subdivide property among all surviving children. Some of the larger land parcels in Argentina were granted under *mayorazgo*, which stated that the entailed estate could not be broken up as ordinary Spanish inheritance laws demanded. In Patagonia's most productive region, the Alto Valle in the Negro-Limay-Neuquén river triangle, 70 percent of all farms have 10 or less hectares. Of Patagonia's 231,000 hectares of irrigated land, nearly 90 percent is located in Neuquén and Río Negro provinces, with the bulk of that percentage in the Alto Valle (República Argentina

1994). Río Negro province particularly has experienced a steady decline since 1980 in the contribution of both agriculture and resource extraction to provincial GDP. From 30 percent of provincial GDP in 1980, by 1993 the primary sector in Río Negro had fallen to less than a 20 percent share (Table 8.2).

Patagonia's major agricultural crops are apples, pears, grapes, and tomatoes. About two-thirds of the irrigated land along the Río Negro is devoted to fruit orchards (Figure 8.8). Brazil and several European countries import the majority of the Alto Valle's fruit production, Brazil preferring red apples and the European countries the green varieties. Recently, a new fruit-growing area in the southwest corner of La Pampa province has been developed around the town of 25 de Mayo, utilizing the waters of the Río Colorado. One of the more serious problems facing Patagonia's fruit growers is the long-term implications of MERCOSUR trade policies. Brazil has developed a highly subsidized apple industry in recent decades, and open competition within the context of the common market could give Patagonia's fruit growers an advantage. However, it is unlikely that Brazil will allow its domestic apple industry to be devastated by increased Patagonian imports and tariffs are likely to remain in place for the foreseeable future.

Natural Resources. Patagonia is believed to be rich in natural resources and many of Argentina's textbooks and research journals continue to emphasize this belief (for example, Daguerre et al. 1992; Lorenzini et al. 1993). Mining and quarrying provided less than 2 percent of Argentina's gross domestic product in 1992, and exports of all raw non-food materials, except petroleum, accounted for 7.5 percent of total exports in 1993 (República Argentina 1994). Chubut, Neuquén, and Río Negro provinces combined contributed only 25 percent of the total value of Argentina's production of metalliferous minerals in 1991. Patagonia supplied less than 15 percent of Argentina's total production of non-metalliferous metals in 1993. Iron ore, uranium, lead, zinc, gold, oil, natural gas, and coal are the major natural resources extracted from Patagonia.

Santa Cruz province supplies the majority of Argentina's coal, although its quality is not suitable for export to the major industrial countries. Coal mined at Río Turbio is sub-bituminous and is shipped nearly 2,000 kilometers to the steel mills of Ramallo, in Buenos Aires province. Most of the workers at the Río Turbio mines are Chilean and they reside in and around Puerto Natales across the border in Chile. Petroleum discovered in

TABLE 8.2 Gross Domestic Product in Río Negro Province by Sector, 1980 and 1993

Sector	1980	Percent	1993	Percent
	(In thousands of pesos at constant 1986 prices)			
Agriculture	18,635	12.73	18,615	10.64
Resource Extraction	24,957	17.04	15,366	8.78
Manufacturing	8,958	6.12	7,782	4.45
Public Utilities	4,302	2.94	5,178	2.96
Construction	7,330	5.00	10,694	6.11
Commercial Services	32,237	22.01	37,025	21.16
Transportation	4,189	2.86	9,317	5.32
Financial Services	28,656	19.57	39,949	22.83
Personal Services	17,180	11.73	31,074	17.75
Total:	146,444	100.00	175,000	100.00

Source: República Argentina (1995).

FIGURE 8.8 Fruit Orchards in the Alto Valle, Neuquén.

Comodoro Rivadavia in 1907 provided a tremendous boost to the region's economy and, up until the 1990s, royalties for petroleum and natural gas production accounted for a substantial percentage of funds received annually by the provinces from the federal government. Three major oil and gas fields exist in Patagonia. The Golfo San Jorge and the Neuquén basins each contained about 40 percent of the country's proven oil reserves in 1993, with the Austral basin a distant third with about 3 percent. These three basins also contained 75 percent of the country's proven natural gas reserves. The Austral basin holds the promise of significant future reserves, especially around the Malvinas (Falkland) Islands. Belief in this future potential continues to encourage Argentina to seek a permanent solution in its favor over the status of the Malvinas (Falkland) Islands. Indeed, Carlos Menem still argues that the return of the islands to Argentina is one of the top priorities of his current administration.

Privatization of the oil, gas, and mining sectors has featured as a dominant component of the Menem government's economic restructuring policies since 1991. Provincial administrations receive a lump-sum settlement from the federal government as their share of the privatization proceeds. But what happens to the provincial economies when the privatization windfall has been exhausted? Many provincial governments have complained that over the long-term they will be worse off financially under the current privatization agreements than if the resources remained in the hands of the state.

Pastoral activities, forestry, fishing, and hunting are other important sectors of Patagonia's contemporary natural resource-based economy. Cattle and angora goats are raised primarily in northern Patagonia, whereas sheep herding is spread more widely across all of the region. Nearly 40 percent of the region's sheep are raised on large *estancias* of 10,000 or more hectares, where flocks of 10,000 or more sheep are not uncommon. Most sheep and goat herders, however, have less than 1,000 animals. Pastoral activities are not labor intensive and have not contributed much to the Patagonian economy in recent decades. Forestry, in contrast, has grown in importance in recent years. Large reforestation projects are underway along the Andean slopes in Santa Cruz and Neuquén provinces. Together, the five Patagonian provinces in 1993 contained less than 4 percent of the total number of hectares in Argentina in natural forest and less than 10 percent of the total hectares reforested (República Argentina 1994; Carlevari and Carlevari 1994). Imports of forestry products into Argentina continue to outpace exports by a three to one margin. Fishing and hunting remain relatively minor components of the national economy, although both ocean and coastal fishing from Patagonian ports have increased since 1990, especially from Ushuaia, Puerto Madryn, and Puerto Deseado.

Industrial Promotion Schemes and Growth-Pole Strategies

Geopolitical considerations in the 1950s, coupled with growing migration from the rural interior to the industrializing cities of the Pampeana, encouraged Argentina's military government to promote industrial development in Patagonia. Plans to colonize and settle interior provinces characterized by socioeconomic disparities also focused on Patagonia. The federal government encouraged settlement particularly in southern Patagonia not only to take advantage of mineral resources in the area but also to solidify national territorial claims in areas that had many Chilean residents. Industrial promotion and colonization schemes were augmented with growth-pole strategies in the early 1970s, when certain industries were linked with cities designated as development poles (Morris 1972). Argentina's growth-pole policies were adopted from ideas formulated in France during the 1950s and 1960s concerning the role of selected urban centers in stimulating regional growth and modernization.

Argentina's first industrial promotion scheme established a tax-free zone in Patagonia south of the 42nd parallel (Schvarzer 1990). Trelew, the closest urban center to Buenos Aires south of this parallel, benefitted initially from industrial development. Migrants flocked to Trelew to take advantage of higher-paying jobs in the factories. Between 1956 and 1970, the town's population grew from 5,000 to 25,000 inhabitants. However, industrial promotion in Trelew did not create new, dynamic industries; it simply shifted production from one province to another. In the 1960s, detailed developments plans from each province were required as part of a Patagonian and national regional development strategy (República Argentina 1965). Yet integrated, industrial-based regional development never occurred in Patagonia because of a lack of coordination between provincial governments, the embedded power of the oligarchy, corruption, tax evasion, and operating inefficiency within the industries (Morris 1972; Artana 1991).

In the 1970s, the concept of development poles with energy auto-sufficiency focused growth on Puerto Madryn just north of Trelew. Argentina's first aluminum plant was constructed here, with hydroelectricity generated from the Río Chubut the major source of power. However, bauxite had to be imported from Guyana and Jamaica at exorbitant transportation costs. The aluminum plant also attracted migrants from the interior and Puerto Madryn's population multiplied tenfold during the 1970s and 1980s. Yet national industrial development plans were never integrated or coordinated with regional, provincial, or local development plans (if these existed), and Puerto Madryn suffered from shantytown growth and serious water and sewer problems. Moreover, regional transportation deficiencies continued to pose serious barriers to the cheap, efficient, and rapid movement of people, goods, and information within Patagonia and between the industrial sites and Buenos Aires.

Tierra del Fuego also benefitted in the 1970s from industrial promotion schemes. Declared a free-trade zone, the island attracted *maquillas* or assembly plants that specialized in electronic appliances to the urban centers of Río Grande and Ushuaia. Color televisions, for example, were imported as "kits," assembled in Río Grande's factories, and then sold in the domestic market. As a consequence of industrial promotion schemes, Tierra del Fuego experienced Argentina's highest rates of population growth between 1970 and 1991. From 13,000 inhabitants in 1970, the population exploded to just under 70,000 in 1991 (see Table 3.3). Since 1992, however, the Menem government has lowered tariffs on consumer electronic goods as part of the MERCOSUR trade agreements and of Argentina's trade liberalization strategies. Manufacturing in Tierra del Fuego declined from 63 percent of provincial GDP in 1988 to less than 35 percent in 1991, and preliminary figures from the 1994 national economic census suggest that reductions in GDP share have continued (República Argentina 1995). Violent strikes and vituperative demonstrations in 1994 and 1995 by *maquilla* workers protesting government policies may be a portent of future problems for Tierra de Fuego *(Latin American Weekly Report* 1994-1995).

Tourism

Patagonia is an ecotourist's dream, relatively isolated, sparsely populated, and containing 12 of Argentina's 28 national parks, reserves, and other protected areas. Dozens of provincial parks and reserves add to the amount of territory under government protection in the region. Government officials, business people, entrepreneurs, and service providers in Patagonia view tourism as a potential savior of the local economy. International and domestic tourism in Argentina have grown steadily since the 1970s and increasing numbers of visitors are discovering Patagonia. The region is marketed as a year-round destination, offering winter alpine activities and summer camping, backpacking, hiking, and fishing. Five distinct tourist zones chararacterize Patagonia: the Río Negro coast and Valdés Peninsula; the Lake district centered on San Carlos de Bariloche; Glacier National Park in southwestern Santa Cruz; the Santa Cruz coast and Cabo Virgenes; and Tierra del Fuego. These zones, as well as myriad other sites accessible to tourists in Patagonia, are described in much detail in the many travel guides available (for example, Bernhardson and Massolo 1995).

Probably the three most important tourist activities in terms of contribution to the regional economy are wildlife viewing, skiing, and touring the region's lakes and national parks. The Valdés peninsula lies approximately 75 kilometers east of Puerto Madryn in Chubut province and is one of South America's finest wildlife reserves. Within the reserve area, visitors can view Magellanic penguins, seabirds, rheas, guanacos, elephant seals, and the southern sea lion (Figure 8.9). Pods of killer whales also frequent the waters around the Valdés peninsula. In western Río Negro province, San Carlos de Bariloche functions as the main urban center of Argentina's Lake District and is typical of many European alpine resorts. The city sits at the eastern end of Lake Nahuel Huapi's south shore and it is laid out in a fairly conventional grid pattern (Figure 8.10). Uncontrolled growth over the past several decades has eroded Bariloche's original attraction to visitors; for example, uncontrolled commercial development has marred the once-attractive lakefront area. Skiing dominates the winter season and hiking, camping, and climbing are the major summer activities. Running along the entire western section of Patagonia is a series of lakes and glaciers, many situated within national or provincial parks. Lake Moreno in Nahuel Huapi National Park is typical of this region's physical environment (Figure 8.11).

Several challenges face tourism's development in Patagonia. The most important is accessibility and mobility. International visitors have no direct access to the region; they must arrive in and transit Buenos Aires. Disances are great between Buenos Aires and the major tourist centers of Patagonia and air transport is the only viable mode of travel for most visitors. Within Patagonia, passenger trains are almost non-existent, but international-quality buses cover all the major intercity routes and serve most of the major tourist centers. Many visitors rely on automobiles to tour the area, as most major highways have been paved in recent decades, yet access to many lesser-known parks remains difficult particularly along the Argentina-Chile border.

FIGURE 8.9   Sealife on the Valdés Peninsula, Chubut, Patagonia.

FIGURE 8.10   Aerial View of San Carlos de Bariloche, Patagonia.

FIGURE 8.11 Lake Moreno in the Nahuel Huapi National Park.

FIGURE 8.12 Route 40 in Western Patagonia.

Moreover, car rental prices are exorbitantly high for most international tourists. Recent investment in road rehabilitation and maintenance along national highway 40, however, has improved north-south linkages along the western section of Patagonia (Figure 8.12), and cross-border travel between Argentina and Chile has become easier since the 1980s. Another challenge relates to the chronic overvaluation of the Argentine peso, as Patagonia currently is one of the most expensive tourist destinations in the Western Hemisphere. Coupled with a lack of investment in tourist infrastructure in recent years, these challenges may serve to retard tourism's growth potential over the next decade.

Geopolitical Considerations

Ongoing friction with Britain over the Malvinas (Falkland) Islands and concerns about Chilean intrusion into Patagonia have shaped Argentina's geopolitical policies throughout the twentieth century. The Patagonian region occupies a key position in the country's contemporary geopolitical strategies and three areas of concern merit attention: South Atlantic territorial claims, boundary disputes, and the concept of a forward capital. Within the global context, many developed countries recently have set aside past geopolitical ambitions in order to focus their energies on regional integration, multinational relationships, socioeconomic restructuring, and cross-border infrastructural development. Yet Argentina remains fixated with a need to solidify its territorial limits, to occupy territory to which it feels it has historical or legal claim, and to promote Argentine nationalism. The rallying cry of *Las Malvinas Son Argentinos* (the Malvinas belong to Argentina) continues to resound through school rooms, in the popular media, in the corridors of political power, and directly from the mouth of the country's president. Moreover, most textbooks, maps, journal articles about, and analyses of, Argentina's territorial situation project state control over a sizeable portion of Antarctica, the South Atlantic islands, and the continental shelf. While these issues may be important to the Argentine psyche and to national identity, far more important development problems exist, particularly in Patagonia and other interior regions.

Claims for Antarctica and the Malvinas. Argentina's conflict with Britain over the Malvinas (Falkland) Islands resulted in a short and devastating war in 1982 and the discrediting and eventual downfall of the military government. The Malvinas (Falklands) lie approximately 400 kilometers northeast of Tierra del Fuego and are geologically related to Patagonia. Argentina also claims title to the South Georgia and South Sandwich Islands, about 1500 and 2000 kilometers east of the Malvinas (Falklands) respectively. Competing claims to the Malvinas (Falklands) can be traced back to the early nineteenth century, when Argentina gained independence from Spain and subsequently relied on the principle of *uti possidetis juris* (as you now possess, so shall you possess) to solidify its national territory (Dolzer 1993). The 2,000 or so residents of the Malvinas (Falklands) are primarily of English descent and have expressed a desire not to be governed by Argentina. Perhaps the solution to this issue would be to give the islands nominal independence or to place them under some type of United Nations trusteeship so that neither Britain nor Argentina imposes political control over the residents.

Another territorial issue of some importance concerns Argentina's claims to Antarctica. Since the 1950s, the country has claimed a pie-shaped section of Antarctica between the 25th and 74th meridians and from the 60th parallel to the South Pole. Several scientific bases have been established in this zone since the 1960s and Argentina has gone to extraordinary lengths to solidify and legitimize its national claim. For example, the government arranged for a pregnant Argentine woman to give birth to her child in one of the Antarctic science stations and for two military personnel to be married on Antarctica. Both events were designed to give legitimacy to an Argentine Antarctic territory. Indeed, statistical descriptions of Patagonia to this day include the nearly one million square kilometers of Antarctic territory claimed by Argentina (República Argentina 1994). Argentina is a signatory to a 1961 treaty, and to its 1991 30-year extension, that prohibits all non-scientific activity south of the 60th parallel and that seeks to preserve Antarctica as the "common heritage of humankind." Tourism activities continue to grow in importance in the Antarctic region, and Ushuaia on Tierra del Fuego serves as Argentina's gateway to the frozen continent (Figure 8.13).

Boundary Disputes with Chile. Political and economic relations between Argentina and Chile have improved dramatically since 1991, although the potential for conflict over extant boundaries still exists, particularly in Patagonia. In the Patagonian Andes, dispute arose over differing interpretations of the physical boundary separating the two countries. Argentina preferred the line that corresponded to the highest peaks (*la línea orográfica*), which placed the national border well within territory claimed

FIGURE 8.13   The Main Thoroughfare of Ushuaia, Tierra del Fuego.

by Chile. In contrast, Chile claimed the line that corresponded to the continental divide or division of waters (*la línea hidrográfica*). This placed the international boundary will within Argentine territory. On several occasions over the past 100 years, Chile and Argentina have come close to all-out war over Patagonian boundaries. In 1984, Pope John Paul II mediated an accord between the two neighbors that seemed to resolve the boundary disputes. The Treaty of Peace and Friendship settled the major issue of the Beagle Channel in Tierra del Fuego and both parties agreed not to pursue other boundary claims (Morris 1985). However, in late 1990 and early 1991, Argentinos were surprised to read in their local newspapers that renewed debate had arisen over 24 boundary locations ranging from Jujuy to Tierra del Fuego. Fresh negotiations with Chile resulted in a 1991 accord, finally signed in 1994, that defined a polygonal line through the Patagonian ice-fields and the Laguna del Desierto as the new political boundary between the two countries. For now, disputes with Chile over boundary lines in Patagonia appear to be fully resolved, although mutual suspicion still remains.

A New Federal Capital in Patagonia? The third geopolitical consideration that continues to occupy the attention of planners and strategists in

Argentina is the overwhelming dominance exerted over the country by Buenos Aires and attempts to alleviate this dominance by constructing a forward capital in Patagonia. An unbalanced relationship between a dominant urban center (often the political capital) and its national hinterland often can hinder a country's regional development. With the federal government located in a city as dominant as Buenos Aires, it often becomes extremely difficult to separate national planning goals from regional and local issues. In addition, the physical presence of the federal government in the dominant city often gives that city an advantage, which can lead to excessive influence by the megacity over the political, economic, social, and cultural life of the country.

Argentina long has suffered from such a problem, with Buenos Aires often described as a Goliath standing on the shoulders of an impoverished and dwarfed interior. Several countries have tried to address the undue influence of a dominant urban center by relocating federal functions to a new capital city (for example, Abuja, Ankara, Brasilia, Canberra, Dodoma, Islamabad, and Yamoussoukro). Other countries have attempted to decentralize government activities or to divide national government functions between two or more locations (Cape Town and Pretoria, Santiago and Valparaíso, and La Paz and Sucre). Even the European Community has divided administrative activities between Brussels, Strasbourg, and other urban centers.

In Argentina, plans either to devolve federal government functions from Buenos Aires to an interior city or to construct a new capital have their genesis in the nineteenth-century clashes between unitarists and federalists. Federalists were extremely concerned with the dominance exerted by Buenos Aires over the entire country, whereas Unitarists supported a strong national capital in Buenos Aires. When the Federal District of Buenos Aires was created in 1880, lawmakers and politicians acknowledged that debate over the power exerted by Buenos Aires and about the location of Argentina's capital would continue. Indeed, serious plans to separate the decision-making power of the federal government from Buenos Aires' economic and political power began to surface in the early 1960s (Aguirre 1983, 1987). After years of debate and inaction, the government of Raúl Alfonsín announced in April, 1986, plans to construct a new national capital in the Patagonian city of Viedma. Situated on the Río Negro, which forms both a natural and political boundary between the Pampeana and Patagonia, Viedma would serve as a gateway city, argued supporters of the plan, and would give impetus to policies designed to develop the resources of Patagonia. A new federal capital could help to reduce the influence of Buenos Aires over Argentina and it could help to develop a much needed Patagonian growth pole. Moreover, relocating the capital would allow the government to shed thousands of needless bureaucratic jobs in Buenos Aires. Construction of a new federal capital also had a social aim. Supporters of the new city argued that the unlimited growth of Buenos Aires had "perverted social concord, increased criminality, and greatly disturbed family structures" (Scovazzi 1993, 524). A new capital in Patagonia could help to reverse the unmanageable growth of Buenos Aires and lead to a more harmonious and balanced urban system.

Initial support for the project proved strong, but historical inertia, entrenched political and economic interests, and a debilitating recession combined to kill the plan. Officially still a viable project, the relocation of Argentina's federal capital to Viedma or any other interior city is unlikely in the near future. Argentina's contemporary urban planners, economists, and bureaucrats generally do not see either relocation or devolution as a viable strategy for reducing the influence of Buenos Aires over the nation or for spreading the megacity's economic impetus to the hinterland. Indeed, Larry Sawers (1996), in a recent study that analyzed the structural problems of Argentina's interior, strongly argued against any type of decentralization or devolution away from Buenos Aires. Sawers pointed out that inefficiencies and corruption in the interior would only exacerbate economic backwardness. Moreover, the estimated price tag of building a new federal capital--ranging anywhere from US$300 billion to US$5 trillion depending on the source--would make it a fiscal impossibility for most governments.

Future Development Prospects

Despite the prevailing myth that Patagonia represents an underdeveloped frontier, replete with bountiful natural resources, its present prosperity rests almost exclusively on tremendous subsidies from the federal government. As Larry Sawers (1996:225) convincingly demonstrated, revenue sharing between Argentina's federal and provincial governments heavily favors Patagonia. In 1991, Patagonia received US$569 per capita from the federal treasury, 200 percent of the national average. At the provincial level, Chubut received US$442, Neuquén US$465, Río Negro US$511, Tierra del Fuego US$1021, and Santa Cruz received US$1,099 per capita. This compares extremely unfavorably to the per capita share of US$190 received by Buenos Aires province. Less than 30 percent of provincial spending in

Patagonia for 1992 was financed directly from provincial taxes. Moreover, Patagonian provincial governments, like most of Argentina's other interior governments, spend a high percentage of their current account spending on personnel. Chubut, for example, expended 73 percent of its 1992 budget on payroll costs (Sawers 1996:246). A major development problem for Patagonia, therefore, is that funds received from the federal government are channelled primarily into supporting the provincial government employment rolls rather than into building the infrastructure necessary for socio-economic development.

Embedded in the Menem government's economic restructuring strategies are plans to wean the interior provinces off federal financial support. Foreign investment, the liberalization of international trade agreements, and improved transportation in Patagonia are three key components of these plans. Better provincial tax collection and reductions in provincial government payrolls also figure prominently in federal strategies to encourage interior fiscal austerity and independence. Notwithstanding the problems created by decades of financial subsidies from the federal government, the most serious development issue facing Patagonia over both the short- and long-term is environmental degradation.

Coping With Environmental Degradation

Agriculture, forestry, tourism, and natural resource extraction all have an influence on, and are influenced by, environmental change in Patagonia. Over the past 100 years, human use and abuse of the region's physical environment has created an ecological disaster area. Coupled with natural events such as earthquakes and the 1991 eruption of the Mt. Hudson volcano, as well as the long-term effects of global climate change, human alteration of the Patagonian environment has critical development implications. Irrigated agriculture in the Río Negro basin has created salinization, alkalization, water logging, and flooding problems. Inadequate investment in irrigation infrastructure and in the maintenance of the system has created excessive water loss, groundwater pollution, and topsoil erosion (Manzanal and Rofman 1989; Sawers 1996). Damming rivers for flood and irrigation control has had negative consequences for Patagonia. Silt settles out of the water and does not replenish the soils downstream of the dams, swamps are created behind the dams, mosquitos breed more rapidly in the reservoirs, and aquatic plants grow quickly in the irrigation canals as a result of a reduction in suspended silts in the flowing water.

Soil erosion from the fierce Patagonian winds continues to pose challenges to farmers. Declining soil fertility has reduced overall agricultural yields in northern Patagonia, forced an increase in the use of chemical fertilizers, and accelerated the abandonment of agricultural land. In the Chubut valley, for example, little agricultural activity remains today compared to 100 years ago (Lorenzini et al. 1993). The introduction of sheep, cattle, and goats into the fragile Patagonian ecosystem has devastated much of the region's natural pastures. Sheep and goats pull vegetation up by the roots, and the hooves of these domesticated animals compact the soil and encourage the desertification process. Desertification in Chubut and Santa Cruz provinces is particularly severe and it has contributed to the steady reduction in the total number of sheep raised in Patagonia since the 1940s (República Argentina 1994).   Overpasturing, argued Bonnnie Tucker (1994), is the principal cause of desertification in the region today.

Forestry also contributes to environmental degradation. Throughout the Andes foothills, decades of unsustainable logging have reduced the forests' genetic pool, accelerated disease and pest damage, reduced forest cover, and exposed huge areas of the slopes to wind and water erosion (Garriz 1992). Although reforestation is underway in the provinces of Neuquén and Santa Cruz, no long-term rehabilitation or management strategies exist for the forestry sector. Other natural resource extraction activities also have caused environmental degradation. Petroleum and natural gas exploration, extraction, and refining have destroyed vegetation, polluted coastal waters, disturbed aquatic systems, and fouled urban land.   Industrialization programs developed for Patagonia never considered the environmental impacts of industry. Around industrial sites, the pollution of soils, vegetation, and groundwater has reached critical levels. Moreover, industrial promotion schemes encouraged rapid urban growth, yet no towns or cities in Patagonia had any management strategies to deal with the environmental consequences of growth. Shantytowns, poor water quality, inadequate sewage and solid waste disposal practices, and an overreliance on automobiles all have contributed to urban environmental deterioration in recent decades.

Increased tourism also has had environmental impacts, particularly in fragile ecosystems where solid and human wastes can wreak extensive long-term damage. Although a number of Argentina's private environmental agencies have focused attention on Patagonia's damaged environment since 1991, federal and provincial governments have seemed unwilling or unable to address seriously the environmental problem. President Carlos

Menem did create the Department of Natural Resources and Human Environment in November 1991, and both the president and the governors of the 23 provinces signed the Federal Environmental Pact in May, 1993, which proposes to reach a level of environmental development equal to or better than that of 1990 by the beginning of the next century. However, no integrated national or regional environmental policies have been forthcoming, and environmental issues in Patagonia currently are being addressed on a local, piecemeal basis. Patagonia in the mid-1990s, therefore, stands at a development threshold. Unfortunately for the region's 1.5 million inhabitants, the economy of the region still rests on massive federal government subsidies, and overall prospects for positive change within the context of national liberalization policies are not encouraging.

9

The Problem of Submerging Rural Areas

Poverty, underdevelopment, and declining standards of living have been synonymous with the northern interior provinces for the better part of the last two centuries. These outer rural areas contain a great variety of landscapes and populations, and they are of significant economic, demographic, and cultural importance to Argentina. However, the stagnant northern provinces have remained almost invisible to politicians, researchers, and residents of the Pampeana provinces, especially over the past half-century. As Larry Sawers (1996) pointed out, most analysts of Argentina's development problems have either ignored the interior completely or have dismissed its important with such clichés as "isolated pockets of poverty" (see Waisman 1987, Sábato 1988). In reality, the interior contains only isolated pockets of growth and development. Juan Roccatagliata's (1993a) recent edited volume on the economic geography of Argentina, for example, mentions the development problems of the northern interior provinces but provides little detailed analysis of these problems. Neglect of the northern rural provinces has inhibited the ability of planners, governments, and researchers alike to find solutions to Argentina's national development problems.

Different socioeconomic histories in the northern provinces have produced a variety of land-use patterns, transportation and communication linkages, and economic functions. During the pre-colonial period, sedentary indigenous peoples practiced irrigated agriculture in the Northwest. In the Northeast, indigenous hunter-gatherers dominated the landscape. For much of the Spanish colonial period, the Northwest settlements controlled southern South America and the region was the most densely populated area of the Southern Cone. Throughout the nineteenth century, the rural north remained isolated from the Atlantic core region by high transport costs, provincial tariffs, and costly conflict with neighboring provinces and states. In recent decades, national regional development policies have paid only lip service to the problems of the northern provinces, and they have become mired in poverty and environmental deterioration.

This chapter's analysis is divided into two sections. The first analyzes the Northeast and the second the Northwest. Each section examines the socioeconomic profile of the constituent provinces and explores the potential impact of national socioeconomic restructuring on the people and economies of the region.

The Northeast

Chaco, Corrientes, Formosa, and Misiones provinces traditionally have comprised the development region called the Northeast. A more complete description would include the extreme northern sections of Entre Ríos and Santa Fé provinces above 31.5 degrees latitude and the northeastern third of Santiago del Estero province beyond the Río Salado basin. Portions of extreme western Chaco and Formosa should be included in the Northwest region. A functional description of the entire Northeast region should also include areas across Argentina's borders in Paraguay and Brazil. Many towns and villages in these border areas have similar physical, cultural, and economic characteristics. However, such areas are beyond the scope of this study.

The entire Northeast region can be divided into two distinct physical-cultural zones: the *Llanura Platense* or the basin of the Paraná, Paraguay and Pilcomayo rivers; and the subtropical plateau of Misiones and Corrientes provinces east of the Río Aguapey. Misiones is bounded almost completely by rivers, with the interior composed of forested, low mountains around 200 meters in height. Much of central Corrientes province is marshland and subtropical savannah, and the most intensive agricultural activity is located along the Río Paraná. West of the Paraná and Paraguay rivers, the savannah gives way to arid scrubland, where ranching and some forestry remain the dominant economic activities. To the extreme west lies *El Impenetrable*, an area of thick, intertwined vegetation with few trees. During the dry season this area becomes a desert, but during the rainy season *El Impenetrable* turns to swamp.

Settlement and Communication Patterns

As with Patagonia, much of the Northeast region remained under-developed and isolated from the economic core until well into the twentieth century. After the founding of Corrientes on the Río Paraná in 1588 as an entrepôt settlement on the Asunción-Buenos Aires trade route, socioeconomic development of the immediate hinterland seemed assured. However, the region fell into a state of torpor, as few economic possibilities existed beyond the petty capitalist activities of the town. To the northeast of Corrientes, the Jesuits established a number of missions. San Ignacio, Candelaria, Loreto, Apóstoles, Concepción, Yapeyú, and San Javier were the most important Jesuit settlements in the Northeast and, at their peak, about 55,000 people lived in the missions (Rock 1985). Apart from proselytizing the indigenous Guaraní to Catholicism, the missions cultivated cotton, natural herbs, and vegetables. After the Jesuit expulsions in 1767-1768, economic and demographic decline set in, and within a few years most of the missions lay in ruins.

To the west of the Paraná-Paraguay rivers, the present-day provinces of Chaco and Formosa remained mostly unoccupied by the Spanish and their successors until the second phase of the Conquest of the Desert in the 1880s. Resistencia and Formosa were founded in 1878 and 1879 respectively as military forts from which the government challenged the scattered groups of indigenous hunter-gatherers who populated the area. However, Resistencia had an earlier incarnation in the 1750s as the Jesuit settlement of San Fernando del Río Negro, and it served as the starting point for woodcutters who eventually cleared the Chaco for graziers and agricultural colonists. These two forts later became the capitals of their respective provinces.

Argentine sovereignty over much of the Northeast region remained tentative until the War of the Triple Alliance against Paraguay ended in 1870. Chaco and Formosa were seized from Paraguay as a prize of war, and most of present-day Misiones province was ceded to Argentina by Brazil and Paraguay. In 1881, the federal government created the Misiones Territory, separating it from the province of Corrientes. On the eve of this separation, however, the Corrientes provincial government sold 70 percent of the land area of Misiones, about 2 million hectares, to 29 individuals. Thus the pattern of large landholdings already found in other regions of Argentina was replicated in the Northeast.

At the 1869 census, 128,545 people lived in the Northeast, or 7.4 percent of Argentina's total population. By the end of the nineteenth century, nearly 50,000 people lived in Misiones, over 200,000 resided in Corrientes, and several thousand hardy settlers had colonized parts of Chaco and Formosa. German colonists around Eldorado in the upper Paraná area of Misiones were the most successful immigrants, but other European nationalities plus Asians, Arabs, and Brazilians also contributed to the area's growth. During the 1950s, many Japanese migrants settled successfully in central Misiones, and in recent years Brazilians have dominated in-migration. In 1991, the Northeast accounted for only 8.7 percent of Argentina's national population, approximately 2.8 million people. Nearly 400,000 people live in Chaco province, and the remaining 2.4 million are split relatively evenly between Formosa, Corrientes, and Misiones provinces. Rural depopulation of the region has been endemic since the 1940s. Posadas and Corrientes are the largest urban areas in the Northeast, each with populations around 260,000 in their respective greater metropolitan areas. Resistencia, a few kilometers across the Río Paraná from Corrientes by the General Belgrano bridge, is approaching 250,000 inhabitants in size. Other important urban centers include Formosa, the provincial capital, with a population near 100,000; Presidencia Roque Sáenz Peña, an important agricultural center about 200 kilometers west of Resistencia, with 50,000 inhabitants; and Goya, the second largest city in Corrientes province, with approximately 50,000 residents. Population densities throughout most of the Northeast are extremely low, with the exception of the major urban centers.

Transportation Networks

Railroads began to link the Northeast region to the rest of Argentina during the early years of the twentieth century. Initial railroad construction in the region had begun in the 1890s, when investors funded a line designed to link the city of Corrientes to the Pampeana core. The standard-gauge General Urquiza railroad from Buenos Aires reached Posadas in Misiones province during 1912 and connected to the Paraguayan railroad from Asunción via a ferryboat across the Río Paraná. A branch of this line extended into northwest Corrientes to connect with the railroad extending south from the provincial capital. A direct east-west link between Posadas and Corrientes along the Río Paraná failed to extend more than a few kilometers east of Corrientes. An extension of the railroad along the Río Paraná northeast from Posadas toward Iguazúa also had been planned, but the project never obtained adequate funding to continue. Today, a combination road-rail bridge allows for direct links between Paraguay and Argentina, although rail service across the river has been inactive for years. Planned connections between the General Urquiza railroad and the Brazilian network at Monte Caseros and Paso de los Libres also never materialized, in part because the Brazilians operated a meter-gauge line from the border to Porto Alegre. Today, a bridge at Paso de los Libres carries a rail line across the Río Uruguay, but integrated service with Brazil remains an unfulfilled dream.

West of the Río Paraná, the narrow-gauge Belgrano railroad extended from west to east across Chaco and Formosa provinces. A northern branch connected Formosa to northeastern Salta province at Embarcación and a southern branch linked Resistencia to southeastern Salta at Metán. Numerous local lines off the southern branch reached important agricultural centers in eastern Chaco province, and a north-south spur connected to the Tucumán-Santa Fé main line in southern Santiago del Estero province. A north-south extension of the Belgrano system also linked Resistencia to Santa Fé along the western side of the Río Paraná. In the early 1990s, most of these railroads had no passenger service and the more remote local lines essentially had been abandoned. Privatization of the Urquiza network east of the Río Paraná is projected to revitalize freight operations in the Northeast, but massive infusions of investment capital are needed before any of the lines approach the level of operating efficiency found in North America or in Europe.

All of the national highways that link the provincial capitals and major urban centers are paved but are in poor condition. Especially vulnerable to damage is the major highway linking Buenos Aires and the Northeast provinces to Brazil. This route has experienced a dramatic increase in heavy truck traffic over the past five years as a consequence of MERCOSUR-driven increases in trade. Under the federal government's privatization program, most major routes are to be sold to private investors. However, the only infrastructural improvements on many of the highways privatized since 1991 have been the construction of toll booths. Many of the Northeast's provincial and rural roads remain unpaved, most constructed of consolidated materials or simply of dirt. During the rainy season, many secondary roads in Chaco and Formosa provinces are impassable for weeks at a time. Regular air service links the provincial capitals and a handful of important towns such as Iguazú to Buenos Aires. Other communications facilities in the Northeast, such as telephones, computers, facsimile

machines, and mail remain inefficient and starved of infrastructural investment. The Northeast will continue to be severely disadvantaged socially
and economically because it lacks the basic transport and communication
services and infrastructure that are the foundation of modern, developed
economies.

The Northeast's Economic Patterns

The foundation of the Northeast's contemporary economy rests on pastoral activities, crop cultivation--particularly cotton, rice, and yerba maté--
forestry, and some industry. In recent years, tourism and hydroelectric
power generation have contributed to the regional economy.

Agriculture and Pastoral Activities. Yerba maté production dominates
the economy of Misiones. The leaves of this plant are brewed into a potent
tea that has become the national drink of Argentina. Production of yerba
maté is concentrated in northeast Corrientes and southwest Misiones primarily on *minifundios* of less than 25 hectares. About 98 percent of production is distributed within the domestic market and two percent is
exported to countries such as the United States, Lebanon, Syria, Chile,
Uruguay, and Australia, where large communities of Argentinos are found.
Abolition of the Regulatory Commission for the Production and Sale of
Yerba Maté (CRYM) in 1991 as part of the Menem government's economic
restructuring policies has had, and will continue to have, serious consequences for maté production in the Northeast. Other price support and
tariff reductions signal difficult years ahead for the Northeast's agriculturalists. Tung oil, tobacco, and tea are the important secondary crops of
Misiones and some citrus fruits, soybeans, tomatoes, and manioc also
contribute to the local and regional economy.

Cattle and sheep have dominated the Corrientes economy since the nineteenth century. The province contains approximately 8 percent (4.1 million
head) of the national cattle herd and about 7.5 percent, or 1.4 million, of
Argentina's sheep stocks. Nearly 95 percent of all agricultural land in
Corrientes province is dedicated to pastoral activities, yet cattle and sheep
combined contribute less than 50 percent of the gross agricultural product
of the province (Bruniard and Bolsi 1992; Carlevari and Carlevari 1994;
República Argentina 1994). Crop cultivation is restricted to the immediate
vicinity of the Ríos Paraná and Uruguay, particularly in the southwest
corner of the province. Frequent flooding, soil erosion, and soil infertility
present ongoing challenges to farmers in Corrientes.

Rice has become the most important commercial crop and Corrientes now produces about one-third of the national rice harvest (Carlevari and Carlevari 1994). Argentine rice is expensive to produce and growers have not taken advantage of recent advances in rice genetics. As a consequence, yields from the Northeast are much lower than those achieved by the major rice-growing and exporting countries (Sawers 1996). The rice industry in the Northeast also suffers from a lack of investment in modern machinery, a failure to utilize more productive land, and from serious inefficiencies in harvesting and distribution. Other important crops in Corrientes include tobacco, which has declined rapidly since the 1970s, citrus fruit, and small amounts of cotton, corn, and subsistence crops. In the 1980s, citrus fruits replaced tobacco as the most important agricultural crop and now contribute approximately 25 percent of the gross agricultural product of the province. Oranges, mandarins, and lemons are the dominant crops, but the region faces stiff competition in the domestic market from the Cuyo and the Alto Valle area of Patagonia. In Corrientes, the overall share of the primary sector improved slightly between 1986 and 1992, growing from just under 12 percent to approximately 16 percent of the province's gross domestic product (Table 9.1).

Formosa and Chaco are the poorest and least developed provinces of Argentina and much of the land is not conducive to extensive commercial agriculture. Cotton and cattle are the mainstays of the contemporary economy, although a persistent crisis in the cotton industry since the 1960s has encouraged some diversification to soybean, corn, sunflower, and sorghum production. Environmental conditions limit the production of cotton to a narrow belt that stretches from the Paraguayan border, through the mid-section of Formosa and Chaco, and into northern Santa Fé and northeastern Santiago del Estero (Manzanal and Rofman 1989). This area produces 92 percent of Argentina's cotton, most of which remains in the domestic market as Chaqueñan cotton particularly is too poor in quality for export. Just under 350,000 hectares of land are under cotton cultivation in this area, with about 70 percent of the total agricultural land in both Formosa and Chaco planted in cotton (Carlevari and Carlevari 1994). Problems facing cotton producers in the Northeast include obsolete machinery, inadequate levels of capital investment, soil degradation, a chronic shortage of labor, stiff competition from more efficient cotton-growing areas in the world economy, and an ongoing deterioration in the physical environment.

Bracketing the cotton belt to the east and west are cattle ranches and small farms. Approximately 4 million head of cattle and 150,000 sheep

TABLE 9.1   Gross Domestic Product in Corrientes Province by Sector, 1986 and 1992

Sector	1986	Percent	1992	Percent
	(In thousands of pesos at constant 1986 prices)			
Agriculture	12,465	11.28	19,340	15.64
Resource Extraction	645	0.58	426	0.34
Manufacturing	22,432	20.30	25,743	20.82
Public Utilities	2,487	2.25	2,711	2.19
Construction	9,007	8.15	7,811	6.32
Commercial Services	12,727	11.52	9,483	7.67
Transportation	4,062	3.68	5,588	4.52
Financial Services	12,211	11.05	11,802	9.54
Personal Services	34,476	31.19	40,761	32.96
Total:	110,512	100.00	123,665	100.00

Source: República Argentina (1995).

roam the natural pastures of the two provinces. Overgrazing and soil erosion afflict much of the western portions of Formosa and Chaco, but to the east modern cattle raising techniques from the pampas have not inflicted as much environmental damage. Pastoral activities in the eastern section of Formosa and Chaco have contributed to rural depopulation in the area, as cattle ranching is not labor intensive. Moreover, the area has been heavily over-logged and few opportunities exist in natural resource extraction. Only in Misiones province, where reforestation is under way to support growth in the cellulose paste and paper industries, is the forestry sector reasonably healthy.

Hydroelectricity and Growth Pole Strategies. Industrial activity in the Northeast, with the exception of agricultural-related processing, has been non-existent for most of the twentieth century. Industrial promotion schemes and growth-pole strategies introduced between the late 1960s and the end of the 1970s focused on Patagonia and the Northwest, not on the Northeast region. Although the Argentine government viewed Misiones as a cornerstone province in its national geopolitical strategy, Chile was perceived as presenting much more of a threat than either Brazil or Paraguay. Moreover, during this period Brazil had become heavily involved in opening the Amazon Basin to development and did not appear to be paying much attention to the Misiones border region. Failure of Brazil's Amazon program and the southward expansion of industrial activity from the São Paulo area into the states of Paraná, Santa Catarina, and Rio Grande do Sul at the end of the 1970s helped to refocus the Argentine government's attention on the Northeast. These three Brazilian states experienced dramatic industrial and demographic growth during the 1980s (Diniz 1994). Brazil also began construction in the early 1970s on a huge hydroelectric complex in partnership with Paraguay on the Río Paraná just a few kilometers north of the Argentina-Brazil-Paraguay border. The world's largest hydroelectric project until completion of Argentina's Yacyretá facility, the Itaipú dam created a 220-meter deep reservoir covering 1,350 square kilometers and it has an installed capacity of 12.6 million kilowatts.

Between 1980 and 1985, the Northeast region received 34.5 percent of Argentina's total investment promotion funds. Misiones province alone received 93 percent of the funds allocated to the Northeast, and Posadas was designated a growth-pole city (República Argentina 1985). However, rather than investing in industrial activities complementary to Brazil's southeastern economy, the government channeled funds into agricultural processing, cellulose paste and paper manufacturing, and low-quality durable consumer goods. In addition, funds continued to flow into the construction of the world's largest hydroelectric facility at Yacyretá on the Río Paraná at the Misiones-Corrientes provincial border, a project first proposed in 1973 during the last Perón administration. A joint project between Paraguay and Argentina, the two countries created a commission in 1974 called *El Ente Binacional Yacyretá* to oversee the judicial, financial, and administrative aspects of the construction. With an original cost estimate of US$1.5 billion, the final price tag of the Yacyretá project may approach US$12 billion. Even President Carlos Menem has called Yacyretá a "monument" to corruption and vowed during his 1989 presidential campaign to halt construction. However, the Menem government since has solicited further international loans for the project and construction continues.

On September 2, 1994, the presidents of Paraguay and Argentina officially inaugurated the Yacyretá hydroelectric facility. When the system's 20 turbines are fully operational in 1998, approximately 20,000 Gigawatts of electricity will be produced, enough to satisfy over 40 percent of Argentina's electricity demand. The reservoir created by the dam covers 142,000 hectares and it has submerged the Río Paraná for 200 kilometers upstream from the dam (Durán et al. 1995). Many low-lying areas on both sides of the river, including Posadas in Misiones and Encarnación in Paraguay, have been inundated, requiring the relocation of nearly 40,000 people.

The long-term objective of the Yacyretá project is to stimulate industrial development around the Posadas-Encarnación growth-pole, although a concrete strategy detailing exactly what industries will be attracted and how these industries will contribute to regional socioeconomic development has yet to be produced. Moreover, environmental concerns about Yacyretá have never been addressed satisfactorily. Research indicates that the reservoir will create a new habitat for anopheline mosquitos, posing an increased malaria risk in a region where the disease had been on the verge of eradication. Questions also have been raised about the necessity of constructing such a dam when the Itaipú facility already supplies more than enough energy for the area. Other concerns center on the silt that will collect behind the dam over the coming decades and what impacts this will have on soil fertility, flow patterns, and fish habitats downstream.

Despite the construction of two of the world's largest hydroelectric facilities, the Northeast region is the focus of two other hydroelectric projects. The *Proyecto del Paraná Medio* calls for a series of dams on the lower Río Paraná that would create a huge reservoir from the 29th parallel to just north of the Santa Fé and Paraná metropolitan areas. A second scheme called the *Proyecto Iberá* envisions flooding the Iberá marshes in north-central Corrientes province to control flooding in the lower Paraná basin and to create a navigable waterway linking the upper Paraná to the Río Uruguay (Carlevari and Carlevari 1994). Again, no real environmental analysis of the long-term impact of these projects has been conducted and Argentina's government is unable to explain precisely what long-term benefits these projects could bring to either the country or to the Northeast.

Tourism. The final major component of the Northeast's economy is tourism, with international and domestic tourists drawn to the region's two major attractions: a world-famous natural feature and an important historic cultural landscape. Both of these attractions are in Misiones province, and few tourists venture into the area west of the Río Paraná. Sitting amidst subtropical rainforest along the border between Argentina and Brazil, Iguazú Falls is a series of cataracts that stretch over two kilometers along the Río Iguazú. The cataracts occur where the Río Iguazú flows over a basaltic plateau that ends abruptly just east of the confluence with the Río Paraná. Beyond the basaltic plateau, sedimentary terrain has been eroded by the water to a depth of over 70 meters, creating a spectacular series of waterfalls (Figure 9.1). Most of the National Park area's commercial development has occurred on the Brazilian side of the cataracts, although most visitors prefer to view the Falls from the Argentine side.

The ruined Jesuit missions offer tourists an intriguing historic cultural landscape to explore in the central section of Misiones province. Many visitors headquarter in Posadas and tour the missions located with a 100-kilometer radius of the city. San Ignacio Guazú, Santa Ana, and San Ignacio Miní are the favorite destinations. The ruins of San Ignacio Guazú were rediscovered in 1897 and are the most impressive in the Northeast; they underwent extensive restoration in the 1940s and 1950s (Bernhardson and Massolo 1992). As with other areas of Argentina, tourism is viewed by many as a panacea for the economic ills that afflict the region. However, poor transportation facilities, inadequate infrastructure, and a lack of investment in tourist activities continue to restrict the tourism's growth in the Northeast.

Future Development Prospects

Agriculture remains limited in the Northeast, with inadequate investment, deteriorating environmental conditions, and poor quality production serious barriers to positive growth in the future. Crops produced in the Northeast have great difficulty competing in the highly competitive regional and global marketplaces and have only survived into the 1990s by receiving massive federal government subsidies. Secondary and tertiary sector opportunities are extremely limited, although potential does exist for Corrientes and Misiones provinces to benefit from increased interaction with Paraguay and Brazil as a result of the MERCOSUR trade agreement. The major transportation corridor between Argentina and its MERCOSUR partners runs through the northeastern section of the country. Planned improvements in transportation infrastructure and services along this corridor may provide a firm foundation for socioeconomic improvements in the region. However, the key component of improved interaction between Brazil and Argentina is the Southern Cone Superhighway, projected to run south from Rio de Janeiro along the Atlantic coast to Montevideo in Uruguay and then across the Río de la Plata estuary to Buenos Aires. If this project comes to fruition, the Northeast provinces, particularly Misiones and Corrientes, may be further isolated from the socioeconomic core as most of the international traffic would bypass the region completely.

FIGURE 9.1   Iguazú Falls, Misiones Province.

Development potential for the Northeast also has been linked to the Paraná-Paraguay River Basin project. The five countries that share the Basin have proposed a plan to create a vast inland waterway system called the Hidrovía that would link Puerto Suárez and west central Brazil to the Atlantic via Paraguay and Argentina. At the official 14th Reunion of the Ministers of Public Works and Transportation of the Southern Cone convened in Campo Grande, Brazil, in 1988, the five governments agreed to establish an intergovernmental committee to coordinate the project (Padula 1993). Supporters of the Hidrovía project argue that regional development in the Basin cannot occur without this vital fluvial commercial link to the global maritime network, and that transportation costs could be cut by up to 60 percent (Carlevari and Carlevari 1994). Detractors argue that no cost-benefit analysis has been conducted to prove how regional development might occur as a result of the Hidrovía. Moreover, opponents argue, the environmental damage caused by the construction could be monumental in impact and scope. For example, concerns have been raised by indigenous groups and others about environmental threats to the Gran Pantanal, an important wetlands region in west central Brazil (Caviedes and Knapp 1995). Other concerns have focused on the project's impact on farmland in the lower Paraná basin and on pollution problems in the Río de la Plata estuary.

By any measure, the Northeast is the poorest of Argentina's poor interior regions. Despite the billions of dollars invested in the region's agriculture, hydroelectric projects, industrial promotion schemes, and transport infrastructure, little improvement in the basic quality of life for the Northeast's nearly 3 million inhabitants has been evident. The region's gross domestic product is thought to be less than 60 percent of the national average, although the federal government has few reliable up-to-date statistics on GDP by province. In 1989, GDP from the Northeast accounted for only 4.92 percent of the national total, with Corrientes alone accounting for 41 percent of regional GDP (República Argentina 1995).

Most basic indicators of poverty for the Northeast far exceed both national and Pampeana averages. In 1991, 64.3 percent of the region's population lived in deficient housing and 42.3 percent of all inhabitants suffered from unsatisfied basic needs (República Argentina 1991). These figures compared unfavorably to the core Pampeana provinces, where only 22 percent lived in deficient housing and less than 20 percent of the total population suffered from unsatisfied basic needs. Over 75 percent of the rural population in Chaco, Corrientes, and Formosa lived in dirt-floor housing in 1991. Primary school dropout rates for the Northeast are three times as high as in the Pampeana core, illiteracy rates are higher, and unemployment or underemployment rates continue to climb, especially in the major urban centers. With poverty embedded in the region's socio-economic structures, the environment fast deteriorating, little investment in modern agricultural techniques and technologies, and few industrial or service-oriented opportunities, the immediate future for the Northeast looks bleak. President Menem's economic restructuring strategies and globalization policies have had little positive impact on the Northeast since 1990.

The Northwest

Most definitions of the Northwest include the six provinces of Catamarca, Jujuy, La Rioja, Salta, Santiago del Estero, and Tucumán. A more accurate description of the region disregards the political boundaries and incorporates certain physical, cultural, and economic features that distinctly define this spatial milieu. In this more functional definition, the extreme westernmost portions of Chaco and Formosa provinces are included, and the eastern half of Santiago del Estero and the southeastern corners of Catamarca and La Rioja provinces are excluded. The Northwest, as re-defined, encompasses approximately 540,000 square kilometers or about

20 percent of Argentina's continental surface and is characterized by three major physical zones.

To the west, the deserts and valleys of the high Andean plateau and the Andean *precordillera* (foothills) are separated by north- to south-trending mountain ranges. The *precordillera* rises to a height of 5,000 meters, while the High Andes have peaks over 6,500 meters. The geological formations of the region hinder inter-valley communication and isolate settlements in the western areas from the major urban centers located in the eastern valleys. The extreme eastern section of the Northwest is characterized by arid and semi-arid scrublands and is a continuation of the broad plain that borders the Paraná and Paraguay rivers. The third major physical zone incorporates the modestly fertile valleys that lie between the mountains and the scrublands. For example, the Tucumán-Orán wedge or *Ramal* has a subtropical climate with adequate rainfall for agriculture. Although rainfall is spread unevenly throughout the year across the region, irrigation and dam projects have enabled the Northwest's central strip to become the most active production and population nucleus of the north (Santillán de Andrés and Ricci 1992).

Just under four million people inhabit the Northwest, concentrated primarily in the Jujuy and Lerma valleys and in the eastern piedmont of the Aconquija clustered around Tucumán. Overall densities in these areas surpass 100 inhabitants per square kilometer, with densities higher in the urban cores. Eight urban areas in the Northwest account for just over two million people, more than half of the entire region's population, thus replicating the degree of urban primacy found at the national level. In the high puna and along the more elevated sections of the major *quebradas* (tributary stream valleys), such as Humahuaca in the north and Santa María-Guachipas to the south, population densities are much lower and rarely exceed 2 persons per square kilometer. Rural populations are grouped in small villages sheltered from the mountains or where they can capture sufficient water for drinking and irrigation. Other small settlements are located near mining areas to the extreme west.

Figure 9.2 details the main population centers of the Northwest and highlights the general north-south orientation of traffic flow. Both settlement and traffic flow patterns are dictated to a significant degree by the physical environment. The dominant urban center of the Northwest is San Miguel de Tucumán, founded in 1565. Throughout the colonial period, Tucumán functioned as an important gateway city between present-day Bolivia and the Atlantic coast. Today, the city contains nearly 750,000

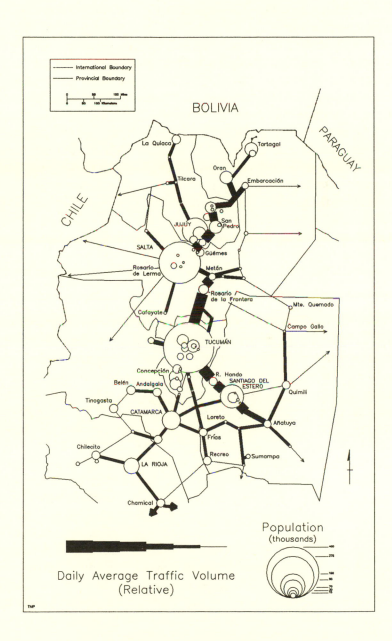

FIGURE 9.2   Population Centers and Average Daily Traffic Flows in the Northwest, 1991. *Source*: After Santillán de Andrés and Ricci (1992).

inhabitants in its environs and is the center of the Northwest's sugar industry. It also functions as the most important economic, political, and educational center in the Northwest, with the built environment showing visible evidence of global economic and cultural influences (Figure 9.3). About 320 kilometers north of Tucumán lies Salta, the region's second most important city with 375,000 inhabitants. Salta has retained its colonial atmosphere, with numerous colonial-period buildings, and it functions as the most important tourist center of the region (Figure 9.4). Sugar, tobacco, and other agricultural products are the mainstay of the local economy, while growth-pole policies in recent decades have encouraged modest industrialization. Both the Santiago del Estero-La Banda and San Salvador de Jujuy-Palpalá urban agglomerations have populations over 150,000. Industrial activities also have developed in these cities over the past 30 years as a result of national growth pole policies, although without any significant impact on the area's economy.

Patterns of Economic Development

During the colonial period, the economic rhythm of the Northwest depended heavily on the silver mining activities of Potosí. A downturn in silver production caused economic depression throughout the Northwest. Indigenous societies scattered about the region supplied maize, potatoes, beans, squash, and quinoa for local and Potosí consumption during the initial stages of Spanish settlement. In the seventeenth century, the Northwest supplied Potosí with fruit, melons, grapes, cotton, dyestuffs, and honey, as well as sheep and cattle from the pampas grasslands to the south (Cobb 1949). Material life in colonial times revolved around the production of commodities for interregional trade and not for intraregional or local markets. The economy of the Northwest became highly specialized and symbiotically linked to the commerce spurred by silver production. A cycle of silver-for-imports fostered local self-sufficiency, hindered local and intraregional trade and specialization, and became an almost insurmountable barrier to regional socioeconomic development. Silver, and the demand for goods and services that its production generated, helped to structure a Pan-Andean socioeconomic space characterized by interregional market networks that laid the foundation for subsequent uneven regional development (Sempat Assadourian 1983; Stern 1985).

With the loss of the Bolivian market after 1810 as a consequence of national independence movements, small-scale artisanal manufacturing

FIGURE 9.3   Global Economic Influences in the City of Tucumán.

FIGURE 9.4   Skyline of the City of Salta.

declined steadily. By the 1870s, the exchange of mules and silver had been destroyed and most rural communities had fallen back on subsistence agriculture. Large land holdings controlled by a few elite families became the norm and the region's local manufacturers and skilled artisans, for the most part, were replaced by landless, nomadic peoples. Only in the provincial capitals did the transition from traditional to more commercial and industrial activities take place. Tucumán, for example, began a process of economic diversification, as new industries such as saw mills, tanneries, tobacco growing, and cane alcohol production took hold (Brown 1979). The railroad's arrival in Tucumán in 1876 spelled the end of small-scale textile manufacturing. Local products could not compete with imports from Europe or from the pampas either in the local or in the regional and national marketplace. Coupled with special tariff protection extended to the sugar industry in 1877, reductions in shipping time and costs triggered by the railroad led to a dramatic growth in sugar production. Tobacco production also benefitted from tariffs and railroads.

Sugar and Tobacco. Sugar and tobacco have dominated the economy of the Northwest since the late nineteenth century. Table 9.2 details the dramatic change in the percentage of cultivated land in sugar cane between 1874 and 1914 in the Tucumán area. From only a 5 percent share in 1874, sugar cane production exploded to occupy 70 percent of the total cultivated land area by 1914. In contrast, the staple products of maize and wheat accounted for 72 percent of agricultural production prior to the railroad's arrival. By 1914, wheat production had all but disappeared and maize production had fallen to 27 percent. In terms of volume, sugar production grew from a few metric tons in the 1870s to approximately 540,000 metric tons by the 1940s. During the 1980s and into the 1990s, sugar production hovered between 1.1 and 1.6 million tons annually (República Argentina 1994). However production has shown a declining trend since the 1980 harvest, a direct result of liberalizing forces in the economy.

Tucumán province presently accounts for about 55 percent of all sugar production in Argentina, Jujuy contributes 25 percent, and Salta province accounts for about 13 percent. The remaining 7 percent comes from several isolated areas, including western Corrientes and Misiones (Lorenzini et al. 1993; Sawers 1996). Almost all sugar grown in the Northwest comes from irrigated land, and most of the irrigation networks are heavily subsidized by the federal and provincial governments. The Northwest also supplies 70 percent of the national production of tobacco, and approximately 65 percent

TABLE 9.2 The Percentage of Cultivated Land in Tucumán by Major Product, 1874-1914

Product	1874	1882	1895	1905	1914
Sugar Cane	5	14	53	44	70
Maize	42	40	35	33	27
Wheat	30	26	1	5	*
Rice	7	7	*	2	1
Tobacco	2	2	3	3	*
Alfalfa	7	7	5	4	*
Other Crops	7	4	3	9	1
Total**	100	100	100	100	100

* Less than one percent.
** Columns may not add to 100 percent due to rounding.
Source: After Balán (1982:41).

of all land under tobacco cultivation is located in the region. In Salta and Jujuy, large estates using wage labor dominate the production of sugar and tobacco, and average yields are higher than in Tucumán province. At the beginning of the 1990s, over 90 percent of all sugar farmers in Tucumán grew sugar cane on *minifundios* with less than 20 hectares and they accounted for approximately 35 percent of the province's total harvest. Similarly, over 50 percent of the tobacco grown in Tucumán is produced on farms of less than 5 hectares, and only 1 percent of tobacco growers in the province had farms greater than 25 hectares (Manzanal and Rofman 1989).

Throughout the twentieth century, sugar and tobacco cultivation in the Northwest have created a culture of poverty. Working and living conditions for sugar and tobacco workers are deplorable. Bolivian migrants are the primary source of seasonal labor for both sugar and tobacco harvesting (Figure 9.5). These migrants receive pitiful wages and they are forced to live in unsanitary, crowded conditions for the five-to-six month harvest period. Throughout the sugar and tobacco zones of the Northwest, workers live in compounds without electricity, sewage disposal, or running water. Houses are constructed of mud and canvas, with cane or, occasionally, wood or metal roofs. In most cases, three to four families are crowded into a four-square-meter room. Many of the larger tobacco farms in Tucumán employ migrant workers who travel primarily from Catamarca and Santiago del Estero provinces.

FIGURE 9.5   Bolivian Migrant Heading Home from the Sugar Harvest, Humahuaca, Jujuy Province.

Both sugar and tobacco production in the Northwest are feeling the impact of changes in national, regional, and global production and demand. Health concerns have reduced the demand for both commodities in the industrialized, developed countries. For example, per capita sugar consumption in the United States, long an importer of sugar from Argentina, has declined since the 1950s and corn sugar is replacing cane and beet sugar. The European Community has changed from a net importer of sugar in the 1950s and 1960s to the world's second largest sugar exporter (Manzanal and Rofman 1989; Carlevari and Carlevari 1994). Brazil, one of Argentina's regional competitors and a partner in the Southern Cone Common Market, extends significant protection to its sugar industry and any liberalization of the sugar trade is liable to have negative impacts on the Northwest. Prospects for tobacco production also are bleak, especially in light of growing anti-smoking policies in the developed countries and competition from low-cost producers in other developing countries.

Other Agricultural and Natural Resource Production. Although sugar and tobacco continue to dominate the Northwest's economy, progress has been made in recent years with the production of other agricultural crops. Tomatoes, beans, citrus fruits, and cotton are grown for the local and national markets. Citrus production now accounts for about 10 percent of Tucumán's annual agricultural output and approximately 5 percent of agricultural production in Salta and Jujuy provinces (Yanes and Gerber 1989; Carlevari and Carlevari 1994). Between 1987 and 1992, for example, Tucumán produced 81 percent of the national lemon crop and Salta produced 35 percent of the grapefruit crop. Since the 1960s, huge tracts of land in the northeast corner of Santiago del Estero province have been converted to irrigated cotton, and the area now produces 15 percent of Argentina's cotton crop. Some land in Salta, Tucumán, and Jujuy also has been converted from sugar to cotton production in recent years.

Agricultural production in the provinces of Catamarca and La Rioja is dominated by *minifundios*. Principal crops grown in these provincial oases include alfalfa, peaches, asparagus, walnuts, cotton, and some tobacco (Santillán de Andrés and Ricci 1992). Throughout Salta and Jujuy provinces, thousands of *minifundios* are found along the north-south valleys in the central section of the region. In the Río Calchaquí valley of western Salta, for example, alfalfa, fruits, and vegetables are grown for the local and regional markets. Along the main highway north to Bolivia in the Quebrada de Humahuaca, *minifundios* produce corn and alfalfa for local consumption and grow onions for sale in the regional markets (Santillán de Andrés and Ricci 1992). Soy, kidney, and black beans are cultivated on a narrow strip of land called the Umbral al Chaco, literally the beginning of the Chaco region, which sits between the foothills of the Andes and the eastern arid plains.

Natural resource extraction includes logging, oil and gas production, and mining. Much of the Northwest's forests were over-logged during the first decades of the twentieth century and very little reforestation has occurred since. Less than 40,000 hectares of reforested land exists in the Northwest, less than 5 percent of the total reforested area in Argentina, and most of this reforestation is found in Salta and Jujuy provinces. The Northwest accounts for less than 6 percent of the total forested land in Argentina (Carlevari and Carlevari 1994), and current plans call for the logging of the remaining forests in the region (*Buenos Aires Herald* May 15, 1994). Approximately 25 percent of Argentina's proven natural gas reserves was located in the Northwest in 1993, primarily in Salta, along with about 6 percent of the nation's proven oil reserves (República Argentina 1994). Slightly less than 10 percent of Argentina's total non-metalliferous mineral production came from the Northwest in 1993, but the region accounted for over 75 percent of all metalliferous mineral production in Argentina. Silver and zinc are mined in Jujuy, boracite in Jujuy and Salta (Argentina is the third largest producer of boracite after the United States and Turkey), gold in Catamarca, and limestone in Jujuy and Catamarca. Most of the mineral production of the Northwest is absorbed within the domestic economy.

Industrial Promotion Schemes

Agricultural-based poverty in the Northwest encouraged the federal government to focus regional development strategies on the region in the late 1960s. Social polarization in the Northwest was, and remains, extreme and levels of social hostility toward the end of the 1960s were very high. In Tucumán, for example, the militant Peronist Armed Forces set up a guerilla camp near Taco Ralo and later expanded operations to the main urban centers (Hodges 1988). The military government that seized power in 1966 attempted to rectify public sector inefficiencies by creating a modernizing autocracy based on the Brazilian model that would transform the Northwest's society from above (Rock 1985). The National System of Development Planning and Action (CONADE) was created to reverse the process of industrial concentration in the Pampeana and to address the serious inequalities that existed between the interior regions and the littoral. The government produced an emergency development plan for the North- west that attempted to reverse the trends of rural-urban migration, unem- ployment, and regional economic stagnation (República Argentina 1966). In a clear display of its power and intentions, the military government forcibly closed eleven sugar mills in Tucumán and amalgamated many larger ones. The policy aimed at resolving chronic problems associated with *minifundios*, unremitting poverty, and a rising tide of unemployment resulting from an overproduction of sugar. New labor-intensive industries such as textiles, electrical manufacturing, and sugar-related processing sprang up in Tucumán and over 3,000 jobs were created between 1967 and 1970. Yet many of these jobs came from other sectors of the economy, and unemployment among displaced farmers and sugar-industry workers remained extremely high (Morris 1972).

By 1975, the benefits of industrial promotion had spread to Jujuy, Salta, and Santiago del Estero, yet most of the new factories remained concen- trated in Tucumán. The area between the cities of Salta, Güemes, San Pedro, and Jujuy received growth-pole status in 1971, although little development occurred because socioeconomic linkages focused on Buenos Aires and not on the surrounding hinterland. In 1979, the military government introduced a new industrial promotion scheme for La Rioja province and offered huge tax concessions for any industry that would locate there (Díaz 1989). However, a general pattern of economic benefits for the Northwest from industrial promotion schemes began to emerge only after the restoration of democracy in 1983. Increases in manufacturing employment were short lived, unfortunately, because the industrial promotion schemes coincided with the general process of global industrial restructuring that reached Argentina in the early 1980s. For example, between 1980 and 1985 Tucumán lost 12,000 industrial jobs, while Salta and Catamarca each lost around 1,000 jobs. Only Jujuy showed a positive change during this period with 2,000 industrial jobs gained (República Argentina 1985). Manufacturing's contribution to the region's gross domestic product has declined since the 1970s. In Salta, for example, manufacturing accounted for 33 percent of the province's GDP in 1980 but only 28 percent in 1992 (Table 9.3). The fastest growing sector of the Salta economy since 1980 has been social and personal services, with accounted for nearly 21 percent of provincial GDP in 1992.

Many of the industrial jobs lost came from regional companies who could no longer compete in the national and global marketplace (Yanes and Gerber 1990). Ramón Díaz's (1991) recent study of exports from La Rioja province highlighted the problems related to the cost of shipping goods to market in Buenos Aires or to other countries. La Rioja's proximity to the Pacific ports of Valparaíso and Antofagasta is negated because all-weather routes have not been developed across the Andean passes. The railroad network in La Rioja is in poor repair; there are no passenger services and freight trains are rare and extremely slow. Exporters in La Rioja must rely on expensive air transport or must ship their products by truck. Unfortunately, few intraregional links exist to spread the benefits of industrial promotion to the hinterlands, and few north-south links exist to facilitate trade with adjoining provinces or with Bolivia, Brazil, Chile, Paraguay and Peru. Inadequate transportation, the lack of external economies, and competition from the economies of agglomeration provided by the Pampeana cities continue to plague industrial development in the Northwest.

Tourism

As with other interior provinces in Argentina, provincial leaders in the Northwest perceive tourism as a key component of economic development.

TABLE 9.3   Gross Domestic Product in Salta Province by Sector, 1980 and 1992

Sector	1980	Percent	1992	Percent
	(In thousands of pesos at constant 1986 prices)			
Agriculture	19,703	15.64	23,468	15.50
Resource Extraction	1,658	1.32	3,166	2.09
Manufacturing	41,595	33.02	42,722	28.21
Public Utilities	2,544	2.02	4,725	3.12
Construction	8,621	6.84	7,805	5.15
Commercial Services	19,012	15.10	22,340	14.75
Transportation	1,671	1.33	1,961	1.29
Financial Services	11,333	9.00	13,805	9.12
Personal Services	19,811	15.73	31,447	20.77
Total:	125,948	100.00	151,439	100.00

Source: República Argentina (1995).

Several prehispanic sites are found in the region, and the areas around Tilcara, Tolombón, and Santa Rosa de Tastil have attracted archaeologists, anthropologists, and tourists alike. The most visited areas of the Northwest are the valleys of Humahuaca, Santa María-Guachipas, and Calchaquíes, which are famous for their geomorphology and spectacular colored rock formations as well as for their rich cultural environments. Purmamarca in Jujuy province, for example, has a beautiful seventeenth-century colonial church and is the site of a colorful weekly market (Figure 9.6). Salta's Train of the Clouds also attracts visitors. The line runs west from Salta into the high *puna* landscape via 33 bridges, 13 viaducts, 21 tunnels, and two zig-zags. National and provincial parks, colonial churches, and several micro-climatic areas round out the myriad opportunities available to tourists in the Northwest.

Tourism development in the region is not without its problems. Infrastructure is lacking in many parts of the Northwest, particularly transport and accommodation. Moreover, tourism threatens to change the economic foundation of many villages. Small-scale manufacturing in recent years has shifted to the production of tourist-related merchandise, such as souvenirs, pots, shirts, and trinkets, to the detriment of basic goods needed in the local economy. Larger-scale tourist infrastructure often is financed from Buenos Aires or by overseas investors and local entrepreneurs often are excluded from participating in the development process.   More sophisticated

FIGURE 9.6 Tourist-Influenced Weekly Market in Purmamarca, Jujuy Province.

packaged tourism also requires a higher standard of basic services, which many areas in the Northwest are unable to provide. Nonetheless, despite these many difficulties, tourism has evolved over the past several decades to become an important sector of the Northwest's economy.

Transportation Development

One of the key elements to the Northwest's underdevelopment is the absence of adequate transport and communication infrastructure and services. The contemporary transport problem has its roots in the nineteenth century, when railroad technology arrived in Argentina and was hailed as the key to economic, political, and social growth. Railroads, more than any other technological advance in the nineteenth century, epitomized Argentina's crusade to incorporate European ideologies into the country's development. Enthusiasm for the ability of railroads to expand frontiers, civilize populations, transform economies, and unite disparate provinces into a single nation ran rampant throughout Argentina. In the interior, railroads were seen as a way to economic salvation after the crisis years of the early independence period. Connecting interior settlements and their hinterlands to the Atlantic ports would transform them into profitable and populated areas of production. Socioeconomic benefits would accrue to the entire interior, development in the European-Buenos Aires mold would proceed apace, and the political-economic dominance of Buenos Aires would be nullified.

Despite the positive impact of the railroad on certain sectors of the economy between 1876 and the 1950s, regional development in the Northwest failed to materialize. Dreams by nineteenth-century visionaries of the power of railroads, roads, and telegraph lines to civilize the Northwest, transform its economy, and bring region-wide social and political integration never were translated fully into reality (Keeling 1992, 1993). Transport and communication improvements in the Northwest did not facilitate widespread advancement in either a geographical or social sense, nor did they build the institutional means whereby the local population could increase its production and income.

Railroad development in the Northwest complemented the elites' dominance of the land by favoring large producers and by reinforcing the geographic isolation of the region's rural economic activity. Railroads did not encourage the creation of a territorial dispersed hierarchy of market centers; this caused the regional economy to become bifurcated and internally fragmented. The local means of production remained small, technologically deprived, and poor. In contrast, the landowners' world of cities, industry, imports, and exports, a world that relied on a backward and exploited rural population, thrived as a result of the railroad. Heralded as the interior's economic salvation, railroads could not negate the culturally embedded influences of a regressive social system, unjust land tenure practices, exploitive labor conditions, endemic political corruption, usurious credit practices, and technological underdevelopment. These problems remain evident in the Northwest's contemporary social structure.

The railroad's growth pattern in Northwest Argentina created a dendritic market system which encouraged socioeconomic polarization and an over-reliance on export trade. The Pampeana cities functioned as import-export points and centers of consumption. The provincial capitals of the Northwest, connected to the Pampeana cities by the railroads, acted as collection points for exportable primary production and as distribution points for imported consumer goods. The local marketplaces came to be dependent on the provincial capitals for both transport and an entire range of other social and economic facilities. Continued rural isolation and the sugar monocrop that dominated the regional economy restricted the growth of urban centers in the Northwest. The provincial capitals could offer only a geographically and socially limited range of goods, services, employment opportunities, and technological change. The elites appropriated the profits of commercial agriculture stimulated by the railroad, yet offered the regional community nothing in return.

Railroads could have stimulated region-wide development in the Northwest only as part of a strategy designed to produce an interconnected network of market towns. A coherent spatial, temporal, and cultural hierarchy of settlements was required that could function as production, trade, and service centers offering employment and access to other basic needs and opportunities. Thus, 120 years after the railroad arrived in Tucumán, and despite the economic development induced by the railroad and subsequent transport and communication improvements, the majority of the Northwest's population remain poor and isolated. Residents of the Northwest's cities, towns, and villages live a life decades removed from Buenos Aires and the Pampeana core, with regional inequalities evident across a broad spectrum of Northwest society.

Contemporary Transport and Communication Problems. Five critical transport and communication problems pose barriers to contemporary development efforts in the Northwest. First, privatization of the railroad network has eliminated almost all remaining passenger services to and within the Northwest, with the exception of a Tucumán-Buenos Aires service supported by the provincial government. Even this service is tenuous and liable to be withdrawn at a moment's notice. Moreover, railroad freight services on the narrow-gauge Belgrano system that serves the Northwest and parts of the Northeast are in a state of flux as the government prepares the system for privatization. In 1994, the Northwest contributed less than 8 percent of Argentina's total railroad freight tonnage. Much of the system is in a state of disrepair and needs massive investment in order to restore track beds and rolling stock to minimum safe operating standards. Second, cross-border linkages to neighboring countries are inadequate to take advantage of increased suprastate regional economic interaction. Although a number of plans have been proposed to strengthen economic links with Chile and Bolivia, little new infrastructure has been forthcoming over the past decade. Third, few paved roads exist beyond the main trunk routes that link the major urban centers. Those paved roads that do exist are poorly maintained and inadequate for intensive intraregional accessibility and mobility. Especially problematic are the transverse routes that connect the north-south valleys across extremely difficult terrain

(Figure 9.7). Infrastructure has deteriorated in recent years, and almost no investment in rehabilitating or maintaining key structures has taken place (Figure 9.8). Privatization of secondary and tertiary roads in the Northwest is not really an option because insufficient traffic exists as a base for toll-driven maintenance. Provincial and local governments are bankrupt and cannot afford long-term investment in transportation improvements without aid from the federal government.

Fourth, transport and communication networks at the provincial and regional level replicate the dendritic pattern found at the national level. Multimodal, intraregional, and intercity services are poorly developed throughout much of the Northwest. For example, business travelers who wish to travel by air from Salta or Tucumán to Mendoza or Posadas, or to a neighboring country, must transit through Buenos Aires. This system is inefficient and does not encourage intra- or interregional trade. Airline managers, however, support this type of routing because they argue that insufficient demand exists between the major secondary urban centers of the interior. Most freight now travels by road, while most individuals who do not have access to an automobile use the region's extensive passenger bus service. The highest quality and frequencies of bus service are found on the routes that link provincial capitals to Buenos Aires. Second in service frequency and quality is bus service to and from the major cities within the provinces. At the bottom of the service frequency and quality hierarchy are services to and between the smaller rural communities.

Finally, most interior provinces lack the basic telecommunications technology available in most developed countries. For example, the distribution of private telephones and access to computer networks such as the Internet is highly skewed in favor of Buenos Aires and the major Pampeana cities. The Northwest provincial capitals have less than 85 telephone lines in service per 1,000 inhabitants, compared to over 300 per 1,000 inhabitants in the Federal District of Buenos Aires. Overall, telephone densities in the Northwest range from 15 to 45 lines in service per 1,000 inhabitants (Ministry of the Economy 1996). Most rural residents must rely on a single telephone in a village or must journey to a neighboring settlement to find a telephone. Widespread computer use is rare in the Northwest and is confined to government agencies, some universities, and very few businesses. Poor communication does not foster a developmental atmosphere; it helps to keep rural communities mired in poverty and unable to take advantage of simple technological advancements in agriculture or manufacturing that could contribute to economic advancement. In summary, since 1990, the

FIGURE 9.7 Typical Rural Road Across the Cordillera in Salta Province.

FIGURE 9.8 Rural Bridge in Salta Province.

economic globalization policies of Argentina's federal government have had few, if any, positive impacts on the Northwest, particularly in the transport and communication sector. No multimodal, integrated plan exists that addresses transport and communication problems in the Northwest, either from a regional development perspective or within the context of a national development strategy.

Development Problems and Prospects

The future of the Northwest provinces in 1996 looked bleak. Economic restructuring policies have had little positive impact on the majority of the Northwest's residents and social polarization rates remain among the highest in Argentina. Privatization policies have not encouraged infrastructural development or service improvements in the Northwest, provincial governments have not been weaned off their reliance on federal government funds, and monocropping still dominates the socioeconomic structure. Throughout the region, the environment continues to deteriorate, diseases such as cholera and Chagas inflict huge numbers of people, and a culture of poverty remains embedded in many communities. There are some positive signs of development in the region, mostly related to future economic potential. Tourism has the capability to impact positively some local communities, particularly in Salta and Jujuy. Changing regional socioeconomic relationships as a consequence of MERCOSUR and other regional trade alliances also could help to reinvigorate the Northwest. Plans are in development for a series of Atlantic-Pacific corridors that could help the Northwest to reorient its economy away from the Pampeana provinces and Buenos Aires. However, any real improvements in socioeconomic conditions in the Northwest depend on the ability of both the provincial and federal governments to recognize and address the root causes of poverty and maldevelopment.

Environmental degradation is almost universal throughout the Northwest. Irrigation has encouraged widespread salinization, alkalization, and waterlogging across the region, which in turn have reduced the productivity of the fields. Water is heavily subsidized and little effort has been made to control usage abuse. The Northwest's irrigation system is underutilized, yet construction continues with government funds. For example, in 1992 the federal government announced a scheme to construct an extensive network of dams, reservoirs, canals, and channels that would divert water from Tucumán and Santiago del Estero into La Rioja and Catamarca provinces for crop irrigation (Pascuchi 1992). At a cost of US$2 billion, or US$5,000 for every person living in the recipient provinces, this project is reminiscent of the former Soviet Union government's mind-boggling scheme to divert the northward flowing waters of Siberia south to the cotton fields of Kazakhstan. Argentina's government conducted no environmental impact study for the diversion scheme nor any cost-benefit analyses of the project. Why hasn't the government invested this money in social infrastructure, transportation, or education, all of which would have a much more positive long-term impact on the region?

Soils throughout the Northwest have deteriorated since the 1950s and most are of poor quality. Severe erosion has encouraged the formation of gullies and has accelerated topsoil loss. Widespread logging and the over-pasturing of animals contribute to soil erosion and have degraded natural forests and grasslands. Deforestation in the region contributes to serious flooding throughout the Río Paraná basin, especially in Chaco and Formosa provinces (Bayón and Dugan 1994). Desertification now threatens the region's irrigated valleys and is especially severe in western Catamarca and in Salta. In addition, natural resource extraction, agricultural processing (particularly sugar), and industrial activities have polluted groundwater, rivers, and soils across the Northwest. Contamination by heavy metals such as boron, mercury, cadmium, and lead, and by synthetic toxins such as PCBs and petroleum byproducts has reached crisis levels (Lara and Durán 1993b; Durán et al. 1995; Sawers 1996). Urban vehicular pollution also has reduced the quality of life in the cities of Tucumán, Salta, and Jujuy.

Deterioration of the environment and its negative impact on agricultural activities at all scales has further embedded a culture of poverty in the Northwest's society and economy. The Menem government's attempt to reduce the flow of funds to the interior provinces, coupled with the essentially bankrupt status of most provincial governments, means that the resources needed to reverse environmental degradation, restructure agriculture, and to attack the root causes of poverty do not exist. Chronic social polarization afflicts the region. Most of the land is controlled by huge estates and over 80 percent of the population lives near, at, or below the official poverty line. For example, in 1991 about 70 percent of the rural population in the Northwest lived in housing with dirt floors, and over half of the region's entire population suffered from housing deficiencies (República Argentina 1991).

Primary school dropout rates exceed 20 percent of the school-age children in the Northwest and over 60 percent of the region's children suffer from an insufficient daily calorific intake. On average, about 40 percent of the total population in the Northwest does not have direct access in the home to potable water, sewage facilities, electricity, or heating. Moreover, the recession that has gripped the economy since Menem's economic re-structuring began in 1990 has closed off the safety valve of migration to the Pampeana cities. Buenos Aires offers no real opportunities to rural migrants from the Northwest, as living conditions in the myriad *villas miserias* that cluster around the periphery of the capital are as poor as in the Northwest cities. The popular view from the core that the Northwest is afflicted only by isolated pockets of poverty is patently absurd. In the mid-1990s, only rare and isolated pockets of development could be found throughout the Northwest. A substantial portion of the population lives in extreme poverty and the overall prospects for the region are not encouraging.

Summary

The long-term future of Argentina's submerging interior regions seems to suggest little relative improvement compared with other types of area. Agriculture is unlikely to provide an adequate base for regional economic support, and manufacturing cannot yield net increases in jobs in the northern provinces without a strong program of transport, communication, education, and distribution network improvements. Infrastructure in these four critical areas desperately is needed throughout the interior. A likely scenario for the immediate future in the North is a gradual growth in service employment, some of it in tourism-related activities, but most related to servicing the growing urban population clusters and migrants from contiguous countries. This process will reflect the demographic changes and economic restructuring occurring in rural communities and it will create a region of plural interests which requires extremely sensitive, integrated planning and policy making. Treating the interior as a homogenous plan-ning environment which should aspire to be like Buenos Aires and the Pampeana will only compound the existing problems of the northern pro-vinces. Furthermore, over the long run such actions could well prove to be an economic, political, cultural, demographic, and environmental disaster for Argentina's national development.

PART FOUR

Argentina in the Twenty-First Century

10

Future Argentina

Many times over the past 150 years, successive generations of Argentinos stood breathless on the threshold of anticipation as their country stood poised at the proverbial "fork in the road." Yet rarely did dreams of successful socioeconomic development, growth, and change fully become reality. Argentina's ruling elite frequently chose to adopt rather than to adapt prevailing theories and models of development, often with an astonishing disregard for the social, political, economic, and spatial realities of the nation. Particularly from the 1930s onwards, Argentina's various governments consistently chose the "wrong" road for the country and succeeded in propelling Argentina to the very brink of socioeconomic collapse. Over the past fifty years, for example, Argentinos have endured political chaos, brutal human rights violations, misguided economic policies, increased social polarization, the spatial bifurcation of the country, and the deterioration of national wealth and overall quality of life. Argentina evolved from a country with a brilliant future at the beginning of the twentieth century to one with a brilliant past at the close of the century. In 1990, just a decade away from the twenty-first century, Argentinos stood out of breath on the threshold of economic disaster and social disintegration.

After the election of Carlos Saúl Menem, Argentinos again stood breathless on the threshold of anticipation as Argentina embarked upon a new journey down a road characterized by economic globalization, free trade, neoliberal policies, and state disengagement from many aspects of society and economy. In the mid-1990s, initial macroeconomic performance indicators suggest that this time Argentina's government made the right choice. Financial stability, strong GDP growth, increased articulation with hemispheric and global economies, and encouraging signs of a broader democratic base are just a few of the success stories trumpeted by the Menem government as it began a second term of office in 1996. Change, however, has not been achieved without profound and often disturbing impacts on the people of Argentina. President Menem has argued loudly and vociferously that the short-term pain experienced by many Argentinos is the price that the country must pay for long-term socioeconomic gain. Critics of both the Menem government's neoliberal policies and of the prevailing model of global capitalism argue that, in reality, Argentina is experiencing short-term gain for the elite, while long-term pain for the masses becomes embedded in the socioeconomic structures of the country.

Against this background, my study's primary aim has been to document the patterns and processes of recent changes in the geography of Argentina. Particular attention has been focused on the economic restructuring policies implemented since 1990 and on the spatially uneven ways in which their effects are being felt across Argentina. I have attempted to examine in detail Argentina's three pillars of regional development, as well as the country's system of transport and communication, which serves as the foundation upon which the three pillars of growth and change rest. In part three of the study, I explored how Argentina's national restructuring policies are exerting different influences on different types of places. I explained why, despite solid macroeconomic success at the national level, Argentina's interior regions remain poorly developed, impoverished, and unable to benefit directly from national socioeconomic restructuring strategies.

In this final chapter, I present some future directions and policy issues that are relevant to Argentina's continuing journey along the road of neoliberal socioeconomic change. This is not a concluding chapter, however, but rather the end of the beginning. The dynamic, constantly evolving nature of the global economy makes it impossible to predict with any degree of accuracy the long-term success or failure of economic restructuring in Argentina or of the country's desire to incorporate its economy and society more fully into the global system. Rather, the chapter serves as a summary of the journey so far and as an indicator of the key components of change. Finally, I offer some suggestions concerning the key policy issues that I believe face Argentina and its citizens as the country stands poised to enter the twenty-first century.

Argentina's Five Fundamental Myths

In the book's preface, I set out five myths or beliefs that have shaped perceptions and research about Argentina over the past fifty years. The first myth revolves around the idea of an Argentina endowed with a rich array of human and natural resources. Theoretically, this strong resource base should have allowed the country to develop in the manner of the North Atlantic economies. However, Argentina has failed to take advantage of its human resources over the past two decades. The country's education system, particularly the universities, has suffered from ideological purges, inadequate infrastructural investments, and a real failure to define a national curriculum that could lead Argentina into the twenty-first century. Moreover, globalization policies are exerting downward pressure on wage labor rates and pushing increasing numbers of workers into the informal economy. Natural resources exist in quantities and quality inadequate to generate substantial profits within the global commodity system. Where profits have been generated, they have not been reinvested into natural resource regions in order to promote economic diversification. In addition, the global economy no longer demands the quantities of agricultural products produced in the Pampeana region. Inefficiencies and a lack of technology in Argentina's agricultural sector have made the country uncompetitive in global and regional economies.

The second myth concerns the perception that Argentina's core region has systematically exploited the interior provinces. Socioeconomic exploitation, in turn, led to the impoverishment of the interior regions and ultimately created a bifurcated country. Many scholars have pointed to Buenos Aires' dominance over the country and to the dramatic disparities in development between interior and coast as evidence of this exploitation. In reality, as Larry Sawers (1996) pointed out, poverty and underdevelopment in the interior actually have been a tremendous drain on national resources and have hindered the national development of Argentina. Massive subsidies throughout the twentieth century have flowed from the Pampeana to the interior, and the interior provinces have enjoyed a disproportionate level of influence in the federal government. Despite the flow of money and political influence to the interior, embedded structures of corruption, elitism, rural poverty, and inadequate infrastructure have combined to impoverish further the interior's economy and society.

Argentina's third myth pertains to the general perception of the country as European in development and culture. Models of order and progress were adopted wholesale from Europe in the nineteenth century by the Argentine elite, who made a concerted effort to replicate Paris in Buenos Aires and to mimic the modernization philosophies and strategies of France and Britain. Massive migration from Europe encouraged the myth of Europeanness, which in turn led to heightened levels of antagonism between the interior and the Pampeana. Development problems in Argentina's interior, however, always have been closely related to the problems found in neighboring countries and bear little resemblance to European development problems. Rural to urban migration from the interior to the Pampeana after the 1940s accelerated the latinamericanization of "European" Argentina and presented serious theoretical and practical challenges to the myth that Argentina could, should, and ought to develop in the image of Europe. In the 1990s, Argentina is more Latin American than European, and its development theories and strategies should reflect this reality.

Myth number four refers to the belief that only isolated pockets of poverty and underdevelopment exist beyond the Pampeana. However, as I detailed in part three of this study, nothing could be further from reality. The interior is characterized by relatively few isolated pockets of development. The idea that substantial portions of Argentina could be wracked by the type of poverty and underdevelopment experienced in Bolivia, Haiti, or Guatemala is an anathema to many Argentinos. Over the decades, scholars and governments alike in Argentina have chosen to turn a blind eye to the interior's reality. As long as this myth prevails among Argentina's scholars, planners, policy makers, and government bureaucrats, meaningful programs to address the interior's poverty and underdevelopment will remain few and far between.

The final myth shaping development, growth, and change in contemporary Argentina is that globalization, free trade, and privatization strategies have the power to transform the country, to end its socioeconomic bifurcation, and to insert it more forcefully into the global system. Although macroeconomic statistics suggest that these strategies are working, there is alarming evidence that serious socioeconomic problems are reemerging in Argentina. Environmental deterioration, growing urban poverty, resource depletion, social polarization, and an increasing concentration of wealth in the hands of corporations and elite families argue against the myth that Argentina's restructuring has been an unqualified success so far. What issues, then, should the government and citizens of Argentina be addressing as the country moves toward the next millennium?

Future Directions and Policy Issues

Although uncertainty exists about the long-term implications of Argentina's current restructuring program, there are specific concerns that must be addressed if the country is to grow and change in an environmentally and humanly sustainable way. As a geographer, observer, and frequent visitor to Argentina, I posit to the country's planners and policy makers that five key issues stand out as crucial to future development success. These key issues are not unique to Argentina, but are faced in varying degrees by almost every country in the global system. However, solutions to Argentina's problems do require a recognition of the distinct social, cultural, and economic spaces that shape contemporary Argentina. Policies and programs that are good for Buenos Aires and the Pampeana are not necessarily suitable for the Northwest or for Patagonia.

First, transportation and communication are the foundation of Argentina's future development. If investment is made in social and economic infrastructure without a concomitant investment in transport and communication, then I argue that little development progress will occur. Argentina will remain a bifurcated state, with poverty and isolation the norm for interior regions. However, if transport and communication improvements are made without related investments in education, health, industry, and agriculture then regional development in the interior is unlikely to occur. Migrant flows to major urban centers would be accelerated, backwash would further devastate rural areas, and bifurcation would remain embedded in the national structure. Transport and communication must develop hand-in-hand with other projects and they must form part of a holistic, multimodal, regional development strategy. Although privatization has had many successes in the transport and communication arena, not least of which is the shedding of huge deficits from the federal budgets, policy makers must remember that accessibility and mobility are necessary for all sectors of society in all locations. Moreover, governments must be committed to stringent regulation and to providing a workable national development plan for transport and communication that allows the benefits of privatization to spread while ensuring an equitable operating arena.

Critics may argue that this focus on transport and communication infrastructure smacks of modernization theory, which has come under strident attack in recent decades. However, I do not suggest that the transport-economic development nexus should evolve through a progression of stages approximating the phases of growth experienced by the industrialized, urbanized countries of North America and Europe. Rather, transport planning in Argentina must recognize the unique regional and local social, economic, and cultural milieus within which infrastructure should be developed.

The second key issue for the future of Argentina relates to the devolution and decentralization of political processes. Larry Sawers (1996) argued that decentralization of political-economic power is not the answer to Argentina's structural problems. He pointed out that although decentralization of federal activities has become a new fad, whose strategies are supposed to end economic backwardness in the interior (see Mattos 1989), there has never been any clear explanation of how devolution actually will work. I agree with Sawers' assessment of the absence of concrete devolutionary strategies, but I fundamentally disagree with his belief that decentralization will not work in Argentina. Part of the problem is that, although purportedly governed by a federal system, Argentina since the 1880s has functioned as a highly centralized unitary state, with almost all the political, financial, and social policies that affect the provinces emanating from Buenos Aires. No other country outside the Soviet Union's centralized system of trade and governance had as much federal government involvement in the political economy as Argentina up until 1991.

The interior provinces must be weaned off their reliance on federal government subsidies. However, devolving greater financial and political power to the interior is not the only answer. Interior provinces must take greater financial and political responsibility for their societies and economies and must operate within a strict long-term budget that identifies and addresses major areas of social deficit. Yet decentralization cannot work without concomitant investments in transportation, education, basic technologies, social services, and the environment. Corruption must be eliminated from the interior political system and elite dominance of local and regional political-economic structures must be weakened. Wholesale relocation of federal government functions from Buenos Aires to some interior city or group of cities is unnecessary and unlikely ever to occur. A more useful strategy would be a long-term program designed to shift components of the federal bureaucracy that are critical to regional development to the interior provinces. Whatever devolution strategies are applied to the interior, a fundamental issue is the increased participation of the average Argentino in the development of community, region, and country. Argentina does not yet have a true democracy. Millions of people remain excluded from the democratic process by inadequate access to the political, economic, and social structures that shape communities and societies. This must change in order for Argentina to move forward in a more equitable and sustainable fashion.

Third, Argentina's policy makers must balance the desire to participate more forcefully in the global export system against the internal development needs of the country. More attention should be paid to the agricultural sector, especially in the interior provinces, and the devaluation and negative stereotyping of rural, agricultural lifestyles must end. Agricultural production in the interior must be modernized if Argentina's current economic restructuring policies are to have any real success beyond the Pampeana region. Inequality in land ownership throughout the interior, for example, has produced and reinforced poverty over the past two hundred years. Land reform programs have never been attempted in Argentina, in part because policy makers simply have denied that such problems existed. Although *minifundios* typically are inefficient and unprofitable by traditional economic measures, many rural strategists who promote bottom-up development argue that society benefits over the long-term from the promotion of small-scale agriculture. In addition, improvements in access to credit, agricultural extension services, transportation, and basic sustainable technologies are necessary throughout the rural interior.

Argentina's planners also must do more to promote a more spatially balanced system of industrial production and distribution. Again, critical to the success of industrial deconcentration is the development of integrated, multimodal transport and communication services and infrastructure. New economic links to the north and west must be promoted, and better education facilities must be provided in the interior towns and cities to prepare Argentinos for interaction with an increasingly more sophisticated and technologically advanced global economy.

A fourth key issue for the future of Argentine society is the need to provide more basic social infrastructure, especially in the interior regions and in the urban periphery. Access to water, sewer, electricity, shelter, education, transport, and health care is fundamental to the balanced growth of a society. The spatially unbalanced way in which these services historically have been provided in Argentina exacerbated the development of a bifurcated state and created a situation whereby isolated islands of wealth became surrounded by a turbulent sea of the impoverished masses. Poverty stricken urban shantytowns in particular can quickly become breeding grounds for violent anti-government protests if their residents are not valued as productive members of society and are excluded for the political-economy process.

Finally, Argentina's planners and policy makers immediately should begin to address some important environmental issues. Degradation of the physical environment has reached, and gone beyond in some areas, a crisis situation. Indiscriminate industrial pollution has devastated many water-ways and fouled the soils. Marginal agricultural practices have overtaxed the capacity of the land in many interior regions and have encouraged desertification. In the cities, a lack of urban planning and an over-reliance on the automobile as the preferred mode of mobility have created dirty, noisy, unpleasant environments. Many government bureaucrats have ignored the growing environmental crisis in part because polluted air, water, and soils do not affect them on a daily basis. It is difficult to react to an enemy that is not completely visible. Moreover, the prevailing neo-liberal, free-market development model in Argentina places a higher priority on economic order and stability than on environmental sustain-ability. In discussions and meetings with planners and economists in Argentina, my questions about environmental policies were usually answered with "let's worry about turning the economy around first and then we'll deal with the environment." Unfortunately, it may be too late by the time serious policies to address environmental degradation in Argentina are finally implemented.

For Argentina and its citizens, there is no turning back from the socio-economic restructuring policies introduced by the Menem government. However, whether or not Argentina chose the "correct" fork in the road at the beginning of the 1990s ultimately will be determined by events that are unfolding today. My hope is that this study has served not only to shed light on contemporary conditions in Argentina and to bring the country's geography to the fore, but also to stand as a benchmark against which to compare future Argentina. Above all, I hope that the journey you have taken through Argentina via this book encourages you to follow the unfolding history of its people, economy, and culture.

Bibliography

Abbott, C. (1993). Through flight to Tokyo: Sunbelt cities and the new world economy, 1960-1990, pp. 183-212 in Arnold R. Hirsch and Raymond A. Mohl, eds., *Urban Policy in Twentieth-Century America*. New Brunswick, NJ: Rutgers University Press.

Abdala, Manuel Angel (1994). The regulation of newly privatized firms: An Illustration from Argentina, pp. 45-70 in Werner Baer and Melissa H. Birch, eds., *Privatization in Latin America: New Roles for the Public and Private Sectors*. New York: Praeger.

Aguirre, Alfredo A. (1983). El traslado de la Capital Federal en el pensamiento argentino. *Participar* (Buenos Aires) Año VI (52):22-26.

Aguirre, Alfredo A. (1987). El desafío del traslado. *Participar* (Buenos Aires) Año IX (71):12-13.

Aguirre, Patricia (1994). How the very poor survive: The impact of hyperinflationary crisis on low-income urban households in Buenos Aires, Argentina. *GeoJournal* 34(3):295-304.

Ainstein, Luis (1992). *Megacities in the Third World: A Research Agenda on Buenos Aires and the Question of National Urban Policy*. São Paulo: United Nations University.

Amin, Ash, and Nigel Thrift (1992). Neo-Marshallian nodes in global networks. *International Journal of Urban and Regional Research* 1694:571-587.

Amin, Samir (1976). *Unequal Development: An Essay on the Social Formations of Peripheral Capitalism*. London:

Artana, Daniel (1991). La promoción económica en la Argentina: Introducción y síntesis de los principales resultados, pp. 13-25 in Alberto Porto, ed., *Regulación de Actividades Económicas y Financieras*. Buenos Aires: Instituto di Tella.

Balán, Jorge (1982). Regional urbanization and agricultural production in Argentina: A contemporary analysis, pp. 35-58 in A. Gilbert, J.E. Hardoy, and R. Ramírez, eds., *Urbanization in Contemporary Latin America*. New York: Wiley.

Barret, Paul (1983). *The Automobile and Urban Transit*. Philadelphia: Temple University Press.

Basco, C.A., T.L. Cerenza, J.E. Iturriza, and E.O. Valenciano (1988). *Transporte e Integración*. Buenos Aires: Banco Interamericano de Desarrollo, Instituto para la Integración de América Latina.

Bayón, Ricardo, and Patrick Dugan (1994). Floods, wetlands, and the environment. *Buenos Aires Herald* January 30:5.

Becker, Bertha K., and Claudio A. Egler (1992). *Brazil: A New Regional Power in the World-Economy*. New York: Cambridge.

Bennett, R.J. (1980). *The Geography of Public Finance*. London: Methuen.

Benoit, P., J. Benoit, F. Bellanger, and B. Marzloff (1993). *Paris 1995: Le Grand Desserrement*. Paris: Romillat.

Bernhardson, Wayne, and María Massolo (1995). *Argentina, Uruguay, and Paraguay: A Travel Survival Kit*. London: Lonely Planet Publications.

Berón, L. (1981). *La Contaminación: Factor de Desequilibrio Ecológico*. Buenos Aires: Secretaría de Media Ambiente.

Bortagaray, Lucía L. (1992). Comercio e intercambio, pp. 387-423 in Juan A. Roccatagliata, ed., *La Argentina: Geografía General y los Marcos Regionales*. Buenos Aires: Planeta.

Bortagaray, Lucía L., and Alberto H. Peláez (1993). El sistema productivo, pp. 93-125 in Juan A. Roccatagliata, ed., *Geografía Económica Argentina*. Buenos Aires: El Ateneo.

Bourdé, Guy (1974). *Urbanisation et Immigration en Amérique Latine: Buenos Aires (XIXe et XXe siécles)*. Paris: Romillat.

Brailovsky, A.E., and D. Foguelman (1992). *Agua y Media Ambiente en Buenos Aires*. Buenos Aires: Editorial Fraterna.

Brecher, Jeremy, and Tim Costello (1994). *Global Village or Global Pillage: Economic Reconstruction From the Bottom Up*. Boston: South End Press.

Brodersohn, M.S. (1967). *Regional Development and Industrial Location Policy in Argentina*. Buenos Aires: Instituto Torcuato di Tella.

Brown, J.C. (1979). *A Socioeconomic History of Argentina: 1776-1860*. New York: Cambridge University Press.

Bruniard, Enrique, and Alfredo S. Bolsi (1992). Región agro-silvoganadera con frentes pioneros de ocupación del Nordeste, pp. 527-577 in Juan A. Roccatagliata, ed., *La Argentina: Geografía General y los Marcos Regionales*. Buenos Aires: Planeta.

Buenos Aires Herald (1988-1994). Various Issues.

Bunge, Alejandro E. (1918). *Ferrocarriles Argentinos: Contribución al Estudio del Patrimonio Nacional*. Buenos Aires: Imprenta Mercatali.

___ (1940). *Una Nueva Argentina*. Buenos Aires: Kraft.

Business Week (1990). Going private with no holds barred, September 24:60-61.

Business Week (1995). Menem: The Devil's real name is devaluation, August 28, 1995: 45.

Canitrot, Adolfo (1993). Crisis and transformation of the Argentine State (1978-1992), pp. 75-102 in William C. Smith, Carlos H. Acuña, and Eduardo A. Gamarra, eds., *Democracy, Markets, and Structural Reform in Latin America: Argentina, Bolivia, Brazil, Chile, and Mexico*. New Brunswick, NJ: Transaction Publishers.

Capitanelli, Ricardo G. (1992). Patagonia, un medio duro, dominio de ovejas, con focos pioneros de ocupación e industrias promovidas, pp. 699-746 in Juan A. Roccatagliata, ed., *La Argentina: Geografía General y Los Marcos Regionales*. Buenos Aires: Planeta.

Carlevari, Isidro J.F., and Ricardo D. Carlevari (1994). *La Argentina '94: Estructura Humana y Económica*. Buenos Aires: Ediciones Macchi.

Carter, Michael R., Bradford L. Barham, and Dina Mesbah (1996). Agricultural export booms and the rural poor in Chile, Guatemala, and Paraguay. *Latin American Research Review* 31(1):33-65.

Caviedes, César N., and Gregory Knapp (1995). *South America*. Englewood Cliffs, NJ: Prentice-Hall.

CEPAL (1995). *Las Empresas Transnacionales de una Economía en Transición: La Experiencia Argentina en Los Años Ochentos*. Santiago: Comisión Económica Para América Latina y El Caribe (CEPAL).

Champion, A.G., and A.R. Townsend (1990). *Contemporary Britain: A Geographical Perspective*. New York: Edward Arnold.

Chatwin, Bruce (1977). *In Patagonia*. New York: Penguin.

Clark, C. (1966). Industrial location and economic potential. *Lloyds Bank Review* 82:1-17.

Cobb, G.B. (1949). Supply and transportation for the Potosí mines, 1545-1640. *Hispanic American Historical Review* 29(1):25-45.

Cohen, Saul B. (1991). Global geopolitical change in the post-cold war era. *Annals of the Association of American Geographers* 81(4):551-580.

Corradi, Juan E. (1985). *The Fitful Republic: Economy, Society, and Politics in Argentina*. Boulder: Westview Press.

___ (1995). Menem's Argentina, Act II. *Current History* 94(589):76-80.

Crossley, J. Colin (1983). The River Plate countries, pp. 383-455 in Harold Blakemore and Clifford T. Smith, eds., *Latin America: Geographical Perspectives*, 2nd. edn. New York: Methuen.

Cuccorese, H.J. (1969). *Historia de los Ferrocarriles en la Argentina*. Córdoba: Ediciones Macchi.

Daguerre, Celia, Diana Durán, and Albina L. Lara (1992). *Argentina: Mitos y Realidades*. Buenos Aires: Lugar Editorial.

Daus, Federico A., and Ana del C. Yeannes (1992). La macroregion pampeana agroganadera, con industrias urbana y portuarias, pp. 479-526 in Juan A. Roccatagliata, ed., *La Argentina: Geografía General y Los Marcos Regionales*. Buenos Aires: Planeta.

Díaz, Ramón J., ed. (1989). *La Rioja: Encrucijada de Áridez y Esperanza*. Buenos Aires: Editorial Magisterio.

Díaz, Ramón J. (1991). *Exportaciones de la Provincia de La Rioja, Año 1989*. La Rioja: Universidad Provincial de La Rioja.

Díaz-Alejandro, C.F. (1970). *Essays on the Economic History of the Argentine Republic*. New Haven: Yale University Press.

Diniz, Clélio Campolina (1994). Polygonized development in Brazil: Neither de-centralization nor continued polarization. *International Journal of Urban and Regional Research* 18(2):293-314.

Direction of Trade Statistics Yearbook (1993). *World Trade 1992.* Washington, D.C.: International Monetary Fund.

Dolzer, Rudolf (1993). *The Territorial Status of the Falkland Islands (Malvinas): Past and Present.* New York: Oceana.

Dornbusch, Rudiger (1995). Progress report on Argentina, pp. 223-238 in Rudiger Dornbusch and Sebastian Edwards, eds., *Reform, Recovery, and Growth: Latin American and the Middle East.* Chicago: The University of Chicago Press.

Durán, Diana, Graciela De Marco, Albina L. Lara, Susana Sassone, and Celia de Bertone Daguerre (1995). *Geografía de la Argentina.* Buenos Aires: Troqvel.

ECLAC (1994). *Economic Panorama of Latin America (Annual Report).* Santiago: Economic Commission for Latin America and the Caribbean (ECLAC), United Nations.

___ (1995). *Preliminary Overview of the Economy of Latin America and the Caribbean, 1995.* Santiago: Economic Commission for Latin America and the Caribbean (ECLAC), United Nations.

Economic Information on Argentina (1983). A way out to the Pacific through the province of Jujuy, Vol. 128:62-63.

Economist (1994). Argentina Survey, November 26:1-18.

___ (1995). Dreams of roads and railways, Vol. 334(7905):47-48 (March 11).

Erbiti, Cecilia (1993). El sistema espacial: Estructura de los asentamientos, pp. 44-69 in Juan A. Roccatagliata, ed., *Geografía Económia Argentina.* Buenos Aires: El Ateneo.

Erro, Davide G. (1993). *Resolving the Argentine Paradox: Politics and Development, 1966-1992.* Boulder: Lynne Rienner.

Ferraro, R.M. (1973). *El Desarrollo Regional Argentino: Problemática y Posibilidades.* Buenos Aires: Editorial Plus Ultra.

Ferrer, Aldo (1967). *The Argentine Economy.* Berkeley: University of California Press.

Fifer, J. Valerie (1994a). Chile's pioneering location: Pacific Rim and Southern Cone. *Geography* 79(2): 129-46.

___ (1994b). Andes crossing: Old tracks and new opportunities at the Uspallata Pass. *Yearbook 1994: Journal of the Conference of Latin Americanist Geographers* 20: 35-48.

Fleming, William J. (1987). *Regional Development and Transportation in Argentina.* New York: Garland Publishing.

Flichman, G. (1982). *La Renta del Suelo y el Desarrollo Agrario Argentino.* Buenos Aires: Siglo XXI.

Fodor, Jorge, and A. O'Connell (1973). La Argentina y la economía atlántica en la primera mitad del siglo viente. *Desarrollo Económico* XIII(49):375-94.

Foster, Derek (1988). The world's fifth-largest wine producer, Argentina is turning out world-class wines and looking for a larger share of the international market. *Americas* 40(2):30-35.

Friedman, G. (1991). *The Coming War With Japan*. New York: St. Martin's Press.

Friedmann, John (1993). Where we stand: A decade of world city research. Paper presented to the World Cities in a World-System conference, 1-3 April, Sterling, VA.

___ (1995). The world city hypothesis, pp.317-331 in Paul L. Knox and Peter J. Taylor, eds., *World Cities in a World-System*. Cambridge: Cambridge University Press.

Friedmann, J., and G. Wolff (1982). World city formation: An agenda for research and action. *International Journal of Urban and Regional Research* 6(3):309-344.

Gamba-Stonehouse, Virginia (1992). Science in policy and policy for science: Some experiences from Argentina. *Technology in Society* 14:151-165.

Garelli, Stephane (1996). *The Fundamentals of World Competitiveness*. Http://www.imd.ch/wcy/1996/garelli.html.

Garriz, Patricia I. (1992). Los cultivos bajo riego y el control de la desertificación: Demasiado interrogantes con abultadas respuestas hoy, pp. 179-182 in Patricia I. Garriz, ed., *Crecimiento y Productividad de los Cultivos*. Neuquén: Universidad Nacional de Comahue.

Garten, J.E. (1992). *A Cold Peace: America, Japan, Germany, and the Struggle for Supremacy*. New York: Times Books.

Gibb, Richard, and David Smith (1994). The regional economic impact of the Channel Tunnel, pp. 155-176 in Richard Gibb, ed., *The Channel Tunnel: A Geographical Perspective*. New York: Wiley.

Gilbert, Alan (1994). *The Latin American City*. London: Latin American Bureau.

Gills, Barry, and Joel Rocamora (1992). Low intensity democracy. *Third World Quarterly* 13(3):501-523.

Green, Paula L. (1993). DC consultant wins contract for Argentine bridge study. *Journal of Commerce and Commercial* 398(28127):2.

Griffin, Ernst, and Larry Ford (1993). Cities of Latin America, pp. 225-265 in Stanley D. Brunn and Jack F. Williams, eds., *Cities of the World*, 2nd edn. New York: Harper Collins.

Hardoy, Jorge E. (1972). *Las Ciudades en América Latina: Seis Ensayos Sobre la Urbanización Contemporánea*. Buenos Aires: Instituto Torcuato Di Tella.

Harris, C. (1954). The Market as a factor in the localization of industry in the United States. *Annals of the Association of American Geographers* 44:315-348.

Hartshorn, Truman (1971). The spatial structure of socioeconomic development in the Southeast, 1950-1960. *Geographical Review* 61(3):250-275.

Hodges, Donald C. (1988). *Argentina, 1943-1987: The National Revolution and Resistance*. Albuquerque: University of New Mexico Press.

Hudson, Ray, and Allan M. Williams (1995). *Divided Britain.* London: Wiley.

IBRD (1987). *Argentina: Economic Recovery and Growth.* Washington, DC: International Bank for Reconstruction and Development (IBRD).

Imai, Keiko (1992). Decentralizing government deficit finance in Argentina. *The Developing Economies* XXX(4):430-449.

IMD (1996). *World Competitiveness Yearbook 1996: Country Competitiveness Profile: Argentina.* Http://www.imd.ch/wcy/1996/countries/argentina.html.

Instituto de Estudios de la Marina Mercante Argentina (1962). *La Marina Mercante Argentina, 1962.* Buenos Aires: IDEMMA.

Johns, Michael (1992). The urbanization of peripheral capitalism: Buenos Aires, 1880-1920. *International Journal of Urban and Regional Research* 16(3):352-374.

Keeling, David J. (1992). *You Cannot Get There From Here: Transport and Communication Deficiencies in the Regional Development of Northwest Argentina.* Ann Arbor: UMI Dissertation Publications.

___ (1993). Transport and regional development in Argentina: Structural deficiencies and patterns of network evolution. *Yearbook 1993: Journal of the Conference of Latin Americanist Geographers* 19:25-34.

___ (1994). Regional development and transport policies in Argentina: An appraisal. *The Journal of Developing Areas* 28(4):487-502.

___ (1995). Transport and the world city paradigm, pp. 115-131 in Paul L. Knox and Peter J. Taylor, eds., *World Cities in a World-System.* Cambridge: Cambridge UniversityPress.

___ (1996). *Buenos Aires: Global Dreams, Local Crises.* London: Wiley.

Kondratieff, N. (1935). The long waves in economic life. *Review of Economic Statistics* 17(2):105-115.

La Nación (Buenos Aires) (1989, 1991, 1993, 1994). Various Issues.

Lara, Albina L., and Diana Durán (1993a). Estructura regional y organización territorial, pp. 266-283 in Juan A. Roccatagliata, ed., *Geografía Económica Argentina.* Buenos Aires: El Ateneo.

___ (1993b). Sistema ecológico, medio ambiente y recursos naturales, pp. 17-43 in Juan A. Roccatagliata, ed., *Geografía Económica Argentina.* Buenos Aires: El Ateneo.

Latin American Travel Advisor (1994). Various Issues. Quito: LatinAmerican Travel Consultants.

Latin American Weekly Report (1994-1996). London: Latin American Newsletters.

Lewis, Colin M. (1993). Cycles and macroeconomic policy since the 1930s, pp. 103-123 in Colin M. Lewis and Nissa Torrents, eds., *Argentina in the Crisis Years, (1983-1990).* London: Institute of Latin American Studies.

Lewis, Paul H. (1990). *The Crisis of Argentine Capitalism.* Chapel Hill, The University of North Carolina Press.

López del Amo, Fernando (1990). *Ferrocarril, Ideología y Política Ferroviaria en el Proyecto Liberal Argentino (1852-1916)*. Madrid: Centro Español de Estudios de América Latina.

Lorenzini, Horacio N., Raúl Rey Balmaceda, and María J. Echeverría (1993). *Geografía de la Argentina*. Buenos Aires: A-Z Editora.

Ludueña, M.A. (1993). Región Metropolitana Buenos Aires: Estructuración, problemática y aspecto de cambio, pp. 284-330 in Juan A. Roccatagliata, ed., *Geografía Económica Argentina*. Buenos Aires: El Ateneo.

Manzanal, Mabel, and Alejandro B. Rofman (1989). *Las Economías Regionales de la Argentina: Crisis y Políticas de Desarrollo*. Buenos Aires: Centro Editor de América Latina.

Manzetti, Luigi (1994). Institutional decay and distributional coalitions in developing countries: The Argentine riddle reconsidered. *Studies in Comparative International Development* 29(2):82-114.

Mattos, Carlos (1989). La descentralización. ¿Una nueva panacea para enfrentar el subdesarrollo regional? pp. 335-363 in Elsa Laurelli and Alejandro Rofman, eds., *Descentralización del Estado: Requerimientos y Políticas en las Crisis*. Buenos Aires: Ediciones CEUR.

McGuire, James W. (1996). Strikes in Argentina: Data sources and recent trends. *Latin American Research Review* 31(3):127-150.

Milberg, Agustin F. (1993). Good riddance to rent controls in Argentina. *Urban Land* 52(11):44-45.

Ministry of the Economy (1996). *Internet Service: www.mecon.ar*. Buenos Aires: Ministry of the Economy and Public Works.

Mochkowsky, J. (1991). La situación habitacional de los sectores populares, pp. 55-64 in Rubén Gazzoli, ed., *Alojamiento para Sectores Populares Urbanos: Buenos Aires, Montevideo, San Pablo y México*. Buenos Aires: Editorial Plus Ultra.

Morris, Arthur S. (1972). The regional problem in Argentine economic development. *Geography* 57(4):289-306.

___ (1975). *Regional Disparities and Policy in Modern Argentina*. Glasgow: Institute of Latin American Studies, University of Glasgow, Occasional Paper No. 16

Morris, Michael A. (1985). The 1984 Argentine-Chilean Pact of Peace and Friendship. *Oceanus* 28(2):93-96.

Munck, Ronaldo (1994). Workers, Structural Adjustment, and *Concertación Social* in Latin America. *Latin American Perspectives* 21(3):90-103.

Murray, M.P. (1988). *Subsidizing Industrial Location: A Conceptual Framework with Application to Korea*. Baltimore: Johns Hopkins University Press.

Myrdal, Gunnar (1957). *Economic Theory and Underdeveloped Regions*. London: Duckman.

Nash, Nathaniel C. (1992). The days dwindle down to poverty and suicide. *The New York Times*, November 17:A4.

New York Times (1992). Argentina: A survey of its opportunities (advertisement). September 22:C9-C15.

Official Airline Guides (1972, 1982, 1992, 1993, 1996). Worldwide Edition. Chicago: Reuben H. Donnelly.

Oil and Gas Journal (1996). Construction progressing on GasAndes pipeline. Vol. 94(15):28.

Ortiz, R.M. (1946). El Ferrocarril en la Economía Argentina. Buenos Aires: Ediciones Problemas.

___ (1964). Historia Económica de la Argentina. Buenos Aires: Pampa y Cielo.

Padula, Cristina C. (1993). El proceso de integración, pp. 331-361 in Juan A. Roccatagliata, ed., Geografía Económia Argentina. Buenos Aires: El Ateneo.

Pascuchi, Javier (1992). A timely reminder of past mistakes. Buenos Aires Herald, April 19:2.

Perroux, F. (1955). Note sur la notion des 'pôles de croissance.' Economie Appliquèe 1(2):307-20.

Quiroga, Jorge S. (1995). Proyecto para unir el Cono Central de Sudamérica en 1995. Iquique, Chile: Municipalidad de Iquique.

República Argentina (1946). Origen y Desarrollo de los Ferrocarriles Argentinos. Buenos Aires: El Ateneo (Dirección de Informaciones y Publicaciones Ferrovarias).

___ (1960, 1991). Censo Nacional de Población y Vivienda. Buenos Aires: Instituto Nacional de Estadística y Censos (INDEC).

___ (1965). Plan National de Desarrollo, 1965-1969. Buenos Aires: Consejo National de Desarrollo (CONADE).

___ (1966). Plan de Emergencia para el Noroeste Argentino, 1967. Buenos Aires: Consejo Federal de Inversiones (CFI).

___ (1969). Organización del Espacio de la Región Metropolitana de Buenos Aires: Esquema Director Año 2000. Buenos Aires: Oficina Regional de Desarrollo Area Metropolitana.

___ (1971). Plan Nacional de Desarrollo y Seguridad, 1971-1975. Buenos Aires: Consejo Nacional de Desarrollo (CONADE).

___ (1984). La Pobreza en la Argentina. Buenos Aires: Instituto Nacional de Estadística y Censo (INDEC).

___ (1985). Censo Económico 1985. Buenos Aires: Secretaría de Desarrollo Industrial y Gobiernos Provinciales (SDIGP).

___ (1990). La Pobreza Urbana en la Argentina. Buenos Aires: Instituto Nacional de Estadística y Censo (INDEC).

___ (1993a). Reflexiones y Orientaciones para la Formulación de una Política de Ordenación Territorial. Buenos Aires: Subsecretaría de Acción de Gobierno.

___ (1993b). Argentina: A Growing Nation. Buenos Aires: Ministerio de Economía y Obras y Servicios Públicos.

___ (1994). Statistical Yearbook: Republic of Argentina, 1994. Buenos Aires: Instituto Nacional de Estadística y Censos (INDEC).

República Argentina (1995a). *Estimaciones y Proyecciones de Población: Total del País (Versión Revisada), 1950-2050.* Buenos Aires: Instituto Nacional de Estadística y Censos (INDEC).

___ (1995b). *Censo Económico 1994: Resultados Preliminares.* Buenos Aires: Instituto Nacional de Estadística y Censos (INDEC).

Review of the River Plate (1961). Various Issues (Buenos Aires).

Rich, D. (1980). *Potential Models in Human Geography.* Norwich: University of East Anglia Press.

Richter, Frank (1996). Railroad restructuring paying off in Argentina. *Progressive Railroading* 39(5):37-47.

Roccatagliata, Juan A. (1986). *Argentina: Hacia un Nuevo Ordenamiento Territorial.* Buenos Aires: Editorial Pleamar.

___ (1992a). Los transportes y las comunicaciones, pp. 355-384 in Juan A. Roccatagliata, ed., *La Argentina: Geografía General y Los Marcos Regionales.* Buenos Aires: Planeta.

___ (1992b). Regionalización, pp. 429-449 in Juan A. Roccatagliata, ed., *La Argentina: Geografía General y Los Marcos Regionales.* Buenos Aires: Planeta.

___, ed. (1993a). *Geografía Económica Argentina.* Buenos Aires: El Ateneo.

___ (1993b). Transporte. Algunas consideraciones actuales, pp. 193-240 in Juan A. Roccatagliata, ed., *Geografía Económica Argentina.* Buenos Aires: El Ateneo.

___ (1994). *Geografía y Políticas Territoriales: La Ordenación del Espacio.* Buenos Aires: Editorial Ceyne.

Rock, David (1985). *Argentina: 1516-1982.* Berkeley: University of California Press.

___ (1993). *Authoritarian Argentina: The Nationalist Movement, its History and its Impact.* Berkeley: University of California Press.

Sábato, Jorge (1988). *La Clase Dominante en la Argentina Moderna: Formación y Características.* Buenos Aires: Grupo Editorial Latinoamericano.

Sanmarchi, Marta D. (1989). Las disparidades regionales en el nivel preprimario argentino. *Signos Universitarios* 15:113-146.

Santillán de Andrés, Selva, and Teodoro R. Ricci (1992). La región del Noroeste Argentino: Paisajes heterogeneos con economía mixta, pp. 567-600 in Juan A. Roccatagliata, ed., *La Argentina: Geografía General y los Marcos Regionales.* Buenos Aires: Planeta.

Sargent, Charles S. (1974). *The Spatial Evolution of Greater Buenos Aires, Argentina, 1870-1930.* Tempe: Arizona State University Press.

Sarmiento, Domingo F. (1868). *Life in the Argentine Republic in the Days of the Tyrants.* New York: Hafner Press.

Sassone, Susana María (1989). Migraciones limítrofes en la Argentina. *Signos Universitarios* 15:149-198.

Saútu, Ruth (1993). The role of the private sector in the industrialisation of Argentina, pp. 159-177 in Colin M. Lewis and Nissa Torrents, eds., *Argentina in the Crisis Years (1983-1990)*. London: The Institute of Latin American Studies.

Sawers, Larry (1996). *The Other Argentina: The Interior and National Development*. Boulder, CO: Westview.

Scalabrini Ortiz, Raúl (1957). *Política Británica en el Río de la Plata*. Buenos Aires: Fernández Blanco.

___ (1983). *Historia de los Ferrocarriles Argentinos*. Buenos Aires: Editoral Plus Ultra.

Schneider, Joe (1994). Thou shalt not kill. *Buenos Aires Herald*, May 13:10.

Schivelbusch, Wolfgang (1986). *The Railway Journey: The Industrialization of Time and Space in the 19th Century*. Berkeley: University of California Press.

Schvarzer, Jorge (1990). *Promoción Industrial en Argentina: Características, Evolución y Resultados*. Buenos Aires: CISEA.

___ (1992). The Argentina riddle in historical perspective. *Latin American Research Review* 27(1):169-181.

Scobie, James R. (1971). *Argentina: A City and A Nation*, 2nd. edn. New York: Oxford University Press.

___ (1988). *Secondary Cities of Argentina: The Social History of Corrientes, Salta, and Mendoza, 1850-1910*. Stanford: Stanford University Press.

Scovazzi, E. (1993). Carmen de Viedma. *International Journal of Urban and Regional Research* 17(4):516-525.

Sempat Assadourian, Carlos (1983). *El Sistema de la Economía Colonial: El Mercado Interior, Regiones y Espacio Económico*. Mexico: Editorial Nueva Imágen.

SEPLADE (1978). *Estrategias para el Desarrollo y Modernización del Eje Metropolitano*. Buenos Aires: Secretaría de Planeamiento y Desarrollo de la Provincia de Buenos Aires (SEPLADE).

Shumway, Nicolas (1991). *The Invention of Argentina*. Berkeley: University of California Press.

Simon, David (1990). Introduction, pp.xiii-xix in David Simon, ed., *Third World Regional Development*. London: Chapman.

Sims, C. (1996). Opposition party wins mayoral election in Argentine capital. *New York Times* July 2, Vol. 145:A3.

Smith, N. (1984). *Uneven Development*. New York: Basil Blackwell.

Stern, S.J. (1985). New directions in Andean economic history; a critical dialogue with Carlos Sempat Assadourian. *Latin American Perspectives* 44(12-1):133-148.

Stoetzel, J.R. (1993). BN,MK to move commuters. *Progressive Railroading* 36(2):68-70.

Storper, Michael, and Richard Walker (1989). *The Capitalist Imperative: Territory, Technology, and Industrial Growth*. New York: Basil Blackwell.

Stewart, J.Q. (1947). Empirical mathematical rules concerning the distribution and equilibrium of population. *Geographical Review* 37(4):461-485.

Taylor, Peter J. (1989). *Political Geography: World-Economy, Nation-State, and Locality.* New York: Longman.

Thomas Cook (1995). *Overseas Timetable.* Peterborough, UK: Thomas Cook Publications.

Thrift, Nigel (1986). The geography of international economic disorder, pp. 12-67 in Ronald J. Johnston and Peter J. Taylor, eds., *The World in Crisis?* New York: Blackwell.

Thurow, Lester (1992). *Head to Head: The Coming Economic Battle Among Japan, Europe, and America.* New York: William Morrow.

___ (1996). *The Future of Capitalism: How Today's Economic Forces Will Shape Tomorrow's World.* New York: Morrow.

Torres, H.A. (1993). La aglomeración de Buenos Aires: Centralidad y suburbanización (1940-1990). *Estudios Geográficos* 54(211):301-322.

Tucker, Bonnie (1994). Will Patagonia's 'gold' turn green? *Buenos Aires Herald* September 25, p. 7.

United Nations (1993). *Human Development Report.* New York: Oxford (U.N. Human Development Program).

U.S. News and World Report (1990). A talk with Carlos Menem, May 7, p. 43.

Waisman, Carlos H. (1987). *Reversal of Development in Argentina: Postwar Counterrevolutionary Policies and their Structural Consequences.* Princeton: Princeton University Press.

Waldmann, Peter (1993). The Peronism of Perón and Menem: From justicialism to liberalism?, pp. 92-101 in Colin M. Lewis and Nissa Torrents, eds., *Argentina in the Crisis Years (1983-1990).* London: Institute of Latin American Studies.

Walter, Richard J. (1982). The socioeconomic growth of Buenos Aires in the twentieth century, pp. 67-126 in Stanley R. Ross and Thomas F. McGann, eds., *Buenos Aires: 400 Years.* Austin: University of Texas Press.

Williams, Glyn B. (1991). *The Welsh in Patagonia: The State and the Ethnic Community.* Cardiff: University of Wales Press.

World Bank (1993). *World Development Report.* New York: World Bank.

Wright, Andrew G. (1996). Multipartner tango (Aguas Argentinas' public works project in Buenos Aires, Argentina). *ENR* Vol. 236(22):38.

Wynia, Gary W. (1992). *Argentina: Illusions and Realities.* New York: Holmes and Meier.

Yanes, Luis A., and Marcos Gerber (1989). El Noroeste argentino: Heterogeneidad productiva y crecimiento regional, pp. 13-56 in Luis A. Yanes and Ana María Liberali, eds., *Aportes para el Estudio del Espacio SocioEconómico.* Buenos Aires: Editoral El Coloquio.

___ (1990). Crisis de acumulación, regulación estatal y valorización del espacio en Argentina. *Territorio* 3:3-54.

Zamorano, Mariano (1992). Región cuyana de los oasis agroindustriales, pp. 613-661 in Juan A. Roccatagliata, ed., *La Argentina: Geografía General y los Marcos Regionales*. Buenos Aires: Planeta.

About the Book and Author

Since 1989, Argentina has experienced perhaps its most significant period of change since federation in 1880. Under the leadership of Carlos Menem and the Justicialista political party, contemporary Argentina is emerging from the chaos of long-term instability to reassert itself as a viable player in both regional and global systems.

In this perceptive book, David Keeling analyzes Argentina's emergence within the modern world economy against the backdrop of the country's regional development processes. Combining systematic and area-based approaches, he discusses international and national trends that have shaped the social and economic geography of Argentina in profound and fundamental ways.

Drawing on new material from recent demographic and economic censuses and on the Menem government's privatization and deregulation policies, Keeling asks whether participation in the new world economy has forced workers, communities, and cities in Argentina to downgrade environmental, labor, and social conditions. He also traces national economic and societal trends by region, showing how these trends will continue to affect regions and localities to the end of the decade and into the twenty-first century. Keeling concludes by assessing how changes in Argentina—a semi-peripheral country and emerging regional power—could affect the restructuring of its role in the new regional and world economies.

David J. Keeling is assistant professor of geography at Western Kentucky University.

Index